HTML For Dummies, 3rd Edition

Cheat Sheet

Document Structure

<HTML> ... </HTML>	HTML
<HEAD> ... </HEAD>	Head
<TITLE> ... </TITLE>	Title
<BODY> ... </BODY>	Body
<BASE>	Base
<ISINDEX>	Isindex
<LINK>	Link type
<NEXTID>	Next document
<META>	Structure

Graphics

<IMG>	Image
<MAP>	Client-side imagemap parameters
<AREA> Hotzone	Imagemap

Links

<A> ... </A>	Anchor
<APPLET>...</APPLET>	Java
<PARAM>	Applet parameters
<OBJECT>...</OBJECT>	Insert Object
<SCRIPT>...</SCRIPT>	Insert Script

Lists

<DIR> ... </DIR>	Directory list
<OL> ... </OL>	Ordered list
<UL> ... </UL>	Unordered list
<LI>	List item
<MENU> ... </MENU>	Menu list
<DL> ... </DL>	Glossary list
<DT>	Definition term
<DD>	Definition datum

Layout Elements

 	Line break
<HR>	Horizontal rule
<P>	Paragraph
<ADDRESS> ... </ADDRESS>	Address
<BASEFONT>	Default font size
<FONT>...</FONT>	Font Appearance
<BLOCKQUOTE> ... </BLOCKQUOTE>	Blockquote
<PRE>...</PRE>	Preformatted text
<CENTER>...</CENTER>	Center
<DIV>	Divison
<STYLE>	In-line style info
<SPAN>...</SPAN>	Span

Tables

<TABLE>...</TABLE>	Table block
<CAPTION>...</CAPTION>	Table caption
<TH>...</TH>	Column head
<COLGROUP...</COLGROUP>	Column grouping
<COL>	Column
<THEAD>	Table head
<TBODY>	Table body
<TFOOT>	Table footer
<TR>	Table row
<TD>	Table data

P9-DGH-518

For Dummies: Bestselling Book Series for Beginners

HTML For Dummies® 3rd Edition

Cheat Sheet

Forms

<FORM> ... </FORM>	Form block
<INPUT>	Input widget
<TEXTAREA> ... </TEXTAREA>	Text area
<SELECT> ... </SELECT>	Input pick list
<OPTION>	Selectable item
<LABEL>...</LABEL>	Control Label
<FIELDSET>...</FIELDSET>	Field Set

Document Headings

<H*> ... </H*>	Level * head

Frames

<FRAME>	Frame denotation
<FRAMESET> ... </FRAMESET>	Frame group
<NOFRAMES> ... </NOFRAMES>	Alternate text

Text Controls

<B> ... </B>	Boldface
<BIG>...</BIG>	Big text
<CITE> ... </CITE>	Short citation
<CODE> ... </CODE>	Code font
<DFN> ... </DFN>	Defined term
<EM> ... </EM>	Emphasis
<I> ... </I>	Italic
<S>...</S>	Strikethrough
<SMALL>...</SMALL>	Small text
<STRONG> ... </STRONG>	Strong
_{...}	Subscript
^{...}	Superscript
<U>... </U>	Underline

Comments

<!-- ... -->	Comment

For Dummies: Bestselling Book Series for Beginners

™

BESTSELLING BOOK SERIES

References for the Rest of Us!®

Are you intimidated and confused by computers? Do you find that traditional manuals are overloaded with technical details you'll never use? Do your friends and family always call you to fix simple problems on their PCs? Then the For Dummies® computer book series from Wiley Publishing, Inc. is for you.

For Dummies books are written for those frustrated computer users who know they aren't really dumb but find that PC hardware, software, and indeed the unique vocabulary of computing make them feel helpless. For Dummies books use a lighthearted approach, a down-to-earth style, and even cartoons and humorous icons to dispel computer novices' fears and build their confidence. Lighthearted but not lightweight, these books are a perfect survival guide for anyone forced to use a computer.

Already, millions of satisfied readers agree. They have made For Dummies books the #1 introductory level computer book series and have written asking for more. So, if you're looking for the most fun and easy way to learn about computers, look to For Dummies books to give you a helping hand.

Wiley Publishing, Inc.

HTML
FOR
DUMMIES®
3RD EDITION

by Ed Tittel and Stephen N. James

Wiley Publishing, Inc.

HTML For Dummies® 3rd Edition

Published by
Wiley Publishing, Inc.
909 Third Avenue
New York, NY 10022
www.wiley.com

About the Authors

Ed Tittel is the coauthor of numerous books about computing and the World Wide Web, including *The Foundations of World Wide Web Programming with HTML and CGI,* and *The Hip Pocket Guide to HTML.* (The first book's authors include Mark Gaither, Mike Erwin, and Sebastian Hassinger; the second book's coauthor is James Michael Stewart, who also contributed substantially to this book, even though his name does not appear on the cover.) These days, Ed's aiming his efforts at Internet programming-related topics, both as a writer and as a member of the NetWorld + Interop program committee.

Ed has been a regular contributor to the trade press since 1987 and has written over 200 articles for a variety of publications, including *Computerworld, Infoworld, Maximize, Iway,* and *NetGuide.* He's a regular contributor to *Windows NT* magazine and works for several online 'zines, including *Interop Online.*

Ed also enjoys working at home, where his real job is keeping Dusty, his large and rambunctious Labrador Retriever, company. When he's not pounding the keyboard, he's either out walking Dusty, playing pool, or cooking up something in his kitchen for friends and family.

Contact Ed at etittel@zilker.net or visit his Web site at http://www.lanw.com.

Stephen Nelson James is the coauthor (with Ed Tittel) of the best-selling *HTML For Dummies,* and also of *ISDN Networking Essentials* and *PC Telephony for Home and Small Office.* He has also authored numerous computer-related magazine articles, software user's manuals, and WWW pages. Steve is a former environmental biologist and ex-president/CEO of FYI, Inc., a software development company. When he's not writing or surfing the Net, you can find him out on the roads in the hills around Austin doing what he really loves to do best: riding his bicycle!

Contact Steve at snjames@wetlands.com.

Authors' Acknowledgments

Our biggest thanks go to our readers, who made the first and second editions such a great success. Their feedback should continue to improve this third edition as well! We have way too many folks to thank, so we'd like to begin by thanking everybody who helped us whom we don't mention by name. Actually, we couldn't have done it without you, even if we don't name you here! Thanks for your help, information, and encouragement.

Ed Tittel

I want to share my thanks with a large crew. First off, there's my family — you were there for me when it counted. Thanks! Second, a talented crew of technical people helped me over a variety of humps, large and small. I would like to specifically mention Mark Gaither, Michael Stewart, and Natanya Pitts. You guys are the greatest! Third, there's a whole crowd of other folks whose information has helped me over the years, especially the originators of the Web — most notably, Tim Berners-Lee, Dan Connolly, and the rest of the CERN team. I'd also like to thank the geniuses, sung and unsung, at NCSA, Netscape, and any place else whose Web collections I visited, for helping pull the many strands of this book together. I'd also like to thank Steve James for sticking with me from the first edition to the third! Finally, I'd like to thank my lucky stars for making it possible for me to work at home and make writing a part of my daily routine.

Stephen Nelson James

First and foremost, a heartfelt thank you to Ed Tittel for his inspiration and enthusiasm during the sometimes tedious revisions necessary to create this edition of *HTML For Dummies.* As always, my eternal gratitude to my family, Trisha, Kelly, and Chris, for their understanding and support of my writing habit. And finally, a very sincere thank you to all of you who purchased *HTML For Dummies,* first and second editions, and made this third edition possible. Please continue to keep our e-mail filled with your great comments and suggestions.

Together, we want to thank the editorial staff at IDG Books, especially Jennifer Davies, our copy editor; Tim Gallan, one of the best project editors we've ever had the chance to work with; Mike Kelly, the guy who made it all happen; Diane Steele, who let us keep this "strange torpedo" moving; and the other editorial and production folks, including Gina Snyder and Linda Boyer.

Please feel free to contact either of us, care of IDG Books: IDG Books Worldwide, 919 East Hillsdale Blvd., Suite 400, Foster City, CA 94404.

Publisher's Acknowledgments

We're proud of this book; please send us your comments through our online registration form located at www.dummies.com/register/.

Some of the people who helped bring this book to market include the following:

Acquisitions, Development, and Editorial

Project Editor: Tim Gallan

Acquisitions Editor: Michael Kelly

Media Development Manager: Joyce Pepple

Associate Permissions Editor:
Heather H. Dismore

Copy Editor: Jennifer Davies

Technical Editor: Lee Musick

Editorial Manager: Leah P. Cameron

Editorial Assistant: Michael D. Sullivan

Production

Project Coordinator: Regina D. Snyder

Layout and Graphics: Linda M. Boyer, Elizabeth Cárdenas-Nelson, Dominique DeFelice, Pamela Emanoil, Kelly Hardesty, Angela F. Hunckler, Heather Pearson, Brent Savage, Ian A. Smith

Proofreaders: Jennifer K. Overmyer, Melissa D. Buddendeck, Carrie Voorhis, Christine D. Berman, Joel K. Draper, Rachel Garvey, Robert Springer, Karen York

Indexer: Richard Shrout

General and Administrative

Wiley Technology Publishing Group: Richard Swadley, Vice President and Executive Group Publisher; Bob Ipsen, Vice President and Group Publisher; Joseph Wikert, Vice President and Publisher; Barry Pruett, Vice President and Publisher; Mary Bednarek, Editorial Director; Mary C. Corder, Editorial Director; Andy Cummings, Editorial Director

Wiley Manufacturing: Ivor Parker, Vice President, Manufacturing

Wiley Marketing: John Helmus, Assistant Vice President, Director of Marketing

Wiley Composition Services for Branded Press: Debbie Stailey, Composition Services Director

Contents at a Glance

Introduction 1

Part I: Building Better Web Pages 7
Chapter 1: The Web's THE Place to Be! 9
Chapter 2: Getting Hyper 27
Chapter 3: What's in a Page? 39
Chapter 4: Build Your First Web Page 53

Part II: A Tour of HTML Basics 59
Chapter 5: What's a Markup Language? 61
Chapter 6: Pigeonholing Page Contents: HTML Categories 73
Chapter 7: Introducing the Unrepresentable: HTML Entities 163
Chapter 8: Stick Out Your Neck! HTML Extensions 173
Chapter 9: Using HTML Tables Effectively 179
Chapter 10: Building Basic HTML Documents 187

Part III: Advanced HTML 201
Chapter 11: Beyond Basics: Adding Flair and Impact to Your Pages 203
Chapter 12: Going High-Rise: Building Complex Pages 221
Chapter 13: Strictly Pro Forma: Using Forms for Feedback 239
Chapter 14: The Map's the Thing! 255
Chapter 15: Navigation Aids 267

Part IV: Publishing on the Web 281
Chapter 16: Testing, Testing, 1-2-3 283
Chapter 17: Going Live with Your Web Site 293
Chapter 18: What Do the Users Think? 301

Part V: It's Tool Time: HTML Development Tools and Environments 307
Chapter 19: Tools of the Trade: HTML and Web Publishing Tools 309
Chapter 20: Using UNIX Uniformly 321
Chapter 21: More Macintosh Madness 331
Chapter 22: Webbing Up Windows 341

Part VI: The Part of Tens 351
Chapter 23: The Top Ten HTML Dos and Don'ts 353
Chapter 24: Ten Design Desiderata 359
Chapter 25: Almost Ten Ways to Exterminate Web Bugs 365
Chapter 26: Ten "Build or Buy" Tips for Web Services 371

Appendix: About the CD 377

Index 387

End-User
License Agreement 405

CD Installation Instructions 407

Cartoons at a Glance

By Rich Tennant

page 59

page 201

page 7

page 307

page 281

page 351

Fax: 978-546-7747
E-mail: richtennant@the5thwave.com
World Wide Web: www.the5thwave.com

Table of Contents

· ·

Introduction 1

    About This Book 1
    How to Use This Book 2
    Assume = Makes an A** Out of U & Me 3
    How This Book Is Organized 3
        Part I: Building Better Web Pages 3
        Part II: A Tour of HTML Basics 4
        Part III: Advanced HTML 4
        Part IV: Publishing on the Web 4
        Part V: It's Tool Time: HTML Development Tools
          and Environments 5
        Part VI: The Part of Tens 5
    Icons Used in This Book 5
    Where to Go from Here 6

Part I: Building Better Web Pages 7

Chapter 1: The Web's THE Place to Be! 9

    From Small Things, Big Things Sometimes Come 9
        What is the Web, and where is it strung? 10
        And now, a word from our sponsor 10
    Before the Web: Other Internet Navigation Tools 10
        FTP (no, it's not about flowers — that's FTD!) 11
        Burrowing around in Gopherspace 11
        The beauty of mailing lists and electronic mail 12
        Usenet 13
        Wide-Area Information Service (WAIS) 13
    Why Is the Web a "Big Deal"? 13
    Of Browsers and Search Tools 14
        Lynx 14
        Mosaic 15
        Netscape Navigator 15
        Internet Explorer 16
    Uniform Resources on the Web 16
        URLs hold the keys to the Web 16
        Making those URL keys fit 18

Danger! Explosive Growth 18
A Scintillating Survey of the Web, Worldwide 19
    Jumping-off points galore 19
    Search pages, anyone? 19
Under the Hood: How the Web Works 20
Networking Takes Protocols 21
    How Webs talk: the HyperText Transfer Protocol (HTTP) ... 21
    The straight dope on HTTP 23
HTML: HyperText Markup Language 24
Accessing the Web 25

Chapter 2: Getting Hyper 27

HTML Basics 27
Of Links and Sausages 28
    Jumping around inside documents 28
    Jumping across documents (and services) 29
You've Used Hypertext, Without Knowing It 30
Beyond Text, There's Multimedia 31
    Hyperhelpers: useful "helper" applications 33
    The value of visuals 35
    Mavens of multimedia 36
Bringing It All Together with the Web 37

Chapter 3: What's in a Page? 39

It's All in the Layout 40
What Are You Trying to Say? 41
    Who's listening? 41
    Design springs from content — and intent 42
        A matter of intent 42
        Establish key messages 42
        Think about superstructure and information flow ... 43
    Grab the audience's attention 44
    They're after the goods . . . don't get in the way! 44
    What should they remember? 45
Meet the Elements of Page Design 45
    Tagging text 46
    Titles and labels 46
    Text and hypertext links 47
    Overcoming two-dimensional thinking 48
        Stringing pages together the old-fashioned way ... 48
        Hierarchies are easy to model in HTML 49
        Multiple tracks for multiple audiences 50
        A bona-fide Web wonder: the "hotlist" or "jump page" ... 51
        Extending the Web, a piece at a time 52

Chapter 4: Build Your First Web Page 53

Start with the Right Tools 53
The Edit-Review Cycle 54
Working with Templates 57
What Comes Next? 58

Part II: A Tour of HTML Basics 59

Chapter 5: What's a Markup Language? 61

A Markup Language Is Not a Form of Graffiti 61
A syntax is not a levy on cigarettes! 62
Elements of HTML syntax 63
Standard Generalized Markup Language (SGML) 65
Generalized Markup Covers Many Sins 66
Building better pieces and parts 67
Where HTML fits under the SGML umbrella 67
Welcome to HTML! 68
Delivering content to a variety of platforms 68
The four-plus faces of HTML 69
HTML Elements! 70
Go to the head of the document 70
The bulk's in the body 71
The good stuff's in the graphics and links 71
A footer may be optional, but it's still a good idea...... 71
Ladies and Gentlemen, Start Your Engines! 72

Chapter 6: Pigeonholing Page Contents: HTML Categories 73

HTML Syntax Redux 73
Syntax conventions are no party! 74
Decoding a complex metacharacter example: ALIGN = ? 76
Interesting HTML properties 77
No embedded blanks, please! 77
What's the default? 78
The nesting instinct 78
A matter of context 79
HTML Categories 80
HTML Tags 86
The run-down on attributes 86
Common attributes 87
Tag information layout 87
<IMG> Inline image 87
Tag layout commentary 90

The HTML tag team 90
  <A> ... </A> Anchor 90
  <ADDRESS> ... </ADDRESS> Attribution info 93
  <APPLET> ... </APPLET> Java Applet 93
  <AREA> Hotzone 95
  <B> ... </B> Bold style 96
  <BASE> Basis for relative addressing 97
  <BASEFONT> Base font 98
  <BIG> ... </BIG> Big text 98
  <BLOCKQUOTE> ... </BLOCKQUOTE> Quote style 99
  <BODY> ... </BODY> Mark off HTML document body 100

 Force line break 101
  <CAPTION> ... </CAPTION> Table caption 102
  <CENTER> ... </CENTER> Center text 103
  <CITE> ... </CITE> Citation markup 103
  <CODE> ... </CODE> Program code text 104
  <COL> Column 105
  <COLGROUP> A Column group 106
  <DD> Definition description 108
  <DFN> ... </DFN> Definition 108
  <DIR> ... </DIR> Directory list 109
  <DIV> ... </DIV> Logical division 109
  <DL> ... </DL> Definition list 110
  <DT> Definition term 111
  <EM> ... </EM> Emphasis 112
  <FIELDSET> ... </FIELDSET> Form field set 113
  <FONT> ... </FONT> Font settings 113
  <FORM> ... </FORM> User input form 114
  <H*> ... </H*> Header levels 1 through 6 116
  <HEAD> ... </HEAD> Document head block 117
  <HR> Horizontal rule 117
  <HTML> ... </HTML> Main document head 119
  <I> ... </I> Italicize text 119
  <IMG> Inline image 120
  <INPUT> Input object 122
  <ISINDEX> Document is indexed 124
  <KBD> ... </KBD> Keyboard text style 125
  <LABEL> ... </LABEL> Form field label 126
  <LI> List item 127
  <LINK> 128
  <LISTING> ... </LISTING> 129
  <MAP> ... </MAP> Client side image map 129
  <MENU> ... </MENU> 130
  <META> 131
  <OBJECT> ... </OBJECT> Non-http object 132

<OL> ... </OL> Ordered list 135
<OPTION> Form list choice 135
<P> 136
<PARAM> Applet and object parameters 137
<PLAINTEXT> ... </PLAINTEXT> 137
<PRE> ... </PRE> Preformatted style 138
<S> ... </S> Strikethrough text 139
<SAMP> ... </SAMP> Sample text 140
<SCRIPT> ... </SCRIPT> Inline script 140
<SELECT> ... </SELECT> Select input object 141
<SMALL> ... </SMALL> Small text 143
<SPAN> ... </SPAN> Style area 143
<STRONG> ... </STRONG> Strong emphasis 144
<STYLE> ... </STYLE> Style sheet 144
_{...} Subscript 145
^{...} Superscript 146
<TABLE> Table 146
<TBODY> ... </TBODY> Table body 148
<TD> ... </TD> Table cell 149
<TEXTAREA> ... </TEXTAREA> Text input area 151
<TEXTFLOW> ... </TEXTFLOW> Applet alternative 153
<TFOOT> ... </TFOOT> Table footer 154
<THEAD> ... </THEAD> Table body 155
<TH> ... </TH> Column head 156
<TITLE> ... </TITLE> Document title 158
<TR> ... </TR> Table row 158
<TT> ... </TT> Teletype text 160
<U> ... </U> Underline text 160
<UL> ... </UL> Unordered list style 161
<VAR> ... </VAR> Variable text style 161
<XMP> ... </XMP> Variable text style 162

Chapter 7: Introducing the Unrepresentable: HTML Entities 163

Entities Don't Have to Be an Alien Concept 163
Producing Special Characters 164
Nothing Ancient about the ISO-Latin-1 HTML 166

Chapter 8: Stick Out Your Neck! HTML Extensions 173

If Your Browser Can't See It, Is It Really There? 174
The State of the HTML Art 174
A "simple explanation" for browser diversity 174
Vive la différence: adding value . . . or adding confusion? 175
What's in Store for HTML? 175
Nonstandard HTML Extensions 176
Added tag attributes 176

Chapter 9: Using HTML Tables Effectively 179

   HTML <TABLE> Overview 180
   HTML Table Markup 180
      The parts of a <TABLE> 181
      The basic table attributes 183
   Building Your Own Tables 184
      Laying out tabular data for easy display 184
      Multirow and multicolumn 185
      Mixing graphics and tables makes for interesting pages 185
      Nesting 185
   Some Stunning Table Examples 186

Chapter 10: Building Basic HTML Documents 187

   The Template's the Thing! 188
   Page Layout: Top to Bottom 189
   What's in a Name? Thinking Up Good Titles and Headings 191
      Titles 191
      Headings 192
   Building Better Document Bodies 193
      Textual sound bites — NOT! 194
      Balanced composition 194
      Controlling long pages 195
      The bottom line on bodies 195
   Good Bones: Building Strong Paragraphs 196
   Listward Ho: Using a List Structure 196
   Hooking Up: Linking Your Pages 198
      Links to pages within your Web are relative 198
      Links to the world outside of your Web are physical 199
      Choose your hyperlinks with care 200

Part III: Advanced HTML *201*

**Chapter 11: Beyond Basics: Adding Flair and Impact
to Your Pages** 203

   Borrowing Can Lead to Sorrow 203
   Eye-Catchers: Logos, Icons, and Other Little Gems 204
      Horizontal rules — but rainbow lines bring smiles 207
      Colored dots beat list dots 208
      Icons 209
      Logos and graphics as hyperlinks 209
   Building Graphic Page Layouts 211
      Working with graphics files 212
      GIF and JPEG file formats 213
         Seeing through the graphic to the background 213
         A new pic's resolution 214
      Rules for graphical thumbs 214

Footers Complete Your Page 215
    Use a URL line as part of your page 217
    Copyright 218
    Counting coup: versions, dates, and times 218
Pointers to the Author or Owner 219
    The e-mail link for feedback 219
Comment Your HTML Documents for Posterity 220

Chapter 12: Going High-Rise: Building Complex Pages 221

There's No Place Like Home 221
    Organization 222
    It's story (board) time, boys and girls! 224
First Things First: List 'em Out 224
    Sketch the Web 225
    Board the whole story 225
Anchors Away: Jumping Around Your Documents 226
    Linking to text in another page 226
    Linking to text within a page: table of contents links 227
Jumping to Remote Pages 229
    Hypertext links to outside resources 229
    Jump pages 230
    A special <LINK> 230
The Nesting Instinct: Lists within Lists 231
Analyzing Sophisticated Pages 233
    HTML For Dummies home page 233

Chapter 13: Strictly Pro Forma: Using Forms for Feedback 239

What HTML Forms Are For 239
Living within Your Forms Limitations 240
    Beware of browsers! 240
    Sorry, servers 240
What's in a Form? 241
    Forms involve two-way communication 242
    Tag! You're a form 243
Using Form Tags 244
    Setting the <FORM> environment 244
        There's no rhythm to METHOD 244
        Lights, camera . . . ACTION 244
        Let's make an assumption 244
    Knowing what's (in)coming: the <INPUT> tags 245
        TYPE-casting still works! 245
        Other <INPUT> attributes 246
        A TEXT-oriented <INPUT> example 246
    Being <SELECT>ive 248
    <TEXTAREA> lets users wax eloquent . . . or profane! 250
Formulating Good Attitudes 253

Chapter 14: The Map's the Thing! 255

Where Are You? (Using Clickable Maps) 255
Cosmic Cartography: What It Takes to Present Maps on the Web 257
  Warning: different maps for different servers 258
  Dealing with shapes in maps 259
Building and Linking to CERN Map Files 260
  The menu bar map file 260
  Using map files 261
Building and Linking to NCSA Map Files 261
  The button bar map file 261
  Using map files 262
Final Touches 262
  Creating and storing map files 262
  Defining a clickable map in your HTML document 263
"The Map Is Not the Territory" 263
Of Clickable Maps and URLs 264
Late-Breaking News! Client-Side Image Maps! 265

Chapter 15: Navigation Aids 267

The <META> Tag 268
There's a Spider on the Web! 270
  Webcrawlers and search engines 270
  Don't wait for the spider to come to you — register! 271
Keeping the Bugs Away 271
  <META> CONTENT 271
  Robots, go home! 272
Searching Documents for Details 273
The Bigger Things Get, the Easier It Is to Get Lost! 274
Documentary Integuments: Indexes, Jump Tables, and Internal Links ... 276
Doing Things the Database Way 276
Stay Away from Diminishing Returns 277
Virtual Compass 277
Rack and Pinion Steering 278
Where's the Search Lead? 279

Part IV: Publishing on the Web 281

Chapter 16: Testing, Testing, 1-2-3 283

Why Test Your Pages? 283
What You Think Doesn't Count 284
Expect (And Test for) the Unexpected 285
In Vitro Vitrification: Alpha Testing Methods 285
  Webbuilder, test thine own Web thyself 287
  Iteration, iteration, iteration 288

Type it or write It; then do it 289
Alpha test plan 289
Purpose 289
Scope 289
Test overview 290
Goals 290
Schedule and resources 290
Tester form 290
System configurations 291
Test method and evaluation 291
Performance and functionality testing 292
Limits and boundary checking 292

Chapter 17: Going Live with Your Web Site **293**

Prelaunch Checklist 293
All in the Family 295
Elbow Room 296
Throwing Caution to the Wind 298

Chapter 18: What Do the Users Think? **301**

Beta Testing 301
Beta testers 302
Cycling ahead of the gremlins 303
Gamma Testing and Beyond? 303
There's nothing crazy about a sanity check! 304
Stick it to me: the importance of feedback 304
Building a report card 305
Serious feedback methods 305
Knowing When to Quit (Testing) 306

**Part V: It's Tool Time: HTML Development Tools
and Environments** **307**

Chapter 19: Tools of the Trade: HTML and Web Publishing Tools ... 309

Making Coding Easier: HTML Editors 310
Why you should know HTML 310
Making an editor work for you 311
The Doctor Is In: Page Checkups 312
HTML validation: bad code is bad news 313
What browsers forgive, a validator may not! 313
A Kinder, Gentler HTML Validator 314
Of course you can spel: spell check your pages! 315

Don't lose the connection: link checking 316
    MOMSpider 316
    WebWalker 317
    CheckBot 317
Keeper of the Zoo: Tools for Managing Your Site 318

Chapter 20: Using UNIX Uniformly 321

Diving for Treasure in the UNIX HTML Tools Sea 322
Standing Alone Amidst the UNIX HTML Editors 322
    A.S.H.E. 323
    Phoenix 324
    HoTMetaL Pro 324
    AOLPress 326
    EMACS modes and templates 326
Filtering and Converting Your UNIX Files 328
    WebMaker 328
    WebWorks Publisher 329
UNIX Web Server Search 330

Chapter 21: More Macintosh Madness 331

Surveying the Orchard: Macintosh HTML Tools 331
Biting into Stand-Alone HTML Editors for Macintosh 332
    Webtor 332
    HTML Pro 333
    Claris Home Page 333
    NetObjects Fusion 334
    PageMill 334
    HoTMetaL Pro 334
    AOLPress 335
    Netscape Navigator Gold 337
Tackling Text Editor Extensions and Templates 337
    BBEdit 338
    BBEdit HTML extensions 338
    BBEdit HTML tools 338
Magnificent Miscellaneous Mac Tools 339
Web Server Primer 339
    WebSTAR / MacHTTP Web server 339
    Netwings 340
    httpd4Mac 340

Chapter 22: Webbing Up Windows 341

Surveying the Field of HTML Software Tools 342
WYSIWYG Web Authoring Systems 342
    FrontPage 97 343
    Netscape Composer 346

HTML Code Editors 347
    HomeSite 2.5 347
Word Processors as HTML Editors 348
Filters and File Converters 349
    HTML Transit 349
    WebMaker 3.0 350

Part VI: The Part of Tens .... _351_

Chapter 23: The Top Ten HTML Dos and Don'ts 353

Remembering Your Content! 353
Structuring Your Documents 354
Keeping Track of Tags 354
Making the Most from the Least 355
Building Attractive Pages 356
Avoiding Browser Dependencies 356
Evolution, Not Revolution 357
Navigating Your Wild and Woolly Web 357
Beating the Two-Dimensional Text Trap 358
Overcoming Inertia Takes Constant Vigilance 358

Chapter 24: Ten Design Desiderata 359

Creating Page Layouts 359
Building a Graphical Vocabulary 360
Using White Space 360
Formatting for Impact 361
Enhancing Content 361
Making Effective Use of Hypermedia 362
Aiding Navigation 362
Forming Good Opinions 363
Knowing When to Split 363
Adding Value for Value 363

Chapter 25: Almost Ten Ways to Exterminate Web Bugs 365

Making a List and Checking It Twice 365
Mastering the Mechanics of Text 366
Lacking Live Links Leaves Loathsome Legacies 366
Looking for Trouble in All the Right Places 367
Covering All the Bases 368
Tools of the Testing Trade 368
Fostering Feedback 369
Making the Most of Your Audience 369

Chapter 26: Ten "Build or Buy" Tips for Web Services 371

Understanding Objectives 372
Counting Your Pennies 372
Projecting and Monitoring Traffic 372
How Much Is Too Much? 373
Managing Volatility 373
Communicating Corporately 374
Reaching Your Audience 374
"Web-ifying" Commerce 375
Understanding Your Options 376
Overcoming Success 376

Appendix: About the CD *377*

Index *387*

End-User
License Agreement *405*

CD Installation Instructions *407*

Introduction

• •

*W*elcome to the wild, wacky, and wonderful possibilities inherent in the World Wide Web. In this book, we introduce you to the mysteries of the HyperText Markup Language used to build Web pages, and initiate you into the select, but growing community of Web authors.

If you've tried to build your own Web pages before but found it too forbidding, now you can relax. If you can dial a telephone, or find your keys in the morning, you too can become an HTML author. (No kidding!)

When we wrote this book, we took a straightforward approach to telling you about authoring documents for the World Wide Web. We've tried to keep the amount of technobabble to a minimum and stuck with plain English as much as possible. Besides plain talk about hypertext, HTML, and the Web, we've included lots of sample programs and tag-by-tag instructions for building your very own Web pages.

We've also included a peachy CD with this book that contains each and every HTML example in usable form and a number of other interesting widgets for your own documents. In addition, this CD also includes the magnificent and bedazzling source materials for the *HTML For Dummies,* 3rd Edition, Web pages, which you might find to be a source of inspiration and raw material for your own uses!

About This Book

Think of this book as a friendly, approachable guide to HTML and to building readable, attractive pages for the World Wide Web. Although HTML isn't hard to learn, it can be hard to remember all the details needed to write interesting Web pages. Some sample topics you'll find in this book include the following:

- ✔ The origins and history of the World Wide Web
- ✔ Designing and building Web pages
- ✔ Creating interesting page layouts
- ✔ Testing and debugging your Web pages

Although you might think that building Web pages requires years of training and advanced aesthetic capabilities, we must point out that this just ain't so. If you can tell somebody how to drive from their house to yours, you can certainly build a Web document that does what you want it to. The purpose of this book isn't to turn you into a rocket scientist — it's to show you all the design and technical elements you need to build a good-looking, readable Web page, and give you the know-how and confidence to do it!

How to Use This Book

This book tells you what the World Wide Web is all about and how it works. Then, it tells you what's involved in designing and building effective Web documents to bring your important ideas and information to the whole world, if that's what you want to do.

All HTML code appears in monospaced type like this:

```
<HEAD><TITLE>What's in a Title?</TITLE></HEAD>...
```

When you type in HTML tags or other related information, be sure to copy the information exactly as you see it between the angle brackets (< and >) because that's part of the magic that makes HTML work. Other than that, you'll find out how to marshal and manage the content that makes your pages special, and we'll tell you exactly what you need to do to mix the elements of HTML with your own work.

Due to the margins in this book, some long lines of HTML markup, or designations of World Wide Web sites (called URLs, for Uniform Resource Locators), may wrap to the next line. On your computer though, these wrapped lines will appear as a single line of HTML, or as a single URL, so don't insert a hard return when you see one of these wrapped lines.

```
http://www.infomagic.austin.com/nexus/plexus/lexus/sexus/
    this_is_a_deliberately_long.html
```

HTML doesn't care if you type tag text in uppercase, lowercase, or both (except for character entities, which must be typed exactly as shown in Chapter 7). In order for your own work to look like ours as much as possible, you should enter all HTML tag text in uppercase only.

Assume = Makes an A** Out of U & Me

They say that making assumptions makes a fool out of the person who's making them and the person who's the subject of those assumptions. Nevertheless, we're going to make a few assumptions about you, our gentle reader:

- ✔ You can turn your computer on and off.
- ✔ You know how to use a mouse and a keyboard.
- ✔ You want to build your own Web pages for fun, profit, or because it's part of your job.

In addition, we assume you already have a working connection to the Internet and one of the many fine Web browsers available by hook, by crook, or by download from that selfsame Internet. You don't need to be a master logician or a wizard in the arcane arts of programming, nor do you need a Ph.D. in computer science. You don't even need a detailed sense of what's going on in the innards of your computer to deal with the material in this book.

If you can write a sentence and know the difference between a heading and a paragraph, you will be able to build and deploy your own documents on the World Wide Web. If you have an imagination, and the ability to communicate what's important to you, you've already mastered the key ingredients necessary to build useful, attractive Web pages. The rest is details, and we'll help you with those!

How This Book Is Organized

This book contains six major parts. Each part contains three or more chapters, and each chapter contains several modular sections. Any time you need help or information, just pick up the book and start anywhere you want, or use the table of contents and index to look up specific topics or key words.

Here is a breakdown of the six parts and what you'll find in each one:

Part I: Building Better Web Pages

This part sets the stage and includes an overview of and introduction to the World Wide Web, its history, and the software that people use to mine its treasures. It also explains how the Web works, including the HyperText Markup Language to which this book is devoted, and the server-side software and services that deliver information to end-users.

HTML documents, also called Web pages, are the fundamental units of information organization and delivery on the Web. Here, you'll also find out what HTML is about and how hypertext can enrich ordinary text. Then, you'll take a walk on the Web side, and build your very first HTML document. You'll also work through a primer on basic Web page layout and design to help you begin the process of building your own HTML documents and sites.

Part II: A Tour of HTML Basics

HTML mixes ordinary text with special strings of characters, called markup, that instruct browsers how to display HTML documents. In this part of the book, we cover markup in general, and HTML in particular. This includes logical groupings for HTML tags, and a complete dictionary of HTML tags. By the time you're finished with Part II, you'll have a good overall idea of what HTML is and what it can do.

Part III: Advanced HTML

Part III takes all the elements covered in Part II and puts them together to help you build commercial-grade HTML documents, which includes building complex pages, developing on-screen forms to solicit information and feedback, and creating clickable image maps to let graphics guide your user's on-screen navigation.

Part IV: Publishing on the Web

Once you've built your HTML documents, the real fun begins as your work meets the ultimate test: what users like or don't like about it. As you're getting ready to release your Web site to a possibly indifferent world, you'll be prepared to catch and kill potential bugs yourself. You'll also be armed with strategies to enlist user feedback, to help you effectively communicate online, and to avoid having to deal with too many problems once you've taken your work public.

After you've tested and debugged your work, it's time to publish your documents. In this part of the book, we show you how to blow your own horn and let the world know not just where your pages are, but why they're worth a visit. You'll also be prepared to deal with the potential onslaught of users, and to decide whether you'll put your pages on somebody else's Web server, or build your own.

Part V: It's Tool Time: HTML Development Tools and Environments

When it comes to building HTML, you can do it alone, with only your trusty text editor. But it doesn't have to be that way: In this part, you'll be exposed to the many different tools available to help you build the Web pages of your dreams, and to manage those pages once they're built. We'll tell you about our own favorite Web-related tools as well. And along the way, you'll have a chance to see what's available for UNIX, Macintosh, Windows, and other computing platforms by way of HTML editors and related tools, and Web servers and related services.

Part VI: The Part of Tens

In the concluding part of the book, we sum up and distill the very essence of what you've read. Here, you'll have a chance to review the top dos and don'ts for HTML markup, to rethink your views on document design, and to catch and kill any potential bugs and errors in your pages before anybody else sees them. Finally, you'll end your adventure by revisiting your Web server situation, as you reconsider whether your pages should reside on an Internet provider's Web server or whether you should build a Web server of your very own.

Icons Used in This Book

This icon points out information you shouldn't pass by — don't overlook these gentle reminders (the life you save could be your own).

This icon flags useful information that makes HTML markup, Web page design, or other important stuff even less complicated that you feared it might be.

This icon signals technical details that are informative and interesting, but not critical to writing HTML. Skip these if you want (but please, come back and read them later).

This icon lets you know that there's some additional related information elsewhere in the book.

Be cautious when you see this icon. It warns you of things you shouldn't do. The bomb is meant to emphasize that the consequences of ignoring these bits of wisdom can be severe.

When you see this spiderweb symbol, it flags the presence of Web-based resources that you can go out and investigate further.

When we refer to resources on the CD-ROM, we use this icon.

Where to Go from Here

This is the part where you pick a direction and hit the road! *HTML For Dummies* is a lot like the story of the seven blind men and the elephant: It almost doesn't matter where you start; you'll be looking at lots of different stuff as you prepare yourself to build your own Web pages. Who cares if anybody else thinks you're just goofing around — we know you're getting ready to have the time of your life.

Enjoy!

Part I
Building Better
Web Pages

The 5th Wave   By Rich Tennant

"Hold your horses. It takes time to build a
home page for someone your size."

In this part . . .

This part includes an introduction to the World Wide Web, explaining its history and the software that people use to mine its treasures. We also cover how the Web works, including the HyperText Markup Language to which this book is devoted, and the server-side software and services that deliver information to end-users. We show you what HTML is about and how hypertext can enrich ordinary text. Then you get to design and build your very first HTML document.

Chapter 1
The Web's THE Place to Be!

● ●

In This Chapter

▶ Defining the World Wide Web

▶ Examining other Internet search tools

▶ Making the most of the Web — browsers and search tools

▶ Examining Web background and terminology

▶ Looking at exploding Web growth

▶ Interpreting Web pages

▶ Accessing the Web

● ●

To understand HTML (*HyperText Markup Language*), you must first understand the environment that it serves and the world in which it operates. HTML is a text-based markup language that provides the under-pinnings for one of the most exciting information search and navigation environments ever developed: This environment is called the World Wide Web (Web, WWW, or W3, for short). The Web represents a major step forward in making all kinds of information accessible to average folks like you.

From Small Things, Big Things Sometimes Come

Tim Berners-Lee and a group of colleagues at the European Laboratory for Particle Physics (CERN) in Geneva, Switzerland, had no idea what they were starting when they began hacking together a way for physicists to share research results with each other. Nevertheless, they started a strange and wonderful phenomenon that has taken the whole Internet community by storm. Originally, they wanted to build an online system so ordinary users could share data, without having to master arcane commands or esoteric interfaces. But by 1992, users outside CERN were also creating Web pages.

This led to the advent of powerful, graphical browsers for a broad range of desktop computers and workstations. By 1993, the Web had become the most popular and powerful Internet tool of all.

To get started on the Web, you need a way to access the Internet, a Web browser, and information about where to enter the Web. After that, you can scan the information that shows up on your screen and follow chains of information for the rest of your life (without ever again having to come up for air).

But wait a minute! Before you get lost in its infinite strands, you may want to consider a few more details about the Web's workings. (But don't let us stop you from trying it out — just check in right here when you come back!)

What is the Web, and where is it strung?

You probably have a vague idea that the Web is a vast, amorphous blob of text, image, audio, and video data that is scattered across networks and computers worldwide. Hence comes the name, World Wide Web.

And now, a word from our sponsor . . .

According to Tim Berners-Lee, one of the Web's chief architects (and a founding father for its original development), "The World Wide Web is conceived as a seamless world in which ALL information, from any source, can be accessed in a consistent and simple way." (You can find this statement in a Web page written by Berners-Lee at: `http://www.w3.org/pub/WWW/WWW/Talks/General/Concepts.html` entitled *W3 Concepts*.) By working with HTML, you can not only roam this seamless world, you can even contribute to the growth and proliferation of the Web!

Before the Web: Other Internet Navigation Tools

To understand the extraordinary impact the Web has on the Internet, you may want to take a look at previous Internet navigation tools. These other tools require considerably more user expertise than do Web browsers. While you're taking this trip down memory lane, please keep the following in mind: Although Web browsers supplant the functionality of many navigation tools, they work with these tools as well. Through HTML links, browsers call on other services to locate and retrieve files, messages, and other goodies from the vast Internet storehouse.

FTP (no, it's not about flowers — that's FTD!)

FTP (*File Transfer Protocol*) is a cross-platform protocol for transferring files to and from computers anywhere on the Internet. *Cross-platform* means that you don't have to use the same kind of computer operating system to access files on a remote system. Figure 1-1 shows a graphical FTP menu. Notice the PC file system on the left (what's on your machine) and the remote file system on the right (what's on the FTP server). By navigating the directories shown, you can copy files between the two systems, as your access rights allow. (In English, "navigating the directories" means finding the location in a file system where the files you're after reside, and "access rights" refers to your ability to see, copy, delete, or write files within the FTP server's directories.) You can access and transfer FTP-based files directly from within a Web browser.

Burrowing around in Gopherspace

Gopher is the creation of a team of dedicated programmers at the University of Minnesota, home of "The Golden Gophers." More than a totemic animal, Gopher is a good tool when browsing files on the Internet. Gopher servers are extensively interlinked, much like the Web. In addition, all Gopher interaction occurs through a consistent menu interface that makes all Gopher systems look alike. You can search by keyword or filename so that you have more flexibility in finding your way around. Like FTP, you can also access Gopher resources through a Web browser.

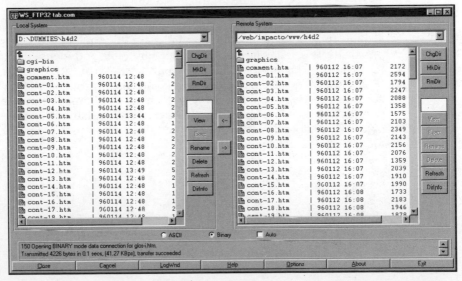

Figure 1-1:
A graphical view of FTP.

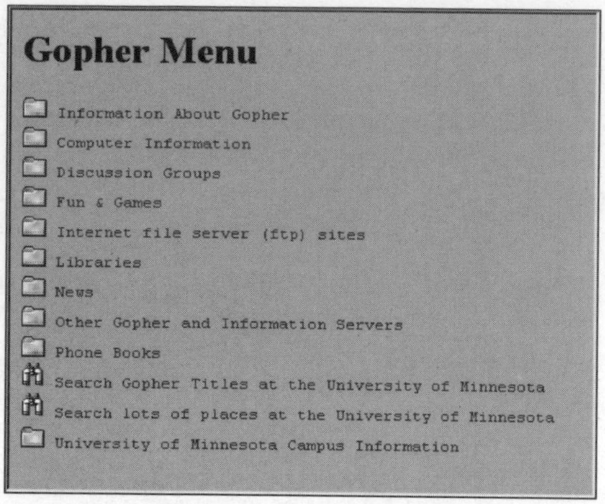

Gopher Menu

- 📁 Information About Gopher
- 📁 Computer Information
- 📁 Discussion Groups
- 📁 Fun & Games
- 📁 Internet file server (ftp) sites
- 📁 Libraries
- 📁 News
- 📁 Other Gopher and Information Servers
- 📁 Phone Books
- 🔍 Search Gopher Titles at the University of Minnesota
- 🔍 Search lots of places at the University of Minnesota
- 📁 University of Minnesota Campus Information

Figure 1-2:
The prime
Gopher
at the
University of
Minnesota.

The beauty of mailing lists and electronic mail

A little-known bit of trivia is that much information on the Internet is available through e-mail and through tools like FTP and Gopher. By stating the proper requests to the right e-mail servers — thereby accessing mail service programs such as *listserv* and *majordomo* — users with sufficient savvy can get to just about anything on the Internet. And — you guessed it — you can also access e-mail with most modern Web browsers, too!

Usenet

Usenet is a worldwide messaging system where anyone can read and post articles to a group of individuals who share the same interests. Usenet organizes its articles into named groups by topic and focus. These groups have varying degrees of internal organization — from strict moderation to freeform conversation. In some cases, you can approach Usenet with a specific question and come away with an answer immediately, but other queries can go unanswered for weeks on end. Persistence, coupled with an appreciation for Usenet's workings and the rules of proper Internet behavior, also called *netiquette,* are your keys to success.

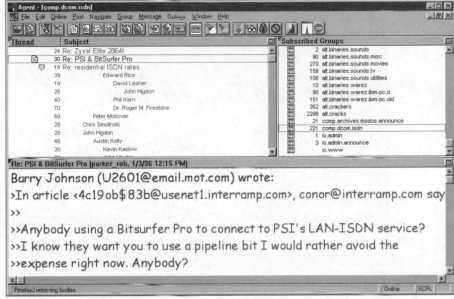

Figure 1-3:
Usenet
messages
from comp.
dcom.isdn.

Wide-Area Information Service (WAIS)

WAIS (pronounced "ways" or "wase") is one of a handful of Internet search tools that can spread itself across the network to scour multiple archives and handle multiple data formats. This tool searches tirelessly throughout the entire Internet for the information you request. WAIS can help you find things, especially when you're not sure of precise filenames, menu entries, or other name-specific information.

To find out more about the Internet, take a trip to your local bookstore. You'll find no shortage of Internet-related titles there. (We counted more than 100 on our last visit!) Pay particular attention to John R. Levine, Carol Baroudi, and Margaret Levine Young's *The Internet For Dummies,* 4th Edition (1997) and Levine and Young's *MORE Internet For Dummies,* 3rd Edition (1997), both from IDG Books Worldwide, Inc.

Why Is the Web a "Big Deal"?

We hope that you can come up with answers to this question on your own by now. But we'll run this one down, just to be sure: The World Wide Web is a major development in information access on the Internet. The W3 is a big deal because it covers an astonishing amount of ground. Also, the World Wide Web makes it easy and intuitive for users to find their way around huge collections of data while hiding most of the ugly details involved.

Any one reason would make the Web important and useful; all of them together make it a genuine step forward in the way we use and share information as a part of our daily lives.

Of Browsers and Search Tools

For most end users, their Web access software — called a browser or a Web client — is the most important piece of Internet software that they use. Today, you can find many browsers for PCs running Windows, a more limited selection for DOS-only machines, and options for Macintosh, UNIX, and other kinds of computers. All graphical Web browsers share a common point-and-click approach to interacting with information. Even character-based browsers, like Lynx, make it easy to pick and follow links by selecting the appropriate highlighted text. Here's a quick look at some of the players.

Lynx

Lynx is a text-only Web browser. That is, it cannot display graphical or multimedia elements (although you can configure it to display graphics by using an external file viewer on appropriate systems). Even so, Lynx provides useful Web functionality for users on so-called *dumb terminals* because it supports keyboard navigation and boldface display of hypertext links (which is where we think that the program got its name: Lynx = links; get it?).

Figure 1-4:
Lynx uses
text displays
effectively
for Web
pages.

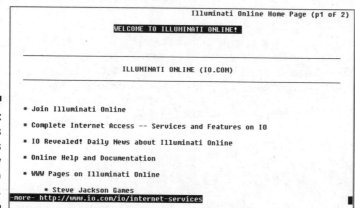

Mosaic

Mosaic is a graphical Web browser developed by a team of programmers at the National Center for Supercomputing Applications (NCSA). One of the original programmers, Marc Andreesen, eventually left NCSA to form his own Internet service company — Netscape. Mosaic was the first graphical browser for the Web, and it continues to hold its own against other browsers. You can find many flavors of Mosaic today, including ones for X Windows (primarily for UNIX), Microsoft Windows, and the Macintosh. Mosaic was the first *full-featured* graphical browser and has spawned many clones.

Netscape Navigator

Netscape Navigator, the brainchild of Marc Andreesen, is the Internet's most popular graphical Web browser. Take one look and you see clear evidence of its developers' wisdom and experience. In addition, Netscape Navigator includes advanced features not found in other Web browsers, and its list of features, advancements, and add-ons boggles the mind — with additions made almost daily. Available both as shareware and in a commercial release, Navigator provides one of the best and most popular Web interfaces that we've encountered anywhere.

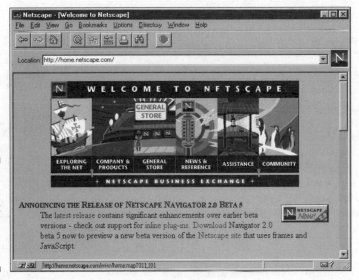

Figure 1-5: More than 50 percent of Web surfers use Netscape.

Internet Explorer

You get a version of Internet Explorer (IE), the Microsoft entry into the Web browser arena, as part of Windows 95 or Windows NT. You can also obtain the most recent release from the Microsoft Web site at `http://www. microsoft.com`. Although it's a relative newcomer in this game, IE is number two in the popularity sweepstakes. Like Netscape Navigator, IE has proprietary HTML tag elements in its list of features. But IE's extensions also include some proprietary, but powerful, programming extensions, and its inclusion with the best-selling desktop and server operating systems (that is, Windows 95 and Windows NT) means that IE is a force to be reckoned with and exerts considerable power over future directions for Web browser features and functions.

Uniform Resources on the Web

The most significant feature of the World Wide Web is its ability to shield and even protect users from the unfriendly UNIX-derived environment on the Internet. With the Web, locating information is simple: Web resources have special names — called *URLs* or *Uniform Resource Locators* — that describe the protocols needed to access the resource and then point to these resources' Internet locations.

URLs hold the keys to the Web

As you examine a URL for a specific HTML file, it looks something like this:

```
http:/www.w3.org:80/hypertext/WWW/Addressing/
            Addressing.html#spot
|-1-|--2--|3|------4------|----5----|-6-|
```

This URL is composed of six parts that work as follows:

1. **Protocol/data source:** For network resources, this part is usually the name of the protocol used to access the data that resides on the other end of the link. The syntax for this part of the name is as follows:

   - **ftp://** points to a file accessible through the File Transfer Protocol.

   - **gopher://** points to a file system index accessible through the Gopher protocol.

   - **http://** points to a hypertext document (typically, an HTML file) accessible through the HyperText Transfer Protocol.

   - **mailto:** links to an application that allows you to compose a message to send through e-mail to a predefined address.

- **news://** points to a Usenet newsgroup and uses the Network News Transfer Protocol (NNTP) to access the information.

- **telnet://** links to a remote log-in on another Internet computer, typically to select from a predefined menu.

- **WAIS://** points to a Wide Area Information Server on the Internet and provides access to a system of indexed databases.

- **file://** indicates that the file is local and is not a public Web page (that is, not available outside your directory or local network). Use this syntax for local data (typically, HTML files from your desktop machine's hard disks or other drives), but note that the syntax varies from browser to browser. If you're desperate for a more complete discussion of accessing local files, see the sidebar "URL syntax and punctuation for local file access" in this chapter.

2. **Domain name:** The domain name for the Web server where the desired Web page or other resource resides.

3. **Port address:** In most cases, the default port address for http is *:80* (and you can omit it), but you may see URLs with other numbers; when present, this number identifies a process address that a Web session needs to use. In general, if a number appears in the URL, it's a good idea to include it (even if the number is the default *:80*).

4. **Directory path:** The location of the Web page in the Web server's file system.

5. **Object name:** The actual name of the HTML file for the desired Web page or the name of any other resource that you require.

URL syntax and punctuation for local file access

When trying to access local files, you can first look for a menu selection in your browser that lets you search your local file system (like "Open File" or "Open Local File"). If that doesn't work, we've had pretty good results with the following approach:

```
file:///<drive ID>|<directory
   spec>/<filename>
```

Notice the three forward slashes after the colon. After the drive ID (which would be a letter for DOS or the volume name for Macintosh, NetWare, and so on), use a vertical bar character (I) in place of a colon.

Then when specifying the directory path (spec), use forward slashes (/) to separate directory levels. Follow the path with the exact name of the file, and you are able to access it with your browser.

If the preceding strategy doesn't work for you, look in your browser's Help file for enlightenment: Often, it's just waiting a few screens away. Search on a phrase such as "Open file" or "Open local file," and you should get the information that you need.

6. **Spot:** Sometimes, getting users to the HTML file isn't enough: You want to drop them at a particular location *within* the file. By preceding the name of an HTML *anchor* with a pound sign (#) and tacking it onto a URL, you direct the browser to jump right to a specific location. Using this structure is handy for large documents, where users might otherwise need to scroll a long way to get to the information they desire.

Making those URL keys fit

All in all, the most important thing to remember about URLs is to enter them *exactly as they're written* because they don't work if they're not exactly correct. When you use a Web browser, cutting and pasting URLs into a hotlist, bookmark, or text file is better than typing them out because you reduce the possibility of introducing an error.

For more information on URLs, consult this one:

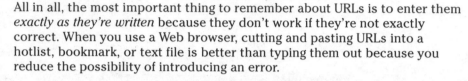

```
http://www.w3.org/hypertext/WWW/Addressing/Addressing.html
```

This resource describes the details for URL syntax and supported protocols and points to specifications and other documents on the subject. A word to the wise: The W3C site gets a lot of traffic, so you may get *timed out* trying to connect. (In English, timed out means you wait forever, and then your browser tells you it can't retrieve the page!) We've had good luck getting there during off-hours, like 3 a.m. eastern standard time.

Danger! Explosive Growth

The word *exploding* conjures an image of something that isn't safe to crawl onto, but exploding is just what the Web is doing in terms of growth. Even though its introduction (in 1991) makes it one of the newest Internet applications around, the Web has already become the most popular Internet application of all time. According to numerous sources, the Internet enjoys an annual growth rate of more than 1,000 percent (or it increases 10 times each year, if you like smaller numbers).

Wherever you get your statistics about the Web, you will find a unanimous opinion that Web usage is growing dramatically and user ranks are swelling robustly. The only real question then becomes, "How can I possibly manage to find what I really need out there on the Web?" For Web publishers, this question translates into, "How can I let the people know where my pages are?"

The following URL can provide pointers to the references we consulted to compile our statistics. It's a list of pointers (a.k.a. *hotlist,* in Web-speak) from the Library of Congress to collections of Web and Internet:

```
http://lcweb.loc.gov/global/internet/inet-stats.html
```

A Scintillating Survey of the Web, Worldwide

At this point, you should have some idea about the Web's origins; now you can take a quick look at some of the many treasures that the W3 offers.

Jumping-off points galore

Every browser comes with a predefined home page; many offer excellent starting points for Web exploration. Three browsers in particular — Netscape Navigator, Internet Explorer, and NCSA Mosaic — offer outstanding home pages with "Starting Points," topic indexes, and search engines designed to help you locate items of interest. However, the Web is a mystical thing — whose circumference is nowhere and whose center is everywhere — so no "perfect starting point" really exists.

Search pages, anyone?

You can find a variety of search pages on the Web. These pages provide links to background applications, called *search engines*, that can examine loads of data repositories on the Internet and, based on keywords that you supply, can return URLs matching the topics that you want.

The major search pages are nicely represented in a number of places, but we find the Yahoo! "Searching the Web" page to be most useful. The URL for this page is

```
http://www.yahoo.com/Computers_and_Internet/Internet/
World_Wide_Web/Searching_the_Web/
```

Try it on for size; pick a search engine and attempt a search with a term of particular interest. (For best results, pick something specific like *coriander*, instead of something general like *spices*.)

As you travel around the Web, pay attention to page layouts and to the use of indexes, graphics, and hotlists. You can glean a great deal from these examples, both good and bad. You can also select View Source from your browser's menu to see the HTML code that represents each of these pages!

Under the Hood: How the Web Works

Now that you know what the Web is, where it came from, and what a big deal it has become, it's time to start grappling with how it actually works. Despite the volume of connected information and the different ways of presenting and delivering that information, the Web works through a single basic set of mechanisms.

The Web is more than just the browser that you use on your desktop. The hidden structure of the Web is just as important as the utility that you use to access it. The Web has two labor-handling divisions: storage/retrieval and display/input. The Web *server* (located elsewhere on the network) typically handles the storage and retrieval part. The browser on the user's work-station (sometimes called a *client*) handles the display of information and recognition of input, when appropriate.

In the grand scheme of the computer world, this approach to handling information delivery is called *client/server computing*. Client/server has become an industry buzzword; nevertheless, the approach does confer some appreciable benefits:

✔ Because this approach divides the processing load, clients concentrate on providing the best possible user interface. Also, the client's location on your desktop simplifies the offering of cool graphical displays and powerful visual controls.

✔ Likewise, servers concentrate on maximizing their ability to handle lots of requests; this division of labor lets Web servers handle tens of thousands to millions of resource requests per day with ease.

✔ Another benefit of client/server derives from the location where servers store the information that clients use: Residence on a server makes information easy to share; permits better control; and lets information providers decide how much power and capability to provide.

✔ By keeping dollars and data concentrated in one place — namely, on the server — the client/server approach helps maximize server perfor-mance (where it's going to do the greatest good for the most users). A server environment also ensures information protection through backups, rigorous control over data access, and accurate logging of request statistics (known as *hits*).

In short, clients handle the job of user interaction, and servers provide rapid retrieval and delivery of information. Client/server capabilities are well-realized on the World Wide Web, which features powerful, graphical clients (browsers) and fast, powerful servers. By working together, these elements contribute to the Web's burgeoning popularity.

Networking Takes Protocols

In diplomatic circles, a protocol is a set of rules that keeps professionals, friends, and enemies alike, from making fools of each other (or themselves). For networks, methods of bulletproof communication are equally necessary and appreciated. Thus, you shouldn't be surprised to find out that the rules and formats that govern the methods by which computers communicate over a network are also called *protocols*.

How Webs talk: the HyperText Transfer Protocol (HTTP)

HTTP is an Internet protocol for a specific application — the World Wide Web. It provides a way for Web clients and servers to communicate, primarily through the exchange of messages from clients (like "Give me this." or "Get me that.") and servers (like "Here's the page you asked for." or "Huh? I can't find what you're looking for.").

To fully understand HTTP, you need to fully understand TCP/IP. A longish sort of acronym, *TCP/IP* stands for Transmission Control Protocol/Internet Protocol, which is the name given to the full set of protocols used on the Internet. But to begin writing good Web documents, you don't need to know much about either topic. Nevertheless, we have included a list of reference materials for you masochists out there.

Acronymophobes, beware!

One thing you've got to realize if you're going to become a real Webmaster is that when you climb onto the Web, you're joining the Internet community. If there's ever been an unabashed bastion for acronyms — those multi-letter combinations that nerds use to refer to things like personal computers (PCs), a disk operating system (DOS), random access memory (RAM), or a compact disc, read-only-memory (CD-ROM) — it's the Internet crowd.

Because we're talking about Web lore, the term *Webmaster* is a ubiquitous name for a person who holds the Web protocols on high, is a veteran of the Web trenches, and lives, eats, and breathes the Web. You may be lucky and good enough to be called a Webmaster yourself — some day!

So, if your most fiendish nightmare is of drowning in a bowl of alphabet soup, maybe you'd better rethink your Web-oriented efforts! That's because networking in general, and the Internet in particular, is a field that revels in acronyms. When it comes to discussing Internet protocols, you can find no better gathering spot for bizarre alphanumeric combinations.

Welcome to the Nebulous Zone . . .

It's a place where different kinds of computers can freely exchange information with one another, where mere implementations bow to the demands of an all-encompassing standard. TCP/IP is a world unto itself: More bits use TCP/IP in a day on today's Internet than are required to store every piece of printed material known to mankind before 1950.

When it comes to TCP/IP, there's a lot to learn and a lot to know. Covering TCP/IP in any depth is way beyond the scope of this book. Therefore, we'd like to give you some choice references:

✔ The Internet is the subject of at least two other *...For Dummies* books: *The Internet For Dummies*, 4th Edition (1997) by John R. Levine, Carol Baroudi, and Margaret Levine Young; and *MORE Internet For Dummies,* 3rd Edition (1997) by Levine and Young. Both books are a good place for beginners to start investigating the basics of TCP/IP.

✔ John Quarterman and Smoot Carl-Mitchell are the authors of *Practical Internetworking with TCP/IP and UNIX* (Addison-Wesley 1993). This book is aimed at the system or network administrator for a TCP/IP network who wants to understand how and why things work.

✔ *TCP/IP For Dummies* by Marshall Wilensky and Candace Leiden (IDG Books Worldwide, Inc. 1995) is a great place to continue your TCP/IP investigations. In addition to covering the topic in wonderfully amusing detail, the book provides a gentle introduction to TCP/IP that is hard to beat.

✔ Matthew Flint Arnett is the first of 14 coauthors for *Inside TCP/IP* (New Riders Press 1994), another book aimed at helping those who run TCP/IP networks or internetworks, or those who oversee Internet connections.

✔ O'Reilly & Associates covers TCP/IP with a Nutshell handbook for UNIX system administrators, *TCP/IP Network Administration*, by Craig Hunt.

✔ A truly definitive look at TCP/IP comes from Douglas E. Comer, author of *Internetworking with TCP/IP*, a 3-volume set (Prentice-Hall 1996, 2nd Edition., 1991, 1993; Volumes 2 and 3 were authored with David L. Stevens). Comer's books are widely regarded as the best general references on the subject.

✔ Another comprehensive two-volume treatise on TCP/IP is available from W. Richard Stevens, called *TCP/IP Illustrated*, Volumes 1 and 2 (assisted by Gary R. Wright on the second volume, Addison-Wesley 1994). These books are more up to date than Comer's and offer detailed "war stories" taken straight from life on the Internet.

✔ The ultimate authority on TCP/IP comes from a standards body called the Internet Architecture Board (IAB). Within the IAB, the Internet Engineering Task Force (IETF) drafts and maintains Internet standards of all kinds, including those for protocols, in the form of numbered documents called "Requests for Comment" (RFCs). The following table has more information on RFCs.

For a listing of all current protocol-related RFCs, consult RFC 1800 "Internet Official Protocol Standards," which is available in at least three ways. (If 1800 isn't current anymore, it tells you it's been obsoleted by a new document, and you can follow a link to the new reigning standard.)

If you take the time to examine the RFC collection, you'll be going straight to the horse's mouth, where TCP/IP and related matters are concerned!

Three methods for examining RFCs	
Service	*Method*
e-mail	Send e-mail to `mailserv@ds.internic.net` and type **file/ftp/rfc/rfc1800.txt** in the message body.
FTP	Anonymous FTP to `ds.internet.net` (password = your e-mail address); look in directory RFC/ for the file named RFC1800.TXT.
Web	`<URL: http://www.cis.ohio-state.edu/htbin/rfc/ rfc1800.html>` for the contents of RFC 1720. `<URL: http://www.cis.ohio-state.edu/hypertext/ information/rfc.html>` has general RFC information.

The straight dope on HTTP

Protocols that link clients and servers together must handle requests and responses. Consequently, you'll not be surprised to know that information exchanges on the Web happen in four parts, all classed as specific message types for HTTP.

- **Connection:** Occurs as a client tries to connect to a specific Web server (your browser may display a status message like `Connecting to HTTP Server`). If the client can't connect, the attempt usually times out, and the browser displays a `Connection timed out` message.

- **Request:** The client asks for a Web resource. The request includes the protocol to use the name of the object to find and information about how the server should respond to the client.

- **Response:** Now it's the server's turn. If the server can deliver the requested object, it responds with a delivery in the requested form. If it can't deliver the object, the server sends an error message explaining why not.

- **Close:** After the server transfers information to respond to a request, the connection between client and server is closed. You can easily reopen a connection with another request — for example, by clicking on a link in the current object — that jumps you back to reestablish the connection.

After it completely transfers a requested object, HTTP has done its job. Then the browser must interpret and display what the server has delivered, and another strand in the Web unfurls.

HTML: HyperText Markup Language

After the Web server returns the response to a Web request, the browser takes over to interpret and display the information.

HTML is a *markup language* that describes the structure of a Web document's content plus some behavioral characteristics. All Web browsers can understand and interpret this language. HTML is itself defined using a more complex markup language known as the *Standard Generalized Markup Language*. (SGML; that's as much as you need to know about SGML to write Web documents.)

HTML is a way of representing text and linking that text to other kinds of resources — including sound files, graphics files, multimedia files, and so on — that allows the concurrent display of different kinds of data and lets different resources augment and reinforce one another.

As delivered by a Web server, HTML is nothing more than a plain-vanilla text file that includes two kinds of text:

- ✔ **The content:** Text or information for display or playback on the client's screen, speakers, and so on.
- ✔ **The markup:** Text or information to control the display or to point to other information items in need of display or playback.

Also, a browser must be prepared to convert a third kind of data — encoded files — and hand them off to the right kind of helper application if necessary. This hand-off may involve a graphics program for an icon or image, a sound player program to handle audio, a video player program to play back a video file, or any other program necessary to reproduce a particular kind of information. Increasingly, however, such extensions are finding their way into Web browsers and are supported directly within the same general program.

HTML files include both control information (tags) and content (text), which together describe the appearance and contents of Web pages. HTML also provides mechanisms to tie in other Internet protocols and services on the Web — like FTP, Gopher, Usenet, e-mail, WAIS, Telnet, and HTTP — so Web pages can deliver many kinds of resources.

Accessing the Web

A crucial ingredient in gaining access to the Web — the one that lives up to the "World Wide" in its name — is an attachment to the Internet. In fact, the biggest constraint on your enjoyment of the Web is likely to be the size of the pipe that connects you to the Internet (and it to you). When we say pipe, we mean how much data the connection between you and the Web server can accommodate (a.k.a. *bandwidth*); like a water pipe, the bigger the connection between you and your server, the faster things can move. Because waiting for screens to complete is a big drag, the faster the data goes, the better you'll like it!

Following are the two basic ways to go for your Internet link-ups:

- ✔ Over the telephone system and into another computer or network that's connected to the Internet.
- ✔ Over a network and onto the Internet (or onto another computer that's properly connected).

You need to contact your ISP (*Internet Service Provider*) to get detailed information on how to maximize your speed and access to the Web.

Chapter 2

Getting Hyper

• •

In This Chapter

▶ Understanding basic HTML concepts

▶ Linking up the strands in the Web

▶ Looking for hypertext examples

▶ Getting past hypertext — to hypermedia

▶ Going for the graphics

▶ Dealing with multimedia display/playback

▶ Bringing multiple media together on the Web

• •

*T*he real secret behind the HyperText Markup Language is that there is no secret: Everything's out in the open with HTML, just waiting for the right interpretation. The beauty of HTML is its simple content — it's just a stream of plain characters — that makes virtually any text editor a potential HTML generator. The challenge of using HTML is working within its boundaries because HTML relies on the order in which characters occur and the way that they're used to produce the right results.

Even though HTML can be forgiving (when you use *some* browsers to view documents with *certain* omitted or misstated elements), the best way to use HTML is to understand and work within its structure. Because your readers can use so many different browsers, the only way to get consistent Web page appearance and behavior is to know the rules for creating HTML documents and to use them to your users' advantage!

This chapter presents the fundamental ideas behind HTML and introduces the concepts and operation of hypertext. Along the way, we hope that you begin to appreciate some of the basic principles behind building well-structured, readable Web pages.

HTML Basics

HTML's name reflects the two key concepts that make it work (and that make the World Wide Web such an incredible phenomenon):

> ✔ **HyperText:** A way of creating multimedia documents as well as a method for providing links within and between documents.
>
> ✔ **Markup Language:** A method for embedding special tags that describe the structure as well as the behavior of a document (not a way of discussing a preschooler's efforts with crayons on the wall).

The simplicity and power of HTML markup lets anyone create Web documents for private or public use. The power of hypertext, with its built-in support for multimedia and document links, creates the incredible breadth and reach of the Web. Making Web documents is so easy and straightforward that anyone can do it — as long as you can play by the rules.

Of Links and Sausages

HTML supports links within the same document as well as to completely different data elements elsewhere on the Web. Both types of links work the same way: Put the correct HTML tags around text or graphics to create an *active* (linked) area; when users visit your Web site and click the active area, they're transported to another spot within the same file, to another document in the same Web site, or off to some other Web site. Figure 2-1 shows an *HTML For Dummies* hotlist that includes links to several resources on HTML. Each of these links connects to a valuable source of HTML information.

Methods used to denote links vary from one browser to the next, but all browsers give some kind of visual clue that you're selecting an active area on the screen. You may see text underlined in a bright color, a font change to boldface, or a graphic outlined in a contrasting color. You might see image maps with the only direct visual clues being a changing set of coordinates (in the browser's status line) that correspond to the location of your cursor on-screen. Using this kind of link is a bit like playing an adventure game: You're not always sure where you're going or what you'll find after you get there!

Jumping around inside documents

One type of link connects points inside the same document; these links are called *internal anchors*. Webmasters often use this kind of link to move users from a table of contents (at the top of an HTML file) to related sections throughout a document. Also, you can use this method to jump directly to the start of the document from its end — this beats the heck out of scrolling through a long file!

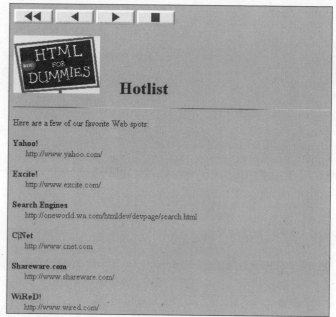

Figure 2-1:
A simple
HTML link
example.

Jumping around is a key advantage of hypertext — namely, the capability to circumvent the linear nature of paper documents and to provide rapid, obvious ways to navigate within (or among) documents. Sure, you can do the same thing with the table of contents or the index of a paper book by looking up what you want and then flipping the pages to the correct section. But hypertext automates this task for you so that you can effortlessly jump around inside and between documents by creating links that are a snap (or actually, a click) to use.

Jumping across documents (and services)

By using a combination of links and Uniform Resource Locators (URLs), HTML can link your page to other Web pages, no matter where they are on the Web. Because URLs can reference a variety of protocols and services on the Internet (not just other HTML files), you can link through telnet, WAIS, Gopher, FTP, Usenet newsgroups, or even e-mail.

The same hypertext technology that lets you jump around inside a document also lets you reach any other resource available through the Web, as long as you know its exact URL (address). HTML's simple, text-tagging technique erases the difference between here and there. With a single click of the mouse or selection of the right text field, you are there, or the information is here. . . . Anyway, you get it.

Creation of the Web as we know it today comes from the work of individual Web weavers that include links to other documents from their Web sites. That is, individual documents may constitute the contents of the Web, but the links among those documents reveal the Web's true interconnectedness. Hyperlinks make up the strands in the Web that tie people, ideas, and locations together.

 Whenever you reference a URL in an HTML document, cut and paste that URL from a browser if at all possible. You save time on typing — some URLs can get pretty long — and even better, you can be sure to get the reference right. For an additional check, test the URL with a browser to make sure that it's still valid before you copy it.

You've Used Hypertext, Without Knowing It

At this point, you may be saying something like, "What is this hypertext stuff?" Although you may see hypertext as strange and exotic, you're probably much more familiar with it than you think. Your own desktop computer undoubtedly contains several hypertext applications that you use regularly.

For example, if you're a Microsoft Windows user, every time you run the Windows Help utility, you're using a hypertext application. In addition, Figure 2-2 shows a screen that covers some of Microsoft Word for Windows technical support options. Notice the five buttons on the upper portion of the screen shot: "Contents," "Search," "Back," "Print," and "Index." These buttons work much like the navigation tools for a Web browser; they can let you return to where you've been (Back), or examine the range of available links within a document (Contents and Search). The underlined phrases are links to text within the help system. They work much like the HTML links via your browser. In fact, Microsoft is in the process of switching its Help system over to use HTML directly even as you read this!

Macintosh users can identify HyperCard or SuperCard as forms of hypertext, and they may also recognize our references to application Help utilities. You others just have to take our word for it and not assume that these are games of chance! Here again, hypertext applications have concepts in common with the Web, including some kind of home page, various navigation tools (shaped arrows and specific commands), multimedia data, and plenty of links to select.

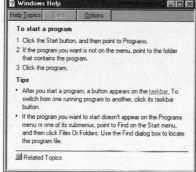

Figure 2-2:
The
Microsoft
Windows
Help engine
is a well-
known
hypertext
example.

Likewise, UNIX users who are familiar with FrameMaker or other multimedia authoring tools can find some common ground with the Web's hypertext capabilities. Yet again, the concepts of a home page, document navigation and linkage, and integrated multimedia help to realize the notion of hypertext and how it operates.

The difference between the preceding examples and the Web are the kinds of links that they support: Only the Web offers the ability to jump across the Internet and follow links to other Web documents and servers. Enabling this feature is what gives HTML its unique value and, of course, what's made the Web so popular.

Beyond Text, There's Multimedia

If you include non-text files (like sound, graphics, and video) in Web pages, you must employ a certain amount of alchemy. Shipping Web information in a format called *MIME* (*Multipurpose Internet Mail Extensions*) makes it possible for a Web server to deliver multiple forms of data to your browser in a single transfer. Actually, MIME is a technique designed to bundle attachments within individual e-mail files. The following paragraphs tell a little more about how this works.

After a MIME file with attachments shows up at your workstation, additional processing begins immediately. The text portion of the message file arrives first. It contains a text-only HTML page description that lets the browser get right to work building and displaying the text portions of the page. Because the text arrives first, you may see placeholders or icons for graphics when you first see a Web page. Eventually, graphics or other forms of data replace these placeholders as their related attachments arrive.

While a user views a Web page, the browser receives attachments in the background. As they arrive, the browser identifies these attachments by file type or by description information contained within an attachment tag (as specified by the MIME format). After the browser identifies a file, it can handle the file's playback or display. Table 2-1 shows a list of common file types used on the Web, including expansions for the inevitable acronyms that such files often invoke.

Table 2-1	Common Sound, Graphics, and Motion-Video Formats on the Web	
Extension	*Format*	*Explanation*
Sound Formats		
RA	RealAudio	Used with RealAudio Web Server and RealAudio Player add-on for browsers.
SBI	Sound Blaster Instrument	Used for a single instrument with Sound Blaster cards (multi-instrument: IBK).
SND, AU	8 kHz mulaw	Voice-grade sound format used on workstations (such as Sun, NeXT, HP9000, and so on).
WAV	Microsoft Waveform	Sound format used in Windows for event notification.
Still-Video (Graphics) Formats		
GIF	Graphics Interchange Format	Compressed graphics format commonly used on CompuServe, easy to render multiplatform. Can be interleaved or not, depending on how image is created.
JPEG, JPG	Joint Photographic Experts Group	Highly compressed format for still images, widely used for multi-platform graphics.
PDF	Portable Document Format	Adobe's format for multiplatform document access through its Acrobat software.
PS	PostScript	Adobe's type description language, used to deliver complex documents over the Internet.
XBM	X-Windows Bitmap	Image bitmap used by X-Windows, primarily on UNIX workstations.
Motion-Video Formats		
AVI	Audio Video Interleaved	Microsoft's Video for Windows standard format; found on many CD-ROMs.

Extension	Format	Explanation
Motion-Video Formats		
DVI	Digital Video Interactive	Another motion-video format, also found on CD-ROMs.
FLI	Flick	Autodesk Animator motion-video format.
MOV	QuickTime	Apple's motion video and audio format; originated on the Macintosh, but also available for Windows.
MPEG, MPG	Motion Picture Experts Group	Full-motion video standard using frame format similar to JPEG with variable compression capabilities.

Many Web sites contain large amounts of information on file formats and programs; here are two of the best that we turned up by searching on the string "common Internet file formats" at `http://www.excite.com`.

✔ **Common Internet File Formats:** This site contains an annotated list of audio, graphic, and multimedia file formats with links to applications that use them and was compiled by Eric Perlman and Ian Kallen for Internet Literacy Consultants.

`http://www.matisse.net/files/formats.html`

✔ **GRAPHICS:** This site is maintained by Martin Reddy at the University of Edinburgh and contains "everything you ever wanted to know" about graphics and links to additional resources.

`http://www.dcs.ed.ac.uk/%7Emxr/gfx/`

Hyperhelpers: useful "helper" applications

When referenced by a Web page, non-text data shows up as attachments to an HTML file. Sometimes the browser itself handles playback or display, as in the case of simple, two-dimensional graphics (including .GIF and .JPEG files). Even so, these attachments may be handled by other applications (especially for character-mode Web browsers like Lynx).

When other kinds of files need special handling (beyond the scope of most browsers), the browser passes these files to other applications for playback or display. Such *helper* or *plug-in* applications have the built-in smarts to handle both the formats and the processing needed to deliver the contents of specialized files on demand.

The process normally works something like this:

1. The browser builds a page display that includes an active region (underlined or outlined in some way) to indicate the attachment of a sound, video, or animation playback.

2. If the user selects the active region (the link), the browser calls on another application or plug-in to handle playback or display.

3. The other application or plug-in takes over and plays back or displays the file.

4. After the helper completes the display or playback, the browser reasserts control, and the user can continue (or select the active region again, and get another playback or display).

A standard part of browser configuration supplies the names and locations of helper programs, or configures specially tailored add-ons called plug-ins, to assist the browser when such data arrives. If the browser can't find a helper application or plug-in, it simply won't respond to an attempt to display or play back the requested information. For plug-ins, however, most browsers are smart enough to recognize what they're missing, and some (like Navigator and IE) even ask you if you want to add them to your current configuration.

For example, RealAudio is a common sound player plug-in for Web browsers, primarily for PCs running some flavor of Windows. As part of the configuration that occurs when a plug-in is installed, associations between particular file types (like the .SBI and .WAV file extensions common on the PC) and the plug-in may be automatically established. After this association is created, the browser automatically invokes the plug-in when it encounters files with those extensions. This causes the sounds to play (which, we assume, is a good thing).

For comprehensive listings of PC, Mac, and UNIX plug-ins or helper applications as well as links to their sources, start your search at one of the following URLs:

```
http://browserwatch.iworld.com/
http://tucows.myriad.net/acc95.html
http://wwwhost.cc.utexas.edu/learn/use/helper.html
```

Also check out both the Netscape and Internet Explorer pages at their respective sites for information about the latest plug-ins (for example, Netscape has a link to a set of pages labeled "Navigator Plug-ins" in the "Download Software" section of its home page at http://home.netscape.com).

Some useful helper applications for Windows include:

- ✔ **For still graphics:** LView is a good, small graphics viewer that can handle .GIF, .PCX, and .JPEG files. It also supports interesting image editing capabilities.

- ✔ **For video:** You can use QuickTime for Windows (for QuickTime movies) or MPEGplay for .MPEG video files.

- ✔ **For PostScript viewing:** GhostView for Windows works with a companion program called GhostScript that allows users to view or print PostScript files from any source, including the Web. Because so many documents on the Internet have the PostScript format, we find these to be useful programs.

All in all, a good set of plug-ins or helper applications can make your browser even more effective at bringing the wonders of the Web to your desktop. With the right additions, your browser can play back or render just about anything you run into!

The value of visuals

Without a doubt, graphics add impact and interest to Web pages, but that extra punch comes at a price. You can get carried away with the appeal of pictures and overdo their use on your Web page.

Overdoing graphics applies as much to those small images you use for buttons and on-screen controls as it does to the large images you use to dress up a Web page.

Therefore, when you use graphics, remember these two things:

- ✔ Not everybody who reads your page can see the graphics. Users may not see graphics because they use a character-mode browser (which can't display graphics) or because they switch off their graphics displays (a common option on most Web browsers designed to conserve bandwidth and improve the ability to move data and decrease response time).

- ✔ Graphics files — even compressed ones — can sometimes be quite big, often ten or more times larger than the HTML files to which they're attached. Moving graphics takes time and consumes precious bandwidth. Also, it penalizes users with slower modems far more than those attached directly to the Internet via a higher-speed link.

Sometimes graphics are essential — for example, when using a diagram or illustration to explain your material. In other situations, impact is important — such as on a home page, where you make your first impression. Under these circumstances, using graphics is perfectly appropriate, but be sensitive to the different capabilities and bandwidths of your users.

Here are some rules for using graphics effectively in your Web pages. (As you examine the work of others, see what happens to your attitude when you find that they have violated some or all these rules.)

- ✔ Keep your graphics small and uncomplicated whenever possible. This reduces file sizes and keeps transfer times down.

- ✔ Keep file sizes smaller by using compressed formats (like .GIF and .JPEG) whenever you can.

- ✔ Create a small version (called a *thumbnail*) of a graphic to include on your Web page (an easy way to do this is by sizing your image on-screen, and then taking a screen shot when you display it in the proper dimensions, usually 100x100 pixels or so). If you must use larger, more complex graphics, link the thumbnail to a full-size version of the graphic. This spares casual users from having to download the large version every time they access your page (and keeps Internet usage under control, making you a better *netizen!*).

- ✔ Keep the number of graphic elements on a page to a minimum. Practically speaking, this means at most a half dozen graphic items per page, where most items are compact, icon-like navigation controls and the others are content-specific graphics. Here again, the idea is to limit page complexity and to speed transfer times.

Sometimes, the temptation to violate these rules is nearly overwhelming. If you must break the rules, be sure to run your results past some disinterested third parties. (You find out more about testing techniques in Part IV of this book.) Watch them read your pages if you can. Listen carefully to their feedback to see whether you've merely bent these rules — or smashed them to smithereens!

Also, remembering that not everybody who accesses the Web can see your graphics may help keep you humble. For users who don't have graphical browsers, try to think of ways to enhance their reading experience even without using graphics.

Mavens of multimedia

The rules that go for graphics go *double* for other forms of multimedia. If graphics files are large when compared to HTML text files, then sound and video files are HUGE. They are time-dependent; therefore, the longer they play, the bigger they are, and the longer the browser takes to download them to a user's computer. Although they're appealing and definitely increase the interest level for some topics, sound and video files are not germane to many topics on the Web. Use them sparingly or not at all, unless your Web site is an Internet radio show or movie theater.

With the advent of the smaller, faster display and interactivity tools for the Web (such as Java, VRML, and Shockwave), the Web employs more and more multimedia applications. Java _applets_ work with Netscape, IE, and other browsers to allow quick display of animated graphics and other special effects. VRML (Virtual Reality Modeling Language) is similar to HTML but provides 3-D viewing capabilities and more. Shockwave is the name of Macromedia's plug-in that allows Director movies to play inside Web pages. The use of these tools goes far beyond the scope of this book, but you can look forward to using them in your Web pages after you've mastered the basics of HTML. If you're interested in these tools, check out these URLs for more information:

✔ Java — Sun Microsystems

```
http://www.javasoft.com or http://java.sun.com
```

✔ VRML

```
http://www.vrml.org/
```

✔ Shockwave — Macromedia

```
http://www.macromedia.com
```

Once again, the trick is to make large files available through links instead of including them on pages that everyone tries to download. Labeling such active regions with the file's size is also a good idea so that people know what they're in for if they choose to download. (For example: `Warning! This points to a 40KB sound byte of a barking seal.`)

Bringing It All Together with the Web

Let's step back from multimedia hyperspace and back to the cyberspace world of your future Web page. Now that you understand the basic concepts behind the Web and HTML and have met (briefly) some tools of the trade, you need to read the following paragraph carefully. It embodies the essence of all successful Web pages.

The three most important factors in building good Web pages are content, content, and content. (Get the idea?) If the content is well-organized, engaging, and contains links to interesting places, your Web site can be a potent tool for education and communication. If your Web site is all flash, sharing it can be an exercise in sheer frustration (and humiliation for the Webmaster . . . that's you!). Therefore, if you put your energy into providing high-quality content and link your users to other high-quality, content-filled pages, your Web site will be a howling success. If you don't, your site will be the electronic equivalent of a ghost town!

In the next chapter, you find out what's involved in using — and building — documents for the Web. Step into our parlor for a look at what's in (and on) a Web page.

Chapter 3

What's in a Page?

In This Chapter

▶ Discovering layout basics

▶ Knowing what you want to say

▶ Understanding your users

▶ Figuring out page flow

The trick to understanding HTML lies in knowing how to separate the two components of the HTML file: the *content* and the *controls*. (Controls are also known as *tags* or *markup*.) You can present the majority of *content* in a plain text (ASCII) file with no tagging whatsoever.

If you look at an HTML source file, you see *markup* in the file that doesn't show up when your browser displays the page. Markup consists of the characters that show up within the HTML bracket markers (< >) and controls how characters appear on-screen. If you're puzzled, don't worry — we have plenty of examples throughout the rest of this book.

The really interesting parts of HTML are the combinations of markup and content, such as the commands used to entitle pages or control textual guideposts — headers, graphics, lists of elements, and so on. Before you can read, write, and understand HTML, you must be able to mentally separate the structure of a document from its controls.

Building good Web pages requires that you not only understand the distinction between content and controls but that you use them to their best effect. In this chapter, you begin to appreciate the components of a Web page, and you find out how to bring these pieces together to create readable Web documents.

It's All in the Layout

The human eye and brain are marvelous instruments. They are capable of scanning incredible amounts of material and zeroing in on the things that are most important to the reader. As a Web page designer, your mission (should you choose to accept it) is to aid the reader in locating a page's salient features quickly and efficiently. Nothing communicates this concern — or your lack of it — more quickly than a document's layout.

Layout is the overall arrangement of the elements in a document. Layout isn't concerned with the placement of individual text elements on a page. Instead, layout involves the number of elements, how they're arranged, and how much white space surrounds them.

The layout of a document — whether a Web page, a letter to your sister, or an advertisement in a magazine — is a crucial part of communicating with users. For materials where reader interest is mandatory, layout may not appear to be of concern (this may explain why tax forms are so boring to look at). For documents where interest must be generated, layout is nearly as important as the information that a document delivers.

Think of all the boring textbooks that you've slogged (slept?) through, with pages and pages of text with only the occasional graphic crammed between two half-page paragraphs. By comparison, think of a magazine or television advertisement that you've seen recently. The people who designed the advertising grabbed your interest by creating eye-catching images, using appealing language, and delivering arresting combinations of elements.

When it comes to building Web pages, your job can be as challenging as the one faced by advertising designers. You shouldn't assume that your material is of such great interest to the world that your Web pages can stress content at the expense of layout. You're up against millions of other sites on the WWW. Even if your site's content is completely unique, you can encourage your readers to visit more often and to link your site to theirs by making your layout as inviting as possible.

Because attention to layout adds to the accessibility of any document, you do your users a service by building a good layout. At the same time that you make your page more pleasant to read, you also deliver its content quickly and effectively, which is everyone's goal in the information age.

What Are You Trying to Say?

As markup languages go, HTML is simple and easy to learn. Unfortunately, this fact creates a nearly overwhelming temptation to rush out and start building Web pages right away. In fact, you're probably wondering when we're going to get around to putting HTML tags on text here, aren't you? (Cheer up! We talk about that in Chapter 4.)

Whether you're an individual who's trying to share information with others, or an organization seeking to advertise its products and services, the impetus to publish online ASAP is powerful. Nevertheless, we advise you to step back and do a little analysis and design work, instead of trying to build "killer Web pages" on the fly.

Who's listening?

Knowing your audience is a critical requirement to building Web pages that people can use. If you don't know who's going to visit your Web site and why they should want to, you're just putting together a *vanity page* that a few Web surfers may visit once. Don't get all bent out of shape — vanity pages comprise the majority of the personal pages on the Web. If you have a real reason for building your Web site, you need to know what that reason is and how to emphasize it to potential users.

More importantly, you must base your Web document design on certain assumptions about your audience. Although this is true for both advertisements and for encyclopedias, the focus on form and excitement is a little more intense and urgent for ads than it is for encyclopedias. You could do worse than create the initial interest and impact of an advertisement, but you want to go further than most ads and deliver the depth of content that your audience is most likely to want, even if it isn't encyclopedic in nature.

How can you get to know your audience? Think of it as a form of hunting: Identify your target group and then start hanging around their haunts, whether in cyberspace or in the real world. Watch and listen to them. When you recognize their interests, you can target their needs and duly consider the factors that can hook them into your content. You must deliver solid, usable information to your target group so that they come back for more and spread the word about what you have to offer.

Design springs from content — and intent

Web pages built around long documents with complex ideas take more forethought and are more difficult to design. That's a big surprise . . . NOT! But on the other hand, short, single-concept documents are not necessarily easy to make into good Web pages. No matter how long, short, complex, or simple your content, you need to follow this basic principle: Design springs from content, as form follows function. Also, remember the audience that you intend to reach and then emphasize the high points that your research shows your potential users are interested in. Create an outline before you start writing (or creating HTML, for that matter). An outline can help you organize your information. An outline also determines the order of topics and your needs for graphics, sound, or other multimedia information. Finally, the outline also provides a blueprint as you construct the document that realizes its contents.

By identifying topics and major elements in your document, you highlight relationships between those components (and possibly between its components and other information sources on the Web). Therefore, outlining content plays a key role in establishing links and presenting your users with visual clues on how to read and navigate your document.

A matter of intent

The intent behind a document — to inform, educate, persuade, or question — also plays a major role in your design.

- ✔ If your goal is to inform, reduce the number of eye-catching displays and try to direct your users' vision to the highlights of the information your document contains.

- ✔ If your goal is to persuade or sell, try to hook users' attention with compelling visuals and riveting testimonials, and then you follow through with important details.

- ✔ If your goal is to question something, raise the issues early and provide pointers to additional discussion and related information afterward.

In each case, the goal behind a document strongly conditions its execution and delivery. That's why understanding your intent is so important.

Establish key messages

At the beginning of your document-design process, you must answer the question at the head of this section — "What are you trying to say?" Approach this task by outlining key ideas or messages that you seek to convey and put the most important ones first. Then follow each main idea with any relevant information you need to make your case, prove your point, or otherwise substantiate what you're saying.

If you follow this exercise carefully, much of the content emerges gracefully from your outline. Important relationships among various elements of your document (and other documents) also reveal themselves as you work through the outlining process.

Think about superstructure and information flow

Superstructure refers to the formal mechanics of how you communicate a document's organization and navigation and includes elements such as

- ✔ A table of contents
- ✔ A set of common controls
- ✔ An index
- ✔ A glossary of technical terms

In short, the superstructure is the wrapping that you wind around your content so that users can find their way to the information they want and understand what they're reading or viewing. For any given document, you may not need every element of superstructure, but for most documents — especially longer ones — some elements of superstructure are helpful, and others are absolutely essential.

The TOC (table of contents)

From a lifetime of exposure to printed materials, most readers have come to expect a table of contents at the beginning of a document to lay out the topics and coverage in that document. The beauty of hypertext is that you can build links that take users directly from any entry in the TOC to the corresponding information in the document. Thus, the TOC becomes not just an organizational map for your document but a convenient navigation tool.

Common controls for all screens

To promote readability and familiarity within your Web site, include common controls in each individual document. Common controls can be a set of clickable icons: to page backward or forward, to jump back to the TOC, or to return to your home page. If you include a search tool for keywords in the document, make the tool accessible from any document. Whatever you do, establish a common look and feel for your pages; then your users can navigate more easily. Consistency may be "the last refuge for the unimaginative," but it does promote familiarity and ease of use!

Index or search engine?

Helping users locate key words or individual topics enables them to get the best use from your content. Another great thing about hypertext is that an old-fashioned index may be unnecessary. Because your content is online and accessible to the computer, you can often replace an index with a built-in search engine for your Web pages.

Chapter 15 covers search engines, including tools to index your documents online.

A glossary helps manage specialized terms and language

If you're covering a subject that's full of jargon, technical terms, or other forms of arcane gibberish (beloved of experts and feared by newcomers), include a glossary with your Web pages. Fortunately, HTML includes a text style specifically built for defining terms, which, in turn, helps you to construct a glossary whenever you need one. You still have to come up with the definitions yourself — unless you can find a Web site with a glossary that you can link to your page. Ahh, the beauty of the Web!

Grab the audience's attention . . .

If you've ever watched a movie at a THX-equipped theater, you're probably familiar with the phrase, "The audience is listening." It comes up at the conclusion of the THX demonstration, which usually happens immediately before the feature presentation.

The THX demonstration consists of the simple "THX" graphic that fills the entire screen. A loud, sustained orchestral chord, overlaid with a powerful pipe-organ note, accompanies the graphic. The musical effect starts quietly, builds to a peak over 20 seconds, and then fades away on a low pedal-tone that you swear moves the entire theater. The sensation is similar to standing at the end of the runway while a jet fighter comes toward you and takes off over your head at 200+ mph. It definitely (and almost deafeningly) gets your attention. Having raised the audience nearly out of its seats, the demonstration concludes with "The audience is listening."

Even though we don't recommend this audio effect for most Web pages, we do encourage you to grab your users' attention when they first glimpse at your page. Nothing does this as effectively as a tasteful image coupled with a brief, compelling introduction to your page. Include information that tells why your page is important, what it contains, and how to get around. Get your users interested, get them oriented, and then they'll be hooked!

They're after the goods . . . don't get in the way!

After grabbing your users' attention, help them find your real content. Superstructure needs to be visible, but don't let it get in the way. If you include pointers to direct users to the details, make them obvious and easy to distinguish from the rest of a page. Overly complex designs, layouts, or information flows hamper easy access to the content.

This advice translates into some important rules, particularly for introductory materials. Keep your welcome (home) page simple and elegant. Use short, direct sentences. Keep your focus on the topic(s) at hand. Use the superstructure to emphasize your content. For a complex Web site, include a link to an "About this site" page for those who want to understand the site's structure and function.

What should they remember?

It's well known that people exposed to new materials generally remember ten percent of the concepts — at best. When designing Web documents, keep asking yourself, "What ten percent do I want my users to remember?" This question helps you focus on the important ideas so that you can direct the audience to them and reinforce those ideas throughout your Web pages.

Also true, if somewhat sad, is that most users remember a limited amount of detail as well. Remembering ten percent of the concepts doesn't translate into remembering ten percent of the overall content: Would you remember ten out of a hundred pages in a document that you'd never seen before? This sometimes means presenting less information than you might otherwise be inclined to convey so that you can concentrate on what's really important. Therefore, save yourself time and trouble, and focus on the important stuff right from the outset!

Also, don't be too ambitious in your coverage: Strongly related concepts linger in memory far better than loosely linked or unrelated ones. As with so much else in life, maintaining your focus is a key ingredient for successful communication.

Meet the Elements of Page Design

Okay, you've been exposed to some important design concepts for building Web pages. At this point, you should be ready to meet the elements that make up an HTML document. These elements may sound familiar because many are integral parts of any well-written document. Others may be less familiar, perhaps because of the terminology or because the concepts — like hypertext links — don't equate with normal printed materials.

Nevertheless, the following building blocks make up Web pages. After we give you a tour of these basic elements, we discuss related information flows and design elements.

Tagging text

Including tags along with text is what separates HTML from any ordinary ASCII file. In HTML, tags are enclosed within angle brackets. For example, a document head is indicated by a <HEAD> tag. Most HTML tags travel in pairs, so that <HEAD> actually marks the beginning of a document head and a corresponding </HEAD> marks its end.

Some tags include particular values, called *attributes,* that help describe a pointer or a reference to an external data element. Other attributes label information to be communicated back to a Web server; still others add to the physical description of a display object (for example, the alignment or dimensions of a graphical element).

Attributes provide sources and destinations for links within and across documents: These attributes (called *link anchors* or *anchors,* for short) describe the relationship between two named locations in the Web, whether in the same or different documents.

A linked location is indicated by a document reference (for access to other documents), a location reference (for a point inside the same document), or a combination of the two (for a point inside another document). For more information on such links, please read about <BASE>, <A> (anchor), and <LINK> tags in Chapter 6.

Many HTML tags require that certain attributes be specified; others can take on optional attributes and values, and still others never acquire attributes. You find out what's what as you discover the elements of document design presented in this book.

Titles and labels

Every HTML document needs a title to identify it to its users. Titles have three other important aspects as well:

- ✔ Titles appear in hotlists, which makes them a navigation or selection tool for users who use them.
- ✔ Titles let robots grab a brief description of any HTML document, which makes entries within search databases more accurate and useful.
- ✔ Titles help you manage your documents, especially when they're complex and voluminous.

Whenever you display a Web document, the title shows up in the window's title bar. Figure 3-1 shows the window for an HTML Style Guide with the title, "Style Guide for online hypertext," prominently displayed.

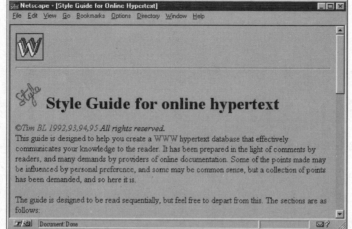

Labels aren't required, but they're a good document organizing tool. Labels help identify sections or topic areas in a document, and they provide better navigation for users, especially when you use them for links. As you see in Parts II and III of this book, if you use the NAME attribute inside an anchor, you can direct an HTML link to a named section in a document, as well as to the head of a document. Anchors also signal to other browsers, "To point to me, reference me by my anchor's NAME attribute."

```
<A NAME="Mexican Dove">Linda Paloma</A>
```

If some author, or even the original author, wants to link to the Linda Paloma area of the current document, all they need to do is create an HTML link definition by using the anchor's NAME (in this case, "Mexican Dove").

Text and hypertext links

Anyone writing HTML has only one kind of link available — a unidirectional association between a source and a target. But one kind of link has four uses:

- ✔ **Intradocument linking** provides a way to move from one location to another inside the same document.

- ✔ **Interdocument linking** provides a way to move from one document to another document.

- ✔ **Linking to an *agent* program** that acts on behalf of the Web server provides a way for an HTML document to handle a query or provide a service (such as information gathering).

- ✔ **Linking to a non-text object** provides a way to access graphics, sounds, video, or some other form of multimedia.

Interestingly enough, links inside HTML files to other types of data — like sound, graphics, and motion video — enable HTML's hypertext aspects. Along with these external links, HTML's inter- and intradocument links create the connections that compose the Web. No matter how they're used, links define the Web's look and feel.

Overcoming two-dimensional thinking

Although hypertext is new and exciting, the legacy of thousands of years of linear text is difficult to overcome. In other words, even though document designers can do nifty and creative things with linking and hypermedia, they have to fight the nearly overwhelming inclination to make their documents read like books. You must exploit the hypertext capabilities of HTML displays and links in appealing and useful ways, or your Web pages won't live up to their potential or the expectations of your users.

In the sections that follow, you have a chance to examine some common organizational techniques for building Web documents; you also encounter documents that can exist only on the Web.

Stringing pages together the old-fashioned way

Some pages demand to be read in sequence: for example, a narrative that builds on previous elements. For such material, string pages together, as shown in Figure 3-2. If you have a document of five pages or more — if you believe Tim Berners-Lee in his *Hypertext Online Style Guide* — you need to chain them together sequentially anyway.

Figure 3-2:
Chain pages together to read them in sequence.

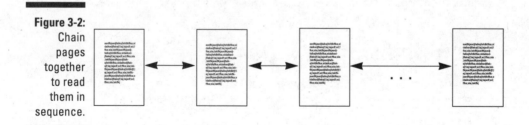

The nice thing about hypertext is that you can chain pages together forward and backward; then you can easily "turn" pages in either direction. Don't be afraid to include other appropriate links in this basic structure (such as links to other HTML documents, a glossary, or other points inside your document).

Hierarchies are easy to model in HTML

If you construct documents from an outline, a hierarchical approach to document links should immediately make sense. Most outlines start with major ideas and divisions that you refine and elaborate to wind up with all the details of a formal document. Figure 3-3 shows a four-level hierarchical document structure that organizes an entire work.

HTML itself has no limits on the levels of hierarchies that you can build; the only limit is your own (and your audience's) ability to handle complexity. For both your sakes, we suggest keeping yours from getting too big or too deep.

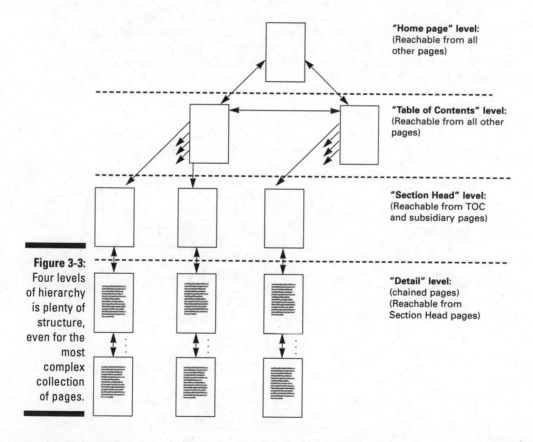

"Home page" level:
(Reachable from all other pages)

"Table of Contents" level:
(Reachable from all other pages)

"Section Head" level:
(Reachable from TOC and subsidiary pages)

Figure 3-3:
Four levels of hierarchy is plenty of structure, even for the most complex collection of pages.

"Detail" level:
(chained pages)
(Reachable from Section Head pages)

Multiple tracks for multiple audiences

It isn't unusual to build a document that includes different kinds of information to meet the needs of different audiences. By using HTML, you can easily interlink basic introductory documents (like a tutorial or technical overview) with more pointed, in-depth reference materials. That way, your home page can point beginners to a tutorial and lead them through an overview before assaulting them with the down and dirty details of your "real" content.

This kind of organization, shown in Figure 3-4, lets you tell experienced users how to bypass introductory materials and access your in-depth content directly. Such an approach lets you design for multiple audiences without lots of extra work.

The organization in Figure 3-4 differs somewhat from that shown in Figures 3-2 and 3-3. It emphasizes links between related documents more than the flow of pages within those documents. In fact, the kind of document pictured in Figure 3-4 would probably combine elements from both a linear and a hierarchical structure in its actual page flows. The tutorial section would be read from front to back (or at least a chapter at a time), but the reference section would be consulted by topic (and only rarely read all the way through).

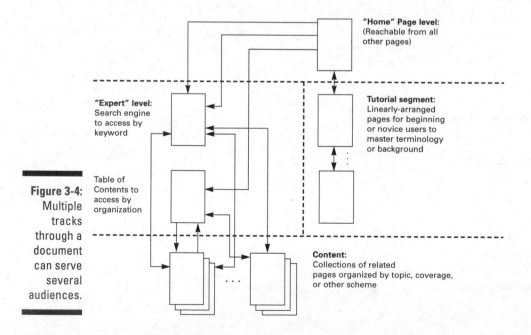

Figure 3-4:
Multiple
tracks
through a
document
can serve
several
audiences.

A bona-fide Web wonder: the "hotlist" or "jump page"

Some of the best resources we've located on the Web consist of nothing more than a list of annotated references to other documents. These lists usually relate to one or more specific topics. You can see this kind of document structure in Figure 3-5, which shows a single page pointing off to multiple pages in various locations. In this example, the picture fails to do complete justice to the concept. For a better illustration, you need to look at a real Web page. Consequently, we advise you to check out the URL listed in the next paragraph — it's quite convincing as an example of what a good hotlist can do!

You can find more good hotlists on the Web than you can shake a stick at. Of course, we suggest that you start by looking at the *IITML For Dummies* Hotlist Page:

```
http://www.outer.net/html4dum/hotlists.htm#top
```

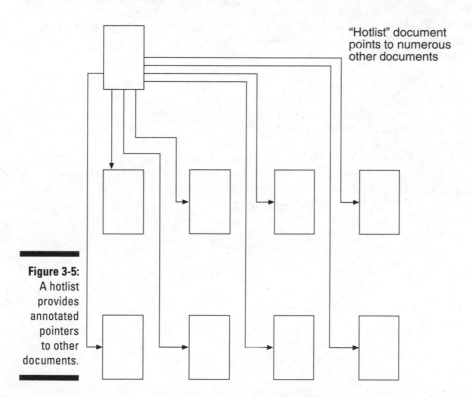

"Hotlist" document points to numerous other documents

Figure 3-5:
A hotlist provides annotated pointers to other documents.

Extending the Web, a piece at a time

Another kind of Web page solicits input from users, who, by their input, help to create an open-ended document. Users contribute comments, additional text, and hypermedia or add to an ongoing narrative. The structure of such a document is hard to predict and, therefore, hard to depict. Suffice it to say that this kind of Web document can grow like a coral colony, more by accretion than by prior organization or design.

For an example of this kind of living, ongoing document, consult the following URL:

```
http://bug.village.virginia.edu/
```

WAXweb is a hypermedia implementation of a feature-length, independent film, *WAX or The Discovery of Television Among the Bees* (David Blair, 85:00, 1991). WAXweb is a large hypermedia database available over the Internet. It features an authoring interface that lets users collaborate in adding onto the story. WAXweb includes thousands of individual elements, ranging from text to music, motion videos, and video transcriptions of motion picture clips. For users with VRML-capable browsers, WAXweb also offers a pretty nifty three-dimensional VRML implementation, as well.

The only limitations on how you structure documents are those imposed by your need to communicate effectively with your audience. After you realize that, you can use the various page flow and organizational techniques that we outline here for their best effects.

Now that you know the first building blocks of Web page design — layout and organization — it's time to initiate you into the world of markup languages. In Chapter 4, you discover what HTML looks like and how to create a simple document. Here comes the good stuff!

Chapter 4

Build Your First Web Page

In This Chapter

▶ Dealing with the tools

▶ Learning the Edit-Review cycle

▶ Working with templates

▶ Understanding what comes next

At this point, you've read enough about HTML that you're probably itching to go out and build a sample page of your own. Your understanding of the details involved and the many capabilities of HTML will improve as you tackle the next sections in the book, but you've learned enough already to try a few simple exercises. That's what we cover in this short, but tightly focused, chapter.

HTML consists of nothing more than plain ASCII text files, filled with special character sequences, called markup, and whatever content you may want to communicate with your audience. (For more on the basics of HTML, check out Chapter 5.) In this chapter, we focus on the mechanics of putting the necessary pieces together to build a minimal but working HTML page. We also describe the typical process of creating the text, viewing it in a Web browser, making corrections or changes, and so on (which we call the "Edit-Review" cycle).

Building good Web pages means understanding how they're created the first time and then maintained thereafter. Roll up your sleeves! This is a strictly hands-on set of exercises to get you up to your elbows in HTML. . . .

Start with the Right Tools

Although you can find a myriad of tools built specifically to help you create and manage HTML pages, we think that a plain text editor does the job pretty well. That's why we recommend that you include a favorite text editor in your HTML toolbox, even if you use other tools. Because even if you decide to use an HTML editor like HoTMetaL, HotDog, FrontPage, or some other HTML-savvy piece of software to create pages, nothing beats a plain-vanilla text editor for rapid post-creation tweaking or maintenance tasks. Even though we have lots of options available to us for building HTML pages, we still use a plain text editor as our tool of choice for most circumstances.

For more discussion of HTML tools of all kinds, please consult Part V of this book (where you find a general tool discussion, along with a discussion of our personal favorites, plus separate chapters for PC, Macintosh, and UNIX users).

For PC users, a text editor like NotePad can do the job quite nicely; for Mac users, SimpleText works pretty well; and for UNIX-heads, an ordinary text editor like *vi* is more than adequate for the task. We base the examples in this chapter on the version of Notepad that ships with Windows 95 and Windows NT.

If you absolutely must use a word processor of some kind, be aware that most such programs do not produce plain text files by default. That's why you have to remember to save any HTML files you create within your program as "text only" or "plain text." And no fair using the built-in "Convert to HTML" option, either!

The Edit-Review Cycle

The process of building an HTML file consists of typing in some HTML markup and some plain old text at the keyboard, saving the file, and then opening that file within a Web browser so you can see what you've wrought. Because it's not at all unusual to see things you missed, misspelled, or just plain don't like, it's normal to continue from that point in a cycle, like this:

1. **Make changes in the text editor.**

2. **Save the changes in the text editor.**

3. **Open (or refresh) the file in a Web browser to check your work.**

This three-step activity typically continues until you obtain the results you're looking for (or until the dinner bell, or some other interruption, pulls you from your work).

Time has no meaning when you're building or tweaking Web pages. Be prepared to lose hours, days, and sometimes even months of your life!

Check out this example. We start with the basic text that any well-formed Web page needs to make it both viewable and legal. Type the following characters into your favorite text editor, and save the resulting file as `test.htm`:

```
<HTML>
<HEAD>
<TITLE>My very first Web Page!</TITLE>
</HEAD>
<BODY>
"Hello World!"
</BODY>
</HTML>
```

After you type this material and save the file as test.htm, open your Web browser and look in the File menu for an entry that says something like Open (Internet Explorer lets you point at a file on your hard drive from this entry) or Open File (Netscape Navigator accepts a local filename here). Figure 4-1 shows what test.htm looks like from Internet Explorer.

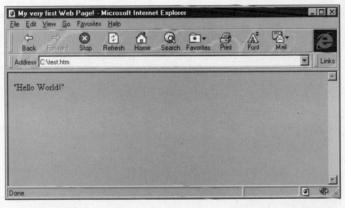

Figure 4-1:
Our first HTML efforts don't really produce much output — or do they?

While the text that shows up in the browser's display window doesn't amount to much, there are several noteworthy elements about this figure. First, notice that the text between the <TITLE> and </TITLE> tags appears in the title bar at the top of the Internet Explorer Window. Also check out how the location of the HTML file you're viewing appears as C:\test.htm in the text box labeled Address just beneath the toolbar, which is above the text display area. Notice also that one of the buttons on that toolbar is labeled Refresh. From here on out, the Edit-Review cycle works like this:

1. **Switch to the text editor and then enter some text.**

2. **Save the file in the text editor.**

3. **Switch to your Web browser and hit the refresh button.**

4. **Check your most recent efforts; if further changes are necessary, go back to Step 1!**

The most often overlooked elements of this process are (a) saving the file after you make changes in the text editor, and (b) remembering to refresh the browser display so that it shows the most recent version of your file. If you can remember to do these things every time, the Edit-Review cycle will become a part of your basic page creation and maintenance activities!

Now give the example a bit more substance by returning to your text editor and making your `test.htm` file look like this one:

```
<HTML>
<HEAD>
<TITLE>Home Page: The Institute of Silly Research</TITLE>
</HEAD>
<BODY>
<H1>Welcome to the ISR!</H1>
The ISR is the world's best-known repository of truly tri-
          fling and insignificant research results. Visit
          our pages regularly to keep up with the exciting
          efforts of our team of talented scholars, and
          their magnificent efforts to extend the bound-
          aries of science and technology to ever more
          meaningless ends.
<H2>The ISR Staff</H2>
Dr. Maury Singleton-Smith, PhD, Director<BR>
Dr. Gwyneth Gastropolis, PhD, Chief of Research<BR>
Dr. Simon Schuster, MD, PhD, Head, Impracticality Dept.<BR>
<H2>ISR's Current Projects</H2>
Beyond Charm and Strangeness: The Nerdon<BR>
Lukewarm Fusion<BR>
Harnessing the Power of Stilton Cheese<BR>
The Dancing Louie Masters<BR>
<HR>
For more information about the ISR, please contact <A
          HREF=mailto:nerdboy@isr.org>Dr. Singleton-
          Smith</A>.
All financial contributions are cheerfully accepted.
</BODY>
</HTML>
```

As you go through the process of entering this text, you may find yourself dealing with HTML mistakes (remember to enclose all tags with < and >, and to precede the text for closing tags with a /). You also may find yourself dealing with typos, omissions, and other kinds of content errors as well. Just remember to shift back into your text editor each time you need to make a change. Then save the new version of the file. When you return to your Web browser, refresh the page, and you can see the results of your latest efforts. Keep at it, and you'll soon have a page every bit as insignificant and meaningless as the one shown in Figure 4-2.

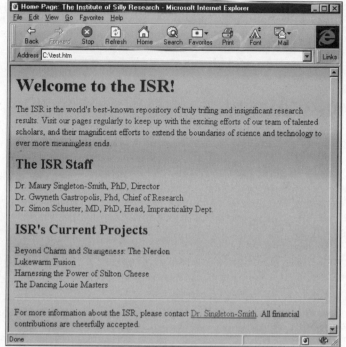

Figure 4-2:
The full-blown home page for the ISR is overwhelming in its triviality!

The real point behind the exercise, of course, is to make you familiar with what's involved in creating and editing an HTML document as you go through the process of building a page for inclusion on a Web site. As the process becomes more familiar, you'll be able to forget about most of these operational issues and concentrate on the content and formatting of your documents. By the time you've created a few pages, all of this will become second nature to you.

Working with Templates

To make the job of building a Web page easier, we've included a number of template files on the CD that accompanies this book (you can find a collection of files in the /Template directory on the CD). You can use these files as a point of departure in your own Web page creation efforts. By copying these files to your hard drive and then editing them, you can get started on the Edit-Review cycle that's so necessary to Web page creation.

Whenever you want to use a template as a point of departure for your work, save it under a different name as soon as you open it in your text editor. That way, you won't have to recopy the files from the CD each time you want to reuse the same template.

What Comes Next?

After you've built an HTML document that looks just right and works the way you want it to, you'll never be able to share it with anyone else unless you move it from your local hard drive to a Web server somewhere. The exact details on how to do this varies tremendously, depending on where your Web pages live, and what kinds of systems and services your Internet Service Provider has to offer. But in general, the process works something like this:

1. **Transfer the HTML file(s), and any graphics or programs they reference, to a Web-accessible directory on your Internet Service Provider's (ISP) machine.**

2. **Access the files through the Web to note any relocation-related problems and make any necessary changes.**

3. **Announce your new pages to the world!**

This is just a general description and doesn't do justice to the necessary details involved. Suffice it to say we've seen FTP- and e-mail-based methods widely used to transfer collections of files, graphics, and programs from users to Web sites, and we've witnessed varying degrees of ISP support and involvement in bringing those materials onto the Web where other people can see them. The best way to understand and master those details is to talk to the technical support folks at your ISP. At least you now know how to build an HTML document that you can look at and tweak on your own machine to your heart's content! In the next chapter, we start to get more serious about HTML, as you grapple with more details of HTML syntax and markup.

Part II
A Tour of HTML Basics

The 5th Wave · By Rich Tennant

"OK, I'VE GOT THIS INTRANET THING DOWN. LIKE HERE—MY REPORT ON INVENTORY MANAGEMENT WILL INCLUDE A VIDEO CLIP FROM www.rottingmeat.com."

In this part . . .

In this part of the book, we cover markup in general, and HTML in particular. This includes logical groupings for HTML tags and a complete dictionary of HTML tags.

Chapter 5
What's a Markup Language?

In This Chapter

▶ Defining HTML markup conventions

▶ Understanding HTML's roots

▶ Introducing the basic HTML control characters, elements, attributes, and entities

*I*n this chapter, you get to see more of what HTML looks like. Hopefully, you'll also begin to appreciate what's involved in a markup language and better understand how to use HTML to create Web pages. Because this chapter is an overview, you won't be able to run right out and start building complex pages after you've read it, but you should have a pretty good idea what pieces and parts make HTML do its thing.

A Markup Language Is Not a Form of Graffiti

HTML represents a way to take ordinary text and turn it into hypertext, just by adding special elements — called markup tags — that instruct Web browsers how to display its contents.

The purpose of a markup language is to give programs (or humans) clues about the structure, content, and behavior of a document. Markup comes in two types: descriptive and procedural. HTML is a *descriptive* markup language. A descriptive markup language describes the structure and behavior of a document. This lets authors concentrate more on content and structure, and less on formatting and presentation. Here's an example:

```
<H1>Cooking for One</H1> -- display level one header
<OL>  - begin ordered (numbered) list
<LI>Take Lean Cuisine out of fridge.
<LI>Place in microwave.
<LI>Set timer for 5 min.
</OL> -- end ordered list
```

The tags H1, OL, and LI describe an object and its components. It's up to a browser to render these properly on your screen. In fact, from browser to browser, each of these objects could be rendered differently. But the important thing is that each browser has a meaningful way to display a first level header (H1) and a numbered list (OL and LI). From a portability standpoint, this is a good thing.

The other kind of markup language, procedural, describes formatting rather than structure. An example is *troff,* the dinosaur UNIX markup language, which looks like this

```
.center .12 .Helvetica .bold Table of Contents
```

These *troff* tags tell the output device to render an object as "centered, 12 point Helvetica bold":

Table of Contents

As you can imagine, this type of markup is not very portable and is difficult to maintain.

HTML tags not only govern how a browser displays the contents of an HTML document, they also control how a browser uses graphics, video, sound, and so on, to create a multimedia experience.

In the same vein, still other HTML tags instruct browsers how to handle and display hypertext links, either within the same HTML file or to other documents or Web-accessible services. The key to building attractive, readable Web pages is knowing how to use HTML markup to highlight and organize your content.

A syntax is not a levy on cigarettes!

When it comes to any kind of formal, computer-readable language, invariably a set of rules governs its terms and their order of placement. This set of rules is called the *syntax* of the language. HTML syntax describes how a Web browser can recognize and interpret the instructions contained in the markup tags.

What makes HTML particularly interesting is that it's all pure text — in fact, HTML can work completely within the confines of the ASCII 7-bit character set (ISO 646), which contains only 128 distinct viewable characters. Nevertheless, HTML can handle display of so-called higher-order ASCII characters, which normally require eight bits to represent directly and are sometimes called the 8-bit ASCII or Latin-1 character set (ISO 8859/1). Quite a bit of work is under way to permit HTML to handle the Unicode character set, which supports up to 65,535 different characters (of which more than 34,000 are defined). The Unicode set includes non-Roman alphabets like Chinese (Han) ideograms, Hebrew characters, and lots of other interesting stuff.

This diversity lets HTML display things like accents, umlauts, and other diacritical marks often associated with non-English languages (or loan words, like résumé), by including instructions on what characters to represent as a part of the markup. In other words, HTML can provide instructions to a browser even if you can't always see things in the same format when you're writing the HTML. For example, `<OL>` and `<LI>` don't look like a numbered list inside a text file, but they do when the browser interprets them.

Elements of HTML syntax

The special control characters that separate HTML markup from ordinary text are the left and right angle brackets: `<` (left bracket) and `>` (right bracket). These characters indicate that the browser should pay special attention to what they enclose. And here's your big chance to learn another buzzword: *parser*. Inside the browser software, a parser reads and constructs display information. In other words, the parser examines characters in an HTML file, decides which elements are markup and which ones aren't, and instructs the browser to take appropriate action based on the markup it detects.

In HTML, left and right angle brackets can enclose all kinds of special instructions called *tags*. We devote the next several chapters of this book to introducing, explaining, and demonstrating the vast majority of known HTML tags.

In the meantime, here's a formal introduction to the way HTML tags look and behave; a tag takes a generic form that looks something like this:

```
<TAG-NAME {ATTRIBUTE{="VALUE"} . . . }>Text{</TAG-NAME>}
```

(By the way, text within tags is case insensitive, but for readability, we use all caps to make HTML tags stand apart from other text.)

Here are the pieces of this generic form:

- `<TAG-NAME>`: All HTML tags have names. For example, H1 is a level one header; OL is an ordered list. Tags are surrounded by angle brackets to mark their contents for special attention from the parser.

- `{ATTRIBUTE{="VALUE"}...}`: Some HTML tags require or permit named attributes to be associated with them. Here the notation using curly braces — for example, {ATTRIBUTE} — indicates that attributes may be present for some tags but not for others. In the same vein, some attributes require that values be associated with them, as when supplying the name of an HTML document for a link; other attributes may not require associated values at all, which is why {`="VALUE"`} is also in curly braces.

For example, in an `<IMG>` tag used to point to a graphics file, a required attribute is `SRC` (source), to provide a pointer to the file where the graphic resides, as in `<IMG SRC="../gifs/redball.gif."` This syntax proves yet again how important it is to stay close to your source! Finally, an ellipsis (. . .) indicates that some HTML tags may include multiple attributes, each of which may or may not take a value.

✔ **Text:** This is content that's modified by a tag. For example, if the tag were a document title, the HTML string

```
<TITLE>HTML For Dummies Home Page</TITLE>
```

would display the words "HTML For Dummies Home Page" in the title bar at the top of a graphical browser's window. Enclosing text within `<TITLE>` and `</TITLE>` tags marks it as the document's title.

✔ **{`</TAG-NAME>`}:** A closing tag name is denoted by a left angle bracket (`<`), followed by a forward slash (`/`), then the tag name, and finally a closing right angle bracket (`>`). Curly braces indicate that this element does not always occur. Because more than 70 percent of HTML tags require a closing tag as well as an opening tag, the omission of a closing tag is an exception, rather than a rule. Don't worry: Most, if not all, browsers simply ignore closing tags if they're not necessary.

The majority of HTML tags don't require assignment of attributes, so don't be too overwhelmed by the full-blown formal syntax. By and large, most tags follow a `<TAG-NAME>Text</TAG-NAME>` layout like `<TITLE>HTML For Dummies Home Page</TITLE>`.

The ampersand (`&`) is another special HTML control character. You can use it to denote a special character for HTML content that may not belong to a 7-bit ASCII character set (like an accent grave or an umlaut), or that could otherwise be interpreted as markup (like a left or right angle bracket). Such tagged items are called character entities and can be expressed in a number of ways. For example, the string `&egrave;` produces a lowercase E with a grave accent mark (è), and the string `&lt;` produces a left angle bracket (<).

Chapter 6 supplies a complete set of HTML character entities. If you work in a language other than English, you may want to consider building macros to replace familiar higher-order ASCII characters in your HTML files. Such macros allow you to automate a search-and-replace maneuver as a post-processing step. Then you can avoid keying seven or eight characters of HTML to produce one output character (this is what computer science nerds like to call *an unfavorable input-output ratio*). Even better, check out some of the HTML authoring tools in Part V. Most of the tools we discuss automate this kind of thing for you.

Warning: Entering the Acronym Zone

Nearly any writing, speech, or documentation that has to do with computers will be rife with technical jargon and gibberish, no matter what the specific subject might be. To make matters even more confusing, the cognoscenti would much rather abbreviate frequently used technical terms like Hypertext Markup Language as HTML or Standard Generalized Markup Language as SGML, instead of having to say all the words for the concept each time it's mentioned.

The use of strings of first letters for technical terms — like ROM for Read-Only Memory,

RAM for Random Access Memory, CPU for Central Processing Unit, and so on — happens across the board in the computer world, so you may as well get used to it! Because this kind of shorthand is called an acronym (which literally means *from the point or head of the name* in Greek), we've got to warn you that you've entered a world where acronyms are commonplace. To make your lives a little easier, dear readers, we've tried to include all of the acronyms that we use in this book in the Glossary at the end. That way, if you forget what a particular string of letters means, you'll at least be able to look it up!

In the next section, we uncover the roots of HTML, namely SGML, Standard Generalized Markup Language.

Standard Generalized Markup Language (SGML)

Technically speaking, HTML is not a programming language, nor can an HTML document be called a program. Normally, a program is defined as a set of instructions and operations to be applied to external data (usually called the input).

HTML combines instructions with data to tell a display program, called a *browser,* how to render the data that a document contains. Even though it's not a programming language per se, HTML provides the structure and layout controls needed to manage a document's appearance as well as the linkage mechanisms necessary to provide hypertext capabilities.

Actually, HTML is defined by a particular type of document — called a *Document Type Definition,* or *DTD* — within the context of SGML. Thus, any HTML document is also an SGML document that represents a specific subset of SGML capability.

Generalized Markup Covers Many Sins

SGML originated with work begun at IBM in the 1960s to overcome the problems inherent in moving documents across multiple hardware platforms and operating systems. IBM's efforts were called GML, for General Markup Language. GML was originally targeted for local use at IBM, rather than as a generic way of representing documents. This development was the first publish-once, multiplatform strategy for document preparation — a concept that's become extremely popular today.

GML's originators — Charles Goldfarb, Ed Mosher, and Ray Lorie (the original "GML") — realized by the 1970s that a general version of markup would make documents portable across systems. Their work led ultimately to the definition and birth of SGML in the 1980s, which is today covered by the ISO 8879 standard.

SGML is a powerful and complex tool for representing documents of all kinds. SGML offers the ability to create document specifications that can then be used to define and build individual documents that conform to those specifications.

Some commercial and government institutions, like the Department of Defense (DoD), have adopted SGML. The DoD mandates that contractors and subcontractors now submit all documentation to the government in SGML. The DoD even mandates the DTDs to which the contractors' documents must conform.

Several quotes from the SGML standard, ISO 8879, may help to illustrate its aims, while underscoring its relationship to HTML. First, about the markup process:

> Text processing and word processing systems typically require additional information to be interspersed among the natural text of the document being processed. This added information, called "markup," serves two purposes:
>
> a) Separating the logical elements of the document; and
>
> b) Specifying the processing functions to be performed on those elements.
>
> Charles F. Goldfarb, *The SGML Handbook,* (Clarendon Press, Oxford, 1990) p. 5.

In stature and in scope, SGML far outstrips HTML; it is used to define complex document types like those used for military standard (Milspec) documents or aircraft maintenance manuals, whose specifications alone can run into thousands of pages.

The notion of *generalized markup* is what makes SGML's document definition system so all-encompassing and powerful. Goldfarb has this to say on that subject:

> ..."generalized markup" [...] does not restrict documents to a single application, formatting style, or processing system. Generalized markup is based on two novel postulates:
>
> a) Markup should describe a document's structure and other attributes rather than specify processing to be performed on it, as descriptive markup need be done only once and will suffice for all future processing.
>
> b) Markup should be rigorous so that the techniques available for processing rigorously defined objects like programs and databases can be used for processing documents as well. (Goldfarb 7-8)

Even though SGML, like HTML, is oriented toward producing documents, the goal is to make those documents behave more like programs — that is, to behave predictably in a computer-oriented world.

Building better pieces and parts

The whole idea behind SGML is to create a formal method to describe the sections, headings, styles, and other components that make up a document so that references to individual items or entries in a document remain subject to such definitions. This definition lets a document be rendered consistently, no matter what platform displays it. In simplistic terms, SGML is a general-purpose tool to describe documents of just about any kind.

In its most generic form, an SGML document comes in three parts:

- A description of the legal character set and the characters used to distinguish plain text from markup tags.
- A declaration of the document type, including a listing of the legal markup tags it may contain.
- The document itself, which includes actual references to markup tags, mixed with the content for the document.

Where HTML fits under the SGML umbrella

All three document parts (see preceding bulleted list) do not have to be included in the same physical file. In fact, HTML works from the same set of definitions for the first two items so that only the contents and tags that make up an HTML document need to be included with the document itself, as described in the third item above.

For HTML, the ISO Latin-1 character set defines character entities for higher-order ASCII characters, along with the angle brackets and forward slash used to indicate markup tags. The declaration of document type comes from a standard DTD for HTML.

Therefore, HTML can be conveyed by pure ASCII text files that conform to the definitions and requirements covered in the first two bulleted items to create instances of documents, the third bulleted item. In other words, all that HTML consists of is content text, character entities, and markup tags.

Welcome to HTML!

Despite its more limited nature, HTML shares several important characteristics with its SGML *parent* — namely

- ✔ A character-based method for describing and expressing content.
- ✔ A desire to deliver that content equally to multiple platforms.
- ✔ A method for linking document components (and documents) to compose compound documents.

Although HTML may be less general than SGML, it still leaves plenty of room for unique and powerful expressions, as any quick perusal of Web pages illustrates. Though it may be less than completely general, HTML's tags and entities can still do justice to a broad range of content!

Delivering content to a variety of platforms

HTML's tremendous power and appeal come from its capacity to service character-mode and graphical browsers with identical content. The look and feel of any document's content remains the same, subject only to the display limitations of the browser being used.

When you add the capability to group multiple, related sources of information together — text, graphics, sound, and video — and the capacity to link documents together, the result is *hypertext*. HTML's combination of a simple concise form, powerful controls, and hypertext linkages helps to explain the overwhelming popularity of the Web as an information retrieval and investigation tool.

The four-plus faces of HTML

In a manner of speaking, all there is to HTML besides content is a collection of character entities and markup tags. Some purists insist on remaining within the confines of the SGML DTD for HTML, but the number and kinds of tags and entities used in various Web environments (especially in some of the more advanced browsers) continue to expand with each passing day and each new version of browser software.

Although some browsers recognize tags and entities unknown to other browsers, HTML includes the convention that all unrecognized markup is ignored. You may lose some of the finer formatting controls with some browsers (like the `<BLINK>` tag), but the content should still be accessible.

Today, HTML has several standardization levels, numbered zero through three, plus a collection of code names:

0 The original text-only markup language developed for prototype browsers at CERN prior to HTML's release to the general public. You shouldn't see any tools that remain at this level, except for historical curiosities.

1 The initial public implementation of HTML markup, which included the ability to reference graphical elements in addition to text controls. Many browsers — for example, Lynx and Cello — still operate at level 1 HTML.

2 The current "official" implementation of HTML markup, which includes all markup elements for level 1, plus tags for interactive forms. Most graphical browsers — like Mosaic, Netscape, and Internet Explorer — support level 2 HTML (and beyond).

3.2 The name of an HTML level that is nearing "official status" just as we're writing this version of the book. HTML 3.2 is nearly final and quite complete at this point; it just hasn't made its way entirely through the standards process at this point. Throughout the rest of this book, 3.2 is our primary reference standard. At one time, 3.2 was known by the code name *Wilbur,* so we may sometimes refer to it by that name.

Cougar The code name for the emerging HTML level that is the focus of intense research and development as we write this book. Cougar includes many significant enhancements and capabilities that are reasonably well-defined, particularly for style sheets and frames. We cover some of its most important aspects in various parts of this book, but we're careful to identify them as "experimental" or "unofficial" standards.

To find out what's current for HTML, you can always go trolling on the Web itself. You should be able to find the current specification, in the form of an HTML DTD, along with online documentation on HTML markup, as well as current information on SGML.

HTML Elements!

Well-structured HTML documents come in three parts, consisting of

- ✔ **A head** that identifies a document as HTML and establishes its title.
- ✔ **A body** that contains the content for a Web page. This parts holds all displayed text on a page (except for the title), as well as all links to graphics, multimedia information, locations inside the same HTML file, or other Web documents.
- ✔ **A footer** that labels a page by identifying its author, date of creation, and version number (if applicable).

In reality, HTML is very forgiving, so you may "get away with" skipping some of these elements. As a matter of good style and practice, however, we strongly recommend that any pages you design begin with the information necessary for all three elements.

Go to the head of the document

An entire HTML document needs to be bracketed by the identification tags <HTML> to open the document and </HTML> to close it. These tags identify the DTD for the document to an SGML-sensitive program and allow it to interpret a document's contents properly. You omit this tag for most browsers, but with the increasing convergence of HTML and SGML, doing so may limit the shelf life of your Web pages.

An optional line may sometimes precede a document head. It is called a *document type prolog* and describes, in SGML, that the HTML document complies to the indicated level of the HTML DTD. Here is an example:

```
<!DOCTYPE HTML PUBLIC "-//IETF//DTD HTML 2.0//EN">
```

Deciphering this line indicates that the HTML document conforms to the HTML 2.0 DTD distributed by the Internet Engineering Task Force (IETF). You can also tell that the DTD is PUBLIC and is not system dependent. Finally, you can tell that the HTML tag set is defined by the English language (the EN in the DOCTYPE statement above). Local SGML parsers can also use this DOCTYPE statement to validate the HTML document; that is, the parsers check the document's syntax for conformance and correctness. This prolog will become increasingly important in the future.

A document title is flagged by the HTML tags <TITLE>, to open the title string, and </TITLE> to close it. The important thing about an HTML document heading is that it should identify itself in an informative and catchy way.

HTML also includes a pair of tags, <HEAD> and </HEAD> to identify the head of a document. As with the <HTML> and </HTML> tags, many browsers happily let you skip this tag, but for readability and structure, we recommend including it anyway. Within this section, you find the actual title and possibly some other document heading tags, which we cover in more detail in Chapters 6 and 8.

The bulk's in the body

The real content for any HTML document occurs in the body section, which is enclosed within <BODY> and </BODY> tags. The body is where you describe your document's layout and structure by using a variety of tags for text headings, embedded graphics, text paragraphs, lists, and other elements. Not surprisingly, the majority of HTML tags occur within a document's body simply because that's where all the beef is!

Chapter 6 covers all HTML tags in brief form (and Chapter 8 covers proprietary extensions, plus obsolete or experimental tags), and Parts II and III of this book provide lots of examples. Remember, this is just the overview.

The good stuff's in the graphics and links

You also find all hypertext content within a document's body section. This content can take the form of references to graphics or other files, as indicated by appropriate use of text tags like <IMG> for in-line graphics. Or, you can have links to other points within the same document or to outside documents by using the *anchor* tags (<A>, </A>) with the appropriate attributes. In fact, because anchors point to generalized URLs (not just other HTML documents), you can also use them to invoke services like FTP to transfer multimedia files from within your Web pages.

Chapters 6, 10, 11, 12, and 14 offer lots of details about using graphics within HTML documents, including good sources for material, appropriate usage, and other sorts of graphical information goodies. By the time you're through with this book, you'll be slinging HTML graphics around with the best Webmasters!

A footer may be optional, but it's still a good idea

Technically speaking, HTML doesn't include a separate tag to denote a page footer — that is, there's no <FOOT> and </FOOT> pair to label the information that would typically appear in a footer. Nevertheless, we strongly recommend that you include a footer on every Web page that you create, just for the record.

"What's in a footer?" you ask. Well, it should contain information to describe the page and its author(s). A good footer helps to identify a document's vintage and contents and lets interested readers contact the author if they spot errors or want to provide feedback.

For your own sake, it's also smart to include date and version information in each of your HTML files. Doing this enables you to recognize what version you're dealing with whenever you look at a page, and it provides a great reminder of how stale your pages may be getting. As any Web-head knows, the older the page, the more likely it's out-of-date!

Chapter 10 provides lots of details about page footers and includes a particularly fine example of what a good footer looks like. Be sure not to miss it.

Ladies and Gentlemen, Start Your Engines!

Okay, so now you've seen the basic elements of HTML. In the chapters that follow, we introduce you to the details, including more tags than you'll see at a Red Tag sale at your local department store. As you come to know and love what HTML can do, you can apply what you're learning to build great Web pages.

Chapter 6

Pigeonholing Page Contents: HTML Categories

In This Chapter

▶ Defining HTML's tag syntax in detail

▶ Categorizing HTML tags

▶ Stepping through HTML, tag-by-tag

*A*t last you've arrived at the first in-depth, no-holds-barred look at HTML markup that appears in this book. In this chapter, we talk some serious turkey about HTML syntax to make sure you can keep up with all the gory details. We also establish some categories for what HTML can do and group the markup tags in meaningful categories (to make them easier to understand and use). The remainder of the chapter is a reference tool, where we describe all the HTML tags in alphabetical order for easy access. Buckle up, and let's go!

HTML Syntax Redux

In the preceding chapter, we talk about a general syntax for HTML tags. At this point, here's what's been presented:

✔ Tags are enclosed in left and right angle brackets — for example, `<HEAD>` marks the beginning of the head of an HTML document.

✔ By convention only (HTML itself has no requirement for upper- or lowercase) we present all tags in uppercase for readability. That's why you see `<HEAD>` but not `<Head>` or `<head>` in the rest of this book, even though all three are perfectly legal — and equivalent — HTML tags. We recommend that you follow this practice yourself because doing so will help you distinguish the tags from the real text.

✔ Tags usually come in pairs, so `<HEAD>` marks the beginning of a document heading block, and `</HEAD>` marks the end. All the text that occurs between opening and closing tags is considered the focus of that tag and is handled appropriately. The majority of HTML tags work this way, so we'll be sure to flag all of the possible exceptions as we introduce them.

✔ Tags can sometimes take on one or more attributes to define data sources or destinations, to specify URLs, or to further specify the characteristics of the text to which a tag will be applied. For example, the `<IMG>` tag for placing graphics can use the following attributes to help specify the source and placement of an image on a page:

- `SRC` = source for image, same as URL

- `ALT` = alternate text to display inline if browser isn't graphics-capable, or graphics are turned off

- `ALIGN = (TOP|MIDDLE|BOTTOM)` and `(\WIDTH=number andr HEIGHT=number\)` controls placement of a graphic. We explain this in more detail later when we tell you what you don't already know!

- `ISMAP` If this attribute is present, it indicates that the graphic is a clickable image map with one or more links to other locations built onto the image. If it's absent, it means the image is not a map.

Some attributes take on values — in this case, `SRC`, `ALT`, and `ALIGN` all require at least one value — while others, like `ISMAP`, do not. Attributes that do not require values are usually true ("turned on") if present and false ("turned off") when omitted. Also, tags may have default values for required attributes that are omitted, so make sure that you check the HTML specification to determine how such defaults are handled.

At this point, you may already know quite a bit about HTML syntax and layout. But there is quite a bit of additional stuff you need to know, some of which we had to use in our discussion in the preceding bullet item. Discussions of this additional stuff contain some goofy characters that aren't part of HTML itself, but are necessary to explain it formally.

In the sections that follow, we begin with formal syntax conventions and then move on to more interesting properties of HTML itself.

Syntax conventions are no party!

While we're providing formal definitions of the various HTML commands, we use typographical notation in an equally formal way. What this means (in plain language) is that you'd better pay attention to how we write some things down because we intend for the notation to describe how terms should be combined, constructed, and used.

Describing a formal syntax means using certain characters in a special way to talk about how to treat elements that appear in conjunction with these characters. This is nearly identical to these HTML notions:

✔ Angle brackets surround a tag (<HEAD>)

✔ A forward slash following the left angle bracket denotes a closing tag (</HEAD>)

✔ An ampersand leads off a character entity and a semicolon closes it (è)

These special characters clue us (and our browser software) into the need for special handling.

The characters we're going to use for our HTML syntax come from conventions developed for a formal syntax — called a Backus-Naur Form (or BNF grammar, for short) — that was developed to completely and formally describe programming languages. Because we're forced to deviate somewhat from BNF, we lay out all of the special characters we use to describe HTML syntax. Table 6-1 contains these characters (which, by the way, are called metacharacters) and their definitions, plus an example for each one.

Table 6-1		**The HTML Syntax Metacharacter Set**	
Char(s)	*Name(s)*	*Definition*	*Example*
I	vertical bar	Separates legal choices	ITEM1IITEM2IITEM3
( )	parentheses	Defines a set of items to treat as a unit	(ITEM1IITEM2) or (ITEM3IITEM4)
\ \	backslashes	Indicates that one or more items can be selected	\ITEM1IITEM2IITEM3\
and	logical and	Indicates that both items must be selected	(ITEM1IITEM2) and (ITEM3IITEM4)
or	logical or	Indicates that one or the other item must be selected	ITEM1 or ITEM2
&r	and/or	Indicates that one or both items must be selected	ITEM1 &r ITEM2
[ ]	square brackets	Indicates nonstandard items, not supported by all browsers	[WIDTH=number]
integer	integer	Indicates whole numbers only	1, 2944, -40

(continued)

Char(s)	Name(s)	Definition	Example
...	ellipsis	Repeat elements as needed	ITEM1IITEM2I...
{}	curly braces	Contain optional elements, not required	{ITEM1IITEM2}

Table 6-1 (continued)

Decoding a complex metacharacter example: ALIGN = ?

Nothing beats an example to make some sense out of this potential gibberish. Recall our definition of the ALIGN attribute for the <IMG> tag:

```
ALIGN = (TOP|MIDDLE|BOTTOM) and (\WIDTH=number &r
          HEIGHT=number\)
```

To make sure you understand what this means, we relate the example as follows:

ALIGN = TOP|MIDDLE|BOTTOM means that ALIGN can take one of the three values: TOP, MIDDLE, or BOTTOM. This is what ALIGN = TOP|MIDDLE|BOTTOM means. Basically, you use it to say whether you want an image at the top, middle, or bottom of a display area on-screen.

Also, ALIGN can also take a member of the set (TOP|MIDDLE|BOTTOM), and it can sometimes take one or both members of the set (\WIDTH=number|HEIGHT=number\).

Sometimes, ALIGN can take either or both of a WIDTH and HEIGHT setting. The backslashes (\ \) around the WIDTH and HEIGHT and the logical and/or (&r) entries indicate either or both. Each of those two entries must be assigned some integer value corresponding to a position relative to the current display area, as indicated by the number part.

As you can see, what we were able to describe in a single complex line of type takes three paragraphs of details to explain completely. The brevity and compactness of formal syntax makes it appealing to computer nerds; as you review the various tags, we hope that you are able to work your way through this syntax to fully grasp what HTML can do. If not, never fear — we provide plenty of examples for each tag throughout so that you can absorb by osmosis what you can't grasp through formalism! Ouch!

Interesting HTML properties

In addition to the formal syntax for HTML that we use throughout the book, the markup language itself has some interesting general properties that are worth covering before you encounter the tags directly.

No embedded blanks, please!

All HTML tags require that the characters in a name be contiguous. You can't insert extra blanks within a tag or its surrounding markup without causing that tag to be ignored (which is what browsers do with tags they can't recognize).

This means that `</HEAD>` is a valid closing tag for a document heading, but that none of the following is legal:

```
< /HEAD>
</ HEAD>
</H EAD>
</HE AD>
</HEA D>
</HEAD >
```

We hope that you get the idea: Don't use blanks inside tags, except where you're using a blank deliberately to separate a tag name from an attribute name (for example `<IMG SRC="sample.gif">` is legal, but `<IMGSRC="sample.gif">` is not).

When assigning values to attributes, however, spaces are okay. Therefore, all four of the following variants for this `SRC` assignment are legal:

```
<IMG SRC="sample.gif">
<!-- Previous line: no spaces before or after = sign -->
<IMG SRC = "sample.gif">
<!-- Previous line: spaces before and after = sign -->
<IMG SRC= "sample.gif">
<!-- Previous line: no space before, one after = sign -->
<IMG SRC ="sample.gif">
<!-- Previous line: 1 space before, none after = sign -->
```

Where one space is legal, multiple spaces are legal. Don't get carried away with what's legal or not, though — try to make your HTML documents as readable as possible and everything else should flow naturally.

We snuck some more HTML markup into the preceding example. After each `<IMG>` tag line, we inserted readable HTML comments to describe what occurred on the preceding line. This lets you infer that the HTML markup to open a comment is the string `<!--` and the string `-->` closes the comment. As you go through the markup section later on, we cover some style guidelines for using comments effectively and correctly.

What's the default?

If a tag can support an attribute, what does it mean when the attribute isn't present? For `ISMAP` on the `<IMG>` tag, for example, you already know that when the `ISMAP` attribute is present, it means *the image is a clickable map*. If `ISMAP` is absent, this means *the image is not a clickable map*.

This is a way of introducing the concept of a *default*, which is not a way of assigning blame, but rather, a way of deciding what to assume when an attribute is not supplied for a particular tag. For `ISMAP`, the default is absent, that is an image is only assumed to be a clickable map when the `ISMAP` attribute is explicitly supplied.

But how do images get displayed if the `ALIGN` attribute isn't defined? As a quick bit of experimentation shows you, the default for most graphical browsers is to insert the graphic at the left-hand margin. These kinds of defaults are important, too, and we'll try to tell you what to expect from them as well.

The nesting instinct

Sometimes it's necessary to insert one set of markup tags within another. You might want a few words within a sentence already marked for special emphasis to be the trigger for a hyper link. For example, the entire heading "Other Important Numbers: Emergency Phone Numbers" will draw the reader's attention if it is rendered in boldface, but you only want the words *Emergency Phone Numbers* to be clickable and lead to another HTML document listing relevant emergency numbers.

When you start enclosing one set of markup within another, it's called *nesting*. When the nesting instinct strikes you, the best rule of thumb is to close first what you've opened most recently. For example, the text tags `<A HREF="ephone.html">...</A>` provide a way of bracketing text linking to another HTML document. If this were to occur within strongly emphasized text, `<STRONG>...</STRONG>`, the proper way to handle the hyper link is like this:

```
<STRONG>Other Important Numbers: <A HREF="ephone.html">
         Emergency Phone Numbers</A></STRONG>
```

That way, you close the nested <A> tag with its mate, before you close out the <STRONG> heading. Some browsers may let you violate this rule, but others may behave unpredictably if you don't open and close tags in the right order. Figure 6-1 shows what this combination of tags looks like. (Notice that the words *Emergency Phone Numbers* appear in heavier type than the rest of the heading.)

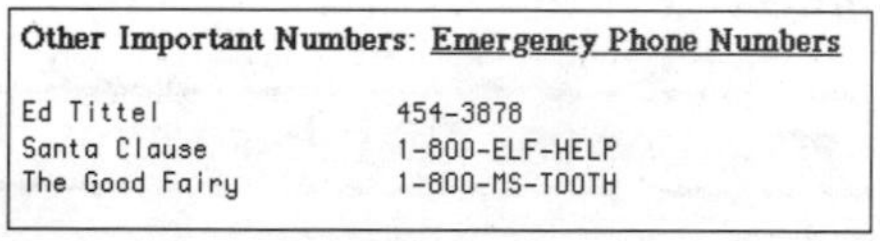

Figure 6-1:
Using nested tags to create a hyper link within strongly emphasized text.

Other Important Numbers: <u>Emergency Phone Numbers</u>

Ed Tittel	454-3878
Santa Clause	1-800-ELF-HELP
The Good Fairy	1-800-MS-TOOTH

Nesting just doesn't make sense for some tags. For instance, within <TITLE> ... </TITLE>, you're dealing with information that shows up only on a window title, rather than on a particular Web page. Text and layout controls clearly do not apply here (and are cheerfully ignored by some browsers, while making others curl up and die).

Always look back to the left as you start closing tags you've already opened. Close the closest one first, the next closest one next, and so on. Check the tag details (later in this chapter) to find out what tags are okay to nest within your outermost open tag. If the tag you want to use isn't on the okay list, then don't try to nest that tag inside the current open ones. Close out what you've got open and then open the tag you need.

Keeping your tags in the right nests keeps your readers' browsers from getting confused! It also makes sure that you hatch only good-looking Web pages.

A matter of context

As you learn which tags can appear inside other tags, you begin to develop an appreciation for the controls and capabilities offered by HTML. In our alphabetical list (later in this chapter) we cover the nesting compatibilities under the heading "Context" to indicate which tags are okay to nest (and by exclusion, which are not).

HTML Categories

Before we take you through the HTML tags in alphabetical order, we'd like to introduce them to you grouped by category. These categories help to explain how and when the tags are used, and what functions they provide.

We hope that the categories presented in Table 6-2 also help you to organize and understand HTML's numerous tags. (For a complete listing of the HTML character entities, please consult Chapter 7.) Because so many tags come in pairs, we use an ellipsis (...) between opening and closing tags to indicate where text and other elements can appear.

Table 6-2	HTML Categories and Their Respective Tags	
Tags	*Tag Names*	*Brief Explanation*
Document Structure	**Basic document layout and linkage structures**	
<HTML> ... </HTML>	HTML	Blocks out an entire HTML document
<HEAD> ... </HEAD>	Head	Blocks out a document's head
<TITLE> ... </TITLE>	Title	Supplies title that labels entire document
<BODY> ... </BODY>	Body	Blocks out a document's body
<BASE>	Base	Indicates complete document URL, establishes location context for other URLs
<ISINDEX>	Isindex	Indicates that document supports CGI script for searches
<LINK>	Link type	Sets relationship between current document and other documents
<NEXTID>	Next document	Indicates the "next" document that follows current to permit HTML documents to be chained together
<META>	Structure	Describes aspects of the page's info structure, contents, or relationships to other documents
Links	**Create links to another document, Java applet, object, or script**	
<A> ... </A>	Anchor	Provides fundamental hypertext link capabilities
<APPLET>... </APPLET>	Java	Calls a Java applet

Tags	Tag Names	Brief Explanation
<PARAM>	Applet parameters	Sets the parameters for a Java applet
<OBJECT>... </OBJECT>	Insert object	Include non-HTTP object in HTML doc
<SCRIPT>... </SCRIPT>	Insert script	Insert script directly into HTML document
Layout Elements	**Control document appearance, add elements**	
 	Line break	Forces a line break into on-screen text flow
<HR>	Horizontal rule	Draws a horizontal line across the page
<P>	Paragraph	Breaks up text into spaced regions
<ADDRESS> ... </ADDRESS>	Address	Author contact information
<BASEFONT>	Default font size	Sets the default font for the entire document
<FONT>...</FONT> block	Font appearance	Defines the size and color of a text
<BLOCKQUOTE> ... </BLOCKQUOTE>	Blockquote	Sets off long quotes or citations
<PRE>...</PRE>	Preformatted text	Preserves spacing and layout of original text in monospaced font
<CENTER>... </CENTER>	Center	Centers text horizontally across the page
<DIV>	Divison	Marks divisions in a document and allows you to apply styles to those divisions
<STYLE>	In-line style info	Provides style information within the HTML document; intended for upward compatibility with style sheets
<SPAN>...</SPAN>	Span	Applies a style as specified in the <STYLE> tag to the text it contains
<BUTTON>... </BUTTON>	Button	Includes HTML within a graphical button

(continued)

Table 6-2 *(continued)*

Tags	Tag Names	Brief Explanation
Graphics	**References to inline images for documents**	
<IMG>	Image	Inserts a referenced image into a document with alternate text, clickable map, and placement controls
<MAP>	Client-side imagemap parameters	Contains client-side image map areas and relate URLs
<AREA>	Imagemap hotspot	Defines the clickable hotspots within a client-side imagemap
Document Headings	**Supply document heading levels, provide important organization and layout elements**	
<H1> ... </H1>	Level 1 head	First-level heading
<H2> ... </H2>	Level 2 head	Second-level heading
<H3> ... </H3>	Level 3 head	Third-level heading
<H4> ... </H4>	Level 4 head	Fourth-level heading
<H5> ... </H5>	Level 5 head	Fifth-level heading
<H6> ... </H6>	Level 6 head	Sixth-level heading
Lists	**Provide methods to lay out item or element sequences in document content**	
<DIR> ... </DIR>	Directory list	Defines unbulleted list of short elements (less than 20 characters in length)
<OL> ... </OL>	Ordered list	Defines numbered list of elements
<UL> ... </UL>	Unordered list	Defines bulleted list of elements
<LI>	List item	Marks a number item within a list of any type
<MENU> ... </MENU>	Menu list	Defines a pickable list of elements
<DL> ... </DL>	Glossary list	Defines a special format for terms and their definitions
<DT>	Definition term	Marks the term being defined in a glossary list
<DD>	Definition datum	Marks the definition for a term in a glossary list

Tags	Tag Names	Brief Explanation
Tables	**Table-related markup tags**	
<TABLE>...</TABLE>	Table block	Defines the beginning an end of table block
<CAPTION>... </CAPTION>	Table caption	Used to format table caption outside of tablo
<TH>...</TH>	Column head	Use to format column header information
<COLGROUP... </COLGROUP>	Column grouping	Defines a group of columns within a table
<COL>	Column	Delineates a column within group of columns defined by <COLGROUP> or a table
<THEAD>	Table head	Marks table header information
<TBODY>	Table body	Marks table body information
<TFOOT>	Table footer	Marks table footer information
<TR>	Table row	Creates a table row
<TD>	Table data	Creates a table cell within a row
Forms	**Forms-related markup tags**	
<FORM> ... </FORM>	Form block	Marks beginning and end of form block
<INPUT>	Input widget	Defines type and appearance for input widgets
<TEXTAREA> ... </TEXTAREA>	Text area	Multiline text entry widget
<SELECT> ... </SELECT>	Input pick list	Creates a menu or scrolling list of input items
<OPTION>	Selectable item	Assigns a value or default to an input item
<LABEL>...</LABEL>	Control Label	Associates an identifying label with a control
<FIELDSET>... </FIELDSET>	Field Set	Groups related fields within a form
Text Controls	**Character formatting tags**	
<B> ... </B>	Boldface	Produces bolded text

(continued)

Table 6-2 *(continued)*

Tags	Tag Names	Brief Explanation
\<BIG\>...\</BIG\>	Big text	Increases font size by one point
\<CITE\> ... \</CITE\>	Short citation	Distinctive text for citations
\<CODE\> ... \</CODE\>	Code font	Used for code samples
\<DFN\> ... \</DFN\>	Defined term	Used to emphasize a term about to be defined in the following text
\<EM\> ... \</EM\>	Emphasis	Adds emphasis to enclosed text
\<I\> ... \</I\>	Italic	Produces italicized text
\<KBD\> ... \</KBD\>	Keyboard text	Text to be typed at keyboard
\<S\>...\</S\>	Strike through	Renders text that is struck through
\<SAMP\> ... \</SAMP\>	Sample text	Sample in-line text
\<SMALL\>...\</SMALL\>	Small text	Decreases font size by one point
\<STRONG\> ... \</STRONG\>	Strong	Maximum emphasis to enclosed text emphasis
\<SUB\>...\</SUB\>	Subscript	Renders text in subscript
\<SUP\>...\</SUP\>	Superscript	Renders text in superscript
\<TT\> ... \</TT\>	Typewriter	Produces a typewriter font text
\<U\>... \</U\>	Underline	Underlines contained text
\<VAR\> ... \</VAR\>	Variable	Marks variable or substitution for some other value
\<XMP\>...\</XMP\>	Example text	Renders text in a fixed width font
Comments	**To document HTML design, techniques, and so on**	
\<!-- ... --\>	Comment	Supports author comments; ignored by browser but digestible by SGML parsers or document management systems

Now, let's review the HTML categories we've just introduced before providing detailed syntax for each tag:

✔ **Document structure:** Numerous tags help to provide structure for HTML documents. They provide an overall HTML label and break up documents into head and body sections. They also provide markup to establish links to other documents and to indicate support for electronic indexing capabilities. While this markup produces little in the way of visible display, it is important to the construction of well-designed Web pages.

✔ **Links:** Links provide the controls to anchor points within a document or to link one document to another, as well as include non-http objects such as applets, scripts, and multimedia files within HTML document. They are the fundamental foundation for the Web's hypertext capabilities.

✔ **Layout elements:** Layout elements introduce specific items within the text of a document, including line breaks, lengthy quotes, and horizontal rules to divide up distinct text areas and preformatted text, and to capture spacing and layout exactly from the source based on a monospaced font (which makes preformatted text kind of ugly). They also include a format for building author information on a page, which is something we recommend for all good Web pages.

✔ **Graphics:** Graphics enter an HTML file through the `<IMG>` command, which we've already covered in some detail. Suffice it to say that `<IMG>` points to the graphics source, provides a text alternative for nongraphical browsing, and indicates whether a graphical element is a clickable map. You also have the option of defining clickable maps directly within an HTML page using the `<MAP>` and `<AREA>` tags.

✔ **Document headings:** Headings provide structure for a document's content, starting with first-level all the way down to sixth-level headings. They provide meaningful clues for document navigation, and when used in conjunction with a hypertext table of contents, can permit readers to quickly jump to other sections.

✔ **Lists:** HTML includes numerous styles for building lists, ranging from numbered to bulleted lists, glossary entries complete with definitions, and selectable menu entries. All of these provide useful tools for organizing lists of items or elements to improve readability.

✔ **Tables:** Tables present columnar data separated by rows in an HTML page. This provides greater flexibility in page design because it essentially divides the entire page into a grid where you can place textual and graphical elements with more precision than HTML usually affords. Tables also give HTML pages a horizontal design element it did not previously have.

✔ **Forms:** Forms provide the essential mechanism for soliciting reader feedback and input on the Web. Forms tags cover how forms are set up, provide a variety of graphical and text widgets for soliciting input, and supply methods to let readers select options from various types of pick lists.

✔ **Text controls:** HTML also offers numerous inline controls for adding emphasis or special appearance to text. It provides tools for describing user input and for including samples of computer code, computer output, variables, and sample text. The idea is to be able to represent different kinds of online text for building materials for online use.

✔ **Comments:** Comments give HTML authors a way to annotate their documents, and browsers will not ordinarily display them. Any assumptions, special conditions, or nonstandard elements should be enclosed in comment to help other readers understand what the document is trying to accomplish and to assist with the testing process.

From managing document structure to controlling the look and feel of text on a page, HTML includes tags to make these things happen. In the next section, we examine the nitty-gritty details of all the various HTML tags.

HTML Tags

The remainder of this chapter is devoted to an alphabetical listing of all the tags in the HTML Cougar DTD.

Because so many browser builders are adding extensions to HTML for their own use, and because future standards will introduce significant changes and enhancements to HTML, this list can be considered neither exhaustive nor complete. Although this listing was complete at press time, the Web changes more quickly than we can write and books can be print. For the latest and most up-to-date information on HTML consult the World Wide Web Consortium Web site at http://www.w3.org/.

The run-down on attributes

In HTML, attributes typically take one of two forms within a tag:

✔ ATTRIBUTE="value": Where value is typically enclosed in quotes (" "), and may be one of the following kinds of elements:

- URL: A uniform resource locator
- name: A user-supplied name, probably for an input field
- number: A user-supplied numeric value
- text: User-supplied text
- server: Server-dependent name (for example, page name defaults)
- (X|Y|Z): One member of a set of fixed values
- #rrggbb: Hexadecimal color notation

✔ ATTRIBUTE: Where the name itself provides information about how the tag should behave (for example, ISMAP in <IMG> indicates that the graphic is a clickable map)

As we discuss attributes for individual tags, you'll see them in a section under the tag name. For each one we provide a definition. We also indicate choices for predefined sets of values or provide an example for open-ended value assignments.

Common attributes

There are a six attributes that you will find listed for more than 85 percent of the tags. We list them here, along with a brief description, to save a few trees and avoid being redundant. All of these attributes have implied values, which means that you don't have to actually list them in your tags unless you want to change their values. For example, the implied value the DIR attribute is ltr which stands for left to right, the direction the tag and its contents will be read. If for some reason you wanted to change the value to rtl (right to left) then you would need to include the attribute and its value.

- **ID="name":** A document-wide identifier that can be used to indicate a specific position within a document.
- **CLASS="text":** A comma-separated list of class names, which indicates that the element belongs to a specific class of style definitions.
- **STYLE="text":** Provides rendering information specific to this element, such as the color, size, and font specifics.
- **TITLE="text":** Defines an advisory title that will displayed as additional help. Balloon text around hyperlinks and graphics are generated using this attribute.
- **DIR="(LTR | RTL)":** Indicates the direction the text will be read in, left-to-right or right-to-left.
- **LANG="name":** Specifies the language in which the element and its contents are written.

Tag information layout

Before we provide our alphabetical list of tags, you need to understand what information we'll be presenting and how it's presented. Using the by-now-familiar image tag (<IMG>) here's what a typical listing will look like:

<IMG> Inline image

Definition: Supplies image source, placement, and behavior information. Used to place in-line graphics on a page.

Attributes:

ALIGN=("TOP"|"MIDDLE"|"BOTTOM"|"LEFT"|"RIGHT")

> Standard use calls for ALIGN to be set to one of the following values:
> TOP, MIDDLE, or BOTTOM to define placement.

ALT="text"

> Supplies an alternate string of text to display (and possibly make
> clickable) if the browser has no graphics capability or if graphics are
> turned off.

BORDER="number"

> Indicates if there will be a border around the graphic and if so how
> many pixels wide it will be. BORDER="0" forces no border while BOR-
> DER="10" renders a border ten pixels wide on all sides of the graphic.

CLASS="text"

HEIGHT="number"

> Defines the graphic's height in pixels. When the browser is loading a
> page, it will reserve a space for the graphic based on height and width
> values given in the attributes. The browser will also size the graphic to
> fit the height and width dimensions even if they are different from the
> actual height and width. This can lead to distorted graphics.

HSPACE="number"

> Provides for horizontal white space, measure in pixels, on either side of
> a graphic to set it apart from the text.

ID="name"

ISMAP

> Indicates by its presence that the image (or its text replacement)
> should be a clickable map. This often invokes special map-handling
> software through the CGI interface on the Web server handling the
> request.

SRC="URL"

> URL is a standard uniform resource locator and specifies the location
> for image file, which is usually .GIF or .JPEG format.

STYLE="text"

TITLE="text"

USEMAP

Indicates which `<MAP>` information store in the document should be used with the image to create a client-side imagemap.

VSPACE="number"

Provides for vertical white space, measured in pixels, on the top and bottom of a graphic to set it apart from the text.

WIDTH="number"

Defines the graphic's width in pixels.

Context: <IMG> is legal within:

<A>, <ADDRESS>, <B>, <BIG>, <BLOCKQUOTE>, <BODY>, <CAPTION>, <CENTER>, <CITE>, <CODE>, <DD>, <DFN>, <DIV>, <DT>, <EM>, <FIELDSET>, <FONT>, <FORM>, <H*>, <I>, <KBD>, <LABEL>, <LI>, <OBJECT>, <P>, <S>, <SAMP>, <SMALL>, <SPAN>, <STRONG>, <SUB>, <SUP>, <TD>, <TEXTFLOW>, <TH>, <TT>, <U>, <VAR>

Note: When referring to heading tags <H1> through <H6>, we abbreviate the whole series as <H*> as we did in the preceding paragraph.

No additional markup can be used within <IMG>:

Suggested style/usage: Keep images small and use them judiciously; graphics should add impact and interest to pages without adding too much bulk (or wait time).

Examples: See file /h4d3e/examples/ch06/img.htm.

Note: Rather than include code snippets and screen shots, we thought you might like to see HTML at work yourself. We've included example code for each and every tag, and attribute where possible, on the CD. Using your browser, just open the file list under the "Examples" section to see how tag information is rendered. To view the HTML choose View Source in your browser or open the .htm file with a text editor.

Tag layout commentary

You'll notice the use of our HTML syntax notation in the "Attributes" section most often. Because <IMG> is a stand-alone tag (that is, there's no closing </IMG>) we don't show a pair of tags here, but tags will be shown in pairs whenever appropriate.

The last item for discussion is the "Context" section. In this section, you see where it's legal to put <IMG> tags inside other markup, between <PRE> ... </PRE> tags, for example. Just because you can use this tag in such a way doesn't mean you have to do so; as always, use markup judiciously to add impact or value to information. Complex compositions seldom delight anyone other than their makers, so try to keep things simple whenever you can.

The HTML tag team

This section shows an alphabetical listing of the most common and widely used HTML tags — taken from HTML Cougar DTD. See Chapter 8 for an in-depth look at nonstandard tags, such as the frames tags and other browser-specific extensions to HTML. The Cougar DTD is not 100-percent supported by current versions of most browsers but should be by the end of 1997. Because of this situation, we've used the Warning icon to alert you to those tags and attributes that aren't widely supported right now. This doesn't mean you can't use them, but until browsers catch up, not every user will be able to see or use them.

<A> ... </A> Anchor

Definition: An anchor marks either the source or the destination of a document link. If it's the destination, it uses the NAME attribute; if it's the source, it uses the HREF attribute.

Attributes:

ACCESSKEY="text (single character)"

> This attribute is used to define a single character that acts as a hotkey to activate the hyperlink. Pressing the hotkey is the same as clicking on the hyperlink. The character will usually be underlined and the "ALT=" and "Command" keys, for PCs and Macs respectively, must be pressed in addition to the hotkey to activate the link.

CLASS="text"

COORDS="number"

Used with the SHAPE attribute to create a regions in an image map, this attribute links the URL defined in the HREF= attribute with coordinates on a graphic specified by the <OBJECT> tag. When a user clicks on any area in the graphic within the coordinates defined by the attribute they are taken to the URL.

DIR="(ltr|rtl)"

HREF="URL"

URL is a standard uniform resource locator specifying the location of another network resource, usually the URL for another HTML file, but it can also be a pointer to services provided by FTP, Telnet, WAIS, e-mail, or Gopher.

ID="name:"

LANG="name"

NAME="text"

Supplies a marked location point within the document to act as a destination for a hypertext link; the text supplied for this attribute acts just like an anchor to hold a place for a link to attach to.

NOTAB

In some browsers, it is possible to tab from link to link. The NOTAB attribute removes the link from the tabbing order so it will be skipped.

ONCLICK="function"

When the link is clicked this attribute calls and activates a script that is specified in the "function" string.

ONMOUSEOUT="function"

When the mouse moves off of the link, this attribute calls and activates a script that is specified in the "function" string.

ONMOUSEOVER="function"

When the mouse moves onto the link this attribute calls and activates a script that is specified in the "function" string.

REL=("SAME"|"NEXT"|"PARENT"|"PREVIOUS")

The REL attribute specifies the relationship between the current anchor and the destination.

"same" indicates that the URL points to the page it's on; "next" indicates that the URL points to the next page in a sequence; "parent"
indicates that the current page is the parent of the destination page;
and "previous" that it points to the prior page.

REV="text"

REV is the reverse of the REL attribute and indicates the destination
and the current anchor.

SHAPE="("RECT"|"CIRCLE"|"POLY"|"DEFAULT")

Used with the COORDS attribute the SHAPE attribute defines the shape
of a hotzone on an image specified by the <OBJECT> tag that, when
clicked, links to the URL defined by the URL attribute.

STYLE="text"

TABINDEX="number"

This attribute defines the link's position in the tabbing order.

TITLE="text"

Context:

<A> ... </A> is legal within the following markup tags:

> <ADDRESS>, <B>, <BIG>, <BLOCKQUOTE>, <BODY>, <CAPTION>,
> <CENTER>, <CITE>, <CODE>, <DD>, <DFN>, <DIV>, <DT>, <EM>,
> <FIELDSET>, <FONT>, <FORM>, <H*>, <I>, <KBD>, <LABEL>, <LI>,
> <OBJECT>, <P>, <PRE>, <S>, <SAMP>, <SMALL>, <SPAN>, <STRONG>,
> <SUB>, <SUP>, <TD>, <TEXTFLOW>, <TH>, <TT>, <U>, <VAR>

The following markup can be used within <A> ... </A>:

> <APPLET>, <B>, <BASEFONT>, <BIG>, <BR>, <CITE>, <CODE>, <DFN>,
> <EM>, <FONT>, <I>, <IMG>, <INPUT>, <KBD>, <LABEL>, <MAP>,
> <OBJECT>, <S>, <SAMP>, <SCRIPT>, <SELECT>, <SMALL>, <SPAN>,
> <STRONG>, <STYLE>, <SUB>, <SUP>, <TEXTAREA>, <TT>, <U>, <VAR>

Suggested style/usage: Anchors should be innermost when used within
nested markup, except when using embedded character controls, font
styles, or line breaks. Relative URLs make for more compact references but
require more maintenance.

Examples: See file /h4d3e/examples/ch06/a.htm.

<ADDRESS> ... </ADDRESS> Attribution info

Definition: <ADDRESS> ... </ADDRESS> tags enclose attribution information about an HTML document, which should usually include things like the author's name and address, signature files, contact information, and so on.

Attributes:

None.

Context:

<ADDRESS> ... </ADDRESS> is legal within the following markup tags:

> <BLOCKQUOTE>, <BODY>, <CENTER>, <DIV>, <FIELDSET>, <FORM>, <OBJECT>, <TD>, <TH>

The following markup can be used within <ADDRESS> ... <ADDRESS>:

> <A>, <APPLET>, <B>, <BASEFONT>, <BIG>, <BR>, <CITE>, <CODE>, <DFN>, <EM>, <FONT>, <I>, <IMG>, <INPUT>, <KBD>, <LABEL>, <MAP>, <OBJECT>, <P>, <S>, <SAMP>, <SCRIPT>, <SELECT>, <SMALL>, <SPAN>, <STRONG>, <STYLE>, <SUB>, <SUP>, <TEXTAREA>, <TT>, <U>, <VAR>

Suggested style/usage: Recommended for inclusion at the end of any document, to supply author contact information for questions or feedback.

Examples: See file /h4d3e/examples/ch06/address.htm.

<APPLET> ... </APPLET> Java Applet

Definition: Embeds a Java Applet in an HTML page.

Attributes:

ALIGN=("LEFT" | "RIGHT" | "TOP" | "MIDDLE" | "BOTTOM")

> Use this attribute to specify how the text should be aligned relative to the text and page. The default alignment is left.

ALT="text"

> Supplies the alternate text will appear in browsers that do not support Java and in text only browsers in place of the applet.

CLASS="text"

CODE="text"

> Identifies the actual Java applet to be displayed in the page.

CODEBASE="URL"

An applet's codebase is the URL of the directory the applet sits in. This attribute tells the browser where to get an applet while the CODE attribute specifies which applet.

DOWNLOAD="number"

There may often be more than one applet embedded in a Web page. This attribute specifies in what order the applet should be downloaded in relation to the other applets.

HEIGHT="number"

Defines the applet's height in pixels.

HSPACE="number"

Provides for horizontal white space, measure in pixels, on either side of the applet to set it apart from the text.

ID="name"

NAME="text"

Gives the applet a name that will identify it to other applets on the page.

STYLE="text"

TITLE="text"

VSPACE="number"

Provides for vertical white space, measure in pixels, on the top and bottom of the applet to set it apart from the text.

WIDTH="number"

Defines the applet's width in pixels.

Context:

<APPLET> ... </APPLET> is legal within the following markup tags:

<A>, <ADDRESS>, <B>, <BIG>, <BLOCKQUOTE>, <BODY>, <CAPTION>, <CENTER>, <CITE>, <CODE>, <DD>, <DFN>, <DIV>, <DT>, <EM>, <FIELDSET>, <FONT>, <FORM>, <H*>, <I>, <KBD>, <LABEL>, <LI>, <OBJECT>, <P>, <PRE>, <S>, <SAMP>, <SMALL>, <SPAN>, <STRONG>, <SUB>, <SUP>, <TD>, <TEXTFLOW>, <TH>, <TT>, <U>, <VAR>

The following markup can be used within <APPLET> ... </APPLET>:

<PARAM>, <TEXTFLOW>

Suggested style/usage: Applets add interactivity and dynamic content to pages without taxing the server or client machine. However, not all browsers support Java and those that do allow the user to disable it. Make sure that you always include alternative text so users see *something* where the applet should be.

Examples: See file /h4d3e/examples/ch6/applet.htm.

<AREA> Hotzone

Definition: Defines the shape of a hotzone in a client-side imagemap.

Attributes:

ALT="text"

Supplies the alternate text that will appear in text-only browsers.

COORDS="number"

The shape of a hotzone is described to the browser by sets of pixel coordinates. This attribute defines those coordinates for the individual hotzone.

HREF="URL"

Identifies the URL the hotzone links to.

NOHREF

Indicate that a click in the hotzone should not invoke an action.

NOTAB

Removes the hotzone from the tabbing order.

ONCLICK="function"

> When the hotzone is clicked, this attribute calls and activates a script that is specified in the "function" string.

ONMOUSEOUT="function"

> When the mouse moves off of the hotzone, this attribute calls and activates a script that is specified in the "function" string.

ONMOUSEOVER="function"

> When the mouse moves onto the hotzone, this attribute calls and activates a script that is specified in the "function" string.

SHAPE="("rect" | "circle" | "poly" | "default")

> Defines the shape of the hotzone.

TABINDEX="number"

> Defines the hotzone's position in the tabbing order.

TITLE="text"

Context:

<AREA> is legal within the following markup tags:

> <MAP>

No additional markup can be used within <AREA>.

Suggested style/usage: Client-side image maps eliminate the need for a server and cgi to create a clickable map. Some earlier versions of browsers and text-only browsers do not support client-side maps, and users who view without graphics cannot take advantage of them either. Always include text-only navigation information in your pages so all users can move through your site easily.

Examples: See file /h4d3e/examples/ch6/area.htm.

<B> ... </B> Bold style

Definition: Encloses text to be boldfaced.

Attributes:

Common attributes only.

Context:

<B> ... </B> is legal within the following markup tags:

<A>, <ADDRESS>, <B>, <BIG>, <BLOCKQUOTE>, <BODY>, <CAPTION>,
<CENTER>, <CITE>, <CODE>, <DD>, <DFN>, <DIV>, <DT>, <EM>,
<FIELDSET>, <FONT>, <FORM>, <H*>, <I>, <KBD>, <LABEL>, <LI>,
<OBJECT>, <P>, <PRE>, <S>, <SAMP>, <SMALL>, <SPAN>, <STRONG>,
<SUB>, <SUP>, <TD>, <TEXTFLOW>, <TH>, <TT>, <U>, <VAR>

The following markup can be used within <B> ... </B>:

<A>, <APPLET>, <B>, <BASEFONT>, <BIG>, <BR>, <CITE>, <CODE>,
<DFN>, <EM>, <FONT>, <I>, <IMG>, <INPUT>, <KBD>, <LABEL>, <MAP>,
<OBJECT>, <S>, <SAMP>, <SCRIPT>, <SELECT>, <SMALL>, <SPAN>,
<STRONG>, <STYLE>, <SUB>, <SUP>, <TEXTAREA>, <TT>, <U>, <VAR>

Suggested style/usage: Boldfacing provide special focus on specific words
or phrases in text, but keep in mind that using it too frequently or for large
text blocks reduces its effectiveness and makes your pages difficult to read.

Examples: See /h4d3e/examples/ch6/b.htm.

<BASE> Basis for relative addressing

Definition: <BASE> normally occurs within <HEAD> ... </HEAD> and provides the URL basis for subsequent URL references in <LINK> or anchor
statements within the body of the document. This makes URLs quicker and
more compact to write if the <BASE> represents a good starting point for
other references. (Ideally, they should all be within one directory level of
this reference.)

Attributes:

HREF="URL"

The fully qualified URL for the current document is required here.

Context:

<BASE> is legal within the following markup tag:

<HEAD>

No additional markup can be used within <BASE>.

Suggested style/usage: Whenever you build complex, multi-page collections,
it's a good idea to use the <BASE> tag in each page and build a directory
structure that's easy to use and navigate.

Examples: See file /h4d3e/examples/ch6/base.htm.

<BASEFONT> Base font

Definition: Describes the base font for the entire document. The setting is currently limited to font size only, although Internet Explorer supports color and font settings as well.

Attributes:

SIZE="number"

> Sets the size of the base font. <BIG>, <SMALL> and <FONT> settings will be interpreted relative to this number.

Context:

<BASEFONT> is legal within the following markup tag:

> <A>, <ADDRESS>, <B>, <BIG>, <BLOCKQUOTE>, <BODY>, <CAPTION>, <CENTER>, <CITE>, <CODE>, <DD>, <DFN>, <DIV>, <DT>, <EM>, <FIELDSET>, <FONT>, <FORM>, <H*>, <I>, <KBD>, <LABEL>, <LI>, <OBJECT>, <P>, <PRE>, <S>, <SAMP>, <SMALL>, <SPAN>, <STRONG>, <SUB>, <SUP>, <TD>, <TEXTFLOW>, <TH>, <TT>, <U>, <VAR>.

No additional markup can be used within <BASEFONT>.

Suggested style/usage: While this tag makes it easy to change the size font your pages are rendered in, use it judiciously. Overly large or small type is difficult to read.

Examples: See file /h4d3e/examples/ch6/basefont.htm.

<BIG> ... </BIG> Big text

Definition: Used to make text one size larger.

Attributes:

Common attributes only.

Context:

<BIG> ... </BIG > is legal within the following markup tags:

> <A>, <ADDRESS>, <B>, <BIG>, <BLOCKQUOTE>, <BODY>, <CAPTION>, <CENTER>, <CITE>, <CODE>, <DD>, <DFN>, <DIV>, <DT>, <EM>, <FIELDSET>, <FONT>, <FORM>, <H*>, <I>, <KBD>, <LABEL>, <LI>, <OBJECT>, <P>, <S>, <SAMP>, <SMALL>, <SPAN>, <STRONG>, <SUB>, <SUP>, <TD>, <TEXTFLOW>, <TH>, <TT>, <U>, <VAR>

The following markup can be used within <BIG> ... </BIG>:

<A>, <APPLET>, <B>, <BASEFONT>, <BIG>, <BR>, <CITE>, <CODE>, <DFN>, <EM>, <FONT>, <I>, <IMG>, <INPUT>, <KBD>, <LABEL>, <MAP>, <OBJECT>, <S>, <SAMP>, <SCRIPT>, <SELECT>, <SMALL>, <SPAN>, <STRONG>, <STYLE>, <SUB>, <SUP>, <TEXTAREA>, <TT>, <U>, <VAR>

Suggested style/usage: You can nest <BIG> tags for increasingly bigger text, but it may be easier to use the <FONT> tag with the SIZE attribute.

Examples: See file /h43/examples/ch6/big.htm.

<BLOCKQUOTE> ... </BLOCKQUOTE> Quote style

Definition: <BLOCKQUOTE> ... </BLOCKQUOTE> is used to set off material quoted from external sources, publications, or other materials.

Attributes:

Common attributes only.

Context:

<BLOCKQUOTE> ... </ BLOCKQUOTE > is legal within the following markup tags:

<BLOCKQUOTE>, <BODY>, <CENTER>, <DD>, <DIV>, <FIELDSET>, <FORM>, <LI>, <OBJECT>, <TD>, <TH>

The following markup can be used within <BLOCKQUOTE> ... </BLOCKQUOTE>:

<A>, <ADDRESS>, <APPLET>, <B>, <BASEFONT>, <BIG>, <BLOCKQUOTE>, <BR>, <CENTER>, <CITE>, <CODE>, <DFN>, <DIR>, <DIV>, <DL>, <EM>, <FIELDSET>, <FONT>, <FORM>, <H*>, <HR>, <I>, <IMG>, <INPUT>, <ISINDEX>, <KBD>, <LABEL>, <LISTING>, <MAP>, <MENU>, <OBJECT>, <OL>, <P>, <PRE>, <S>, <SAMP>, <SCRIPT>, <SELECT>, <SMALL>, <SPAN>, <STRONG>, <STYLE>, <SUB>, <SUP>, <TABLE>, <TEXTAREA>, <TT>, <U>, <UL>, <VAR>, <XMP>

Suggested style/usage: Whenever you use a quote more than one line long from an external source, it's a good idea to use <BLOCKQUOTE>. Don't forget to attribute your sources. (Remember to use <CITE> to highlight the actual publication, if applicable.)

Examples: See file /h4d3e/examples/ch6/blockquo.htm.

<BODY> ... </BODY> Mark off HTML document body

Definition: The <BODY> ... </BODY> tags delimit the body of an HTML document and should completely enclose any content to be shown in the browser.

Attributes:

ALINK="#rrggbb" or "color"

> Specifies the color for active links.

BACKGROUND="URL"

> Provides the location of an image to be tiled in the background of the page.

BGCOLOR=="#rrggbb" or "color"

> Specifies a background color for the page.

CLASS=type

DIR=("ltr"|"rtl")

ID="name"

LANG="name"

LINK="#rrggbb" or "color"

> Specifies a color for links that haven't been visited yet.

ONLOAD="function"

> Calls the script defined in "function" when the page is done loading.

ONUNLOAD="function"

> Calls the script defined in "function" when a user exits a page.

STYLE="text"

TEXT="#rrggbb" or "color"

> Specifies a color for the document text.

VLINK="#rrggbb" or "color"

> Specifies a color for visited links.

Context:

<BODY> ... </BODY> is legal within the following markup tag:

> <HTML>

The following markup can be used within <BODY> ... </BODY>:

> <A>, <ADDRESS>, <APPLET>, <B>, <BASEFONT>, <BIG>,
> <BLOCKQUOTE>, <BR>, <CENTER>, <CITE>, <CODE>, <DFN>, <DIR>,
> <DIV>, <DL>, <EM>, <FIELDSET>, <FONT>, <FORM>, <H*>, <HR>, <I>,
> <IMG>, <INPUT>, <ISINDEX>, <KBD>, <LABEL>, <LISTING>, <MAP>,
> <MENU>, <OBJECT>, <OL>, <P>, <PRE>, <S>, <SAMP>, <SCRIPT>,
> <SELECT>, <SMALL>, <SPAN>, <STRONG>, <STYLE>, <SUB>, <SUP>,
> <TABLE>, <TEXTAREA>, <TT>, <U>, <UL>, <VAR>, <XMP>

Suggested style/usage: <BODY> ... </BODY> is used to set off the body of an HTML document and define text and background settings. It is an explicit structure tag that is required for all HTML.

Examples: See file /h4d3e/examples/ch6/body.htm.

 Force line break

Definition:
 forces a line break in HTML text flow.

Attributes:

CLASS="text"

CLEAR=("NONE"|"LEFT"|"RIGHT"|"ALL")

> This attribute defines how the text immediately following an image will be aligned when the <BR> tag is used. NONE causes the text to flow directly after the image; LEFT and RIGHT display text below the document and left or right justified respectively; and ALL places the text below the image and double justified.

DIR=("ltr"|"rtl")

ID="name"

LANG="name"

STYLE="text"

TITLE="text"

Context:

 is legal within the following markup tags:

> <A>, <ADDRESS>, <B>, <BIG>, <BLOCKQUOTE>, <BODY>, <CAPTION>,
> <CENTER>, <CITE>, <CODE>, <DD>, <DFN>, <DIV>, <DT>, <EM>,
> <FIELDSET>, <FONT>, <FORM>, <H*>, <I>, <KBD>, <LABEL>, <LI>,
> <OBJECT>, <P>, <PRE>, <S>, <SAMP>, <SMALL>, <SPAN>, <STRONG>,
> <SUB>, <SUP>, <TD>, <TEXTFLOW>, <TH>, <TT>, <U>, <VAR>

No additional markup can be used within

Suggested style/usage:
 can force line breaks in text whenever desired. It comes in handy for creating short lines of text and placing text smoothly around graphics.

Examples: See file /h4d3e/examples/ch6/br.htm.

<CAPTION> ... </CAPTION> Table caption

Definition: Contains the caption information for a table or form field set.

Attributes:

ACCESSKEY="text (single character)"

> Defines a single character that acts as a hotkey to move to the table or form field set.

ALIGN=("CENTER" | "LEFT" | "RIGHT")

> Use this attribute to specify how the caption should be aligned relative to the table. The default alignment is CENTER.

CLASS="text"

DIR=("ltr" | "rtl")

ID="name"

LANG="name:"

STYLE="text"

Context:

<CAPTION> ... </CAPTION> is legal within the following markup tags:

> <FIELDSET>, <TABLE>

The following markup can be used within <CAPTION> ... </CAPTION>:

> <A>, <APPLET>, <B>, <BASEFONT>, <BIG>, <BR>, <CITE>, <CODE>, <DFN>, <EM>, <FONT>, <I>, <IMG>, <INPUT>, <KBD>, <LABEL>, <MAP>, <OBJECT>, <S>, <SAMP>, <SCRIPT>, <SELECT>, <SMALL>, <SPAN>, <STRONG>, <STYLE>, <SUB>, <SUP>, <TEXTAREA>, <TT>, <U>, <VAR>

Suggested style/usage: Tables and forms that are clearly labeled will be easy to read. Make your captions short and to the point for maximum effectiveness.

Examples: See file /h4d3e/examples/ch6/caption.htm.

<CENTER> ... </CENTER> Center text

Definition: Centers text across the page.

Attributes:

No attributes.

Context:

<CENTER> ... </CENTER> is legal within the following markup tags:

> <BLOCKQUOTE>, <BODY>, <CENTER>, <DD>, <DIV>, <FIELDSET>, <FORM>, <LI>, <OBJECT>, <TD>, <TH>

The following markup can be used within <CENTER> ... </CENTER>:

> <A>, <ADDRESS>, <APPLET>, <B>, <BASEFONT>, <BIG>, <BLOCKQUOTE>, <BR>, <CENTER>, <CITE>, <CODE>, <DFN>, <DIR>, <DIV>, <DL>, <EM>, <FIELDSET>, <FONT>, <FORM>, <H*>, <HR>, <I>, <IMG>, <INPUT>, <ISINDEX>, <KBD>, <LABEL>, <LISTING>, <MAP>, <MENU>, <OBJECT>, <OL>, <P>, <PRE>, <S>, <SAMP>, <SCRIPT>, <SELECT>, <SMALL>, <SPAN>, <STRONG>, <STYLE>, <SUB>, <SUP>, <TABLE>, <TEXTAREA>, <TT>, <U>, <UL>, <VAR>, <XMP>

Suggested style/usage: This tag is meant to be paragraph-level markup rather than text-level markup so it should be used to affect entire blocks of text rather than single lines or words within a paragraph.

Examples: See /h4d3e/examples/ch6/center.htm.

<CITE> ... </CITE> Citation markup

Definition: Use <CITE> ... </CITE> to highlight document, publication, or other external resource citations.

Attributes:

Common attributes only.

Context:

<CITE> ... </CITE> is legal within the following markup tags:

> <A>, <ADDRESS>, <B>, <BIG>, <BLOCKQUOTE>, <BODY>, <CAPTION>,
> <CENTER>, <CITE>, <CODE>, <DD>, <DFN>, <DIV>, <DT>, <EM>,
> <FIELDSET>, <FONT>, <FORM>, <H*>, <I>, <KBD>, <LABEL>, <LI>,
> <OBJECT>, <P>, <PRE>, <S>, <SAMP>, <SMALL>, <SPAN>, <STRONG>,
> <SUB>, <SUP>, <TD>, <TEXTFLOW>, <TH>, <TT>, <U>, <VAR>

The following markup can be used within <CITE> ... </CITE>:

> <A>, <APPLET>, <B>, <BASEFONT>, <BIG>, <BR>, <CITE>, <CODE>,
> <DFN>, <EM>, <FONT>, <I>, <IMG>, <INPUT>, <KBD>, <LABEL>, <MAP>,
> <OBJECT>, <S>, <SAMP>, <SCRIPT>, <SELECT>, <SMALL>, <SPAN>,
> <STRONG>, <STYLE>, <SUB>, <SUP>, <TEXTAREA>, <TT>, <U>, <VAR>

Suggested style/usage: Use to highlight citations or other references to external data sources.

Examples: See file /h4d3e/examples/ch6/cite.htm.

<CODE> ... </CODE> *Program code text*

Definition: <CODE> ... </CODE> is meant to enclose programs or samples of program code to make it easier to read.

Attributes:

Common attributes only.

Context:

<CODE> ... </CODE> is legal within the following markup tags:

> <A>, <ADDRESS>, <B>, <BIG>, <BLOCKQUOTE>, <BODY>, <CAPTION>,
> <CENTER>, <CITE>, <CODE>, <DD>, <DFN>, <DIV>, <DT>, <EM>,
> <FIELDSET>, <FONT>, <FORM>, <H*>, <I>, <KBD>, <LABEL>, <LI>,
> <OBJECT>, <P>, <PRE>, <S>, <SAMP>, <SMALL>, <SPAN>, <STRONG>,
> <SUB>, <SUP>, <TD>, <TEXTFLOW>, <TH>, <TT>, <U>, <VAR>

The following markup can be used within <CODE> ... </CODE>:

<A>, <APPLET>, <B>, <BASEFONT>, <BIG>, <BR>, <CITE>, <CODE>,
<DFN>, <EM>, <FONT>, <I>, <IMG>, <INPUT>, <KBD>, <LABEL>, <MAP>,
<OBJECT>, <S>, <SAMP>, <SCRIPT>, <SELECT>, <SMALL>, <SPAN>,
<STRONG>, <STYLE>, <SUB>, <SUP>, <TEXTAREA>, <TT>, <U>, <VAR>

Suggested style/usage: To set off samples of program code or other com-
puter-based information within a document body.

Examples: See file /h4d3e/examples/ch6/code.htm.

<COL> Column

Definition: Defines the settings for one or more columns. When used with
the <COLGROUP> tag <COL> specifies the settings for a set of columns
within the larger group.

Attributes:

ALIGN=("CENTER" | "LEFT" | "RIGHT" | "JUSTIFY" | "CHAR")

Use this attribute to specify how text should be aligned left to right
within the column. The CHAR value aligns the column based on a
specific character defined in the CHAR attribute. The default alignment
is CENTER.

CHAR="text" (single character)

Identifies the character the text in the column should align with. The
value is case sensitive and the default is a period.

CHAROFF="number" or "n%"

Defines the offset, in characters or percentage, for the first occurrence
of the alignment character specified by CHAR on any given line. This
attribute can be used to create indentions in lines or paragraphs.

CLASS="text"

DIR=("ltr" | "rtl")

ID="name"

LANG="name"

SPAN="number"

Defines the number of consecutive columns the settings apply to. The
default number is 1.

STYLE="text"

VALIGN=("TOP"|"MIDDLE"|"BOTTOM"|"BASELINE")

> Use this attribute to specify how text should be aligned vertically within the column. The TOP, MIDDLE, and BOTTOM values align cell text at the top, middle, and bottom respectively, of the cell. A BASELINE alignment places all of the first lines in the column's cells on a common baseline. The default is MIDDLE>.

WIDTH="number" or "n%"

> Specifies, in number of characters or percentage, the column's width.

Context:

<COL> is legal within the following markup tag:

> <COLGROUP>, <TABLE>

No additional markup can be used within <COL>

Suggested style/usage: It is much easier to set the common properties for a group of columns in a column group or table once rather than repeatedly using the COL tag.

Examples: See file /h4d3e/examples/ch6/col.htm.

<COLGROUP> A Column group

Definition: Defines the settings for a group of columns within a table.

Attributes:

ALIGN=("CENTER"|"LEFT"|"RIGHT"|"JUSTIFY"|"CHAR")

> Use this attribute to specify how text should be aligned left to right within the group's columns. The CHAR value aligns the column based on a specific character defined in the CHAR attribute. The default alignment is CENTER.

CHAR="text" (single character)

> Identifies the character the text in the columns should align with. The value is case sensitive and the default is a period.

CHAROFF="number" or "n%"

Defines the offset, in characters or percentage, for the first occurrence of the alignment character specified by CHAR on any given line. This attribute can be used to create indentions in lines or paragraphs.

CLASS="text"

DIR=("ltr | | "rtl")

ID="name"

LANG="name"

SPAN="number"

Defines the number of consecutive columns the settings apply to. The default number is 1.

STYLE="text"

ALIGN=("TOP" | "MIDDLE" | "BOTTOM" | "BASELINE")

Use this attribute to specify how text in column cells should be aligned vertically within the column. The TOP, MIDDLE, and BOTTOM values align cell text at the top, middle, and bottom respectively, of the cell. A BASELINE alignment places all of the first lines in the column's cells on a common baseline. The default is MIDDLE>.

WIDTH="number" or "n%"

Specifies, in number of characters or percentage, the width of each column in the group.

Context:

<COLGROUP> is legal within the following markup tag:

    <TABLE>

The following markup can be used within <COLGROUP>:

    <COL>

Suggested style/usage: Use this tag in conjunction with the <COL> tag to set properties for all of the columns within a table and then make specific adjustments in the <COL> settings.

Examples: See file /h4d3e/examples/ch6/colgroup.htm.

<DD> Definition description

Definition: The descriptive part of a definition list element.

Attributes:

Common attributes only.

Context:

<DD> is legal within the following markup tag:

<DL>

The following markup can be used within <DD>:

<A>, <APPLET>, <B>, <BASEFONT>, <BIG>, <BLOCKQUOTE>, <BR>, <CENTER>, <CITE>, <CODE>, <DFN>, <DIR>, <DIV>, <DL>, <EM>, <FIELDSET>, <FONT>, <FORM>, <HR>, <I>, <IMG>, <INPUT>, <ISINDEX>, <KBD>, <LABEL>, <LISTING>, <MAP>, <MENU>, <OBJECT>, <OL>, <P>, <PRE>, <S>, <SAMP>, <SCRIPT>, <SELECT>, <SMALL>, <SPAN>, <STRONG>, <STYLE>, <SUB>, <SUP>, <TABLE>, <TEXTAREA>, <TT>, <U>, <UL>, <VAR>, <XMP>

Suggested style/usage: For glossaries or other kinds of lists where a single term or line needs to be associated with a block of indented text.

Examples: See file /h4d3e/examples/ch6/dd.htm.

<DFN> ... </DFN> Definition

Definition: Identifies a term's first appearance within a document.

Attributes:

Common attributes only.

Context:

<DFN> ... </DFN> is legal within the following markup tag:

<A>, <ADDRESS>, <B>, <BIG>, <BLOCKQUOTE>, <BODY>, <CAPTION>, <CENTER>, <CITE>, <CODE>, <DD>, <DFN>, <DIV>, <DT>, <EM>, <FIELDSET>, <FONT>, <FORM>, <H*>, <I>, <KBD>, <LABEL>, <LI>, <OBJECT>, <P>, <PRE>, <S>, <SAMP>, <SMALL>, <SPAN>, <STRONG>, <SUB>, <SUP>, <TD> <TEXTFLOW>, <TH>, <TT>, <U>, <VAR>

The following markup can be used within <DFN> ... </DFN>:

> <A>, <APPLET>, <B>, <BASEFONT>, <BIG>, <BR>, <CITE>, <CODE>,
> <DFN>, <EM>, <FONT>, <I>, <IMG>, <INPUT>, <KBD>, <LABEL>, <MAP>,
> <OBJECT>, <S>, <SAMP>, <SCRIPT>, <SELECT>, <SMALL>, <SPAN>,
> <STRONG>, <STYLE>, <SUB>, <SUP>, <TEXTAREA>, <TT>, <U>, <VAR>

Suggested style/usage: Important terms should be highlighted when they are introduced in a document.

Examples: See file /h4d3e/examples/ch6/dfn.htm.

<DIR> ... </DIR> Directory list

Definition: List style typically used for lists composed of short elements, such as filenames.

Attributes:

COMPACT

> Renders the directory style list more compact than usual.

Context:

<DIR> ... </DIR> is legal within the following markup tags:

> <BLOCKQUOTE>, <BODY>, <CENTER>, <DD>, <DIV>, <FIELDSET>,
> <FORM>, <LI>, <OBJECT>, <TD>, <TH>

The following markup can be used within <DIR> ... </DIR>:

> <LI>

The following markup cannot be used within an<LI> tag within <DIR> ... </DIR>:

> <BLOCKQUOTE>, <CENTER>, <DIR>, <DIV>, <DL>, <FIELDSET>, <FORM>,
> <HR>, <ISINDEX>, <LISTING>, <MENU>, <OL>, <P>, <PRE>, <TABLE>,
> <UL>, <XMP>

Suggested style/usage: Use <DIR> ... </DIR> to build lists of short elements (usually, shorter than 20 characters long).

Examples: See file /h4d3e/examples/ch6/dir.htm.

<DIV> ... </DIV> Logical division

Definition: Represents a logical division within a document such as a table of contents, section, or chapter, and provides for common formatting.

Attributes:

ALIGN=("LEFT" | "CENTER" | "RIGHT" | "JUSTIFY")

> Use this attribute to specify how the text in the division should be aligned relative to the page. The default alignment is left.

CLASS="text"

DIR=("ltr" | "rtl")

ID="name"

LANG="name"

STYLE="text"

Context:

<DIV> ... </DIV> is legal within the following markup tags:

> <<BLOCKQUOTE>, <BODY>, <CENTER>, <DD>, <DIV>, <FIELDSET>, <FORM>, <LI>, <OBJECT>, <TD>, <TH>

The following markup can be used within <DIV> ... </DIV>:

> <A>, <ADDRESS>, <APPLET>, <B>, <BASEFONT>, <BIG>, <BLOCKQUOTE>, <BR>, <CENTER>, <CITE>, <CODE>, <DFN>, <DIR>, <DIV>, <DL>, <EM>, <FIELDSET>, <FONT>, <FORM>, <H*>, <HR>, <I>, <IMG>, <INPUT>, <ISINDEX>, <KBD>, <LABEL>, <LISTING>, <MAP>, <MENU>, <OBJECT>, <OL>, <P>, <PRE>, <S>, <SAMP>, <SCRIPT>, <SELECT>, <SMALL>, <SPAN>, <STRONG>, <STYLE>, <SUB>, <SUP>, <TABLE>, <TEXTAREA>, <TT>, <U>, <UL>, <VAR>, <XMP>

Suggested style/usage: <DIV> was the first attempt at style sections in HTML and is still part of the DTD primarily to promote backwards compatibility with style sheets.

Examples: See file /h4d3e/examples/ch6/div.htm.

<DL> ... </DL> Definition list

Definition: <DL>... </DL> encloses a collection of definition items <DD> in a definition list, usually used for glossaries or other situations where short, left-justified terms are followed by longer blocks of indented text. Definition lists are usually rendered with the term (<DT>) in the left margin and the definition (<DD>) on one or more lines indented slightly from the term.

Attributes:

CLASS="text"

COMPACT

Indicates that line leading (white space between lines) should be reduced (see example). Warning: This attribute is currently not supported by all browsers.

DIR=("ltr" | "rtl")

ID="name"

LANG="name"

STYLE="text"

Context:

<DL> ... </DL> is legal within the following markup tags:

> <BLOCKQUOTE>, <BODY>, <CENTER>, <DD>, <DIV>, <FIELDSET>, <FORM>, <LI>, <OBJECT>, <TD>, <TH>

The following markup can be used within <DL> ... </DL>:

> <DD> <DT>

Suggested style/usage: For lists of terms and definitions, like glossaries or a dictionary or other situations where left-justified elements are followed by longer indented blocks of text.

Examples: See file /h4d3e/examples/ch6/dl.htm.

<DT> Definition term

Definition: The descriptive part of a definition entry.

Attributes:

Common attributes only.

Context:

<DT> is legal within the following markup tag:

> <DL>

The following markup can be used within <DT>:

> <A>, <APPLET>, <B>, <BASEFONT>, <BIG>, <BR>, <CITE>, <CODE>,
> <DFN>, <EM>, <FONT>, <I>, <IMG>, <INPUT>, <KBD>, <LABEL>, <MAP>,
> <OBJECT>, <S>, <SAMP>, <SCRIPT>, <SELECT>, <SMALL>, <SPAN>,
> <STRONG>, <STYLE>, <SUB>, <SUP>, <TEXTAREA>, <TT>, <U>, <VAR>

Suggested style/usage: For glossaries, definition lists, or other situations where left-justified short entries pair up with longer blocks of indented text.

Examples: See file /h4d3e/examples/ch6/dt.htm.

<EM> ... </EM> Emphasis

Definition: The <EM> tag provides typographic emphasis, usually rendered as italics. While <EM> and <I> often give the same effect, use <EM> except when referring to formatting in the text, as in "The italic parts are mandatory." This improves consistency between documents from various sources if, for example, a reader prefers to use color instead of italics for emphasis.

Attributes:

Common attributes only.

Context:

<EM> ... </EM> is legal within the following markup tags:

> <A>, <ADDRESS>, <B>, <BIG>, <BLOCKQUOTE>, <BODY>, <CAPTION>,
> <CENTER>, <CITE>, <CODE>, <DD>, <DFN>, <DIV>, <DT>, <EM>,
> <FIELDSET>, <FONT>, <FORM>, <H*>, <I>, <KBD>, <LABEL>, <LI>,
> <OBJECT>, <P>, <PRE>, <S>, <SAMP>, <SMALL>, <SPAN>, <STRONG>,
> <SUB>, <SUP>, <TD>, <TEXTFLOW>, <TH>, <TT>, <U>, <VAR>

The following markup can be used within <EM> ... </EM>:

> <A>, <APPLET>, <B>, <BASEFONT>, <BIG>, <BR>, <CITE>, <CODE>,
> <DFN>, <EM>, <FONT>, <I>, <IMG>, <INPUT>, <KBD>, <LABEL>, <MAP>,
> <OBJECT>, <S>, <SAMP>, <SCRIPT>, <SELECT>, <SMALL>, <SPAN>,
> <STRONG>, <STYLE>, <SUB>, <SUP>, <TEXTAREA>, <TT>, <U>, <VAR>

Suggested style/usage: Wherever mild emphasis in text is needed, but be sure to keep usage to a minimum, both in terms of the number of words emphasized and how often text emphasis occurs.

Examples: See file /h4d3e/examples/ch6/em.htm.

<FIELDSET> ... </FIELDSET> Form field set

Definition: Used to group related fields in a form.

Attributes:

Common attributes only.

Context:

<FIELDSET> ... </FIELDSET> is legal within the following markup tags:

> <BLOCKQUOTE>, <BODY>, <CENTER>, <DD>, <DIV>, <FIELDSET>,
> <FORM>, <LI>, <OBJECT>, <TD>, <TH>

The following markup can be used within <FIELDSET> ... </FIELDSET>:

> <A>, <ADDRESS>, <APPLET>, <B>, <BASEFONT>, <BIG>,
> <BLOCKQUOTE>, <BR>, <CAPTION>, <CENTER>, <CITE>, <CODE>,
> <DFN>, <DIR>, <DIV>, <DL>, <EM>, <FIELDSET>, <FONT>, <FORM>, <H*>,
> <HR>, <I>, <IMG>, <INPUT>, <ISINDEX>, <KBD>, <LABEL>, <LISTING>,
> <MAP>, <MENU>, <OBJECT>, <OL>, <P>, <PRE>, <S>, <SAMP>, <SCRIPT>,
> <SELECT>, <SMALL>, <SPAN>, <STRONG>, <STYLE>, <SUB>, <SUP>,
> <TABLE>, <TEXTAREA>, <TT>, <U>, <UL>, <VAR>, <XMP>

Suggested style/usage: Often forms can be separated into related fields to make the form easier to read and complete. Use the <FIELDSET> tag to group these fields and include a caption using the <CAPTION> tag to identify them to users.

Examples: See file /h4d3e/examples/ch6/fieldset.htm.

<FONT> ... </FONT> Font settings

Definition: Defines the font type, color, and size for contained text.

Attributes:

COLOR="#rrggbb" or "color"

> Specifies a color for the text.

FACE="name"

> Specifies a font face (Times for example) for the text.

SIZE="number"

> Specifies the size of the text from 1 to 7 relative to the base font using + or - .

Context:

<FONT> ... </FONT> is legal within the following markup tags:

> <A>, <ADDRESS>, <B>, <BIG>, <BLOCKQUOTE>, <BODY>, <CAPTION>,
> <CENTER>, <CITE>, <CODE>, <DD>, <DFN>, <DIV>, <DT>, <EM>,
> <FIELDSET>, <FONT>, <FORM>, <H*>, <I>, <KBD>, <LABEL>, <LI>,
> <OBJECT>, <P>, <S>, <SAMP>, <SMALL>, <SPAN>, <STRONG>, <SUB>,
> <SUP>, <TD>, <TEXTFLOW>, <TH>, <TT>, <U>, <VAR>

The following markup can be used within <FONT> ... </FONT>:

> <A>, <APPLET>, <B>, <BASEFONT>, <BIG>, <BR>, <CITE>, <CODE>,
> <DFN>, <EM>, <FONT>, <I>, <IMG>, <INPUT>, <KBD>, <LABEL>, <MAP>,
> <OBJECT>, <S>, <SAMP>, <SCRIPT>, <SELECT>, <SMALL>, <SPAN>,
> <STRONG>, <STYLE>, <SUB>, <SUP>, <TEXTAREA>, <TT>, <U>, <VAR>

Suggested style/usage: The <FONT> tag allows you to use specific fonts and colors in your pages, just as you can in a print document. Most browsers allow users to override these settings, so don't count on them to convey content.

Examples: See file /h4d3e/examples/ch6/font.htm.

<FORM> ... </FORM> *User input form*

Definition: For defining an area that contains objects to solicit user input, ranging from selecting buttons or check boxes, to areas for text input.

Attributes:

ACTION="URL"

> URL is a standard uniform resource locator. ACTION specifies the name of a resource for the browser to execute as an action in response to clicking on an on-screen Submit or Reset button.
>
> The URL will typically point to a CGI script or other executable service on a Web server that performs an action in response to being accessed. (*Note:* CGI stands for *Common Gateway Interface* and defines how browsers can communicate with servers on the Web.)

ENCTYPE="MIME type"

> This attribute specifies the format of the submitted data in case the protocol does not impose a format itself. With the POST method, this attribute is a MIME type specifying the format of the posted data. The default value is "application/x-www-form-urlencoded."

METHOD=("GET" | "POST")

> The METHOD attribute tells the browser how to interact with the service designated by the ACTION's URL. If no method is specified, GET is the default.

> If GET is selected, the browser constructs a query URL that consists of the URL of the current page that contains the form, followed by a question mark, followed by the values of the form's input areas and other objects. The browser sends this query URL to the target URL specified by ACTION. The WWW server in the specified target URL uses the information supplied in the incoming URL to perform a search, process a query, or provide whatever services it has been programmed to deliver.

> If POST is selected, the browser sends a copy of the form's contents to the recipient URL as a data block to the standard input service (stdio( ) or STDIN in the UNIX world). This makes it easy to grab and process form data. POST is the preferred method for most HTML programmers because with POST, you can pass much more information in a cleaner fashion to the server than with the GET method.

> Anything the recipient program writes to output will be returned as a new HTML document to the sender for further display or interaction. The recipient program can also save form data to a file on the local WWW server.

ONSUBMIT="function"

> A script specified by "function" is called and executed when the form is submitted.

Context:

<FORM> ... </FORM> is legal within the following markup tags:

> <BLOCKQUOTE>, <BODY>, <CENTER>, <DD>, <DIV>, <FIELDSET>, <LI>, <OBJECT>, <TD>, <TH>

The following markup can be used within <FORM> ... </FORM>:

> <A>, <ADDRESS>, <APPLET>, <B>, <BASEFONT>, <BIG>, <BLOCKQUOTE>, <BR>, <CENTER>, <CITE>, <CODE>, <DFN>, <DIR>, <DIV>, <DL>, <EM>, <FIELDSET>, <FONT>, <FORM>, <H*>, <HR>, <I>, <IMG>, <INPUT>, <ISINDEX>, <KBD>, <LABEL>, <LISTING>, <MAP>, <MENU>, <OBJECT>, <OL>, <P>, <PRE>, <S>, <SAMP>, <SCRIPT>, <SELECT>, <SMALL>, <SPAN>, <STRONG>, <STYLE>, <SUB>, <SUP>, <TABLE>, <TEXTAREA>, <TT>, <U>, <UL>, <VAR>, <XMP>

The following markup can not be used within any markup within <FORM> ... </FORM>:

> <FORM>

Suggested style/usage: Use <FORM> ... </FORM> whenever you want to solicit input from your readers or provide additional back-end services through your Web pages.

Examples: See file /h4d3e/examples/ch6/form.htm.

<H> ... </H*> Header levels 1 through 6*

Definition: Headers come in different styles and weights to help you organize your content for better readability.

Attributes:

ALIGN=("LEFT" | "CENTER" | "RIGHT" | "JUSTIFY")

> Use this attribute to specify how the text in the heading should be aligned relative to the page. The default alignment is left.

CLASS="text"

DIR=("ltr" | "rtl")

ID="name"

LANG="name"

STYLE="text"

Context:

<H*> ... </H*> is legal within the following markup tags:

> <BLOCKQUOTE>, <BODY>, <CENTER>, <DIV>, <FIELDSET>, <FORM>, <OBJECT>, <TD>, <TH>

The following markup can be used within <H*> ... </H*>:

> <A>, <APPLET>, <B>, <BASEFONT>, <BIG>, <BR>, <CITE>, <CODE>, <DFN>, <EM>, <FONT>, <I>, <IMG>, <INPUT>, <KBD>, <LABEL>, <MAP>, <OBJECT>, <S>, <SAMP>, <SCRIPT>, <SELECT>, <SMALL>, <SPAN>, <STRONG>, <STYLE>, <SUB>, <SUP>, <TEXTAREA>, <TT>, <U>, <VAR>

Suggested style/usage: Use headings regularly and consistently to help add structure and provide guideposts to your documents. Some experts don't recommend using a subheader level unless you plan on using at least two of them beneath a parent level. In other words, they recommend that you don't use a single <H3> ... </H3> beneath an <H2> ... </H2> pair. This follows the old principle of outlining, where you don't indent unless you have at least two subtopics to put beneath a topic. We think that the occasional exception is okay, but this remains a pretty good guideline.

Examples: See file /h4d3e/examples/ch6/h.htm.

<HEAD> ... </HEAD> Document head block

Definition: Defines page-level information about an HTML document, including its title, Base URL, index information, next page pointer, and possible links to other HTML documents.

Attributes:

None.

Context:

<HEAD> ... </HEAD> is legal within the following markup tag:

    <HTML>

The following markup can be used within <HEAD> ... </HEAD>:

    <LINK>, <META>, <SCRIPT>, <STYLE>

Suggested style/usage: For strictly interpreted HTML <HEAD> ... </HEAD> is required at the head of an HTML document. Even though many browsers will render documents that lack a <HEAD> ... </HEAD> block at the beginning, it's still good practice to include one, especially if you want to establish a BASE URL when you have numerous graphics or local document links in your page.

Note: Although the <HEAD> ... </HEAD> block produces no browser output other than a document title, it remains an important component of proper HTML page design.

Examples: See file /h4d3e/examples/ch6/head.htm.

<HR> Horizontal rule

Definition: Draws a horizontal rule across the page, usually one or two pixels wide.

Attributes:

ALIGN=("LEFT" | "CENTER" | "RIGHT")

> Use this attribute to specify how the rule should be aligned relative to the page. The default alignment is left.

CLASS="text"

DIR=("ltr" | "rtl")

ID="name"

LANG="name"

NOSHADE

> Includes a colorless rule rather than the standard 3-D shaded one.

SIZE="number"

> Specifies the height of the rule in pixels.

STYLE="text"

WIDTH="number" or "n%"

> Specifies the width of the rule in pixels or a percentage of the window width.

Context:

<HR> is legal within the following markup tags:

> <BLOCKQUOTE>, <BODY>, <CENTER>, <DD>, <DIV>, <FIELDSET>, <FORM>, <LI>, <OBJECT>, <TD>, <TH>

No markup can be used within <HR>.

Suggested style/usage: Wherever good design will benefit from placement of a horizontal rule — typically to emphasize natural divisions between text items or topics or to separate a page header and footer from the body — the <HR> tag can add a lot to page design.

Examples: See file /h4d3e/examples/ch6/hr.htm.

<HTML> ... </HTML> Main document head

Definition: These tags should enclose an entire HTML document as the outermost layer of document structure. For most browsers in use today, this tag is optional, but movements toward more rigorous interpretation of SGML DTDs for HTML indicate that this may not remain true for much longer.

Attributes:

VERSION="version information"

> This reports the DTD version to an application. To date, the default value is "-//W3C//DTD HTML Experimental 19960712//EN".

Context:

<HTML> ... </HTML> is not legal within any other markup tags.

The following markup can be used within <HTML> ... </HTML>:

> <BODY> <HEAD>

Suggested style/usage: Use <HTML> ... </HTML> to enclose all HTML documents.

Examples: See file /h4d3e/examples/ch6/html.htm.

<I> ... </I> Italicize text

Definition: Italicizes all enclosed text.

Attributes:

Common Attributes only.

Context:

<I> ... </I> is legal within the following markup tags:

> <A>, <ADDRESS>, <B>, <BIG>, <BLOCKQUOTE>, <BODY>, <CAPTION>, <CENTER>, <CITE>, <CODE>, <DD>, <DFN>, <DIV>, <DT>, <EM>, <FIELDSET>, <FONT>, <FORM>, <H*>, <I>, <KBD>, <LABEL>, <LI>, <OBJECT>, <P>, <PRE>, <S>, <SAMP>, <SMALL>, <SPAN>, <STRONG>, <SUB>, <SUP>, <TD>, <TEXTFLOW>, <TH>, <TT>, <U>, <VAR>

The following markup can be used within <I> ... </I>:

> <A> <B>
 <CITE> <CODE> <EM> <IMG> <KBD> <SAMP> <STRONG> <TT> <VAR>

Suggested style/usage: Use italics sparingly for emphasis or effect, remembering that its distinctiveness fades quickly with overuse.

Examples: See file /h4d3e/examples/ch6/i.htm.

<IMG> Inline image

Definition: Supplies image source, placement, and behavior information. Used to place in-line graphics on a page.

Attributes:

ALIGN=("TOP" | "MIDDLE" | "BOTTOM" | "LEFT" | "RIGHT")

> Standard use calls for ALIGN to be set to one of the following values: TOP, MIDDLE, or BOTTOM to define placement.

ALT="text"

> Supplies an alternate string of text to display (and possibly make clickable) if the browser has no graphics capability or if graphics are turned off.

BORDER="number"

> Indicates if there will be a border around the graphic and if so how many pixels wide it will be. BORDER="0" forces no border while BORDER="10" renders a border ten pixels wide on all sides of the graphic.

CLASS="text"

HEIGHT="number"

> Defines the graphic's height in pixels. When the browser is loading a page, it will reserve a space for the graphic based on height and width values given in the attributes. The browser will also size the graphic to fit the height and width dimensions even if they are different from the actual height and width. This can lead to distorted graphics.

HSPACE="number"

> Provides for horizontal white space, measured in pixels, on either side of a graphic to set it apart from the text.

ID="name"

ISMAP

> Indicates by its presence that the image (or its text replacement) should be a clickable map. This often invokes special map-handling software through the CGI interface on the Web server handling the request.

SRC="URL"

> URL is a standard uniform resource locator and specifies the location for image file, which is usually .GIF or .JPEG format.

STYLE="text"

TITLE="text"

USEMAP

> Indicates which <MAP> information store in the document should be used with the image to create a client-side imagemap.

VSPACE="number"

> Provides for vertical white space, measured in pixels, on the top and bottom of a graphic to set it apart from the text.

WIDTH="number"

> Defines the graphic's width in pixels.

Context:

<IMG> is legal within:

> <A>, <ADDRESS>, <B>, <BIG>, <BLOCKQUOTE>, <BODY>, <CAPTION>, <CENTER>, <CITE>, <CODE>, <DD>, <DFN>, <DIV>, <DT>, <EM>, <FIELDSET>, <FONT>, <FORM>, <H*>, <I>, <KBD>, <LABEL>, <LI>, <OBJECT>, <P>, <S>, <SAMP>, <SMALL>, <SPAN>, <STRONG>, <SUB>, <SUP>, <TD>, <TEXTFLOW>, <TH>, <TT>, <U>, <VAR>

No additional markup can be used within <IMG>:

Suggested style/usage: Keep images small and use them judiciously; graphics should add impact and interest to pages without adding too much bulk (or wait time).

Examples: See file /h4d3e/examples/ch06/img.htm.

<INPUT> Input object

Definition: <INPUT> defines an input object within an HTML form; these objects come in several different types and also include several different ways to name and specify the data they contain.

Attributes:

ALIGN=("TOP" | "MIDDLE" | "BOTTOM")

Determines how text and images in a form will align for forms that contain images. Otherwise, these settings behave the same as for <IMG>.

CHECKED

> For check boxes or radio buttons, inclusion of this attribute indicates that the box was checked or the button selected, usually as a default.

CLASS="text"

DIR=("ltr" | "rtl")

ID="name"

LANG="name"

MAXLENGTH = "number"

> The maximum number of characters allowed in a TEXT type input item.

NAME = "text"

> The name of the input item, as passed to the CGI script for the form as part of a name, value pair. (This is how the script identifies values with their corresponding form fields.)

NOTAB

> Removes the field from the tabbing order.

ONBLUR="function"

> When the field loses the focus, this attribute calls and activates a script that is specified in the "function" string.

ONCHANGE="function"

> When the information in the field is changed, this attribute calls and activates a script that is specified in the "function" string.

ONCLICK="function"

> When the field is clicked, this attribute calls and activates a script that is specified in the "function" string.

ONFOCUS="function"

> When the field gains the focus, this attribute calls and activates a script that is specified in the "function" string.

ONSELECT="function"

> When the field is selected, this attribute calls and activates a script that is specified in the "function" string.

SIZE="number"

> The size of a TEXT type input item, as measured by the number of characters it contains.

SRC="URL"

> Specifies the URL of the picture to be used when the TYPE value is IMAGE.

STYLE="text"

TABINDEX="number"

> This attribute defines the link's position in the tabbing order.

TITLE="text"

TYPE =
("TEXT"|"PASSWORD"|"CHECKBOX"|"RADIO"|"SUBMIT"|"RESET"|"FILE"|
"HIDDEN"|"IMAGE"|"BUTTON")

> Defines the type of input object being described. TEXT, CHECKBOX, and RADIO define how data entry areas will appear on-screen; PASSWORD is used to prompt for a password; HIDDEN allows the form to pass data to the Web server that users can't see; SUBMIT and RESET provide methods to ship the information on a form to the server, or to clear the data from the form. IMAGE allows you to insert an image as a button that sends data when it is selected, and BUTTON makes the field appear as a button. The default is TEXT.

VALUE = "text"

> The value for the input item, as passed to the CGI script for the form as part of a name, value pair.

Context:

<INPUT> is legal within the following markup tag:

> <A>, <ADDRESS>, <B>, <BIG>, <BLOCKQUOTE>, <BODY>, <CAPTION>,
> <CENTER>, <CITE>, <CODE>, <DD>, <DFN>, <DIV>, <DT>, <EM>,
> <FIELDSET>, <FONT>, <FORM>, <H*>, <I>, <KBD>, <LABEL>, <LI>,
> <OBJECT>, <P>, <PRE>, <S>, <SAMP>, <SMALL>, <SPAN>, <STRONG>,
> <SUB>, <SUP>, <TD>, <TEXTFLOW>, <TH>, <TT>, <U>, <VAR>

No additional markup can be used within <INPUT>

Suggested style/usage: <INPUT> is an essential ingredient for HTML forms of all kinds because it provides the mechanism to solicit input from readers and to deliver it to the underlying forms-handling services supplied by the related CGI script or other forms-handling program.

Examples: See file /h4d3e/examples/ch6/input.htm.

<ISINDEX> Document is indexed

Definition: <ISINDEX> indicates that a searchable index for the document is available on the server, typically in the form of a CGI script that allows searches (normally supplied by a "SEARCH" button somewhere in the document).

Attributes:

DIR=("ltr" | "rtl")

LANG="name"

PROMPT="text"

> Defines a prompt to used in place of the standard message "You can search this index. Type the keyword(s) you want to search for:" followed by a text field users can enter search terms into.

Context:

<ISINDEX> is legal within the following markup tags:

> <BLOCKQUOTE>, <BODY>, <CENTER>, <DD>, <DIV>, <FIELDSET>,
> <FORM>, <HEAD>, <LI>, <OBJECT>, <TD>, <TH>

No markup can be used within <ISINDEX>.

Suggested style/usage: Long, complex documents typically benefit from being searchable, but any kind of document with large numbers of terms or details (for example the HTML specifications or the IETF's RFCs) can benefit from <ISINDEX> support. With <ISINDEX> documents can be queried with a keyword search mechanism by adding a question mark to the end of the URL followed by a list of keywords separated by a plus sign (which, not coincidentally, happens to be called "URL encoding"). For example:

```
http://www.biggus.com/rome/gov/index.html?empire+fall+europe
```

Examples: See file /h4d3e/examples/ch6/isindex.htm.

<KBD> ... </KBD> Keyboard text style

Definition: Indicates that text should be typed in at a computer keyboard. <KBD> ... </KBD> changes the type style for all the text it contains (typically, into a Courier font, or some other font like those typically used in character-mode computer terminal displays).

Attributes:

Common attributes only.

Context:

<KBD> ... </KBD> is legal within the following markup tags:

> <A>, <ADDRESS>, <B>, <BIG>, <BLOCKQUOTE>, <BODY>, <CAPTION>,
> <CENTER>, <CITE>, <CODE>, <DD>, <DFN>, <DIV>, <DT>, <EM>,
> <FIELDSET>, <FONT>, <FORM>, <H*>, <I>, <KBD>, <LABEL>, <LI>,
> <OBJECT>, <P>, <PRE>, <S>, <SAMP>, <SMALL>, <SPAN>, <STRONG>,
> <SUB>, <SUP>, <TD>, <TEXTFLOW>, <TH>, <TT>, <U>, <VAR>

The following markup can be used within <KBD> ... </KBD>:

> <A>, <APPLET>, <B>, <BASEFONT>, <BIG>, <BR>, <CITE>, <CODE>,
> <DFN>, <EM>, <FONT>, <I>, <IMG>, <INPUT>, <KBD>, <LABEL>, <MAP>,
> <OBJECT>, <S>, <SAMP>, <SCRIPT>, <SELECT>, <SMALL>, <SPAN>,
> <STRONG>, <STYLE>, <SUB>, <SUP>, <TEXTAREA>, <TT>, <U>, <VAR>

Suggested style/usage: Whenever you want to illustrate text to be typed in on a computer, please use <KBD> ... </KBD> to set it off from the body text.

Examples: See file /h4d3e/examples/ch6/kbd.htm.

<LABEL> ... </LABEL> Form field label

Definition: This tag adds a label to form fields to associate a descriptor with the label as well as create a control so the field can be selected using hotkeys.

Attributes:

ACCESSKEY="text (single character)"

> This attribute is used to define a single character that acts as a hotkey to activate the form field. Pressing the hotkey is the same as clicking in the field. The character will usually be underlined, and the "ALT=" and "Command" keys, for PCs and Macs respectively, must be pressed in addition to the hotkey to activate the link.

CLASS="text"

DIR="(ltr | rtl)"

FOR="text"

> The ID of the form control the label is associated.

ID="name:"

LANG="name"

ONCLICK="function"

> When the field is clicked this attribute calls and activates a script that is specified in the "function" string.

STYLE="text"

TITLE="text"

Context:

<LABEL> ... </LABEL> is legal within the following markup tags:

> <A>, <ADDRESS>, <B>, <BIG>, <BLOCKQUOTE>, <BODY>, <CAPTION>, <CENTER>, <CITE>, <CODE>, <DD>, <DFN>, <DIV>, <DT>, <EM>, <FIELDSET>, <FONT>, <FORM>, <H*>, <I>, <KBD>, <LI>, <OBJECT>, <P>, <PRE>, <S>, <SAMP>, <SMALL>, <SPAN>, <STRONG>, <SUB>, <SUP>, <TD>, <TEXTFLOW>, <TH>, <TT>, <U>, <VAR>

The following markup can be used within <LABEL> ... </LABEL>:

> <A>, <APPLET>, <B>, <BASEFONT>, <BIG>, <BR>, <CITE>, <CODE>,
> <DFN>, <EM>, <FONT>, <I>, <IMG>, <INPUT>, <KBD>, <LABEL>, <MAP>,
> <OBJECT>, <S>, <SAMP>, <SCRIPT>, <SELECT>, <SMALL>, <SPAN>,
> <STRONG>, <STYLE>, <SUB>, <SUP>, <TEXTAREA>, <TT>, <U>, <VAR>

The following markup can not be used within any markup within <FORM> ... </FORM>:

> <LABEL>

Suggested style/usage: Labels provide a way to associate a description directly with a field in a form as well as way to access the field using a hotkey. This makes forms more interactive and user-friendly.

Examples: See file /h4d3e/examples/ch06/label.htm.

<LI> List item

Definition: An element belonging to one of the various HTML list styles.

Attributes:

CLASS="text"

ID="name"

STYLE="text"

TYPE=("A"|"a"|"I"|"i"|"1")

> Defines the list item marker type: "A" for capital letters, "a" for lower case letters, "I" for large roman numerals, "i" for small roman numerals, and "1" for arabic numerals.

VALUE="number"

> Specifies the number the list should begin with. The default is 1.

Context:

<LI> is legal within the following markup tags:

> <DIR>, <MENU>, <OL>, <UL>

As a singleton tag, no markup can be used within <LI>.

<A>, <APPLET>, <B>, <BASEFONT>, <BIG>, <BLOCKQUOTE>, <BR>, <CENTER>, <CITE>, <CODE>, <DFN>, <DIR>, <DIV>, <DL>, <EM>, <FIELDSET>, <FONT>, <FORM>, <HR>, <I>, <IMG>, <INPUT>, <ISINDEX>, <KBD>, <LABEL>, <LISTING>, <MAP>, <MENU>, <OBJECT>, <OL>, <P>, <PRE>, <S>, <SAMP>, <SCRIPT>, <SELECT>, <SMALL>, <SPAN>, <STRONG>, <STYLE>, <SUB>, <SUP>, <TABLE>, <TEXTAREA>, <TT>, <U>, <UL>, <VAR>, <XMP>

Suggested style/usage: Use to set off elements within lists.

Examples: See file /h4d3e/examples/ch6/div.htm.

<LINK>

Definition: Provides information that links the current document to other documents or URL resources.

Attributes:

CLASS="text"

HREF = "URL"

> The address of the current link destination, accessible through normal Web linkage mechanisms. Works the same as the anchor tag <A>...</A>.

ID="name"

REL=("NEXT" | "PREVIOUS" | "PARENT" | "MADE")

> The REL attribute specifies the relationship between the current anchor and the destination (also known as a "forward relationship type"). "next" indicates that the URL points to the next page in a sequence, "previous" that it points to the prior page, while "parent" indicates that the current page is the parent of the destination page. "made" indicates that the destination page contains information about the maker or owner of the current anchor page.

REV=("NEXT" | "PREVIOUS" | "PARENT" | "MADE")

> REV is the reverse of the REL attribute and indicates the destination and the current anchor. All of the attribute values are the same but apply to the page that the URL points to. Here, "made" indicates that this document contains information about the maker or owner of the destination page.

STYLE="text"

TITLE="text"

Provides advisory information about the title of the destination document (usually the same text as enclosed by the <TITLE> ... </TITLE> tags in that document).

TYPE="text"

Identifies the media type, such as style sheet, of the linked document.

Context:

<LINK> is legal only within the <HEAD> ... </HEAD> tags.

No additional markup can be used within <LINK>.

Suggested style/usage: The use of <LINK> has changed dramatically with the introduction of style sheets.

Examples: See file /h4d3e/examples/ch6/link.htm.

<LISTING> ... </LISTING>

Definition: Creates a list of text in a fixed width font.

Attributes:

None.

Context:

<LISTING> ... </LISTING> is legal within the following markup tags:

<BLOCKQUOTE>, <BODY>, <CENTER>, <DD>, <DIV>, <FIELDSET>, <FORM>, <LI>, <OBJECT>, <TD>, <TH>

No additional markup can be used within <LISTING>.

Suggested style/usage: Data is always easier to read when it is listed in a fixed width font.

Examples: See file /h4d3e/examples/ch6/listing.htm.

<MAP> ... </MAP> Client side image map

Definition: Contains the coordinates and URL information for a client-side image map.

Attributes:

NAME="text"

> A unique identifier for the map referenced by the USEMAP attribute in an <IMG> tag.

Context:

<MAP> ... </MAP> is legal within the following markup tags:

> <A>, <ADDRESS>, <B>, <BIG>, <BLOCKQUOTE>, <BODY>, <CAPTION>, <CENTER>, <CITE>, <CODE>, <DD>, <DFN>, <DIV>, <DT>, <EM>, <FIELDSET>, <FONT>, <FORM>, <H*>, <I>, <KBD>, <LABEL>, <LI>, <OBJECT>, <P>, <PRE>, <S>, <SAMP>, <SMALL>, <SPAN>, <STRONG>, <SUB>, <SUP>, <TD>, <TEXTFLOW>, <TH>, <TT>, <U>, <VAR>

The following markup can be used within <MAP> ... </MAP>:

> <AREA>

Suggested style/usage: All of the hotzone information for any given client-side image map will be listed within in the <MAP> tags. Make sure the name you assign to a map is unique so if you choose to include other maps on the page they will be match with the correct image.

Examples: See file /h4d3e/examples/ch6/map.htm.

<MENU> ... </MENU>

Definition: Encloses a menu list, where each element is typically a word or a short phrase that fits on a single line, rendered more compact than most other list types.

Attributes:

COMPACT

> Renders the list as compact as possible (not currently supported by all browsers).

Context:

<MENU> ... </MENU> is legal within the following markup tags:

> <BLOCKQUOTE>, <BODY>, <CENTER>, <DD>, <DIV>, <FIELDSET>, <FORM>, <LI>, <OBJECT>, <TD>, <TH>

The following markup can be used within <MENU> ... </MENU>:

> <LI>

The following markup can not be used within <LI> tags within <MENU> ... </MENU>:

> <BLOCKQUOTE>, <CENTER>, <DIR>, <DIV>, <DL>, <FIELDSET>, <FORM>, <HR>, <ISINDEX>, <LISTING>, <MENU>, <OL>, <P>, <PRE>, <TABLE>, <UL>, <XMP>

Suggested style/usage: For short, simple lists the <MENU> list style provides the most compact way to display such information. Use the COMPACT attribute to really squeeze things down, if you must.

Examples: See file /h4d3e/examples/ch6/menu.htm.

<META>

Definition: The META element is used within the HEAD element to embed document *meta-information* (or "information about information") not defined by other HTML elements. Such information can be extracted by servers/clients for use in identifying, indexing and cataloging specialized document meta-information. Although it's preferable to use named elements that have well-defined semantics for each type of meta-information, such as title, this element is provided for situations where strict SGML parsing is necessary and the local DTD is not extensible.

Attributes:

CONTENT

>   Used to supply a value for a named property.

HTTP-EQUIV

>   This attribute binds the element to an HTTP response header. If the semantics of the HTTP response header named by this attribute is known, then the contents can be processed based on a well-defined syntactic mapping, whether or not the DTD includes anything about it. HTTP header names are not case sensitive. If absent, the NAME attribute should be used to identify this meta-information and it should not be used within an HTPP response header.

NAME

>   Used to name a property such as author, publication date etc. If absent, the name can be assumed to be the same as the value of HTTP-EQUIV.

Context:

<META> is legal within:

```
<HEAD>
```

No additional markup can be used within <META>.

Suggested style/usage: When your documents are governed by a specific SGML DTD, or if you want to advertise aspects of its content (see examples below), META information can make your information more accessible to spiders and robots for automatic indexing, and more accessible to other programs that you might use to help you manage an HTML document collection.

Examples: See file /h4d3e/examples/ch6/meta.htm.

<OBJECT> ... </OBJECT> Non-http object

Definition: Embeds a non-http object, such as a sound clip, movie, script, or image into an HTML document.

Attributes:

ALIGN=("LEFT"|"TEXTTOP"|"MIDDLE"|"TEXTMIDDLE"|"BASELINE"|"TEXTBOTTOM"| "CENTER"|"RIGHT")

> Use this attribute to specify how the text should be aligned relative to the text and page. The alignment values are a bit different from those discussed previously. LEFT, MIDDLE, and RIGHT flow text around the object, but TEXTTOP, TEXTMIDDLE, CENTER, and TEXTBOTTOM do not produce flowing text, only text aligned with the top, middle, center, or bottom of the object. BASELINE aligns the image with the baseline of the surrounding text. The default value is LEFT.

BORDER="number"

> Indicates if there will be a border around the object and, if so, how many pixels wide it will be. BORDER="0" forces no border; BOR-DER="10" renders a border ten pixels wide on all sides of the object.

CLASS="text"

CLASSID="URL"

> Identifies the type of object.

CODEBASE="URL"

> An object's code base is the URL of the directory the object sits in. This attribute tells the browser where to get an object while the DATA attribute specifies which object.

CODETYPE="text"

Identifies the object's Internet code type.

DATA="URL"

Identifies the object's source file.

DECLARE

Downloads the object but does not activate it. Used when referencing the object in later in the document or as a parameter for another object.

DIR=("ltr"|"rtl")

HEIGHT="number"

Defines the object's height in pixels.

HSPACE="number"

Provides for horizontal white space, measured in pixels, on either side of the object to set it apart from the text.

ID="name"

LANG="name"

NAME="text"

Gives the object a name that will identify it to other objects on the page.

NOTAB

Removes the object from the tabbing order.

SHAPES

Indicates that the object has shaped hotspots with URL references. Used for client-side image maps.

STANDBY="text"

Specified text is displayed while the object is loading.

STYLE="text"

TABINDEX="number"

This attribute defines the link's position in the tabbing order.

TITLE="text"

TYPE="text"

Identifies the object's Internet media type.

USEMAP

Indicates which <MAP> information stored in the document should be used with the object to create a client-side imagemap.

VSPACE="number"

Provides for vertical white space, measured in pixels, on the top and bottom of the object to set it apart from the text.

WIDTH="number"

Defines the object's width in pixels.

Context:

<OBJECT> ... </OBJECT> is legal within the following markup tags:

> <A>, <ADDRESS>, <B>, <BIG>, <BLOCKQUOTE>, <BODY>, <CAPTION>,
> <CENTER>, <CITE>, <CODE>, <DD>, <DFN>, <DIV>, <DT>, <EM>,
> <FIELDSET>, <FONT>, <FORM>, <H*>, <I>, <KBD>, <LABEL>, <LI>,
> <OBJECT>, <P>, <PRE>, <S>, <SAMP>, <SMALL>, <SPAN>, <STRONG>,
> <SUB>, <SUP>, <TD>, <TEXTFLOW>, <TH>, <TT>, <U>, <VAR>

The following markup can be used within <APPLET> ... </APPLET>:

> <A>, <ADDRESS>, <APPLET>, <B>, <BASEFONT>, <BIG>,
> <BLOCKQUOTE>, <BR>, <CENTER>, <CITE>, <CODE>, <DFN>, <DIR>,
> <DIV>, <DL>, <EM>, <FIELDSET>, <FONT>, <FORM>, <H*>, <HR>, <I>,
> <IMG>, <INPUT>, <ISINDEX>, <KBD>, <LABEL>, <LISTING>, <MAP>,
> <MENU>, <OBJECT>, <OL>, <P>, <PARAM>, <PRE>, <S>, <SAMP>,
> <SCRIPT>, <SELECT>, <SMALL>, <SPAN>, <STRONG>, <STYLE>, <SUB>,
> <SUP>, <TABLE>, <TEXTAREA>, <TT>, <U>, <UL>, <VAR>, <XMP>

Suggested style/uage:

Objects extend HTML so almost any type of data can be included in an Web page. Keep in mind that older versions of most browsers do not support objects, and the current implementation in many browsers is not stable.

Examples: See file /h4d3e/examples/ch6/object.htm.

<OL> ... </OL> Ordered list

Definition: An ordered list numbers the elements by order of occurrence.

Attributes:

COMPACT

> Renders the list as compact as possible.

Context:

<OL> ... </OL> is legal within the following markup tags:

> <BLOCKQUOTE>, <BODY>, <CENTER>, <DD>, <DIV>, <FIELDSET>,
> <FORM>, <LI>, <OBJECT>, <TD>, <TH>

The following markup can be used within <OL> ... </OL>:

> <LI>

Suggested style/usage: Ordered lists work well for step-by-step instructions or other information where the order of presentation is important.

Examples: See file /h4d3e/examples/ch6/ol.htm.

<OPTION> Form list choice

Definition: Defines the various options available within a <SELECT> ... </SELECT> tag pair for a forms definition, where users must select a value from a predefined list of options. Also provides a mechanism for selecting a default value, if the user chooses no value explicitly.

Attributes:

CLASS="text"

DIR=("ltr"|"rtl")

ID="name"

LANG="name"

SELECTED

> Defines a default value for a <SELECT> field within a form if the user chooses no value explicitly.

STYLE="text"

TITLE="text"

VALUE="text"

> Defines the value for a specific <SELECT> option, which equals the text string assigned to VALUE.

Context:

<OPTION> is legal only within the <SELECT> ... </SELECT> tag pair.

As a singleton tag, <OPTION> cannot include any markup inside it.

Suggested style/usage: For defining a set of scalar values for a <SELECT> field, and for supplying a default for such sets where appropriate.

Examples: See file /h4d3e/examples/ch6/option.htm.

<P>

Definition: <P> defines paragraph boundaries for normal HTML text, where the break occurs immediately before the text that follows the tag.

Attributes:

ALIGN=("LEFT" | "CENTER" | "RIGHT" | "JUSTIFY")

> Use this attribute to specify how the text in the paragraph should be aligned relative to the page. The default alignment is left.

CLASS="text"

DIR=("ltr" | "rtl")

ID="name"

LANG="name"

STYLE="text"

Context:

<P> is legal within the following markup tags:

> <ADDRESS>, <BLOCKQUOTE>, <BODY>, <CENTER>, <DD>, <DIV>, <FIELDSET>, <FORM>, <LI>, <OBJECT>, <TD>, <TH>

No additional markup is legal with <P>.

Suggested style/usage: Paragraphs are a fundamental unit of text, used to break the flow of ideas or information into related chunks. Good writing style calls for regular use of paragraphs, and for treating each idea or concept separately in its own paragraph.

Examples: See file /h4d3e/examples/ch6/p.htm.

<PARAM> Applet and object parameters

Definition: Specifies parameters settings for Java applets and embedded objects.

Attributes:

NAME="text"

> Provides the parameter name.

TYPE="text"

> Provides the Internet media type.

VALUE="value"

> Identifies the parameter's value in either numbers or text.

VALUETYPE=("DATA"|"REF"|"OBJECT")

> Provides specifics about the VALUE information. DATA indicates the information is data; REF indicates a URL; and OBJECT indicates a URL within the same document. The default is DATA.

Context:

<PARAM> is legal within the following markup tags:

> <APPLET>, <OBJECT>

No additional markup may be used within <PARAM>.

Suggested style/usage: Parameters are used to allow generic applets and objects to be used within multiple documents by providing specific values. There can be more than one parameter for any given applet or object.

Examples: See file /h4d3e/examples/ch6/param.htm.

<PLAINTEXT> ... </PLAINTEXT>

Definition: <PLAINTEXT> ... </PLAINTEXT> renders all text in a fixed-width font. Any HTML markup within the tags is ignored.

Attributes:

None.

Context:

<PLAINTEXT> ... </PLAINTEXT> is legal within the following markup tag:

<HTML>

No additional markup may be used within <PLAINTEXT> ... </PLAINTEXT>.

Suggested style/usage: <PLAINTEXT> is the only tag that not only renders text in a fixed-with font but also ignores all other markup as well.

Examples: See file /h4d3e/examples/ch6/plaintex.htm.

<PRE> ... </PRE> Preformatted style

Definition: <PRE> ... </PRE> provides a way of inserting preformatted text into HTML files. This can be valuable for reproducing formatted tables or other text where you want to preserve its original layout, like code listings where you want to be able to preserve exact formatting and indentation.

Attributes:

CLASS="text"

DIR=("ltr" | "rtl")

ID="name"

LANG="name"

STYLE="text"

WIDTH="number"

This specifies the maximum number of characters for a line and allows the browser to select an appropriate font and indentation setting.

Context:

<PRE> ... </PRE> is legal within the following markup tags:

<BLOCKQUOTE>, <BODY>, <CENTER>, <DD>, <DIV>, <FIELDSET>, <FORM>, <LI>, <OBJECT>, <TD>, <TH>

The following markup can be used within <PRE> ... </PRE>:

<A>, <APPLET>, <B>, <BASEFONT>, <BIG>, <BR>, <CITE>, <CODE>, <DFN>, <EM>, <FONT>, <I>, <IMG>, <INPUT>, <KBD>, <LABEL>, <MAP>, <OBJECT>, <S>, <SAMP>, <SCRIPT>, <SELECT>, <SMALL>, <SPAN>, <STRONG>, <STYLE>, <SUB>, <SUP>, <TEXTAREA>, <TT>, <U>, <VAR>

The following markup can not be used within markup used within <PRE> ... </PRE>:

<BIG>, <FONT>, <IMG>, <SMALL>, <SUB>, <SUP>

Suggested style/usage: When assembling text to use within a <PRE> ... </PRE> block, it's okay to use link tags and text controls. You can obtain line breaks just by using the return key, but because <PRE> text is typically set in a monospaced font (like Courier), try to keep line lengths at 80 columns or less. This tag is great for presenting text-only information, such as .sig files or other e-mail information, or USENET news articles.

Examples: See file /h4d3e/examples/ch6/pre.htm.

<S> ... </S> Strikethrough text

Definition: <S> ... </S> renders enclosed text as struck through.

Attributes:

Common attributes only.

Context:

<S> ... </S> is legal within the following markup tags:

<A>, <ADDRESS>, <B>, <BIG>, <BLOCKQUOTE>, <BODY>, <CAPTION>, <CENTER>, <CITE>, <CODE>, <DD>, <DFN>, <DIV>, <DT>, <EM>, <FIELDSET>, <FONT>, <FORM>, <H*>, <I>, <KBD>, <LABEL>, <LI>, <OBJECT>, <P>, <PRE>, <S>, <SAMP>, <SMALL>, <SPAN>, <STRONG>, <SUB>, <SUP>, <TD>, <TEXTFLOW>, <TH>, <TT>, <U>, <VAR>

The following markup can be used within <S> ... </S>:

<A>, <APPLET>, <B>, <BASEFONT>, <BIG>, <BR>, <CITE>, <CODE>, <DFN>, <EM>, <FONT>, <I>, <IMG>, <INPUT>, <KBD>, <LABEL>, <MAP>, <OBJECT>, <S>, <SAMP>, <SCRIPT>, <SELECT>, <SMALL>, <SPAN>, <STRONG>, <STYLE>, <SUB>, <SUP>, <TEXTAREA>, <TT>, <U>, <VAR>

Suggested style/usage: Strike through is commonly used to indicate corrected or changed information. Too much struck text can be difficult to read.

Examples: See file /h4d3e/examples/ch6/s.htm.

<SAMP> ... </SAMP> Sample text

Definition: <SAMP> ... </SAMP> should be used for sequences of literal characters, or to represent output from a program or other data source.

Attributes:

Common attributes only.

Context:

<SAMP> ... </SAMP> is legal within the following markup tags:

> <A>, <ADDRESS>, <B>, <BIG>, <BLOCKQUOTE>, <BODY>, <CAPTION>,
> <CENTER>, <CITE>, <CODE>, <DD>, <DFN>, <DIV>, <DT>, <EM>,
> <FIELDSET>, <FONT>, <FORM>, <H*>, <I>, <KBD>, <LABEL>, <LI>,
> <OBJECT>, <P>, <PRE>, <S>, <SAMP>, <SMALL>, <SPAN>, <STRONG>,
> <SUB>, <SUP>, <TD>, <TEXTFLOW>, <TH>, <TT>, <U>, <VAR>

The following markup can be used within <SAMP> ... </SAMP>:

> <A>, <APPLET>, <B>, <BASEFONT>, <BIG>, <BR>, <CITE>, <CODE>,
> <DFN>, <EM>, <FONT>, <I>, <IMG>, <INPUT>, <KBD>, <LABEL>, <MAP>,
> <OBJECT>, <S>, <SAMP>, <SCRIPT>, <SELECT>, <SMALL>, <SPAN>,
> <STRONG>, <STYLE>, <SUB>, <SUP>, <TEXTAREA>, <TT>, <U>, <VAR>

Suggested style/usage: Whenever you want to reproduce output from a program, script, or other data source, use <SAMP> ... </SAMP>.

Examples: See file /h4d3e/examples/ch6/samp.htm.

<SCRIPT> ... </SCRIPT> Inline script

Definition: Inserts a VB or JavaScript script.

Attributes:

Language="text"

> Specifies the scripting language used to create the code.

SRC="URL"

> Identifies a URL for the script if it is not included directly within the tag itself.

TYPE="text"

> Specifies the Internet code type.

Context:

<SCRIPT> ... </SCRIPT> is legal within the following markup tags:

> <A>, <ADDRESS>, <B>, <BIG>, <BLOCKQUOTE>, <BODY>, <CAPTION>,
> <CENTER>, <CITE>, <CODE>, <DD>, <DFN>, <DIV>, <DT>, <EM>,
> <FIELDSET>, <FONT>, <FORM>, <H*>, <HEAD>, <I>, <KBD>, <LABEL>,
> <LI>, <OBJECT>, <P>, <PRE>, <S>, <SAMP>, <SMALL>, <SPAN>,
> <STRONG>, <SUB>, <SUP>, <TD>, <TEXTFLOW>, <TH>, <TT>, <U>, <VAR>

No additional markup is allowed within <SCRIPT> ... </SCRIPT>

Suggested style/usage: Scripts can be called by a URL or written within the <SCRIPT> tag. It is usually best to place comment tags <!-- ... --> around scripts included in documents so that older browsers that do not support scripting will not display the code as text.

Examples: See file /h4d3e/examples/ch6/script.htm.

<SELECT> ... </SELECT> Select input object

Definition: The SELECT tags allow users to pick one or more options out of a list of possible values supplied in an input form, where each alternative is represented by an <OPTION> element.

Attributes:

CLASS="text"

DIR=("ltr"|"rtl")

ID="name"

LANG="name"

MULTIPLE

> This attribute appears when users are allowed to select more than one element from the set of <OPTION> values supplied within a <SELECT> ... </SELECT> tag pair.

NAME = "text"

> The name of the input item, as passed to the CGI script for the form as part of a name, value pair (this is how the script identifies values with their corresponding form fields).

NOTAB

Removes the option from the tabbing order.

ONBLUR="function"

When the option loses the focus, this attribute calls and activates a script that is specified in the "function" string.

ONCHANGE="function"

When the information in the field is changed, this attribute calls and activates a script that is specified in the "function" string.

ONFOCUS="function"

When the field gains the focus, this attribute calls and activates a script that is specified in the "function" string.

SIZE="number"

The height of the option list.

STYLE="text"

TABINDEX="number"

This attribute defines the option's position in the tabbing order.

TITLE="text"

Context:

<SELECT> ... </SELECT> is legal only within the following tags:

> <A>, <ADDRESS>, <B>, <BIG>, <BLOCKQUOTE>, <BODY>, <CAPTION>, <CENTER>, <CITE>, <CODE>, <DD>, <DFN>, <DIV>, <DT>, <EM>, <FIELDSET>, <FONT>, <FORM>, <H*>, <I>, <KBD>, <LABEL>, <LI>, <OBJECT>, <P>, <PRE>, <S>, <SAMP>, <SMALL>, <SPAN>, <STRONG>, <SUB>, <SUP>, <TD>, <TEXTFLOW>, <TH>, <TT>, <U>, <VAR>

The following markup can be used within <SELECT> ... </SELECT>:

> <OPTION>

Suggested style/usage: Used to provide pickable lists of scalar values within HTML forms whenever users can pick only from a predetermined set of possible values.

Examples: See file /h4d3e/examples/ch6/select.htm.

<SMALL> ... </SMALL> Small text

Definition: Reduces the size of enclosed text by one size relative to the base font size.

Attributes:

Common attributes only.

Context:

<SMALL> ... </SMALL> is legal within the following markup tags:

> <A>, <ADDRESS>, <B>, <BIG>, <BLOCKQUOTE>, <BODY>, <CAPTION>, <CENTER>, <CITE>, <CODE>, <DD>, <DFN>, <DIV>, <DT>, <EM>, <FIELDSET>, <FONT>, <FORM>, <H*>, <I>, <KBD>, <LABEL>, <LI>, <OBJECT>, <P>, <S>, <SAMP>, <SMALL>, <SPAN>, <STRONG>, <SUB>, <SUP>, <TD>, <TEXTFLOW>, <TH>, <TT>, <U>, <VAR>

The following markup can be used within <SMALL> ... </SMALL>:

> <A>, <APPLET>, <B>, <BASEFONT>, <BIG>, <BR>, <CITE>, <CODE>, <DFN>, <EM>, <FONT>, <I>, <IMG>, <INPUT>, <KBD>, <LABEL>, <MAP>, <OBJECT>, <S>, <SAMP>, <SCRIPT>, <SELECT>, <SMALL>, <SPAN>, <STRONG>, <STYLE>, <SUB>, <SUP>, <TEXTAREA>, <TT>, <U>, <VAR>

Suggested style/usage: <SMALL> is frequently used for copyright and other necessary information that you want to include on your pages without having it intrude.

Examples: See file /h4d3e/examples/ch6/small.htm.

<SPAN> ... </SPAN> Style area

Definition: Used to apply localized formatting to a portion of a document.

Attributes:

Common attributes only.

Context:

<SPAN> ... </SPAN> is legal within the following markup tags:

> <A>, <ADDRESS>, <B>, <BIG>, <BLOCKQUOTE>, <BODY>, <CAPTION>, <CENTER>, <CITE>, <CODE>, <DD>, <DFN>, <DIV>, <DT>, <EM>, <FIELDSET>, <FONT>, <FORM>, <H*>, <I>, <KBD>, <LABEL>, <LI>, <OBJECT>, <P>, <PRE>, <S>, <SAMP>, <SMALL>, <SPAN>, <STRONG>, <SUB>, <SUP>, <TD>, <TEXTFLOW>, <TH>, <TT>, <U>, <VAR>

The following markup can be used within <SPAN> ... </SPAN>:

> <A>, <APPLET>, <B>, <BASEFONT>, <BIG>, <BR>, <CITE>, <CODE>,
> <DFN>, <EM>, <FONT>, <I>, <IMG>, <INPUT>, <KBD>, <LABEL>, <MAP>,
> <OBJECT>, <S>, <SAMP>, <SCRIPT>, <SELECT>, <SMALL>, <SPAN>,
> <STRONG>, <STYLE>, <SUB>, <SUP>, <TEXTAREA>, <TT>, <U>, <VAR>

Suggested style/usage: Use <SPAN> and the STYLE attribute to change margins, text color, and more. However, if you want to apply style specifics to an entire document, style sheets offer a better solution.

Examples: See file /h4d3e/examples/ch6/span.htm.

<STRONG> ... </STRONG> Strong emphasis

Definition: A text control for providing strong emphasis on key words or phrases within normal body text, lists, and so on.

Attributes:

Common attributes only.

Context:

<STRONG> ... </STRONG> is legal within the following markup tags:

> <A>, <ADDRESS>, <B>, <BIG>, <BLOCKQUOTE>, <BODY>, <CAPTION>,
> <CENTER>, <CITE>, <CODE>, <DD>, <DFN>, <DIV>, <DT>, <EM>,
> <FIELDSET>, <FONT>, <FORM>, <H*>, <I>, <KBD>, <LABEL>, <LI>,
> <OBJECT>, <P>, <PRE>, <S>, <SAMP>, <SMALL>, <SPAN>, <STRONG>,
> <SUB>, <SUP>, <TD>, <TEXTFLOW>, <TH>, <TT>, <U>, <VAR>

The following markup can be used within <STRONG> ... </STRONG>:

> <A>, <APPLET>, <B>, <BASEFONT>, <BIG>, <BR>, <CITE>, <CODE>,
> <DFN>, <EM>, <FONT>, <I>, <IMG>, <INPUT>, <KBD>, <LABEL>, <MAP>,
> <OBJECT>, <S>, <SAMP>, <SCRIPT>, <SELECT>, <SMALL>, <SPAN>,
> <STRONG>, <STYLE>, <SUB>, <SUP>, <TEXTAREA>, <TT>, <U>, <VAR>

Suggested style/usage: Use within running text to provide the strongest degree of in-line emphasis available in HTML. Remember, overuse blunts the effect, so use emphatic text controls sparingly in your documents.

Examples: See file /h4d3e/examples/ch6/strong.htm.

<STYLE> ... </STYLE> Style sheet

Definition: Specifies a style information whose parameters will govern the entire document.

Attributes:

DIR=("ltr" | "rtl")

LANG="name"

TITLE="text"

TYPE="text"

> Specifies the MIME type for the file if an external style sheet is referenced.

Context:

<STYLE> ... </STYLE> is legal within the following markup tags:

> <A>, <ADDRESS>, <B>, <BIG>, <BLOCKQUOTE>, <BODY>, <CAPTION>,
> <CENTER>, <CITE>, <CODE>, <DD>, <DFN>, <DIV>, <DT>, <EM>,
> <FIELDSET>, <FONT>, <FORM>, <H*>, <HEAD>, <I>, <KBD>, <LABEL>,
> <LI>, <OBJECT>, <P>, <PRE>, <S>, <SAMP>, <SMALL>, <SPAN>,
> <STRONG>, <SUB>, <SUP>, <TD>, <TEXTFLOW>, <TH>, <TT>, <U>, <VAR>

No additional markup is allowed within <STYLE> ... </STYLE>.

Suggested style/usage: You can define your own parameters for tag display within the <STYLE> tag. For example, H1 could be 12pt Times in Blue and H2 is 10pt Times in Red. Older versions of browser will not register this tag, and many browsers allow users to ignore style implementations.

Examples: See file /h4d3e/examples/ch6/style.htm.

_{...} Subscript

Definition: Renders text in subscript: one font size smaller and slightly lower than the text baseline.

Attributes:

Common attributes only.

Context:

_{...} is legal within the following markup tags:

> <A>, <ADDRESS>, <B>, <BIG>, <BLOCKQUOTE>, <BODY>, <CAPTION>,
> <CENTER>, <CITE>, <CODE>, <DD>, <DFN>, <DIV>, <DT>, <EM>,
> <FIELDSET>, <FONT>, <FORM>, <H*>, <I>, <KBD>, <LABEL>, <LI>,
> <OBJECT>, <P>, <S>, <SAMP>, <SMALL>, <SPAN>, <STRONG>, <SUB>,
> <SUP>, <TD>, <TEXTFLOW>, <TH>, <TT>, <U>, <VAR>

The following markup can be used within _{...}:

> <A>, <APPLET>, <B>, <BASEFONT>, <BIG>, <BR>, <CITE>, <CODE>, <DFN>, <EM>, <FONT>, <I>, <IMG>, <INPUT>, <KBD>, <LABEL>, <MAP>, <OBJECT>, <S>, <SAMP>, <SCRIPT>, <SELECT>, <SMALL>, <SPAN>, <STRONG>, <STYLE>, <SUB>, <SUP>, <TEXTAREA>, <TT>, <U>, <VAR>

Suggested style/usage: Subscript allows you to include accurate mathematical notation in your HTML documents.

Examples: See file /h4d3e/examples/ch6/sub.htm.

^{...} Superscript

Definition: Renders text in superscript: one font size smaller and slightly higher than the text baseline.

Attributes:

Common attributes only.

Context:

^{...} is legal within the following markup tags:

> <A>, <ADDRESS>, <B>, <BIG>, <BLOCKQUOTE>, <BODY>, <CAPTION>, <CENTER>, <CITE>, <CODE>, <DD>, <DFN>, <DIV>, <DT>, <EM>, <FIELDSET>, <FONT>, <FORM>, <H*>, <I>, <KBD>, <LABEL>, <LI>, <OBJECT>, <P>, <S>, <SAMP>, <SMALL>, <SPAN>, <STRONG>, <SUB>, <SUP>, <TD>, <TEXTFLOW>, <TH>, <TT>, <U>, <VAR>

The following markup can be used within ^{...}:

> <A>, <APPLET>, <B>, <BASEFONT>, <BIG>, <BR>, <CITE>, <CODE>, <DFN>, <EM>, <FONT>, <I>, <IMG>, <INPUT>, <KBD>, <LABEL>, <MAP>, <OBJECT>, <S>, <SAMP>, <SCRIPT>, <SELECT>, <SMALL>, <SPAN>, <STRONG>, <STYLE>, <SUB>, <SUP>, <TEXTAREA>, <TT>, <U>, <VAR>

Suggested style/usage: Superscript allows you to correctly annotate names such as M^c as well as include accurate mathematical notation in your HTML documents.

Examples: See file /h4d3e/examples/ch6/sup.htm.

<TABLE> Table

Definition: Creates a table.

Attributes:

ALIGN=("LEFT" | "RIGHT" | "CENTER")

Specifies the alignment of the table. The default is LEFT.

BORDER="number"

Indicates if there will be a border around the table and if so how many pixels wide it will be. BORDER="0" forces no border while BORDER="10" renders a border ten pixels wide on all sides of the graphic.

CELLPADDING="number"

Defines the amount of space within the table cells between the data and the cell sides.

CELLSPACING="number"

Defines the amount of space within the table cells between the table frame and the cells.

CLASS="text"

COLS="number"

Specifies the number of columns within a table. Including this attribute can speed the processing of tables.

DIR=("ltr" | "rtl")

FRAME=("VOID" | "ABOVE" | "BELOW" | "HSIDES" | "LHS" | "RHS" | "VSIDES" | "BOX" | "BORDER")

Defines which part of the table fame, for example, border, will be displayed. VOID removes all borders; ABOVE and BELOW place a border line at the top and bottom of the table respectively; HSIDES creates borders on the top and bottom and VSIDES on the left and right; LHS and RHS places borders on the left and right sides respectively; and BOX creates a border on all sides of the frame.

ID="name"

LANG="name"

RULES=("NONE" | "GROUPS" | "ROWS" | "COLS" | "ALL")

Defines how the inner lines of the tables are drawn. NONE removes all rules; GROUPS creates rules between the table sections defined by the

<THEAD>, <TBODY>, and <TFOOT> tags; ROWS places rules only between rows, but COLS only creates them between columns; and ALL places rules between all rules and columns.

STYLE="text"

WIDTH="number"

Defines the table's width in pixels.

Context:

<TABLE> ... </TABLE> is legal within:

<BLOCKQUOTE>, <BODY>, <CENTER>, <DD>, <DIV>, <FIELDSET>, <FORM>, <LI>, <OBJECT>, <TD>, <TH>>

The following markup can be used within <TABLE> ... </TABLE>:

<CAPTION>, <COL>, <COLGROUP>, <TBODY>, <TFOOT>, <THEAD>

Suggested style/usage: Tables give you more precise control over text and graphical placement. Before a table can display any of its contents, it must load in its entirety, so use lengthy tables judiciously.

Examples: See file /h4d3e/examples/ch06/table.htm.

<TBODY> ... </TBODY> Table body

Definition: A logical division in a table to separate different groups of body information.

Attributes:

ALIGN=("CENTER"|"LEFT"|"RIGHT"|"JUSTIFY"|"CHAR")

Use this attribute to specify how text should be aligned left to right within the cells. The CHAR value aligns the text based on a specific character defined in the CHAR attribute. The default alignment is CENTER.

CHAR="text" (single character)

Identifies the character the text in the cells should align with. The value is case sensitive and the default is a period.

CHAROFF="number" or "n%"

Defines the offset, in characters or percentage, for the first occurrence of the alignment character specified by CHAR on any given line. This attribute can be used to create indentions in lines or paragraphs.

CLASS="text"

DIR=("ltr" | "rtl")

ID="name"

LANG="name"

STYLE="text"

VALIGN=("TOP" | "MIDDLE" | "BOTTOM" | "BASELINE")

> Use this attribute to specify how text should be aligned vertically within the cells. The TOP, MIDDLE, and BOTTOM values align cell text at the top, middle, and bottom respectively, of the cell. A BASELINE alignment places all of the first lines in the column's cells on a common baseline. The default is MIDDLE>.

Context:

<TBODY> ... </TBODY> is legal within the following markup tag:

> <TABLE>

The following markup can be used within <TBODY> ... </TBODY>:

> <TR>

Suggested style/usage: Use <TBODY> to group different types of content within the same table. The GROUPS value of the RULES attribute in the <TABLE> tag will put rules around body groups to show the content is related.

Examples: See file /h4d3e/examples/ch6/tbody.htm.

<TD> ... </TD> Table cell

Definition: Defines a data cell within a table.

Attributes:

ALIGN=("CENTER" | "LEFT" | "RIGHT" | "JUSTIFY" | "CHAR")

> Use this attribute to specify how text should be aligned left to right within the cells. The CHAR value aligns the text based on a specific character defined in the CHAR attribute. The default alignment is CENTER.

AXES="text"

A comma separated list of header information that defines the content of an entire set of cells.

AXIS="text"

Header information that defines the content of the cell.

BGCOLOR=="#rrggbb" or "color"

Specifies a background color for the cell.

CHAR="text" (single character)

Identifies the character the text in the cells should align with. The value is case sensitive and the default is a period.

CHAROFF="number" or "n%"

Defines the offset, in characters or percentage, for the first occurrence of the alignment character specified by CHAR on any given line. This attribute can be used to create indentions in lines or paragraphs.

CLASS="text"

COLSPAN="number"

Indicates the number of columns the cell should span. This causes the cell to overlap into adjoining cell spaces.

DIR=("ltr | | "rtl")

ID="name"

LANG="name"

NOWRAP

Forces the text in the cells to not wrap regardless of its length in relation to the cell width. Any remaining text will disappear beyond the cell's border.

ROWSPAN="number"

Indicates the number of rows the cell should span. This causes the cell to overlap into adjoining cell spaces.

STYLE="text"

VALIGN=("TOP" | "MIDDLE" | "BOTTOM" | "BASELINE")

Use this attribute to specify how text should be aligned vertically within the cells. The TOP, MIDDLE, and BOTTOM values align cell text at the top, middle, and bottom respectively, of the cell. A BASELINE alignment places all of the first lines in the column's cells on a common baseline. The default is MIDDLE>.

Context:

<TD> ... </TD> is legal within the following markup tag:

    <TR>

The following markup can be used within <TD> ... </TD>:

    <A>, <ADDRESS>, <APPLET>, <B>, <BASEFONT>, <BIG>, <BLOCKQUOTE>, <BR>, <CENTER>, <CITE>, <CODE>, <DFN>, <DIR>, <DIV>, <DL>, <EM>, <FIELDSET>, <FONT>, <FORM>, <H*>, <HR>, <I>, <IMG>, <INPUT>, <ISINDEX>, <KBD>, <LABEL>, <LISTING>, <MAP>, <MENU>, <OBJECT>, <OL>, <P>, <PRE>, <S>, <SAMP>, <SCRIPT>, <SELECT>, <SMALL>, <SPAN>, <STRONG>, <STYLE>, <SUB>, <SUP>, <TABLE>, <TEXTAREA>, <TT>, <U>, <UL>, <VAR>, <XMP>

Suggested style/usage: Table data is the core of an HTML table, and it is in the <TD> tags that you will place text and graphics.

Examples: See file /h4d3e/examples/ch6/td.htm.

<TEXTAREA> ... </TEXTAREA> Text input area

Definition: Used to define a text input area for an HTML input form, typically for multiple lines of text.

Attributes:

CLASS="text"

COLS="number"

Defines the number of columns for any given line of text in the TEXTAREA field. Common practice is to limit the number of columns to 72 or less, that being a common limitation for the number of characters a line can hold within the outside page frame of a browser program on-screen. (Eighty is the typical maximum for normal character-mode displays.) This is a required attribute but takes a default of 80.

DIR=("ltr"|"rtl")

ID="name"

LANG="name"

NAME="text"

> Supplies a name for the form field, which will be paired with the value that's ultimately entered for submission to the underlying CGI script or other service program that processes the form. This is a required attribute for which no reasonable default is possible.

NOTAB

> Removes the field from the tabbing order.

ONBLUR="function"

> When the field loses the focus, this attribute calls and activates a script that is specified in the "function" string.

ONCHANGE="function"

> When the information in the field is changed, this attribute calls and activates a script that is specified in the "function" string.

ONFOCUS="function"

> When the field gains the focus, this attribute calls and activates a script that is specified in the "function" string.

ONSELECT="function"

> When the field is selected, this attribute calls and activates a script that is specified in the "function" string.

ROWS="number"

> Defines the number of lines of text that the field can accommodate. Typical values for non-narrative forms range from 2 to 6, but HTML will allow large text areas if needed. (Prudence dictates that page-long input would be better handled by allowing users to upload text files from the editor of their choice, rather than typing into a text field on a form.) This is a required attribute but takes a default of 1.

STYLE="text"

TABINDEX="number"

> This attribute defines the link's position in the tabbing order.

Context:

<TEXTAREA> ... </TEXTAREA> is legal within the following markup tag:

> <A>, <ADDRESS>, <B>, <BIG>, <BLOCKQUOTE>, <BODY>, <CAPTION>,
> <CENTER>, <CITE>, <CODE>, <DD>, <DFN>, <DIV>, <DT>, <EM>,
> <FIELDSET>, <FONT>, <FORM>, <H*>, <I>, <KBD>, <LABEL>, <LI>,
> <OBJECT>, <P>, <PRE>, <S>, <SAMP>, <SMALL>, <SPAN>, <STRONG>,
> <SUB>, <SUP>, <TD>, <TEXTFLOW>, <TH>, <TT>, <U>, <VAR>

No markup is allowed in the <TEXTAREA> tag.

Suggested style/usage: The end tag marks the end of the string used to initialize the field (which can include a default string supplied by the form's author). Thus, even if the field is empty — meaning that <TEXTAREA> and </TEXTAREA> are adjacent to one another — the end tag is essential to indicate a null value for the field.

Use TEXTAREA whenever you have a multi-line input field in a form.

Examples: See file /h4d3e/examples/ch6/textarea.htm.

<TEXTFLOW> ... </TEXTFLOW> Applet alternative

Definition: Contains the text users will see when their browser does not support Java or they have disabled it.

Attributes:

None.

Context:

<TEXTFLOW> ... </TEXTFLOW> is legal only with <APPLET> ... </APPLET>.

The following markup can be used within <TEXTFLOW> ... </TEXTFLOW>:

> <A>, <APPLET>, <B>, <BASEFONT>, <BIG>, <BR>, <CITE>, <CODE>,
> <DFN>, <EM>, <FONT>, <I>, <IMG>, <INPUT>, <KBD>, <LABEL>, <MAP>,
> <OBJECT>, <S>, <SAMP>, <SCRIPT>, <SELECT>, <SMALL>, <SPAN>,
> <STRONG>, <STYLE>, <SUB>, <SUP>, <TEXTAREA>, <TT>, <U>, <VAR>

Suggested style/usage: It is important that all of your users have access to the content you have to offer. Make sure that any information contained in an applet is also provided in the <TEXTFLOW> tags.

Examples: See file /h4d3e/examples/ch6/textflow.htm.

<TFOOT> ... </TFOOT> Table footer

Definition: A logical division in a table to header information.

Attributes:

ALIGN=("CENTER" | "LEFT" | "RIGHT" | "JUSTIFY" | "CHAR")

> Use this attribute to specify how text should be aligned left to right within the cells. The CHAR value aligns the text based on a specific character defined in the CHAR attribute. The default alignment is CENTER.

CHAR="text" (single character)

> Identifies the character the text in the cells should align with. The value is case sensitive and the default is a period.

CHAROFF="number" or "n%"

> Defines the offset, in characters or percentage, for the first occurrence of the alignment character specified by CHAR on any given line. This attribute can be used to create indentions in lines or paragraphs.

CLASS="text"

DIR=("ltr | | "rtl")

ID="name"

LANG="name"

STYLE="text"

VALIGN=("TOP" | "MIDDLE" | "BOTTOM" | "BASELINE")

> Use this attribute to specify how text should be aligned vertically within the cells. The TOP, MIDDLE, and BOTTOM values align cell text at the top, middle, and bottom respectively, of the cell. A BASELINE alignment places all of the first lines in the column's cells on a common baseline. The default is MIDDLE>.

Context:

<TFOOT> ... </TFOOT> is legal within the following markup tag:

> <TABLE>

The following markup can be used within <TFOOT> ... </TFOOT>:

<TR>

Suggested style/usage: Use <TFOOT> to differentiate footer information such as titles and bylines. The GROUPS value of the RULES attribute in the <TABLE> tag will put rules around footer information to set it apart.

Examples: See file /h4d3e/examples/ch6/tfoot.htm.

<THEAD> ... </THEAD> Table body

Definition: A logical division in a table to header information.

Attributes:

ALIGN=("CENTER"|"LEFT"|"RIGHT"|"JUSTIFY"|"CHAR")

> Use this attribute to specify how text should be aligned left to right within the cells. The CHAR value aligns the text based on a specific character defined in the CHAR attribute. The default alignment is CENTER.

CHAR="text" (single character)

> Identifies the character the text in the cells should align with. The value is case sensitive and the default is a period.

CHAROFF="number" or "n%"

> Defines the offset, in characters or percentage, for the first occurrence of the alignment character specified by CHAR on any given line. This attribute can be used to create indentions in lines or paragraphs.

CLASS="text"

DIR=("ltr"|"rtl")

ID="name"

LANG="name"

STYLE="text"

VALIGN=("TOP"|"MIDDLE"|"BOTTOM"|"BASELINE")

> Use this attribute to specify how text should be aligned vertically within the cells. The TOP, MIDDLE, and BOTTOM values align cell text at the top, middle, and bottom respectively, of the cell. A BASELINE alignment places all of the first lines in the column's cells on a common baseline. The default is MIDDLE>.

Context:

<THEAD> ... </THEAD> is legal within the following markup tag:

   <TABLE>

The following markup can be used within <THEAD> ... </THEAD>:

   <TR>

Suggested style/usage: Use <TBODY> to differentiate header information such as titles and bylines. The GROUPS value of the RULES attribute in the <TABLE> tag will put rules around header information to set it apart.

Examples: See file /h4d3e/examples/ch6/thead.htm.

<TH> ... </TH> Column head

Definition: Defines a column header information and formats it differently from other table data.

Attributes:

ALIGN=("CENTER" | "LEFT" | "RIGHT" | "JUSTIFY" | "CHAR")

   Use this attribute to specify how text should be aligned left to right within the cells. The CHAR value aligns the text based on a specific character defined in the CHAR attribute. The default alignment is CENTER.

AXES="text"

   A comma separated list of header information that defines the content of an entire set of cells.

AXIS="text"

   Header information that defines the content of the cell.

BGCOLOR=="#rrggbb" or "color"

   Specifies a background color for the cell.

CHAR="text" (single character)

   Identifies the character the text in the cells should align with. The value is case sensitive and the default is a period.

CHAROFF="number" or "n%"

Defines the offset, in characters or percentage, for the first occurrence of the alignment character specified by CHAR on any given line. This attribute can be used to create indentions in lines or paragraphs.

CLASS="text"

COLSPAN="number"

Indicates the number of columns the cell should span. This causes the cell to overlap into adjoining cell spaces.

DIR=("ltr | | "rtl")

ID="name"

LANG="name"

NOWRAP

Forces the text in the cells to not wrap regardless of its length in relation to the cell width. Any remaining text will disappear beyond the cell's border.

ROWSPAN="number"

Indicates the number of rows the cell should span. This causes the cell to overlap into adjoining cell spaces.

STYLE="text"

VALIGN=("TOP" | "MIDDLE" | "BOTTOM" | "BASELINE")

Use this attribute to specify how text should be aligned vertically within the cells. The TOP, MIDDLE, and BOTTOM values align cell text at the top, middle, and bottom respectively, of the cell. A BASELINE alignment places all of the first lines in the column's cells on a common baseline. The default is MIDDLE>.

Context:

<TH> ... </TH> is legal within the following markup tag:

<TR>

The following markup can be used within <TD> ... </TD>:

<A>, <ADDRESS>, <APPLET>, <B>, <BASEFONT>, <BIG>,
<BLOCKQUOTE>, <BR>, <CENTER>, <CITE>, <CODE>, <DFN>, <DIR>,
<DIV>, <DL>, <EM>, <FIELDSET>, <FONT>, <FORM>, <H*>, <HR>, <I>,
<IMG>, <INPUT>, <ISINDEX>, <KBD>, <LABEL>, <LISTING>, <MAP>,
<MENU>, <OBJECT>, <OL>, <P>, <PRE>, <S>, <SAMP>, <SCRIPT>,
<SELECT>, <SMALL>, <SPAN>, <STRONG>, <STYLE>, <SUB>, <SUP>,
<TABLE>, <TEXTAREA>, <TT>, <U>, <UL>, <VAR>, <XMP>

Suggested style/usage: Column header information helps data organization
and information communication. Choose clear and concise headers for all
columns when appropriate.

Examples: See file /h4d3e/examples/ch6/th.htm.

<TITLE> ... </TITLE> Document title

Definition: Encloses the title for an HTML document, which commonly
appears in the title bar in the browser's window. If a title is not supplied, the
default title is the HTML filename.

Attributes:

Common attributes only.

Context:

<TITLE> ... </TITLE> is legal only with <HEAD> ... </HEAD>.

No markup can be used within <TITLE> ... </TITLE> since it does not normally display within an HTML document, but rather on the title bar of the
window in which the document appears.

Suggested style/usage: We strongly recommend that you define a useful title
for each and every HTML document you write. Because many Web crawlers
and other automated search tools use titles to help locate information for
users, an accurate, descriptive title will help them find your content.

Examples: See file /h4d3e/examples/ch6/title.htm.

<TR> ... </TR> Table row

Definition: Defines a table row.

Attributes:

ALIGN=("CENTER"|"LEFT"|"RIGHT"|"JUSTIFY"|"CHAR")

Use this attribute to specify how text should be aligned left to right within the cells. The CHAR value aligns the text based on a specific character defined in the CHAR attribute. The default alignment is CENTER.

CHAR="text" (single character)

Identifies the character the text in the cells should align with. The value is case sensitive and the default is a period.

CHAROFF="number" or "n%"

Defines the offset, in characters or percentage, for the first occurrence of the alignment character specified by CHAR on any given line. This attribute can be used to create indentions in lines or paragraphs.

CLASS="text"

DIR=("ltr | | "rtl")

ID="name"

LANG="name"

STYLE="text"

VALIGN=("TOP"|"MIDDLE"|"BOTTOM"|"BASELINE")

Use this attribute to specify how text should be aligned vertically within the cells. The TOP, MIDDLE, and BOTTOM values align cell text at the top, middle, and bottom respectively, of the cell. A BASELINE alignment places all of the first lines in the column's cells on a common baseline. The default is MIDDLE>.

Context:

<TR> ... </TR> is legal within the following markup tag:

<TBODY>, <TFOOT>, <THEAD>

The following markup can be used within <TD> ... </TD>:

<TD>, <TH>

Suggested style/usage: Without rows, data wouldn't have a place to call home. These are your cell containers.

Examples: See file /h4d3e/examples/ch6/tr.htm.

<TT> ... </TT> Teletype text

Definition: Encloses text to be displayed in a monospaced (teletype) font (typically, some variety of Courier is used in most browsers).

Attributes:

Common attributes only.

Context:

<TT> ... </TT> is legal within the following markup tags:

> <A>, <ADDRESS>, <B>, <BIG>, <BLOCKQUOTE>, <BODY>, <CAPTION>,
> <CENTER>, <CITE>, <CODE>, <DD>, <DFN>, <DIV>, <DT>, <EM>,
> <FIELDSET>, <FONT>, <FORM>, <H*>, <I>, <KBD>, <LABEL>, <LI>,
> <OBJECT>, <P>, <PRE>, <S>, <SAMP>, <SMALL>, <SPAN>, <STRONG>,
> <SUB>, <SUP>, <TD>, <TEXTFLOW>, <TH>, <TT>, <U>, <VAR>

The following markup can be used within <TT> ... </TT>:

> <A>, <ADDRESS>, <B>, <BIG>, <BLOCKQUOTE>, <BODY>, <CAPTION>,
> <CENTER>, <CITE>, <CODE>, <DD>, <DFN>, <DIV>, <DT>, <EM>,
> <FIELDSET>, <FONT>, <FORM>, <H*>, <I>, <KBD>, <LABEL>, <LI>,
> <OBJECT>, <P>, <PRE>, <S>, <SAMP>, <SMALL>, <SPAN>, <STRONG>,
> <SUB>, <SUP>, <TD>, <TEXTFLOW>, <TH>, <TT>, <U>, <VAR>

Suggested style/usage: Use for monospaced text, where character position is important, or when trying to imitate the look of line-printer or typewriter output.

Examples: See file /h4d3e/examples/ch6/tt.htm.

<U> ... </U> Underline text

Definition: Underlines enclosed text.

Attributes:

Common attributes only.

Context:

<U> ... </U> is legal within the following markup tags:

> <A>, <ADDRESS>, <B>, <BIG>, <BLOCKQUOTE>, <BODY>, <CAPTION>,
> <CENTER>, <CITE>, <CODE>, <DD>, <DFN>, <DIV>, <DT>, <EM>,
> <FIELDSET>, <FONT>, <FORM>, <H*>, <I>, <KBD>, <LABEL>, <LI>,
> <OBJECT>, <P>, <PRE>, <S>, <SAMP>, <SMALL>, <SPAN>, <STRONG>,
> <SUB>, <SUP>, <TD>, <TEXTFLOW>, <TH>, <TT>, <U>, <VAR>

The following markup can be used within <U> ... </U>:

> <A>, <APPLET>, <B>, <BASEFONT>, <BIG>, <BR>, <CITE>, <CODE>,
> <DFN>, <EM>, <FONT>, <I>, <IMG>, <INPUT>, <KBD>, <LABEL>, <MAP>,
> <OBJECT>, <S>, <SAMP>, <SCRIPT>, <SELECT>, <SMALL>, <SPAN>,
> <STRONG>, <STYLE>, <SUB>, <SUP>, <TEXTAREA>, <TT>, <U>, <VAR>

Suggested style/usage: Too much underlined text can be difficult to read and may mislead users who are accustomed to identifying underlining with hyper links. Use sparingly.

Examples: See file /h4d3e/examples/ch6/u.htm.

<UL> ... </UL> Unordered list style

Definition: An HTML list style that produces bulleted lists of items.

Attributes:

COMPACT:

> If present, COMPACT instructs the browser to render this list with only a minimal amount of leading between the lines (this reduces the amount of white space, and makes the listing more compact).

TYPE=("DISC"|"SQUARE"|"CIRCLE")

> Defines the type of bullet to be used in the list.

Context:

<UL> ... </UL> is legal within the following markup tags:

> <BLOCKQUOTE>, <BODY>, <CENTER>, <DD>, <DIV>, <FIELDSET>,
> <FORM>, <LI>, <OBJECT>, <TD>, <TH>

The only markup that can be used within <UL> ... </UL> is <LI>.

Suggested style/usage: To create bulleted lists of items where their order is not important, or where sequence does not apply.

Examples: See file /h4d3e/examples/ch6/ul.htm.

<VAR> ... </VAR> Variable text style

Definition: This text control tag pair is used to highlight variable names in HTML text, to indicate to users that they will be supplying this information when they input text at the keyboard.

Attributes:

Common attributes only.

Context:

<VAR> ... </VAR> is legal within the following markup tags:

> <A>, <ADDRESS>, <B>, <BIG>, <BLOCKQUOTE>, <BODY>, <CAPTION>, <CENTER>, <CITE>, <CODE>, <DD>, <DFN>, <DIV>, <DT>, <EM>, <FIELDSET>, <FONT>, <FORM>, <H*>, <I>, <KBD>, <LABEL>, <LI>, <OBJECT>, <P>, <PRE>, <S>, <SAMP>, <SMALL>, <SPAN>, <STRONG>, <SUB>, <SUP>, <TD>, <TEXTFLOW>, <TH>, <TT>, <U>, <VAR>

The following markup can be used within <VAR> ... </VAR>:

> <A>, <APPLET>, <B>, <BASEFONT>, <BIG>, <BR>, <CITE>, <CODE>, <DFN>, <EM>, <FONT>, <I>, <IMG>, <INPUT>, <KBD>, <LABEL>, <MAP>, <OBJECT>, <S>, <SAMP>, <SCRIPT>, <SELECT>, <SMALL>, <SPAN>, <STRONG>, <STYLE>, <SUB>, <SUP>, <TEXTAREA>, <TT>, <U>, <VAR>

Suggested style/usage: Use to indicate a placeholder for a value that the user will supply when entering text at the keyboard.

Examples: See file /h4d3e/examples/ch6/var.htm.

<XMP> ... </XMP> Variable text style

Definition: Renders text in a fixed-width font to indicate an example.

Attributes:

Common attributes only.

Context:

<XMP> ... </XMP> is legal within the following markup tags:

> <BLOCKQUOTE>, <BODY>, <CENTER>, <DD>, <DIV>, <FIELDSET>, <FORM>, <LI>, <OBJECT>, <TD>, <TH>

No additional markup may be used within <XMP>.

Suggested style/usage: Example text is meant to show example text and so no other markup is allowed within it.

Examples: See file /h4d3e/examples/ch6/xmp.htm.

Chapter 7

Introducing the Unrepresentable: HTML Entities

● ●

In This Chapter

▶ Coloring outside the character boundaries

▶ Producing special characters

▶ Inspecting the ISO-Latin-1 character set

● ●

*1*f you've seen the panoply of HTML tags and have gone through examples in Chapter 6 that included strange notations like < or °, maybe these odd locutions aren't as cryptic as they first appear. Hopefully, you now realize they're simply a way to instruct the browser to look up these symbols and replace them with equivalent characters as it renders a document. The symbol < produces the less-than sign (<) on your computer screen, and the symbol ° produces the degree symbol (°).

Entities Don't Have to Be an Alien Concept

Why are these contortions necessary? We know three important reasons why:

✔ To let browsers represent characters that might otherwise be interpreted as markup.

✔ To let browsers represent higher-order ASCII characters (those with codes over 127) without having to fully support higher-order ASCII or non-ASCII character types. Also, these codes support some characters that are even outside the ASCII character set altogether (as is the case with non-Roman alphabet character sets and some widely used diacritical marks).

✔ To increase portability of SGML documents. Entities are placeholders in the SGML document instance and can be rendered on the fly according to a particular site's requirements. An example is the &COMPANY; entity. One subcontractor could define this entity as *ACME Software*, another as *Alternative Solutions*.

Okay, so now you know what character and numeric entities are for — they let browsers display symbols and not interpret them as markup tags. These entities also let browsers represent a larger range of characters than might otherwise be possible while keeping the actual character set as small as possible.

As you travel into the land of HTML character and numeric entities, you encounter strange characters and symbols that you may never use. On the other hand, if your native language isn't English, you can probably find lots of diacritical marks, accents, and other kinds of character modifications that allow you to express yourself much more effectively!

Producing Special Characters

Three characters act as special signals to let the browser know that it should look up a string in a character table instead of just displaying the string on-screen:

- **Ampersand (&):** If a string starts with &, it flags the browser that what follows is a character code instead of an ordinary string.

- **Pound sign (#):** If the next character after a & is a #, this tells the browser that what follows next is a number that corresponds to the character code for a symbol to be produced on-screen. This kind of code is called a *numeric entity*.

  If the next character is anything other than the pound sign, this tells the browser that the string that follows is a symbol's name and must be looked up in a built-in table of equivalent character symbols. This is called a *character entity*.

- **Semicolon (;):** When the browser sees a ;, this signals the end of the string that represents a character code. The browser then uses whatever characters or numbers follow either the ampersand or the pound sign to perform the right kind of lookup operation and display the requested character symbol. If the browser doesn't recognize the information supplied, most browsers display a question mark (?) instead.

A couple of things about character and numeric entities may differ from your expectations based on what you've found out about HTML tags so far and what you may know about computer character sets:

- When reproducing the string of characters for an entity, HTML is case-sensitive. This means that < is different from <, so you need to reproduce character entities exactly as they're stated in Table 7-1.

That's one reason why we prefer using numeric entities — it's harder to make a mistake. The following code sample and browser display (in Figure 7-1) make this point rather nicely:

```
<HEAD>
<TITLE>Checking character codes</TITLE>
</HEAD>
<BODY>
<H2>Copy character entities exactly...or else!</H2>
<P>
<TT>
<!-- semicolon has a numeric code of 59      -->
<!-- space has a numeric code of 32          -->
<!-- ampersand has a character code of &amp; -->
<!-- less-than has a character code of &lt;  -->
Less-than lowercase&#32;:&#32;&amp;lt&#59;&#32; =
&lt;<BR>
Less-than uppercase&#32;:&#32;&amp;LT&#59;&#32; =
&#32;&LT;<BR>
Less-than mixed-case:&#32;&amp;Lt &#59;&#32; =
&#32;&Lt;<BR>
Less-than mixed-rev&#32;:&#32;&amp;lT&#59;&#32; =
&#32;&lT;<BR>
</TT></BODY></HTML>
```

✔ The numeric codes for reproducing characters within HTML do not come from the ASCII collating sequence; they come from the ISO-Latin-1 character set codes, as shown later in this chapter in Table 7-1.

If you concentrate on reproducing characters exactly as they appear in Table 7-1 or copying the numbers that correspond to the ISO-Latin-1 scheme, you can produce exactly the right effects on your readers' screens.

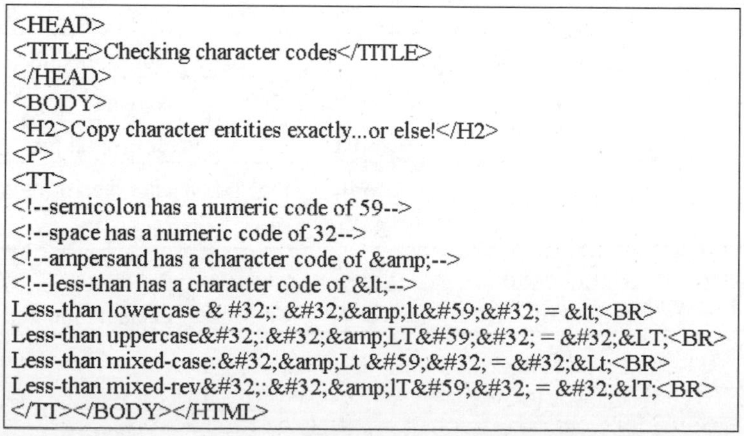

Figure 7-1:
Using and
misusing
character
entities.

```
<HEAD>
<TITLE>Checking character codes</TITLE>
</HEAD>
<BODY>
<H2>Copy character entities exactly...or else!</H2>
<P>
<TT>
<!--semicolon has a numeric code of 59-->
<!--space has a numeric code of 32-->
<!--ampersand has a character code of &amp;-->
<!--less-than has a character code of &lt;-->
Less-than lowercase & #32;: &#32;&amp;lt&#59;&#32; = &lt;<BR>
Less-than uppercase&#32;:&#32;&amp;LT&#59;&#32; = &#32;&LT;<BR>
Less-than mixed-case:&#32;&amp;Lt &#59;&#32; = &#32;&Lt;<BR>
Less-than mixed-rev&#32;:&#32;&amp;lT&#59;&#32; = &#32;&lT;<BR>
</TT></BODY></HTML>
```

Nothing Ancient about the ISO-Latin-1 HTML

The name of the character set that HTML uses is ISO-Latin-1. The *ISO* part means that it's taken from the International Standards Organization's body of official international standards — in fact, all ISO standards have corresponding numeric tags, so ISO-Latin-1 is also known as ISO8859-1. The *Latin* part means that it's derived from the Roman alphabet commonly used worldwide to represent text in many different languages. The number *1* refers to the version number for this standard (in other words, this is the first version of this character set definition).

ISO-Latin-1 distinguishes between two types of entities used to represent characters:

✔ **Character entities:** Strings of characters that represent other characters; for example, < and È show a string of characters (lt and Egrave) that stand for others (< and È).

✔ **Numeric entities:** Strings of numbers that represent characters. These are identified by a pound sign (#) that follows the ampersand. For example, < and È show a string of numbers (60 and 232) that stand for characters (< and È).

Table 7-1 illustrates that there are many more numeric entities than character entities. In fact, every character in the ISO-Latin-1 set has a corresponding numeric entity, but this is not true of the character entities.

Table 7-1	The ISO-Latin-1 Character Set		
Character	*Character Entity*	*Numeric Entity*	*Description*
			Em space - not collapsed
			En space
			Non-breaking space
		&#00; - &#08;	Unused
		&#09;	Horizontal tab
		&#10;	Line feed or new line
		&#11; - &#31;	Unused
		&#32;	Space
!		&#33;	Exclamation mark

Character	Character Entity	Numeric Entity	Description
"	&quot;	&#34;	Quote
#		&#35;	Number sign
$		&#36;	Dollar sign
%		&#37;	Percent sign
&	&amp;	&#38;	Ampersand
'		&#39;	Apostrophe
(		&#40;	Left parenthesis
)		&#41;	Right parenthesis
*		&#42;	Asterisk
+		&#43;	Plus sign
,		&#44;	Comma
-		&#45;	Hyphen
.		&#46;	Period (fullstop)
/		&#47;	Solidus (slash)
0-9		0 - 9	Digits 0-9
:		&#58;	Colon
;		&#59;	Semicolon
<	&lt;	&#60;	Less than
=		&#61;	Equal sign
>	&gt;	&#62;	Greater than
?		&#63;	Question mark
@		&#64;	Commercial at
A-Z		A - Z	Letters A-Z (uppercase)
[		&#91;	Left square bracket
\		&#92;	Reverse solidus (backslash)
]		&#93;	Right square bracket
^		&#94;	Caret
_		&#95;	Underscore
`		&#96;	Grave accent
a-z		a - &#122	Letters a–z (lowercase)

(continued)

Table 7-1 *(continued)*

Character	Character Entity	Numeric Entity	Description
{		&#123;	Left curly brace
|		|	Vertical bar
}		&#125;	Right curly brace
~		&#126;	Tilde
		&#127; -	Unused
¡		&#161;	Inverted exclamation
¢		&#162;	Cent sign
£		&#163;	Pound sterling
¤		&#164;	General currency sign
¥		&#165;	Yen sign
¦		&#166;	Broken vertical bar
§		&#167;	Section sign
¨		&#168;	Umlaut (diaeresis)
©		&#169;	Copyright
ª		&#170;	Feminine ordinal
<<		&#171;	Left angle quote, guillemet left
¬		&#172;	Not sign
-		&#173;	Soft hyphen
®		&#174;	Registered trademark
¯		&#175;	Macron accent
°		&#176;	Degree sign
±		&#177;	Plus or minus
²		&#178;	Superscript two
³		&#179;	Superscript three
´		&#180;	Acute accent
µ		&#181;	Micro sign
¶		&#182;	Paragraph sign
·		&#183;	Middle dot
¸		&#184;	Cedilla
¹		&#185;	Superscript one

Character	Character Entity	Numeric Entity	Description
º		&#186;	Masculine ordinal
>>		&#187;	Right angle quote, guillemet right
¼		&#188;	Fraction one-fourth
½		&#189;	Fraction one-half
¾		&#190;	Fraction three-fourths
¿		&#191;	Inverted question mark
À	&Agrave;	&#192;	Uppercase A, grave accent
Á	&Aacute;	&#193;	Uppercase A, acute accent
Â	&Acirc;	&#194;	Uppercase A, circumflex accent
Ã	&Atilde;	&#195;	Uppercase A, tilde
Ä	&Auml;	&#196;	Uppercase A, diaeresis or umlaut mark
Å	&Aring;	&#197;	Uppercase A, ring
Æ	&AElig;	&#198;	Uppercase AE diphthong (ligature)
Ç	&Ccedil;	&#199;	Uppercase C, cedilla
È	&Egrave;	&#200;	Uppercase E, grave accent
É	&Eacute;	&#201;	Uppercase E, acute accent
Ê	&Ecirc;	&#202;	Uppercase E, circumflex accent
Ë	&Euml;	&#203;	Uppercase E, diaeresis or umlaut mark
Ì	&Igrave;	&#204;	Uppercase I, grave accent
Í	&Iacute;	&#205;	Uppercase I, acute accent
Î	&Icirc;	&#206;	Uppercase I, circumflex accent
Ï	&Iuml;	&#207;	Uppercase I, diaeresis or umlaut mark
Ð	&ETH;	&#208;	Capital Eth, Icelandic
Ñ	&Ntilde;	&#209;	Uppercase N, tilde
Ò	&Ograve;	&#210;	Uppercase O, grave accent

(continued)

Table 7-1 *(continued)*

Character	Character Entity	Numeric Entity	Description
Ó	&Oacute;	&#211;	Uppercase O, acute accent
Ô	&Ocirc;	&#212;	Uppercase O, circumflex accent
Õ	&Otilde;	&#213;	Uppercase O, tilde
Ö	&Ouml;	&#214;	Uppercase O, diaeresis or umlaut mark
×		&#215;	Multiply Sign
Ø	&Oslash;	&#216;	Uppercase O, slash
Ù	&Ugrave;	&#217;	Uppercase U, grave accent
Ú	&Uacute;	&#218;	Uppercase U, acute accent
Û	&Ucirc;	&#219;	Uppercase U, circumflex accent
Ü	&Uuml;	&#220;	Uppercase U, diaeresis or umlaut mark
´Y	&Yacute;	&#221;	Capital Y, acute accent
Þ	&THORN;	&#222;	Capital THORN, Icelandic
ß	&szlig;	&#223;	Lowercase sharp s, German (sz ligature)
à	&agrave;	&#224;	Lowercase a, grave accent
á	&aacute;	&#225;	Lowercase a, acute accent
â	&acirc;	&#226;	Lowercase a, circumflex accent
ã	&atilde;	&#227;	Lowercase a, tilde
ä	&auml;	&#228;	Lowercase a, diaeresis or umlaut mark
å	&aring;	&#229;	Lowercase a, ring
æ	&aelig;	&#230;	Lowercase ae diphthong (ligature)
ç	&ccedil;	&#231;	Lowercase c, cedilla
è	&egrave;	&#232;	Lowercase e, grave accent
é	&eacute;	&#233;	Lowercase e, acute accent
ê	&ecirc;	&#234;	Lowercase e, circumflex accent

Character	Character Entity	Numeric Entity	Description
ë	&euml;	&#235;	Lowercase e, diaeresis or umlaut mark
ì	&igrave;	&#236;	Lowercase i, grave accent
í	&iacute;	&#237;	Lowercase i, acute accent
î	&icirc;	&#238;	Lowercase i, circumflex accent
ï	&iuml;	&#239;	Lowercase i, diaeresis or umlaut mark
eth	&eth;	&#240;	Lowercase eth, Icelandic
ñ	&ntilde;	&#241;	Lowercase n, tilde
ò	&ograve;	&#242;	Lowercase o, grave accent
ó	&oacute;	&#243;	Lowercase o, acute accent
ô	&ocirc;	&#244;	Lowercase o, circumflex accent
õ	&otilde;	&#245;	Lowercase o, tilde
ö	&ouml;	&#246;	Lowercase o, diaeresis or umlaut mark
÷		&#247;	Division sign
ø	&oslash;	&#248;	Lowercase o, slash
ù	&ugrave;	&#249;	Lowercase u, grave accent
ú	&uacute;	&#250;	Lowercase u, acute accent
û	&ucirc;	&#251;	Lowercase u, circumflex accent
ü	&uuml;	&#252;	Lowercase u, diaeresis or umlaut mark
ý	&yacute;	&#253;	Lowercase y, acute accent
þ	&thorn;	&#254;	Lowercase thorn, Icelandic
ÿ	&yuml;	&#255;	Lowercase y, diaeresis or umlaut mark

One thing to note about using this information: If you frequently need to work with character or numeric entities in your documents, it's easier to use some kind of HTML editing tool to handle character replacements automatically. Or, look for a file-oriented search-and-replace utility that you can use as a post-processing step on your files.

For Windows users, point your browser at

```
http://www.shareable.com
```

From there, use the search tool to locate the file fdrepl. This utility works under Windows 3.*x,* 95, and NT.

Part V of this book covers HTML and related tools for a variety of platforms. If you're a serious Web developer or often need to use character codes in your pages, please check out the tools available on your favorite platform. These tools can save you time and effort and make you a happier, more productive Webmaster.

Chapter 8

Stick Out Your Neck!
HTML Extensions

• •

In This Chapter

▶ Understanding what's ineffective

▶ Extending proprietary: Microsoft Internet Explorer extensions

▶ Playing HTML by the rules . . . or not?

• •

*B*y now, you may have seen or written enough HTML to know that it's easy to make the occasional mistake. In case you haven't noticed, most browsers are pretty forgiving about such things. Maybe you thought it was just a case of open-minded software, but it's really part of the way that HTML processing works: The specifications require that any HTML tags that can't be recognized are simply ignored.

Of course, many browsers take that concept even further. Newer ones make all kinds of assumptions about the fallibility of those all-too-human authors who write HTML documents. Among other things, this means that some browsers make educated guesses about where missing closing tags should go — for example, that the closing anchor tag </A> belongs at the end of the next word or line break after the opening <A . . .> anchor tag.

In fact, not all browsers are the same — some recognize markup tags that others don't. In some cases, one browser may track recent additions to an HTML specification more closely than another. In other cases — which you find out more about later in this chapter — a browser may recognize both its standard markup and its own unique "enhancements" to HTML.

If Your Browser Can't See It, Is It Really There?

When it comes to HTML markup, either your browser recognizes it and renders it on-screen, or it doesn't and skips what it considers to be a group of unknown tags. This scenario raises the interesting question at the head of this section. It also helps to explain why some browsers are more popular than others. The bottom line, though, remains the same: If your browser can't recognize various markup elements, it acts like those elements don't exist.

This behavior lets browsers render content in their own way rather than just skipping what's *inside* nonstandard tags. But it does cause some inconsistencies among browsers, so you never know what a page is going to look like until you see it drawn on the screen. These differences among browsers can sometimes be subtle — for example, Netscape puts more white space on pages than Mosaic. In case we haven't said it enough, test your Web pages with as many browsers as possible and always include a character-mode browser in your test.

The State of the HTML Art

HTML is governed by a standard specification for any given version: We discuss these specifications in Chapter 6 as the Document Type Definitions (DTDs) for HTML. At this point, though, you need to understand how the standards-making process works so that you see the perfectly good reasons why browsers differ, even though they claim to support the same HTML standard(s).

A "simple explanation" for browser diversity

The simple explanation for browser differences is that they all track and interpret standards differently. The upshot of working with evolving standards leads to the following assumptions for computer programs like Web browsers:

- ✔ You can usually assume that any new implementation completely replaces the current official (frozen) standard.

- ✔ Developers adopt features and functions already present in developing standards. This is true for a variety of reasons, ranging from personal taste to a firm belief that certain features are more or less guaranteed to be in the "emerging standard" when it finally becomes official.

✔ Some developers even add features and capabilities outside the standard. These additions can range from behaviors that modify parts of an existing standard (like Microsoft's addition of the `BGSOUND` attribute to the `<IMG>` tag) or that add new functionality or controls that were never part of any standard (like frame markup).

The use of evolving standards is a common pattern for software in many industries, from networking protocols (such as the TCP/IP that the Web uses to communicate), to compiler implementations (for standards-governed programming languages like FORTRAN and C). The process can get confusing, but it reflects the living, breathing nature of the state of the art in computer activity.

Vive la différence: adding value . . . or adding confusion?

Some cynics in the room even think that vendors add "enhancements" to standards to try to shape the future direction that standards will take. For their part, most vendors defend such things as ways of "adding value" to a standard and to make their products more attractive to users. In English, this means that they purposely make their browsers different to create unique capabilities that people will pay extra to buy.

It's tough to say whether difference is an attempt to anticipate new standards or to deliberately try to appeal to users. We'd like to sidestep this burning issue and take the opportunity to warn you that standards are like Scripture or the Law — that is, they are subject to interpretation around a core of commonly held beliefs (or an *official standard*) and tend to differ, even though they all start with the same foundation.

What's in Store for HTML?

In general, what's in store for future versions of HTML is

✔ The addition of new markup tags to support sophisticated layout and formatting capabilities.

✔ The obsolescence of simpler, less useful markup.

The only way to check out the state of HTML standards is to go out and look at what's happening. Things are changing fast. You can start with the following URL:

HTML DTDs and terminology

```
http://www.w3.org/pub/WWW/MarkUp/
```

Nonstandard HTML Extensions

The folks at Netscape Communications are the developers of Netscape Navigator, a highly functional, graphically oriented Web browser. Today, Netscape is widely regarded as the most popular browser in use on the Net. Netscape also pioneered the idea of adding their own capabilities to HTML whenever they want to provide otherwise unavailable features or functionality for their browser. These added capabilities are called "extensions." When it comes to such things, Netscape's work has received serious attention.

Although Netscape maintained a large collection of proprietary extensions during the first few years of HTML development, they are now more in line with the current and proposed standards. For the most part, this standards compliance occurred because the standards organizations are moving more quickly now than before in response to the growing demand for multi-functional and standard HTML.

Today, Netscape is no longer the only browser development company that adds capabilities to HTML outside the standards effort; Microsoft also has jumped into the fray with both feet. Not to be outdone by Netscape (or anybody else in the software industry), Microsoft's 32-bit Web browser is called Internet Explorer. Microsoft Internet Explorer has added some useful and inane elements that it supports uniquely.

Added tag attributes

Tag attributes are the names and values that you use to define, specify, or alter the function of a markup tag. In Chapter 6, we tell you that most tags have a handful of attributes that enable authors to customize how they handle and manipulate content. With the recent deployment of the newly proposed HTML DTD (a.k.a. Cougar), most of the elements previously known as extended attributes are now soon to be standards. So we don't have much to talk about in relation to new or nonstandard attributes. In fact, all of the old extensions are now proposed standards (and, therefore, listed in Chapter 6).

But, just because all the previous extensions are now soon-to-be standards, don't think that extensions will cease to exist. *Au contraire, mon frere!* The big boys will continue to push the envelope of HTML by adding new thrills and frills to their browsers. You'll have to keep an eye on the new developments, especially if you plan on creating sites that cater to one brand or another.

The best places to keep watch are

```
http://www.microsoft.com/workshop/author/
http://developer.netscape.com/library/documentation/
```

This concludes our discussion of the innards of HTML. Although the topic is never far away from our minds, in the following chapters we move on to the back-end, server-side of the Web world. We think you'll agree that understanding both sides of the Web equation helps you to build better pages and to take full advantage of the services that the Web can offer. So please read on!

And don't forget to check out the list of nonstandard tags on the CD-ROM in the "Extras" section.

Chapter 9

Using HTML Tables Effectively

● ●

In This Chapter

▶ Gazing over the table landscape

▶ Deciding to table or not to table

▶ Tabling your HTML

▶ Elevating the table tag in proprietary browsers

▶ Polishing your own custom tables

▶ Evaluating some interesting table examples

● ●

*I*n HTML, tables are quite handy for arranging everything from text to images on your Web pages. Most modern browsers support tables. In fact, if a browser does not support tables, take that as a sure sign it's time for that browser to upgrade — it's more than a year old.

Since HTML 3.2, tables have become a fairly standard element in the construction of Web documents. However, Netscape and Microsoft have thrown numerous extensions for tables in the mix. This chapter serves as a general introduction to tables, giving you enough information to use tables on your own. For the really complicated constructions and the extensions not listed in the 3.2 DTD, check out Chapter 2 of our book *MORE HTML For Dummies,* 2nd Edition, (IDG Books Worldwide, Inc.).

Do you really need to use the <TABLE> tag? You can use a list, an image, preformatted text, or a frame instead of a table. Each of these structures has its own good and bad points:

✔ **Lists:** Lists are relatively simple to implement, but they don't give you the formatting capabilities of tables, especially for images.

✔ **Images:** You can make an image in tabular form with borders and colors, but the image then becomes relatively static and difficult to change.

✔ **Preformatted text:** Browsers generally display preformatted text in a nonproportional font that looks terrible.

✔ **Frames:** Frames are complex constructs that may offer an additional dimension instead of a replacement for tables.

The preceding caveats notwithstanding, we believe that tables are great for many uses, such as tabulating financial results, organizing lists of related elements (like dates and birthdays, for instance), and forcing element layouts.

HTML <TABLE> Overview

The <TABLE> tag provides a formatting method that was sorely missing until its introduction. Because you can put almost any other HTML tag into a table cell, the formatting possibilities that tables afford are virtually limitless.

We strongly recommend that you stick with the basic table elements in your tables, unless you're developing documents for a private Web server where you know that your audience is using a particular browser. Sticking to the common denominator (the common table elements) is the best way to ensure the widest audience for your tables. (Because we don't even tell you the nonstandard markup in this chapter, you'll have to go get *MORE HTML For Dummies* to find out what we are talking about anyway.)

If your readership includes members who may be print handicapped or otherwise visually impaired, we strongly recommend you provide an alternative form for your table data. Many browsers that produce Braille or convert text to speech aren't yet able to handle the HTML <TABLE> tag. As a result, many Web sites offer text-only implementations of their tables as an alternative to tabular information. You may want to consider doing the same if such an alternative is appropriate for your audience.

HTML Table Markup

The rest of this chapter shows you the basics and some nifty uses of tables. Be careful to understand the important nesting construction of tables. If you goof up just one nesting order, your information won't display the way you expect it to. A good rule is every time you traverse another level deep into a table, indent the code to offset it from the previous level. Then when you return to a higher level, return to the same indention depth as previous code at the same level. If this doesn't make sense, just keep an eye on our examples in this chapter.

Remember, you can put any HTML body element into the cell of a table. You can even nest multiple tables in a single table cell. And you can use Netscape formatting tags, such as <CENTER>, on an entire table to position the table on your screen. So if you think that some particular formatting might work for your table, give it a try. Your idea may work better than you think, or it may not work at all — the only way to be sure is to experiment!

The parts of a <TABLE>

The basic parts of a table are the `<TABLE>` and `</TABLE>` tags that surround an entire table, the `<TR>` and `</TR>` tags (table row) that define each row of a table, and the `<TD>` and `</TD>` (table data) tags that define each cell of a table. Optional tags include `<CAPTION>` and `</CAPTION>`, which place the contained text above or below your table, and `<TH>` and `</TH>` (table header), which you can use to describe columns and/or rows in your table. The following simple table illustrates all these tags in the most boring way we could imagine. Hey, we can't jump all the way to the jazzy stuff just yet, ya know!

```
<TABLE>
<CAPTION>The default caption placement.</CAPTION>
  <TR>
    <TH> Header: row 1, column 1</TH>
    <TH> Header: row 1, column 2</TH>
  </TR>
  <TR>
    <TD> Cell: row 2, column 1</TD>
    <TD> Cell: row 2, column 2</TD>
  </TR>
</TABLE>
```

If you put the preceding table code in your Web page, you'll have a table, but it won't excite your users much. That's because the table looks like the one depicted in Figure 9-1 when you view it in your browser. Pretty bland, huh?

Figure 9-1:
A basic
`<TABLE>`,
complete
with
`<CAPTION>`
and
headings.

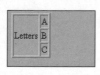

If you can grasp the basic concept of table tag layout and the nesting construction shown in this example, you've already mastered the foundational elements of table building.

See how easy it is to use the table tags to construct a basic table. But now you need to know a little about each of these tags. So in the next sections, we give you the dirt on the tags and their attributes.

<TABLE>...</TABLE>

The <TABLE>...</TABLE> tags provide the container for all other table tags. Browsers ignore the other table tags if they aren't contained inside the <TABLE>...</TABLE> tags. The only attribute of the table tag that the browser widely implements is the BORDER attribute. Netscape also responds to the WIDTH and HEIGHT attributes for the table tag.

The <TABLE> tag accepts the attributes of ALIGN, BORDER, CELLPADDING, CELLSPACING, and WIDTH.

<TR>...</TR>

The table row tags contain the information for all cells within each row of the table. Each set of table row tags represents a single row in the table, regardless of the number of cells in the row. The table row tag can contain both the ALIGN and VALIGN attributes, which if specified, become the default alignments for all cells in the row.

The <TR> tag accepts the attributes of ALIGN and VALIGN.

<TD>...</TD>

Each cell in the table is defined by the table data tags (<TD>...</TD>), which must be nested within table row tags. The following are good tidbits to know about table data tags and how they work:

- ✔ You don't have to worry about making each row contain the same number of cells because short rows are padded with blank cells on the right.
- ✔ A cell can contain any HTML tag normally used within the body of an HTML document.

The <TD> tag accepts the attributes of ALIGN, COLSPAN, HEIGHT, NOWRAP, ROWSPAN, VALIGN, and WIDTH.

<TH>...</TH>

Table header tags (<TH>...</TH>) display text in BOLD with the default of ALIGN="center". Otherwise, they are identical to table data tags — <TD>.

<CAPTION>...</CAPTION>

Place the <CAPTION> tags inside the <TABLE> tags but not inside table rows or cells. Like table cells, any document body HTML can appear in a caption. Captions are horizontally centered with respect to the table, and their lines are wrapped to fit within the width of the table.

The <CAPTION> tag accepts the attributes of ALIGN.

The basic table attributes

You can use several attributes with the table tags. Innovative use of these attributes is the key to making your tables truly outstanding or, at least, visually interesting. Following is a quick overview of these basic attributes; then we show you how to use them.

ALIGN=[top\bottom] / [left\center\right]

When you use the ALIGN attribute with the <CAPTION> tag, specify ALIGN="top" or ALIGN="bottom" to control whether the caption appears above or below the table. The default alignment for the caption is "top."

When you use ALIGN inside of a <TABLE>, <TR>, <TH>, or <TD> tag, ALIGN accepts values of left, center, or right to control the horizontal placement of text within the cells. The default value of ALIGN for these tags is left.

BORDER[=number]

You use the BORDER attribute in the <TABLE> tag to instruct the browser to display borders around the table and all table cells. Space is left for borders around tables so the table width does not change when a border is added. If no number is specified, BORDER defaults to a width of one (1).

CELLPADDING=number

When used within the <TABLE> tag, the CELLPADDING value indicates the amount of space between the border of a cell and the contents of the cell. The default value is one pixel. Setting the cell padding to zero on a table with borders causes the text to touch the border. Padding cells can help you greatly enhance the visual impact of your tables, especially when you couple the padding with cell spacing and border sizing.

CELLSPACING=number

You use the CELLSPACING attribute within the <TABLE> tag to represent the amount of space inserted between individual cells in a table. The default value is two pixels between cells. Couple this with the CELLPADDING attribute and you can really make interesting looking tables.

WIDTH=[number\"percent%"]

You can use the WIDTH attribute inside the <TABLE> tag to set the width of the table as an absolute width in pixels or as a percentage of the browser display area.

When you use the WIDTH attribute in the <TH> or <TD> tag, you set the width of the cell as an absolute width in pixels or as a percentage of the table width.

VALIGN=[top\middle\bottom\baseline]

The VALIGN (vertical alignment) attribute is used inside a <TR>, <TH>, or <TD> tag to control the placement of the cell's contents at the top, middle, or bottom of the cell or to align all elements with a common baseline.

NOWRAP

When you use the NOWRAP in a table cell (<TH> or <TD>), the NOWRAP attribute forces the browser to display all the text for that particular cell on a single line. Using this attribute can cause very wide cells, so be careful.

COLSPAN=number

Use COLSPAN in any table cell (<TH> or <TD>) to specify how many columns of the table the cell should span if you want it to span more than the default of one cell.

ROWSPAN=number

Use ROWSPAN in any table cell (<TH> or <TD>) to specify how many rows of the table the cell should span if you want it to span more than the default of one cell.

Building Your Own Tables

Building tables by hand is time consuming, repetitious work, so be sure that the tabular form will really enhance your content. You can simplify your work, however, by carefully planning the layout of your tabular data and by making use of search, replace, copy, and paste functions in your HTML/text editor.

Laying out tabular data for easy display

First of all, make a sketch of how you want your table to look. Then make a small HTML table with only a few rows of data to test your methodology and to see whether the table appears the way you envisioned it. If you're using multicolumn and multirow spanning heads, you may need to make some adjustments to get them properly spaced to fit your data. Finally, you may want to test your tables with several browsers to see how they look on each browser.

Multirow and multicolumn

Just remember, you must build your tables by rows. If you use ROWSPAN="3" in one table row (<TR>), you must account for the extra two rows in the next two <TR>. The general concept is to leave out the cell in each row or column that will be assumed or spanned into by the ROWSPAN or COLSPAN cell. For example:

```
<TABLE BORDER>
    <TR><TD ROWSPAN=3>Letters</TD><TD>A</TD></TR>
    <TR>                          <TD>B</TD></TR>
    <TR>                          <TD>C</TD></TR>
</TABLE>
```

Mixing graphics and tables makes for interesting pages

Tables are an effective way to present text in a visually pleasing and well-ordered manner so that your readers won't be frightened off by a screen full of dense and impenetrable text. Something about a long, unbroken list of bare numbers quickly drives away all but the truly masochistic. However, putting those numbers into an attractive table, or better yet, several tables interspersed with a few well chosen images, can do wonders for your Web site's attractiveness.

Nesting

Nesting is an important concept in building tables. The method of creating a table relies on nesting one set of tags within another set that is itself nested within yet another set of tags. You can easily get lost and confused when building tables. To keep the confusion down to a minimum, always type in both the opening and closing tags of a tag pair before adding attributes or content. This ensures that you always close your tags.

Another good habit is to code each element of a table on a separate line. Every <TD> tag pair needs to appear on its own line and indented to offset it from the other levels of table markup. Look back at Figure 9-1 to see what we are talking about.

Some Stunning Table Examples

Rather than print out pages and pages of complex table markup from real world Web sites, we've decided to give you a list of sites that make excellent use of tables in their layout and design. After you load these documents into your Web browser, take a look at their source (probably the View Source command from your menu bar). You'll be able to see how complex their markup is (and often how poorly they arrange that markup — but then again, they didn't ask us).

Well, what are you waiting for? Pull up one of these pages:

- C|Net — this entire site uses tables for all the complex layout. Notice how they often use tables within tables within tables.

  ```
  http://www.cnet.com/
  ```

- Yahoo! — the most popular search engine on the Web used tables to display their front page and all of the navigation items on all results pages.

  ```
  http://www.yahoo.com/
  ```

- Holodeck 3 — the quintessential unofficial Star Trek site uses tables to present a fantastic futuristic display of its offerings.

  ```
  http://www.holodeck3.com/
  ```

- Dilbert Zone — the only engineer on the planet to publicly disparage his boss and still keep his job. This daily dose of Dilbert is completely presented by using tables:

  ```
  http://www.unitedmedia.com/comics/dilbert/
  ```

Chapter 10
Building Basic HTML Documents

• •

In This Chapter

▶ Putting it together for the first time

▶ Making templates work for you

▶ Starting page layout at the top

▶ Writing titles and headings with a purpose

▶ Building better bodies for your pages

▶ Building strong paragraphs

▶ Listing with the proper structures

▶ Linking to your Web and beyond

• •

*B*uilding your first Web page is exciting if you keep this thought firmly in mind: You can change anything at any time. Good Web pages are always evolving. Nothing is cast in concrete — change is just a keystroke away.

Now that the pressure is off, you can build your own simple, but complete, home page. Think of it as a prototype for future pages. You can always go back and add a variety of bells and whistles to change your home page into any kind of page you want — be it for a business, an academic institution, or a government agency.

The *layout,* or the way the page looks to the user, creates the first impression of your site. If that first impression isn't pleasing, the first time may also be the last time that the user visits your page. Not to worry, though: Your home page can be pleasing to the eye if you follow the *KISS* (Keep It Simple, Stupid) approach.

The Web itself is a confusing concept to many users. Everything that you do to keep your page intuitively obvious makes your viewers happy and keeps them coming back for more.

Chapter 3 presents the basic concepts of a good Web page. It emphasizes form and content over the HTML controls and presents the elements of page layout and information flow. You may want to check out Chapter 3 before continuing here. If you used Chapter 4 to create a quickie Web page, now is the time to review that Web page and to use what you discover in this chapter to improve it.

The basics are content, layout, first impression, and KISS. Okay, now get on with it.

The Template's the Thing!

Well-constructed Web pages contain the following four sections: title, heading, body, and footer.

If you look at a number of Web pages, you'll undoubtedly see that most contain these sections in one form or another. You may also notice, as your frustration level increases, that Web pages lacking one or more of these elements aren't pleasing to your eye and aren't intuitive in their presentation. Plus, you can't find anything easily. We're not going to let that happen to your pages because you are going to use the following basic template for each HTML document you produce:

```
<HTML>
<HEAD><TITLE>Your Title</TITLE>
</HEAD>
<BODY>
<P>
Your headings and wonderful text and graphics go here.
<P>
<ADDRESS>
Your Name<BR>
Phone number<BR>
Standard Mail Address<BR>
E-Mail Address
</ADDRESS>
<P>
Copyright  &copy; 1998,  Your Name <BR>
Revised -- Revision Date <BR>
URL: <A HREF = "http://this.page's.url.here">
http://this.page's.url.here</A>
</BODY>
</HTML>
```

Getting started on the correct path is really that simple. This template actually works. Figure 10-1 shows what it looks like when viewed with Netscape.

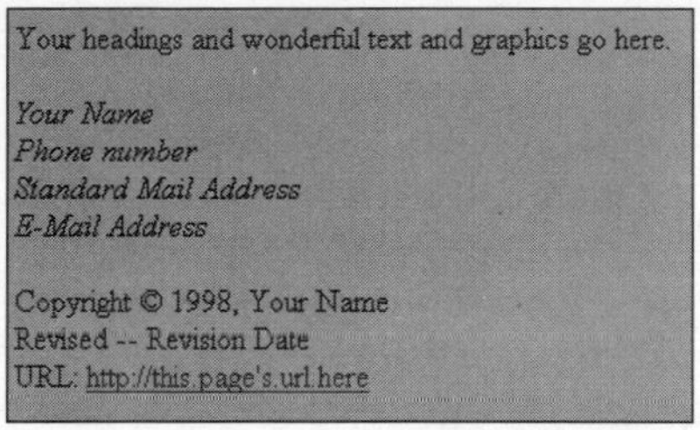

Figure 10-1:
The basic
Web page
template
viewed with
Netscape.

Your headings and wonderful text and graphics go here.

Your Name
Phone number
Standard Mail Address
E-Mail Address

Copyright © 1998, Your Name
Revised -- Revision Date
URL: http://this.page's.url.here

✔ Use your browser to open your Web page HTML document file from your local hard disk.

✔ If you're using Netscape, remember to set the memory and disk caches to zero so that Netscape reloads each new version of your file from the disk, instead of loading the one in its cache. Other browsers cache pages, too, so make sure that you're reading what you just edited — not some older version!

As you can see, your home page is currently plain and simple. That's not going to have folks flocking to see it, is it? That's because you need to add your own wonderful text and graphics. Even though most Internet surfers use GUI browsers, please follow our advice (from Chapter 2) and put your energy into providing high-quality content. Not to worry; in Chapter 11, you get to add some graphics, too.

Page Layout: Top to Bottom

Now that you have a basic template, you can start changing it. To begin the fun, make sure that your first home page doesn't occupy more than a single screen. This screen limit makes the page much easier to edit and test. You can get more than enough information on a single screen and help your audience avoid unnecessary scrolling.

A *single screen* seems like an easy concept, but is it? A single screen is the amount of information that a browser can display on the monitor without scrolling. This amount varies depending upon the readers' browsers and their monitor resolutions. You may decide not to design for the lowest common denominator for both elements, but please understand the following: If you assume that the user can see your page the same way that you see it in *your* browser, you're making a bad assumption. There is no easy answer to this problem, but testing your pages at a relatively low resolution (640 x 480 pixels) with several different browsers can help you see your pages through your readers' eyes. Getting this view is well worth taking the extra time!

Also, you may find it helpful to sketch your design ideas on paper first or to use a drawing program to create a model of your layout and components. (Figure 10-2 shows an example.) This model shows the spatial relationships on the page and the amounts and locations of the ever-important breathing room that page designers call *white space*. Although you can leave too much white space on a page, most designers err in the other direction and wind up with far too little, which causes a page to appear cluttered.

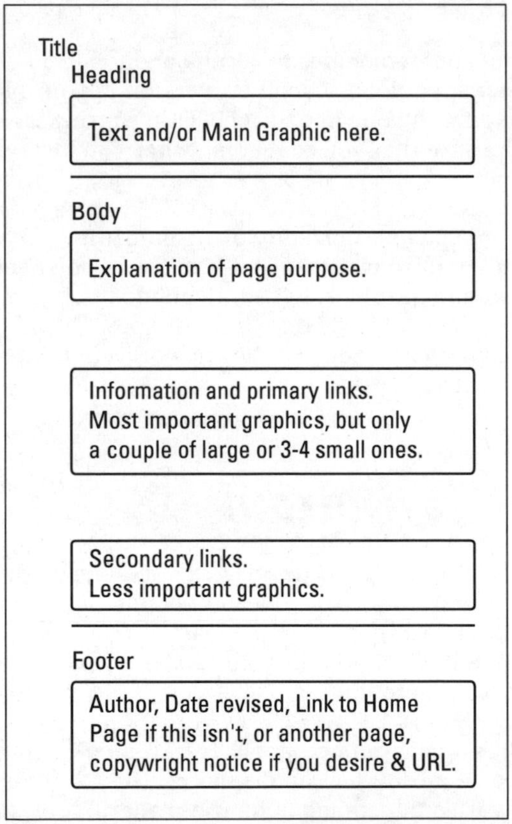

Title
    Heading

> Text and/or Main Graphic here.

    Body

> Explanation of page purpose.

> Information and primary links.
> Most important graphics, but only
> a couple of large or 3-4 small ones.

> Secondary links.
> Less important graphics.

    Footer

> Author, Date revised, Link to Home
> Page if this isn't, or another page,
> copywright notice if you desire & URL.

Figure 10-2:
A sketch of
basic Web
page layout.

You must organize your page logically so that viewers can scan it easily. Because everyone is always in a hurry, put the most important information near the top, in larger type, and with plenty of white space surrounding it. Place the remaining items below as you work your way through the content.

Remember, you're not trying to stuff as much as possible on a single page — you're trying to cover what's important for the topic at hand. If you have lots of material to cover or more topics to deal with, you can easily make more pages and link them to this one. A good rule comes from professional presenters, who say that a single slide should try to convey no more than three to five pieces of related information. We think that the same is true of a single HTML-based screen of information, too!

What's in a Name? Thinking Up Good Titles and Headings

In HTML files, the title provides the most important basis used by the search engines (Yahoo!, Excite, AltaVista, etc.) to index a document. However, after a user enters your Web site, your document's headings provide important visual cues within any page. This happens because the user's browser settings determine the font and page size and also control the line length. If you use appropriate content and layout, you can make the headings on your home page both attractive and informative.

Titles

The title of your page is important. Many Web indexing search engines — the software robots that relentlessly cruise the Web looking for information — use your title to create index records in *their* databases for *your* pages. Also, most browsers use the title in the name field of the *bookmark* or *hotlist* sections, which collect URLs that users want to revisit. That means they'll use your title to figure out what's on your page.

Because you want people to find and read your pages, you need to make titles as descriptive as possible. Try to limit the length of a title so that it fits on a single line. Think of the title as the keywords that describe the contents of your page. Understanding how titles get used can help you build titles that work — we hope you get the idea!

One way to arrive at a truly descriptive title is to type a list of the keywords that best describe your page. Then use them in a sentence. Next, delete the conjunctions, adverbs, and unnecessary adjectives. With a little rearranging, what's left should be a pretty good title.

Here's an example of constructing a title:

- ✔ **Words:** George, classical guitar player, bicycle racing
- ✔ **Sentence:** George is a classical guitarist who races bicycles.
- ✔ **Title:** George's Classical Guitar and Bike Racing Page

This title should fit on one line when viewed by most browsers. Test it with several browsers to see how it looks.

Headings

Discussing headings can get somewhat confusing because each Web page needs to have a heading section after the title and various paragraph headings within the body of the document. In the print world, for example in this book, headings are the emphasized text placed before paragraphs. This section explains the use of paragraph headings.

Headings, along with the title, may be the most important text in your Web page. They are the first text that the viewer scans. If the headings aren't attractive and instantly informative, the viewer may be off to another page with a single click. Well-written headings hook your readers and make them want more.

Concentrate on the content of your headings and the consistency of their meaning and usage throughout your Web pages. Your headings should arise naturally when you analyze your text. They should paraphrase an important concept that you are about to present. If you remove all text from your document (except for the headings), you should be left with a good outline or a detailed table of contents.

If the situation permits, headings may even be humorous. Headings can contain a common theme to help catch the viewer's eye and interest. The best approach to writing headings is to use your imagination and keep your audience in mind. We used this approach with the headings in this book; it is a hallmark of the whole ...*For Dummies* series.

As a quick example, Table 10-1 shows some of the headings from this book in their "plain" and "humorous/theme" forms.

Table 10-1	Headings: Plain versus Extra-Spicy
Plain	*More Interesting*
Building Better Documents	Building Better Document Bodies
Building Good Paragraphs	Good Bones: Building Strong Paragraphs
Logos and Icons	Eye-Catchers: Logos, Icons, and Other Gems

In your Web page, you have only a few headings per screen or page, so make the most of them. Keep the size of like headings consistent throughout your pages to help the viewer understand the level of importance of the information. Although most browsers recognize at least four levels of headings, most well-constructed Web pages use no more than three levels of headings, even for very long documents.

Two schools of thought exist regarding the use of heading sizes. The *information school* says, "Heading tags should be used in increments or decrements of one and always start with <H1>." This approach definitely provides an ordered, standardized structure to your content and makes it easy for Web crawlers to pick out the headings for their indexes.

The *design school* screams, "BORING!" when the information school mentions its incremental approach. Instead, the design school states, "Use headings to draw attention to content. Putting an <H1> next to an <H3> or an <H4> creates more visual interest." As with most HTML design decisions, the choice is yours.

Experiment with heading tags to see what you think looks best. Remember, too much emphasized text diminishes the overall effect. Use it sparingly — emphasis works better when it remains exceptional. If you're a fan of fairy tales, using too many headings is kind of like crying "Wolf!"

Building Better Document Bodies

The body of your HTML document is the core of your Web page. It lies between the header and the footer. Body content depends on the type and amount of information that you want to put online and on what kind of audience you're trying to reach.

Personal Web pages are generally quite different from business, academic, and government ones in the content and form of their bodies, although the layout for each type may be strikingly similar. The bodies of most personal Web pages contain text for, or pointers to, the following elements:

- **Résumé:** Mostly dense text with a picture
- **Personal History:** Mostly plain text
- **Favorite Sports or Hobbies:** Text with an occasional picture and links to sports or hobby sites
- **Favorite Web Sites:** Lists of links to Web sites

The body of a commercial artist's Web pages may contain the following:

- **Pictures, pictures, pictures:** Usually small thumbnail-size pictures that are links to the much larger versions
- **Credentials:** A page containing a résumé, or a list of shows and exhibits, awards, and other professional activities
- **Professional references:** links to online samples of their work on other pages around the Net

The bodies of many government agency pages contain large amounts of text. Unfortunately, many of these documents are simply HTML reproductions of their long, text originals. Some are 100 screens long, or more! Fortunately, some government Webmasters provide a brief description of their text files along with an FTP hyperlink so you can easily download these monsters without having to read them on your screen first.

So, how much text is enough, but not too much, in the body of a Web page? The answer lies in the minds of your viewers. May we suggest, however, that large amounts of scrolling almost always causes them to think, "Too much already!"

Textual sound bites — NOT!

When Web surfers want to read pages and pages of dense text, they buy the book or download the file and print it. For online reading, a large quantity of text isn't much fun, and many users view it as a waste of bandwidth (especially those who dial in with slower connections).

This view doesn't imply that your Web pages should be the textual equivalent of 30-second video bites on TV. It simply indicates that, at the current level of Web development, most users are looking for fast ways to find the information that they want. They aren't going to dig deeply into a sea of text to find it. Your job is to make the good information easily available to your readers by using an appropriate page layout and providing good indexes with hypermedia links within the body of your pages.

Balanced composition

The body on personal Web pages should contain three to five short, well-written paragraphs. If these paragraphs are interspersed with moderately sized headings, enough white space, and small graphics to add visual interest, readers will probably scan them in their entirety.

Good use of separators and numerous links to additional pages are also very much in vogue. Using these techniques should result in a page that's between one and three screens long. Avoid making pages longer than three full screens. Hardly anybody has a 33-inch, high-resolution monitor . . . yet.

Controlling long pages

In general, Web pages composed of more than five screens of text or five screens of URL link lists should be split into multiple pages. If your content insists on being served in long pages, you can greatly increase its readability by linking a table of contents (TOC) to each section and providing a link back to the beginning. This linking structure has an effect similar to splitting the page into multiple page files but still lets your readers capture the entire document as a single file. Also, this structure makes it easier for you to edit the HTML file. You want to balance your convenience against the penalty of moving a single large chunk of data — moving it takes a long time! Just make sure that you aren't overdoing the links.

It looks like we've drifted out of the content stream and into the control stream. The two components tend to blur together when we discuss the layout of long Web page bodies. Nevertheless, content remains your most important concern, but when you have a lot of content, you can make it more approachable with effective use of controls.

The bottom line on bodies

The basic rules for creating great Web page bodies are:

✔ Keep the layout consistent between pages to provide continuity for the reader.

✔ Provide plenty of white space and headings for easy visual scanning.

✔ Write short paragraphs and use them sparingly.

✔ Use meaningful graphics but use them only when absolutely necessary.

✔ Make liberal use of hypertext links to additional pages, instead of making your audience scroll, scroll, scroll.

✔ Vary the placement of the hyperlink words to provide more visual contrast to the page.

✔ Choose meaningful hyperlink words, NOT "Click here."

Good Bones: Building Strong Paragraphs

"Omit needless words," stated William Strunk Jr. He also propounds Rule 17 in *The Elements of Style* (cowritten with E. B. White), which states,

> Vigorous writing is concise. A sentence should contain no unnecessary words, a paragraph no unnecessary sentences, for the same reason that a drawing should have no unnecessary lines and a machine no unnecessary parts. This requires not that the writer make all his sentences short, or that he avoid all detail and treat his subjects only in outline, but that every word tell.

Rule 13 from the same work reads, "Make the paragraph the unit of composition." Combine these two rules and you have the essence of writing clear, accurate prose.

Web users demand the clearest and most concise text you can muster. But alas, not everyone on the Web is an English professor. Many have never heard of (much less, read) *The Elements of Style*. Nevertheless, all Web surfers are readers of some language, so regardless of the language, clarity promotes accurate communication in your writing. To this end, follow these steps to writing better paragraphs:

1. **Create an outline for your information.**

2. **Write one paragraph for each significant point, keeping the sentences short, direct, and to the point.**

3. **Edit your text mercilessly, omitting all needless words and sentences.**

4. **Proofread and spell check.**

5. **Ask a few volunteers to evaluate your work.**

6. **Revise your text and edit it again as you revise it.**

7. **Solicit comments when you publish online.**

Listward Ho: Using a List Structure

Chapter 6 presents the different types of HTML lists. Now we can show you an example of the use of the most commonly used list structure, the unordered list.

The *unordered* or *bulleted* list is handy for emphasizing several short lines of information. The following shows HTML markup for an unordered list (displayed with Netscape in Figure 10-3).

```
<UL>
<LI> This is noticed.
<LI> So is this.
<LI> And so is this.
</UL>
```

Figure 10-3:
An unordered list viewed with Netscape.

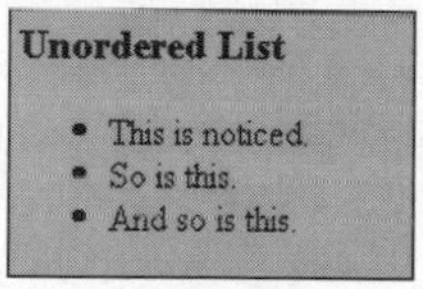

Unordered List

- This is noticed.
- So is this.
- And so is this.

Although you want to keep your page layout simple, lists and even nested lists (to produce outline formatting, as we explain in Chapter 12) can be necessary to optimally display your specific information. However, use lists intelligently and sparingly.

The following HTML document fragment shows the tags for an unordered list in the Web page body. The list serves to emphasize and separate the text lines.

```
You have reached the <I> HTML for Dummies</I> Web Pages,
a charming, and hopefully helpful, addition to the WWW
universe. These pages are designed to aid you in three
key areas:<BR>
<UL>
<LI> To help you find current information on the Web about
            HTML
<LI> To provide working examples and code for all the
Web tricks in the book
<LI> To introduce <I> HTML for Dummies</I> - your
friendliest resource for HTML material offline!
</UL><P>
```

Figure 10-4 shows how this displays in Netscape. The bulleted list definitely emphasizes the body lines and adds to the visual richness of the page.

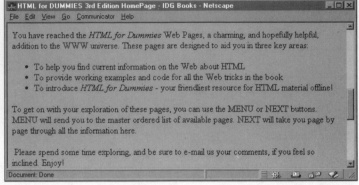

Figure 10-4:
HTML
document
with a
bulleted list
viewed with
Netscape.

Hooking Up: Linking Your Pages

Hypermedia links within the body of your pages bring out the power of the Web. To many users, surfing the Web is the ultimate video game. Following links just to see where they go can be interesting and informative.

As a Web page designer and Web weaver, you obviously want your users to like your pages well enough to tell others, who tell others, and so on. Therefore, you must provide good links both within your own Web pages and to other Internet resources.

Links to pages within your Web are relative

From previous discussions, you may know that links come in two flavors: relative and full. You can use a relative link, such as this one:

```
<A HREF="ftpstuff.htm">Click here to jump straight to
the FTP page!</A>
```

You can use the preceding link within your own Web because the URL referenced is relative to the directory containing the Web page that calls the reference. In this case, the reference is to a file (ftpstuff.htm) in the same directory as the current HTML file (the current URL). The reference is relative to the server's document root plus the path in the file system where the current URL is stored. Got that? Don't worry; you'll understand it better later.

When you create links to HTML documents, you ordinarily use the `.html` extension. Some Web servers require all four characters in the file extension to recognize the `.html` extension in your Web document link. If the page resides on a DOS machine, the server ignores the fourth letter (the `l`). Make sure that you change (to `.html`) the extensions of the `.htm` files that you upload from a DOS or Windows computer to a UNIX server (or make sure it recognizes files that end in `.htm` as valid HTML files).

When you create links to HTML documents, you can use the ".`html`" or the ".`htm`" extension as long as you are consistent. Some platforms, servers, and browsers are forgiving when the "`l`" is left off the extension, but others are not, so be warned. In the past, Web servers required the full four-letter extension for both the filenames and the links that call them. Today, as long as your naming scheme is consistent, you can use either a four- or three-letter extension. But before you take our word for it, ask your Webmaster or system administrator about how your server really works; believe us, they know more about your server than we do!

A bit of advice regarding overuse of links: Use them only when they convey needed information and use each specific link only once per page. Users can get irritable when you make a link out of each occurrence of a commonly used word or phrase on a single page.

Links to the world outside of your Web are physical

A physical or full link, such as

```
<A HREF = " http://www.lanw.com/html4dum/html4dum.htm">
```

gives the entire http URL address. You may use physical URLs for all of your links without any noticeable difference in speed, even on your local server. However, relative links are much shorter to type into your HTML file and may improve your overall productivity.

When including physical URLs for links, we strongly recommend that you link to the resource first and capture the URL using your browser. Then you can paste this URL into your HTML file with little or no chance of introducing a typing error.

Whether it is better to use relative or physical links is a debate for the newsgroups or your local UNIX user's group. You are primarily concerned with the content of the links within your Web, their relationships to each other, and their contribution to your overall Web. Chapter 12 contains more advanced information on using Web links.

Choose your hyperlinks with care

Your home page may have links similar to the one, shown in Figure 10-5, from the *HTML For Dummies* home page. Notice which words in the sentence are included in the hyperlink text (highlighted and/or underlined). You must click on these words to open the link.

Figure 10-5:
Portion of
HTML
document
with a
hyperlink,
viewed with
Netscape.

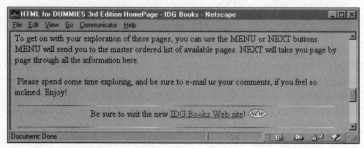

HTML for DUMMIES 3rd Edition HomePage - IDG Books - Netscape

File Edit View Go Communicator Help

To get on with your exploration of these pages, you can use the MENU or NEXT buttons. MENU will send you to the master ordered list of available pages. NEXT will take you page by page through all the information here.

Please spend some time exploring, and be sure to e-mail us your comments, if you feel so inclined. Enjoy!

Be sure to visit the new IDG Books Web site! *(NEW)*

Document: Done

Choose your link text and images carefully. Keep the text short and the graphics small. And never, never, never use the phrase "Click here" by itself as the link text. "Why?" you ask. Because your readers may think that you didn't care enough to write appropriate text with a meaningful word or phrase for the link.

Well-chosen hyperlinks let your users quickly scan hyperlink text and choose links without reading the surrounding nonhighlighted text. The surrounding text is usually included only to provide readers with clarification of the link text anyway. Remember: Users are in a hurry to scan your page and quickly pick out the important links by their unique wording or graphics. Make this task easy for them by using meaningful hyperlinks.

The next chapter goes beyond the Web building that you saw in this chapter. Move "onward, through the fog," to put the finishing touches on your first fantastic home page!

Part III
Advanced HTML

The 5th Wave   By Rich Tennant

IF BOB DYLAN HAD PURSUED A CAREER IN COMPUTERS

"PUT HIM IN FRONT OF A TERMINAL AND HE'S A GENIUS, BUT OTHERWISE THE GUY IS SUCH A BROODING, GLOOMY GUS HE'LL NEVER BREAK INTO MANAGEMENT."

In this part . . .

Part III takes all the elements covered in Part II and puts them together to help you build commercial-grade HTML documents, which includes building complex pages, developing on-screen forms to solicit information and feedback, and creating clickable image maps to let graphics guide your user's on-screen navigation.

Chapter 11

Beyond Basics: Adding Flair and Impact to Your Pages

●●

In This Chapter

▶ Adding logos, icons, and other little gems

▶ Building high-impact graphic pages

▶ Putting your best footer forward

▶ Copyrighting your copy

▶ Including version information

▶ Pointing to the author

▶ Using comments in HTML documents

●●

*E*veryone needs influences and role models when it comes to creation of original content. When you see a Web page with a layout that you especially like, view the page's source to examine the formatting techniques employed. You can use your browser's Save As feature to save the HTML source to your own hard disk for later study, or you can print it.

At the same time, you can add the page to your bookmark file so that you can find it again to look at its images. Most browsers also let you save the images associated with a page to files on your hard disk. However, before you publish somebody else's work on your pages, be aware of copyright laws and always get their permission in writing. (If you're in doubt whether it's okay to reuse something, the safest course of action is, "Don't do it!")

Borrowing Can Lead to Sorrow

Imitation may be the sincerest form of flattery, but stealing other authors' work and including it on your Web pages (as if it were your own) is against the law in most countries. However, learning new techniques from the work of others is the way most Web weavers expand their horizons.

Use the techniques to build your Web pages, with your information, in your own unique manner. You can always e-mail another Web author and request permission to use something of theirs in your page. Many independent Web authors are happy to help you because others helped them in their quest for new Web tools and techniques. Most corporate Web sites are completely copyrighted, and they take a dim view of your using anything from their site without their permission, which they probably won't give you. The Web is increasingly becoming highly commercialized and competitive, so you need to know and respect the legal limitations for others' property.

Eye-Catchers: Logos, Icons, and Other Little Gems

Graphics add impact and interest to your Web pages for users with GUI browsers. Unless the primary focus of your Web pages is computer graphics, use small graphics and only use those where they add extra value to your pages. Again, keep in mind that the only acceptable speed for computer users is instantaneous. The larger the graphic, the slower it loads.

Speaking of small, fast-loading graphics, it's time for you to add some sparkle to your plain-Jane home page. So far, the page has nice-looking headings and simple black bullets next to the list lines (refer back to Figure 10-4). Because the basic layout of the page is well-established, all you need is a few splashes of color in appropriate locations to really spice things up.

Adding an image to your HTML document is as simple as inserting a line using the <IMG> tag:

```
<IMG SRC="graphics/dotred.gif">
```

This line contains the mandatory source reference (URL) to a GIF file named *dotred.gif*. It is a relative reference to the file that the WWW server program expects to find in the same directory as the current page (that is, the page from which the link is called). For example, if the URL that calls for the red dot image is

```
graphics/dotred.gif
```

using the relative URL (as shown) for the red dot would cause the server to look for

```
http://www.lanw.com/html4dum/graphics/dotred.gif
```

Alternatively, you may use the following image tag with the full URL for the red dot:

```
<IMG SRC="http://www.lanw.com/html4dum/graphics/dotred.gif">
```

If you want to link to an image file of a red dot (`dotred.gif`) located in some other Web site, you must use a full URL (sometimes called an absolute URL) in the `<IMG>` tag, like this:

```
<IMG SRC="http://www.someothersite.net/icons/dotred.gif">
```

If you use a full URL as a link, it means that each time the user's browser loads the icon, that browser actually links to the remote location. This increases the time needed for the browser to load the file. If the remote location is not online, the browser can't load the image. Therefore, having your graphic files on your own WWW server usually works better.

An exception to this occurs when you want to include an image from another location that changes over time (weather map, clock, and so on) or a very large image. In the first case, the other site maintains the changing image and your users see it directly from their site, but included in your page. In the second case, you save your server's disk space by pointing to the remote location for the multi-megabyte picture.

The rest of this section discusses several small graphic elements as they are used in the *HTML For Dummies* Web document partially displayed in Figure 11-1. The portion of the document displayed uses five different small graphic elements — a red dot (`dotred.gif`), a rainbow line (`line.gif`), a *new* graphic (`new.gif`) and two buttons (`next.gif` and `menu.gif`). Each of these graphic files is only 1K in size, so they download and display quickly.

Reusing the same graphic on a single Web page doesn't add significant time or disk storage requirements when the user's browser activates caching (storing previously viewed images). Therefore, using the rainbow line and the red dot several times each helps keep load and display times for these images to a minimum. Recycling images makes as much sense for Web pages as it does for the environment!

```
<H1>
Welcome to HTML For Dummies</H1>
You have reached the <I>HTML For Dummies</I> Web Pages,
a charming, and hopefully helpful, addition to the WWW
universe. These pages are designed to aid you in three key
areas: 
<BR>
```

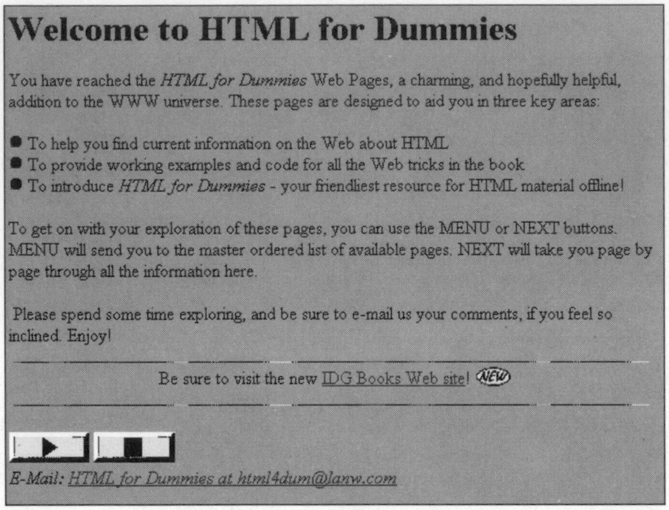

Welcome to HTML for Dummies

You have reached the *HTML for Dummies* Web Pages, a charming, and hopefully helpful, addition to the WWW universe. These pages are designed to aid you in three key areas:

● To help you find current information on the Web about HTML
● To provide working examples and code for all the Web tricks in the book
● To introduce *HTML for Dummies* - your friendliest resource for HTML material offline!

To get on with your exploration of these pages, you can use the MENU or NEXT buttons. MENU will send you to the master ordered list of available pages. NEXT will take you page by page through all the information here.

Please spend some time exploring, and be sure to e-mail us your comments, if you feel so inclined. Enjoy!
_____
Be sure to visit the new IDG Books Web site! *NEW*
_____

E-Mail: *HTML for Dummies at html4dum@lanw.com*

Figure 11-1:
The
Netscape
view of
headers,
links, and
graphics.

```
<BR><IMG SRC="graphics/dotred.gif" HEIGHT=14 WIDTH=14> To
help you find current information on the Web about
          HTML 
<BR><IMG SRC="graphics/dotred.gif" HEIGHT=14 WIDTH=14> To
provide working examples and code for all the Web tricks in
          the book 
<BR><IMG SRC="graphics/dotred.gif" HEIGHT=14 WIDTH=14> To
introduce <I>HTML For Dummies</I> - your friendliest re-
          source for HTML material offline! 
<BR>
<BR>To get on with your exploration of these pages, you can
use the MENU or NEXT buttons. MENU will send you to the
master ordered list of available pages. NEXT
will take you page by page through all the information
          here. 
<BR>
<BR> Please spend some time exploring, and be sure to
e-mail us your comments, if you feel so inclined.
          Enjoy! 
<BR> <IMG SRC="graphics/line.gif" ALT="-==--==--==--==-
          -==-" HEIGHT=1 WIDTH=567> 
<BR><IMG SRC="graphics/space.gif" ALT="_" HEIGHT=1
          WIDTH=130> Be sure to visit the new
<A HREF="http://www.idgbooks.com/">IDG Books Web site</
          A>! <IMG SRC="graphics/new.gif" HEIGHT=17
WIDTH=32 ALIGN=TOP> 
```

```
<BR> <IMG SRC="graphics/line.gif" ALT="-==--==--==--==-
          -==-" HEIGHT=1 WIDTH=567> 
<BR>
<BR><A HREF="contents.htm"><IMG SRC="graphics/next.gif"
ALT="NEXT" BORDER=0 HEIGHT=27 WIDTH=72></A> <A
          HREF="search4d.htm#menu"><IMG SRC="graphics/
menu.gif" ALT="MENU" BORDER=0 HEIGHT=27 WIDTH=72></A> 
<ADDRESS>
E-Mail: <A HREF="mailto:html4dum@lanw.com">HTML For Dummies
at html4dum@lanw.com</A></ADDRESS>
<BR>
```

Horizontal rules — but rainbow lines bring smiles

Separating sections with the rainbow line graphic adds an additional touch of color to our page. We could accomplish this separation with a simple HTML horizontal rule tag <HR>. However, because <HR>'s only display is as a 3-D line (gray, black, and white to give the 3-D effect), you don't get the same visual impact that the brightly colored rainbow line provides. This baby changes from red to violet, blue, green, yellow, orange, and back to red for a much nicer look.

Using the rainbow line to bracket the announcement just above the footer information sets it apart from the surrounding text, thereby drawing the user's attention. When used this way, colored ruler lines are perfect for segmenting your pages into eye-pleasing information blocks. You can make these lines with most "paint" programs in any length, thickness, and color combination imaginable. You can also find many on public access, graphic Web sites where they are available for your use, generally with no strings attached. In fact, feel free to use ours any way you like!

Rather than list any of the more than 7,000 sites with GIFs and JPEGs available for download here, we suggest that you search for "GIF" or "JPEG" on one of the many Web search engines such as

```
http://www.altavista.com
http://www.excite.com
http://www.lycos.com
http://www.webcrawler.com
http://www.yahoo.com
```

Just a couple of thoughts about using colored line images in place of <HR>. It may be quicker and easier to click the HTML editor button that inserts the <HR> into your document than to type the link to the colored line image, especially if you have more than a few of them over many pages. Also, some Web-searching spiders or agents use the <HR> to distinguish breaks in text for their indexes. They won't necessarily recognize the colored line image as a replacement for the <HR> tag.

Colored dots beat list dots

The unordered list structure, used in the previous version of the page to provide black dots (bullets) to the left of the link lines, has been replaced by red dot graphics. These graphics are not just colored dots. They contain highlights and shadows that make them resemble three-dimensional balls. If you want to alternate them in red, white, and blue or some other colors, you can increase their eye-catching effect and differentiate each line from the lines above and below.

One word of caution about replacing lists with colored dots: The HTML 3.2 standard includes the unordered or bulleted list for a reason — that is, to list items in a non-sequential order and set them off by preceding each one with a symbol. The style attribute in the HTML 3.2 DTD lets you set the way you want numbers or bullets to display in your lists. Every browser that adheres to the HTML 3.2 standard should display these bullets in a similar fashion. This can't be said about individual images of colored dots. Thus, if you use your own images to create snappy lists, the standard HTML 3.2 list structure isn't reflected in your document. This may not matter to you though, so try it both ways and see which you like best.

Just as with <HR> versus colored lines, an active spider or agent looking at your page can deduce that an object following an <LI> tag is part of the list it just entered and could organize this information accordingly, but they cannot recognize an imitation list with colored dots. If you're presenting a true list of items, you may want to use the actual HTML list tags. However, if you are more interested in adding some life to your page with colored dots next to some lines, go for it.

Using colored dots and other small icons within lines of text is as simple as inserting the tagged URL in the text at the point where you want it to appear. In the line below, the red dot is created by <IMG SRC="graphics/dotred.gif"> and displayed before To help you. Notice the space between the > and the To. Although browsers generally ignore spaces, Netscape, Internet Explorer, and others may recognize a single space before or after text to help you format sentences properly and keep images from crowding text.

```
<IMG SRC="graphics/dotred.gif"> To help you find current
information on the Web about HTML<BR>
```

Many browsers ignore multiple spaces when they render text, but when you're working in and around HTML tags, careful placement of spaces while writing the code can prevent painstaking reformatting work later on.

Icons

We use the term *icon* here to describe any small graphic image that can be substituted for a unit of text. A few well-designed and carefully located icons can help your users quickly find their way around your Web pages.

Icons stored as GIF files are usually small and load quickly. In most instances, an icon is simply added as a standard image-tagged URL in the position where you want it to appear.

Most icons are so small that you don't need to align text next to them, but for larger images, we discuss alignment later in this chapter. The default for most browsers is to align the text to the bottom of the image.

The *next* and *menu* icons that you can see near the bottom of most of the *HTML For Dummies* Web pages reside in files named `next.gif` and `menu.gif`. These icons let you easily jump to the next page of the site or go directly to the menu page. We added these icons to the HTML document via the lines shown below:

```
<A HREF="contents.htm"><IMG SRC="graphics/next.gif"
ALT="NEXT" BORDER=0 HEIGHT=27 WIDTH=72></A> 

<A HREF="search4d.htm#menu"><IMG SRC="graphics/menu.gif"
ALT="MENU" BORDER=0 HEIGHT=27 WIDTH=72></A> 
```

Logos and graphics as hyperlinks

Logos are special-use graphics. They vary from icon size to much larger, sometimes too large. Remember KISS? Complex logos that take too long to load are nugatory on any Web page.

Use logos to identify your business or institution in a pleasing, eye-catching manner. Don't use them to overpower the page or to irritate the users. A moderately sized logo at the top of the home page is generally acceptable. Using icon-sized logos in the footer of each Web page is equally acceptable. Remember that text-only browsers and GUI browsers with image loading turned off (for faster page loading) won't display your fantastic logos, anyway.

Figures 11-2 and 11-3 illustrate the visual effects of a moderately sized GIF and logo at the top of a page. The *HTML For Dummies* logo file is only 6,000 bytes, so it loads in only a few seconds. Each of the five images (files, contents, search, etc.) below the logo is between 2,000 and 3,000 bytes in size. All of the images are small and therefore fit easily on display screens with resolution as low as 640 x 480 pixels. These figures also illustrate the view with the image loading turned off in Netscape.

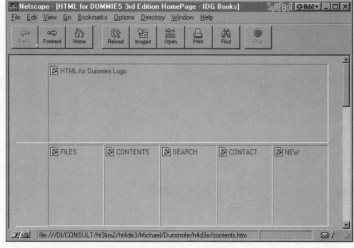

Figure 11-2: HTML document logo viewed with Netscape and image display turned off.

Figure 11-3: HTML document logo viewed with Netscape and images displayed.

The five images under the *HTML For Dummies* Logo at the top of the *HTML For Dummies* home page (shown in Figure 11-3) illustrate the use of graphics as hyperlinks. The following lines from the HTML document that produced the views, shown in Figures 11-2 and 11-3, illustrate how the image icon tag is nested within the link reference tags (between the `<A HREF>` and the `</A>`) to make the icon act as a hyperlink:

```
<A HREF="contents.htm"><IMG SRC="graphics/ht4logoi.gif"
ALT="HTML For Dummies Logo" BORDER=0 HEIGHT=140 WIDTH=500>
</A> <BR>
<IMG SRC-"graphics/space.gif" ALT="" HEIGHT=1 WIDTH=60
         ALIGN=CENTER><A HREF="ftpstuff.htm">
<IMG SRC="graphics/ht4filei.gif" ALT="FILES" BORDER=0
         HEIGHT=145 WIDTH=100></A><A HREF="contents.htm">
<IMG SRC="graphics/ht4conti.gif" ALT="CONTENTS" BORDER=0
         HEIGHT=145 WIDTH=100></A><A HREF="search4d.htm">
<IMG SRC="graphics/ht4seari.gif" ALT="SEARCH" BORDER=0
         HEIGHT=145 WIDTH-100></A><A HREF="contact.htm">
<IMG SRC="graphics/ht4tacti.gif" ALT="CONTACT" BORDER=0
         HEIGHT=145 WIDTH=100></A><A HREF="whatsnew.htm">
<IMG SRC="graphics/ht4newi.gif" ALT="NEW" BORDER=0
         HEIGHT=145 WIDTH=100></A> 
<BR>
```

Notice also the use of the alternate text attribute, `ALT="HTML For Dummies Logo"`, in the first image tag. Text-only browsers display `"HTML For Dummies Logo"` as the hyperlink instead of the icon. Some graphic browsers display an image holder icon and the alternate text when their image display function is turned off, as shown in Figure 11-2.

The creative use of the five (although they look like one) images as the hyperlinks to other pages within the *HTML For Dummies* Web site adds visual interest to the page as well as providing the user with direct links to other parts of the site. If you use a few well-selected icons in this manner, your Web pages stand out and are remembered, in addition to being easier to navigate.

Building Graphic Page Layouts

As you may have gathered, the graphic layout of the Web pages you see in this chapter did not occur by accident. These page layouts were drawn with the best locations for graphics noted. The graphics were carefully chosen and sized to fit the layout and purpose of each page.

As you can see by viewing the *HTML For Dummies* Web site

```
http://www.lanw.com/html4dum/html4du3.htm
```

we added the graphics sparingly to brighten and enhance the visual contrast within the page. Upon first viewing the page, the user sees the *Dummies* logo and five clickable images to different sections of the site. This setup is good because the primary purpose of the page is to focus on the *HTML For Dummies* book.

As the user scans down the page, the rainbow lines, red dots, and highlighted hyperlinks focus the attention on the important parts of the page. The overall layout is conservative yet far more interesting than without the graphics.

The top portion of the page, shown in Figures 11-2 and 11-3, illustrates the additional thought that must go into the design and layout of pages that use larger graphics. The page works well for text-only browsers yet show the much more interesting graphics and logo to users of GUI browsers. If you experiment with the various formatting tags available in HTML and follow the suggestions in this book, you can do the same and much more on your Web pages.

Working with graphics files

You must work with graphics on two distinct levels to arrive at a good page layout and optimum functionality. You must first consider the graphics' size on the screen and complexity for your document layout. Second, you must consider the size of the image files (in bytes) and length of time required to download them.

The original logo file in Figure 11-3 was 1MB and covered the entire screen. Careful cropping, resizing, and resampling (using fewer pixels per inch) resulted in the current file size of only 6,000 bytes. These changes resulted in a dramatic improvement in load time — it's not unusual for a megabyte of data to require minutes to load over a slow link, but a 6,000-byte file moves in seconds, even over slow telephone lines.

You don't have to become an expert at using the old standby graphics manipulation programs such as Paint Shop Pro, Photo Styler, Graphics WorkShop, Wingif, LView Pro, or some of the newer programs that seem to pop up weekly on the Web to produce high-quality images for your Web pages. However, if you are going to do a lot of work with images, you probably want to become fairly adept at one of these shareware programs or a commercial equivalent.

Search for GIF EDITOR on your favorite search engine and you can find links to many useful sites.

GIF and JPEG file formats

Although you can use many different types of graphic files on the Web, virtually all GUI browsers have internal display capabilities for GIF and JPEG formats. Browsers use external helper applications to display the other file types. Also, compressed GIF and JPEG files are the smallest and therefore the fastest to load of all the commonly used file types.

Most good shareware image manipulation programs, such as those mentioned above, can load and save both GIF and JPEG format files. These programs also support the GIF87a and transparent and/or interlaced GIF89a formats. If you're using a Macintosh, the program to use for interlaced GIFs is *GifConverter*.

Whenever you build GIF89a graphics, be sure to test any interlaced graphics on multiple browsers. Some color depths lend themselves better to interlacing (and transparency, too, for that matter) than others. Unfortunately, this seems to be a trial-and-error process and not an exact science; that's why testing your images across multiple browsers on multiple platforms is a must!

Seeing through the graphic to the background

The GIF89 format also introduced the *transparent background* feature. This feature turns off one of the colors of the image — when displayed by a browser — allowing whatever is behind the image to show through at every point where the color is "turned off" or transparent. Usually, this is the background color, but images can be laid over other images or text as well. To the user, your image then appears to float on the browser's background, rather than a square of some other color surrounding the image.

Programs such as *giftrans* for UNIX and DOS and *Transparency* for the Macintosh create images with transparent backgrounds for browsers that support the GIF89 format. For Windows users, *LView for Windows* is also worth checking out in this capacity. This capability really adds to the impact and drama on a Web page.

Slice up your graphics for better response time!

"What is an *interlaced GIF*?" you ask. Well, an interlaced GIF is a method of storing the GIF file so that the browser can load a low-resolution image on the first of multiple passes and then fill in to the normal resolution on the subsequent passes. This method gives the image a "Venetian blind" look as it is drawn.

The total load time for a given image remains the same, but some browsers, such as Netscape, load the text of the page with the first pass of the images. This lets the user begin scrolling and reading while the other three image passes are completed. Therefore, the user gets to your information much faster, which generally results in a happier user.

A new pic's resolution . . .

One last technical aspect of dealing with images involves the number of bits per pixel stored in the file. Although reducing the bits per pixel reduces the resolution (and, therefore, the quality) of the image as seen by the browser, try storing your image with 7 or even 5 bits per pixel if you really need to show a large image as quickly as possible. Alternatively, you can reduce the number of colors in the picture to lower its overall image size. Check your graphics program for more information on either of these techniques.

A standard GIF image requires 8 bits per pixel, which results in 256 colors. Seven bits of information per pixel produces 128 colors, 5 bits 32 colors, etc. Some programs, such as *Paint Shop Pro* (shareware) and *Photoshop* (commercial) even allow a specific number of colors to be set. For example, setting the number of colors to 43 results in 7 bits per pixel, but the remaining 85 empty color definitions are set at 0,0,0 (or undefined), which results in a smaller (and faster) graphic than one set to 7 bits per pixel alone. Most of these programs also tell you how many unique colors appear in an image and let you manipulate the number of colors until you can achieve the best compromise between size and fidelity.

Rules for graphical thumbs

Keep these rules in mind while you design your Web pages:

✓ Sketch your layout with and without the graphics.

✓ Focus on overall page look and content.

- ✔ KISS your images . . . small and simple.

- ✔ Use compressed interlaced GIFs or JPEGs.

- ✔ Link a thumbnail version of an image to the larger file instead of dumping a megabyte-sized file on your unsuspecting users.

- ✔ Include the size of the image file in the text that describes large images.

- ✔ Use graphics sparingly for maximum effect.

- ✔ Images or graphics should enhance the text information.

Footers Complete Your Page

The *Yale C/AIM Web Style Guide* (http://info.med.yale.edu/caim/manual/index.html) provides a concise statement about the use of footers on your Web pages:

> Page footers should always carry basic information about the origin and age of the page. Every Web page needs to bear this basic information, but this repetitive and prosaic information often does not deserve the prominence of being placed at the top of the page.

Unlike the HTML header and body, the footer is not a marked element of an HTML document. By convention, the footer is the bottom portion of the page body.

Footers contribute greatly to your Web pages by providing the authorship, contact information, legal status, version/revision information, and a link to your home page. The footer should contain some or all elements listed here:

- ✔ Author's name

- ✔ Author's institution or company

- ✔ Author's phone number

- ✔ Author's e-mail address

- ✔ Author's postal mailing address

- ✔ Page owner's name

- ✔ Page owner's phone number

- ✔ Page owner's e-mail address

- ✔ Page owner's postal mailing address

- ✔ Legal disclaimer or language designating the page as the official communication of the company or institution
- ✔ Date of page's last revision
- ✔ Official company or institutional seal, logo, or other graphic mark
- ✔ Copyright notice
- ✔ URL of the page
- ✔ Hypertext link(s) to home page or to other pages
- ✔ Hypertext link(s) to other sections of this page

Your basic home page HTML document already contains the minimum suggested footer information for a home page:

```
<ADDRESS>
Your Name<BR>
Phone number<BR>
Standard Mail Address<BR>
E-Mail Address
</ADDRESS><P>
Copyright  &copy; 1998,  Your Name <BR>
Revised -- Revision Date <BR>
URL: <A HREF = "http://this.page's.url.here">
http://this.page's.url.here</A>
```

Even though it is a home page, it contains a link to itself in the URL line. All other local pages in your Web must also contain a link in the footer to your full home page URL, like the example just shown. Why? If a user saves your page as an HTML file and later wants to know its address, there it is on the bottom of the page — both visible and as a link. Nifty, huh? Don't you wish everyone did this?

The name of your home page file depends on your WWW server's requirements. Some servers require a specific name and extension, such as index.html where the extension includes all four letters: html. It's a UNIX thing. Don't worry though; it's easy to do. Check with your ISP to determine the requirements of the WWW server that will house your Web site. Most likely, one of these formats will work:

```
<A HREF="http://www.servername.net/yourdirectory">
<!-- least desirable -->
<A HREF="http://www.servername.net/yourdirectory /">
<!-- better -->
<A HREF="http://www.servername.net/yourdirectory
 /index.html"> <!-- most desirable -->
```

Government agencies and other public institutions frequently want to put what seems like their entire staff directory and departmental history in their footers. At least they're at the bottom of the page. However, if you are going to have a long footer, place a link back to the home page above it so the user doesn't have to scroll as far to find it.

Figure 11-4 illustrates a well-balanced footer for a business-style home page, from the *HTML For Dummies* home page, of course. This footer contains all important footer elements in a visually pleasing layout. Notice that this footer doesn't contain a phone number or snail-mail address, but you may not want folks calling you or writing letters to you at home either. Anyway, on the Net — e-mail rules!

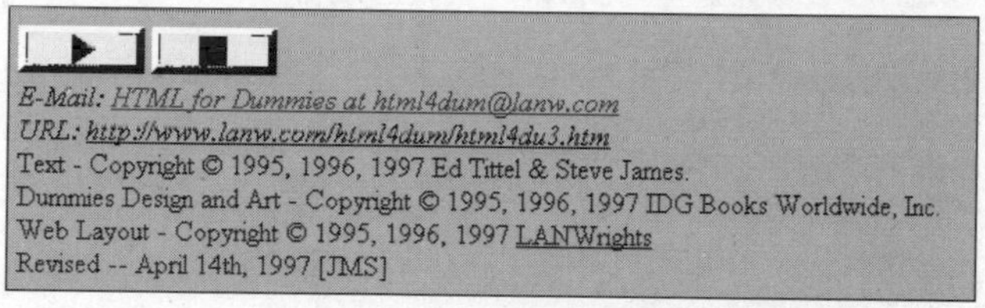

Figure 11-4:
Footer of
the *HTML*
For
Dummies
home page
viewed with
Netscape.

E-Mail: *HTML for Dummies at html4dum@lanw.com*
URL: *http://www.lanw.com/html4dum/html4du3.htm*
Text - Copyright © 1995, 1996, 1997 Ed Tittel & Steve James.
Dummies Design and Art - Copyright © 1995, 1996, 1997 IDG Books Worldwide, Inc.
Web Layout - Copyright © 1995, 1996, 1997 LANWrights
Revised -- April 14th, 1997 [JMS]

Use a URL line as part of your page

Notice that the URL is visible in the footer. It's a good idea to put the URL for each page in the footer in small type. This helps viewers who print your page, but don't add it to their browser's hotlist, find it again on the Web. And adding the URL is a nice finishing touch that tells users that you really do care about them.

Instead of placing all the footer information directly in each page, you may want to put some of it in a page of its own and include a link to that information in the footer instead. This works especially well if your information requires a long legal disclaimer or other complex language. Please check with your legal representative concerning the fine points of using disclaimers on the Web.

Copyright

Copyright law hasn't quite caught up with the explosion in electronic publishing on the Web. However, it won't hurt you or your organization to put your copyright notice at the bottom of any Web page that you don't want freely copied without being attributed to you or without your permission.

The copyright notice shown in Figure 11-4 is simply standard text except for the copyright symbol. Most browsers can display the copyright symbol © if you use the character entity © in the file. Otherwise, you can simulate it with (C) or (c) if your lawyer approves.

Counting coup: versions, dates, and times

Why should you even bother to note when you change your pages? One of the greatest values of publishing on the Web is your ability to change your pages quickly as your content changes. Not only do your users need to know when this occurs, you also need to know which version you're providing so that you can be certain to change old stuff when newer versions are ready.

If it's appropriate to your information, you may want to use version numbers in addition to a revision date. This allows you to refer to a particular page as version 12B, for example, rather than the second revision from December. It's less ambiguous, more direct, and shorter, too!

Placing the revision date in the footer of each page keeps track of its chronology. The format for the date should be January 02, 1998, to avoid confusion. In the USA, this date would be abbreviated 01/02/98. In Europe, this abbreviation would be read as the 2nd of January, 1998. The international ISO 8601 standard date notation is YYYY-MM-DD (year, month, day), which would result in 1998-01-02. Use that format for dates if you want to be globally correct.

If for some reason you don't want to show the revision date on the page, you'll be much happier in the long run if you use the HTML comment tags and hide the revision date inside them.

The time may be added to the date for sensitive information. Because users from all over the world can view your information at any time, 24-hour, UTC (Universal Time, which used to be called GMT — Greenwich Mean Time) is the most appropriate format. The proper format is hh:mm:ss (hour:minute:second). Make sure that you note the time as UTC (that is, 18:30:00 UTC or 18:30:00Z for 6:30 PM). The *Z* stands for *Zulu* in the NATO radio alphabet and refers to the Zulu or Zero meridian of longitude where UTC is measured. Now aren't you so happy to know that little tidbit of information for the next time you're on *Jeopardy?*

Pointers to the Author or Owner

You can choose between an e-mail link or a form as your method for obtaining feedback. Your choice may depend upon which of these options your Web service provider makes available to you. Of the two, e-mail is the simplest and most generally used for personal home pages. Businesses tend to use custom forms in their attempts to obtain more specific information about their users (and to try to turn them into paying customers). We detail the use of forms on your site in Chapter 15.

The e-mail link for feedback

The `mailto:` link is a special link that starts an e-mail program on some servers that lets the user send e-mail to the page owner. Every well-constructed home page has some way for the user to give feedback to the developer or owner of the page. The most general approach is to provide your e-mail address in text inside the HTML `<ADDRESS> . . . </ADDRESS>` tags. Although it isn't supported by all Web server software or even all browsers, the `mailto:` link is another frequently used method. If you want to use it despite its less-than-universal availability, here's how:

```
E-Mail: <A HREF="mailto:html4dum@lanw.com"> HTML For
Dummies at html4dum@lanw.com</A>
```

In this example, the actual hyperlink is `mailto:html4dum@lanw.com` and the second instance of the e-mail address in `HTML For Dummies at html4dum@lanw.com` has been added so that something is highlighted on the page and for readers who can't use the `mailto:` URL. You can customize the wording to your heart's content, outside the actual address portion (`<A HREF = "mailto:html4dum@lanw.com">.</A>`). You can also put text in front of it as shown by the `E-mail:` in the example taken from our own *HTML For Dummies* Web pages. (The preceding e-mail lines are displayed in the *HTML For Dummies* page footer in Figure 11-4.)

Comment Your HTML Documents for Posterity

Do yourself a big favor and annotate your HTML documents liberally with comments. You will thank yourself many times over in the future if you add comments that explain links or lists more fully or state when information needs to be updated.

Comment lines are formatted like this:

```
<!-- comment text -->
```

The comment line starts with <!-- and ends with -->. Most newer browsers ignore the comments inside the HTML document. As a general rule, place comments on a line separate from other HTML text. This way you won't interrupt your HTML text because browsers also ignore white space between HTML tags. To be on the safe side, don't use any special characters (<, >, &, !) within comments, either.

If you've made it this far, congratulations; you are no longer a complete HTML ignoramus. You've already discovered enough to design and create well-balanced, attractive, user-friendly Web pages. You're on a roll, so keep right on going to find out even more fun things to add to your Web pages.

Chapter 12

Going High-Rise: Building Complex Pages

• •

In This Chapter

▶ Expanding your home page into a Web

▶ Moving around inside your documents and local Web

▶ Jumping to remote sites

▶ Framing and tabling for impact

▶ Analyzing sophisticated Web pages

• •

*Y*ou're probably not satisfied with your nice, but simple, single-screen home page. Because of all the wonderful stuff you've seen out there in the Web, you really want to make a Web of pages with all sorts of great material in them, right? That's pretty natural, and it doesn't compromise the KISS principle either. After all, simple is a relative term.

You may recall that we suggested that you'd want to make more pages as you expanded your Web. But the more pages you add, the more difficulty your users will have in finding their way around. While you're growing your Web, your most important job is to make your users' journey through it as enjoyable as possible. In fact, you've already discovered the necessary methods and techniques in previous chapters. Now it's time to put them to use.

This chapter covers important aspects of creating complex Webs. After this discussion, we comment on the elements and layout of a few advanced Web sites.

There's No Place Like Home

Home isn't only your home page; it's your own Web, the local constellation of planets orbiting your home page. It's your local turf in cyberspace, where

Web surfers can find the information that you think is important. But even if your site is fantastic and beautiful, users can be put off if they have trouble navigating your Web site. That's why you need a clear mental picture of its fully developed organization *before* you start expanding things.

Organization

If you listen closely to your content, it can tell you the organizational style that it needs — or rather, demands. Hierarchical style, linear style, and interlinked combinations of these two styles are the standard organizational structures used in most Webs. These Web structures are illustrated in Figures 12-1, 12-2, and 12-3.

It's straightforward to "Web-ify" a linear document, but the converse is not true: Organizing a random collection of ideas and concepts into a linear document is very difficult. When designing and using links within or among Web documents, you need to be clear about the organization and interconnectedness of their content.

The hierarchical, or tree, structure is used as the basis of most Web designs (see Figure 12-1). It's logical and has a familiar look to most computer users (hints: hard disk file trees and GUI help systems). This kind of organization is easy for users to navigate, especially when you include links back to the home page on each page.

Figure 12-1:
The
hierarchical
structure
looks like a
family tree.

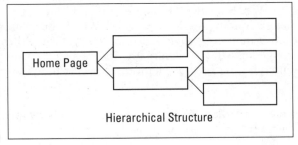

Home Page

Hierarchical Structure

When using a hierarchy, your information should progress from the most general (root) level, or a table of contents on your home page, to the most detailed content in the outermost leaves. Your content dictates the divisions in the tree, but you can include interesting links between seemingly unrelated branches to better inform your users. Also, try providing multiple links to individual pages. In this way, the structure includes aspects of the index of a book, as well as its table of contents.

Keep in mind that readers can enter your Web space from somewhere other than your home page, so make sure that you give navigational clues to *jumped-in* users. You want them to easily find your home page or other relevant pages. It's frustrating to land on a page whose URL you obtained by e-mail from some cohort who says, "Check out this page," only to be forced to blunder around because you can't tell where home is! Preventing your users from experiencing this frustration is an excellent reason to provide navigational clues at the top and bottom of each Web page that you create. For an example of good style (even if we do say so ourselves), check out this URL:

```
http://www.lanw.com/html4dum/
```

Simple, book-like, but also *rigid and confining* are common descriptions of the linear structure (see Figure 12-2). If your information presents a series of steps or follows a process from start to finish, linear structure is a fitting choice for your document organization. A linear structure keeps users on-track and out of trouble. Here, you can make good use of links to "next page," "previous page," and "top or start page."

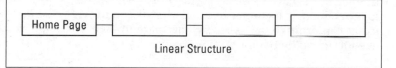

Figure 12-2: Linear structure.

Be sure to put links to your home page (or the starting point) on each page in a linear structure. Without such links, users that drop into the middle of your Web have only the browser's controls to get out. If you trap them this way, they'll talk about you and your Web on the Net — and the talk won't be flattering!

The WWW itself is a Web structure (see Figure 12-3). It's a great example of the fantastic freedom of movement and free-flowing design that are implicit in this kind of loosely linked environment. Providing structure without constraining users' freedom to explore your space is the goal of any well-designed Web structure.

If your information on related subjects is extensive, put hyperlinks within the text to specific paragraphs in other pages where the user can see more detailed information about the content. Be careful how you do this, though. Too much linkage can be just as detrimental as not enough! Hypertext linking is the most time-consuming part of HTML document development. Do it well, and your users will love you forever. We discuss this issue in more detail later in this chapter.

```
┌──────────────────────────────────────────┐
│                    ┌──────────────────┐   │
│                    │ Who are you      │   │
│                    └──────────────────┘   │
│                    ┌──────────────────┐   │
│                    │ What you do      │   │
│                    └──────────────────┘   │
│                    ┌──────────────────┐   │
│                    │ Personal history │   │
│                    └──────────────────┘   │
│   ┌───────────┐    ┌──────────────────┐   │
│   │ Home Page │────│ Your family      │   │
│   └───────────┘    └──────────────────┘   │
│                    ┌──────────────────┐   │
│                    │ Hobbies          │   │
│                    └──────────────────┘   │
│                    ┌──────────────────┐   │
│                    │ Sports           │   │
│                    └──────────────────┘   │
│                    ┌──────────────────────┐│
│                    │ WWW land (jump list) ││
│                    └──────────────────────┘│
│        Web Structure                       │
└──────────────────────────────────────────┘
```

Figure 12-3:
Web
structure.

When you build a complex Web structure, always, always, always put a link to your home page on each page. It's also a great idea to reproduce the URL for each page in its footer in small type. If you provide this information, users can return to any specific page in your Web by using that URL later on, even if they didn't add it to their bookmark lists.

It's story (board) time, boys and girls!

If you made a sketch of your home page along with Chapter 10, then it's time for you to find your pencil and paper again. For this exercise, you get to draw your Web structure. For a personal Web, pencil and paper will probably do nicely.

First Things First: List 'em Out

Make a list of the major pieces of information that you want to include in your Web. These major points will probably be the links on your home page and may be similar to the following:

- Who you are
- What you do

- ✔ Personal history
- ✔ Your family
- ✔ Hobbies
- ✔ Sports
- ✔ WWW land (jump list)

Sketch the Web

In the preceding example, there are relatively few topics to consider, so a combination Web/hierarchical structure looks appropriate. This structure should look familiar, because it's probably similar to the way your directory structure is organized.

By using this sketch to analyze your home page, you can see some links that aren't readily apparent from looking at the HTML document. These links exist between the "Who you are" page and the "What you do," "Personal history," and "Sports" pages as well as between the "Your family" and the "Hobbies" and "Sports" pages. Of course, you need to link all these secondary pages directly to the "Home Page."

Board the whole story

This simple sketch doesn't provide enough information for you to fully visualize your Web. What you really need to do now is to prepare a storyboard for these pages — that is, unless you can mentally picture the elements and links on each of the eight separate pages.

Every movie, TV show, and comic book gets storyboarded before any production takes place. Producing a set of Web pages is a lot like making a TV show, especially if you think of each Web page as a separate scene. Over time, an entire collection of Web documents and associated materials will evolve from your work, making it resemble a whole season's worth of TV episodes instead of a single show.

To prepare a storyboard, simply prepare a sketch of the layout of each Web page with the URLs for links written on each one. For small Webs, some Web authors use a white marker board with colored pens. The colors are handy for showing different types of links, forms, or other HTML elements.

For more complex Webs, many authors use a sheet of paper for each Web page, some string, some push pins, and a large bulletin board (cork type, not BBS). This method allows complex arrangements that can be changed easily.

Also, the storyboard method is invaluable for identifying potential hypertext links, if you attach the text of each Web page to its layout sheet. Whenever you're creating a Web of more than a handful of pages, create a storyboard. Doing this saves you much more time than it takes initially, and after you're finished, you'll appreciate its value.

Anchors Away: Jumping Around Your Documents

We did say that it wasn't too terrible to create Web pages spanning up to three screens, if your information demands the extra room and if you put the most important information on the first screen. You may even expand your home page to more than one screen if you carefully drop your anchors and don't go overboard on the images.

You can use two different anchor tag attributes for movement within your pages. To provide viewers with links to specific parts within a Web page (called intradocument linking), use the `NAME="text"` anchor to provide the destination of an `HREF="#label"` tag. Use the standard `HREF="URL"` (called interdocument linking) to let users jump from page to page. Or to jump to a specific location within another page, you can combine both approaches and use `HREF="URL#label"`.

When following links inside a browser program, you must note an important distinction between interdocument linking and intradocument linking. With interdocument linking (between documents), most browsers land the reader at the first line of the target document. On the other hand, intradocument linking (within the same document) takes you to a place other than the default top of the page, unless there's a named anchor at the top of the page and the URL calls this anchor out.

Here's another interesting quirk about browsers — namely, their behavior with named anchors that occur near the bottom of a document. If an anchor appears near the bottom, most browsers do NOT bring the named anchor to the first line on the screen. This is because the browser usually renders a full screen of text; thus, if the anchor is near the bottom of a document, the link may take you to a point toward the bottom of the screen, rather than the absolute bottom of the document itself.

Linking to text in another page

The *HTML For Dummies* home page provides a good example of how you should use the `NAME="text"` attribute in an anchor tag. The HTML line in the home page document

```
<A HREF="search4d.htm#menu"><IMG SRC="graphics/menu.gif"
ALT="MENU" BORDER=0 HEIGHT=27 WIDTH=72></A>
```

specifies a hypertext relationship between the `menu.gif` graphic (the yellow button with the blue square inside) in the current document and the named anchor `menu` in the target document that is in the `search4d.htm` file. The pound sign (#) indicates that the browser should position the reader not at the top of the page, but at the named anchor in the target document — `menu` in this case. If the anchor isn't found, you get the default instead, which is the top of the document.

The browser displays the information at that location in the file, starting with the heading, "Menu and Order of Pages." This may seem unduly abstract, but you'll catch on if you remember this: The anchor with the `NAME="text"` attribute is the destination for some link. As the author, you have control over how your information is displayed. If you think users will find a nugget of information within a specific page relevant and important, then give it a name with the `NAME` attribute and create a link to it.

Linking to text within a page: table of contents links

You can use the `NAME="text"` attribute to create a really jumping table of contents (TOC) for long text documents. Providing a linked TOC takes a little more time, but it's a great way to impress your users (see Figure 12-4). Remember to provide a link back to the TOC after each block of text in the destination document.

The following HTML code illustrates how to use the TOC links within a large document:

```
<!-- Make this an anchor for return jumps.-->
<A NAME="TOC">Table of Contents</A><P>
<!-- This is the link to the section 1. below.-->
<A HREF="#SEC1">Section 1.</A><BR>
<A HREF="#SEC2">Section 2.</A><BR>
<A HREF="#SEC3">Section 3.</A><BR>
<!-- This is a named anchor called "SEC1".-->
<A NAME="SEC1"><H2> CFR Section 1.</H2></A>
<P> Text of section 1 is here.<BR>
<!-- This is a link back to the TOC at the top of the page-->
<A HREF="#TOC">(TOC)</A> <P>
```

```
<A NAME="SEC2"><H2> CFR Section 2.</H2></A>
<P> Text of section 2 is here.<BR>
<A HREF="#TOC">(TOC)</A><P>
<A NAME="SEC3"><H2> CFR Section 3.</H2></A>
<P> Text of section 3 is here.<BR>
<A HREF="#TOC">(TOC)</A><P>
```

Seeing the (TOC) after each text section may seem strange at first, but your users quickly become accustomed to this method of intradocument linking. We recommend using this approach for longer, more complex documents or for a collection of related documents, but not for shorter pieces. An omnipresent TOC in a short document might seem obtrusive to your readers.

You can use this same general method for links to anything within a single HTML document. It may look strange in the HTML document, but this is the way you create hypertext links within a text paragraph. Only use the `"text"` in each `NAME="text"` once per document, though, to keep the browser from becoming terminally confused. Otherwise, you never know where your users might wind up!

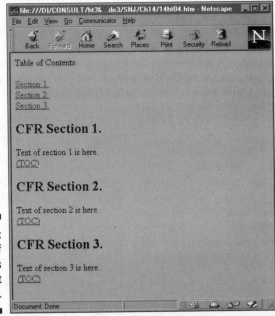

Figure 12-4:
Table of Contents and text links.

TIP

Named anchors should be named with text starting with a character from the set {a-z, A-Z}. They should never be exclusively numeric, like `<A NAME="12">blah</A>`. Make sure to give anchors unique names within the same document. These names are case-sensitive so that: `NAME="Three Stooges"` is not the same as `NAME="ThreeStooges"` is not the same as `NAME="THREESTOOGES"`. You get the idea. . . .

Jumping to Remote Pages

Hypermedia links from text in your pages directly to other Web sites amazes and amuses your users. Although you can't create `NAME="text"` anchors in text at remote sites, you may be able to use anchors already in place there. If you find a linked TOC at another site, you can reference the same links that it uses. Remember, if you can link to it by using your browser, you can copy the link into the text of your Web pages. Just make sure you include the full URL in the `HREF="URL"`.

Hypertext links to outside resources

Links to Web sites outside of your own Web require fully qualified URLs, such as

```
<BR>
URL: <A HREF="http://www.lanw.com/html4dum/
html4dum.htm">http://www.lanw.com/html4dum/html4dum.htm</
A> 
<BR>Text - Copyright &copy; 1995, 1996, 1997 Ed Tittel &amp;
Stephen N. James. 
<BR>Dummies Design and Art - Copyright &copy; 1995, 1996,
1997 IDG Books Worldwide, Inc. 
<BR>Web Layout - Copyright &copy; 1995, 1996, 1997
<A HREF="http://www.lanw.com/">LANWrights</A> 
<BR>Revised — April 14th, 1997 [JMS] 
```

The two links (`HREF`) connect the *HTML For Dummies* home page to itself and to the LANWrights Web site. Why include the page's own URL as a link? It not only shows the user the URL, but it also allows direct linking if users save this page's HTML source to their own computers.

All these tags and links make for difficult reading of the actual HTML code unless you view them through a browser, as shown in Figure 12-5. Through the browser, hypertext words are shown in a different color, underlined, or both, depending on your browser's preference settings.

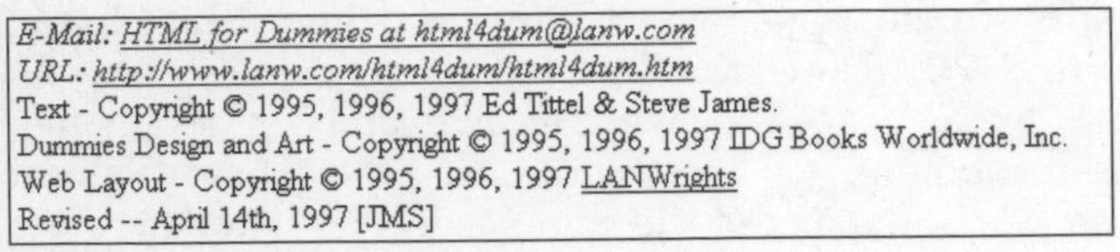

Figure 12-5:
External
links.

> E-Mail: *HTML for Dummies at html4dum@lanw.com*
> URL: *http://www.lanw.com/html4dum/html4dum.htm*
> Text - Copyright © 1995, 1996, 1997 Ed Tittel & Steve James.
> Dummies Design and Art - Copyright © 1995, 1996, 1997 IDG Books Worldwide, Inc.
> Web Layout - Copyright © 1995, 1996, 1997 LANWrights
> Revised -- April 14th, 1997 [JMS]

Jump pages

The term *jump page* refers to a Web page that contains a list of URLs to
other Web pages, usually remote sites. HTML list tags are invaluable when
creating visually pleasing and easily understood lists of links. Jump pages
differ from basic Web pages only because the viewer primarily sees highlighted hyperlinks. This is appropriate for quick scanning, but not for
general reading.

You can use icon images and spacer lines to visually separate sections of
your URL listing. Carefully choose the words you use for each hyperlink,
keeping in mind the main point of the information to which the link refers.
When entering URLs for links, we strongly recommend that you first link to
the destination URLs by using your browser. Then highlight, copy, and paste
the URLs directly into your HTML file to cut down on typos and syntax
errors.

A special <LINK>

The <LINK> tag provides information that links the current Web page to
other Web pages or to other URL resources. When you want to be sure that
your Web pages tell browsers and other WWW software about themselves,
put a <LINK> in the <HEAD>...</HEAD> section.

Chapter 6 shows several attributes that you may use in the <LINK> tag. If
you start using one of the advanced HTML-generating programs, it may
insert several <LINK> tags of various types within the head section of each
page. The programs use these links to keep track of the pages themselves.

Perhaps the most commonly used is NAME="text" to provide an anchor
from other locations. This named anchor is used for reference access from
other locations or documents. Your HTML code should look like this:

```
<HTML>
<HEAD>
<TITLE> The Title of Your Page </TITLE>
<LINK NAME="My Home Page">
```

```
</HEAD>
<BODY>
<H1> The Heading of Your Page That Users See </H1>
and so on...
</BODY></HTML>
```

The Nesting Instinct: Lists within Lists

When you create longer Web pages, you want to keep visual diversity high by using text formatting. If you are preparing your Web site for the newer browser versions, you can work with tables and frames to format your text. However, older versions of GUI browsers and text-only browsers understand the more basic HTML formatting: headings, emphasized text (bold, strong, font size), and indented lists. Lists within lists create the old, familiar outline form when displayed by most browsers. Figure 12-6 shows how a list within a list looks:

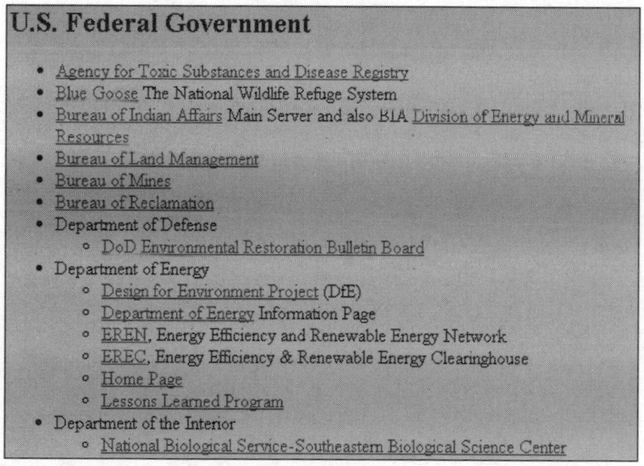

Figure 12-6:
Nested list
example.

The following HTML code created the browser display in Figure 12-6. As you look through this HTML markup, remember that you're seeing only a fragment, not the whole thing:

```
<p><h2>U.S. Federal Government</h2>
<ul>
<li><a href="http://atsdr1.atsdr.cdc.gov:8080/
atsdrhome.html">Agency for Toxic Substances and Disease
              Registry</a>
```

(continued)

(continued)

```
<li><A HREF="http://bluegoose.arw.r9.fws.gov/">Blue Goose
          </A> The National Wildlife Refuge System
<li><A HREF="http://info.er.usgs.gov/doi/bureau-
indian-affairs.html">Bureau of Indian Affairs</a> Main
Server and also BIA <A HREF="http://snake2.cr.usgs.gov/
          ">Division of Energy and Mineral Resources</a>
<li><A HREF="http://info.er.usgs.gov/doi/bureau-land-
          management.html">Bureau of Land Management</a>
<li><A HREF="http://www.usbm.gov/">Bureau of Mines</a>
<li><A HREF="http://info.er.usgs.gov/doi/bureau-of-
          reclamation.html">Bureau of Reclamation</a>
<li>Department of Defense
<ul> <li><a href="http://www.dtic.dla.mil/envirodod/
          envirodod.html">
DoD Environmental Restoration Bulletin Board</a>
</ul>
<li>Department of Energy
<ul>
<li><a href=http://w3.pnl.gov:2080/DFE/home.html>Design for
          Environment  Project</a> (DfE)
<li><A HREF="http://web.fie.com/web/fed/doe/">Department of
          Energy</A> Information Page
<li><a href="http://www.eren.doe.gov/ee/ee.html">EREN</a>,
          Energy Efficiency and Renewable Energy Network
<li><a href="http://www.nciinc.com/~erec">EREC</a>,
Energy Efficiency & Renewable Energy Clearinghouse
<li><a href="http://www.doe.gov">Home Page</a>
<li><a href=http://venus.hyperk.com/trl/ll/ll.html>
Lessons Learned Program</a>
</ul>
<li>Department of the Interior
<ul>
<li><a href="http://www.nfrcg.gov/">National Biological
Service-Southeastern
Biological Science Center</a>
</ul>
</ul>
```

Carefully track the list start (<UL>) and end (</UL>) tags. Directly under the U.S. Federal Government heading you see a start tag, and at the bottom of the listing you see its end tag. This placement of the tags indents and bullets all items that fall between them and are marked with the <LI> tags. This is a normal unordered list. What about all items that are indented a second time and preceded by a box rather than a bullet, you ask?

Each of these sections is contained within another pair of list tags. For example, immediately under the Department of Defense heading is the second level list start tag, and its end tag is immediately before the Department of Energy heading. The text between them, "DoD Environmental Restoration Bulletin Board," is marked with the `<LI>` tag, which causes the browser to indent it farther and place the box in front of it (in Netscape).

Some of the HTML 3.2 responsive browsers keep track of the number of nests you use and change the bullets of each successive nesting to blocks or other symbols. They also use the style tag to let you specify the symbol to be used for each level of your list. It may be easier to visualize nested lists without the `<LI>` lines:

```
<UL> Start level 1.
    <UL> Start level 2.
       <UL> Start level 3.
       </UL> End level 3.
    </UL> End level 2.
</UL> End level 1.
```

Nested lists are a good way to instruct a browser to indent certain lines of text without using the `<PRE>...</PRE>` or `<BLOCKQUOTE>...</BLOCKQUOTE>` tags. Along with the indentations, your readers have to cope with either bullets or numbers, but that's fine for lists, as shown in the earlier example.

Check your favorite browser developer's Web site to determine if they have a version that understands the use of style tags in lists for changing the bullets and numbering. Who knows what they'll think of next?

Analyzing Sophisticated Pages

Now it's time for a quick look at a complex Web page. We also encourage you to surf the Web for pages that strike your fancy. When you find one, view its source to see how the author worked the underlying magic. The Web is one of the few places where you can easily look behind the curtain to see how the illusion is created, so be sure to take full advantage of this opportunity.

HTML For Dummies home page

Our own *HTML For Dummies* home page illustrates what you can accomplish if you use the basic HTML 3.2 tags (without tables or frames) and your imagination. It's eye-catching but not overdone (see Figure 12-7 and compare with Figure 12-8). The information is arranged nicely and gives the user multiple avenues of access. The graphics (logo and link images, or the client-side or CGI image maps) and text commands at the top and the buttons near the bottom make the site easy to navigate quickly. Users who want to "turn the pages" can use the arrow buttons to move linearly through the site. The "menu" page acts as a table of contents from which users can jump anywhere in the site. The "search" function lets users find anything contained in the site and jump directly there.

The entire home page is less than two screens long. It makes liberal use of color and blank space to keep the text readable. The graphics load quickly because each has been designed with only a few colors and simple graphics components. The link images' or image map's functionality is repeated in the text immediately beneath it for users who don't have GUI browsers. The lines, "Click here for a client-side image map version" and "Click here for the standard image map version," display an alternate home page for browsers that understand either client-side or CGI image maps. You won't find a significant visual difference between any of the three image views, with or without the image maps. Only the functionality underneath differs and that is not readily apparent to most users.

The footer contains all the requisite information including the page's own URL, which users may find handy should they capture the HTML source, and later need to return to the online version. The online version is just a click away with the URL included as a hyperlink.

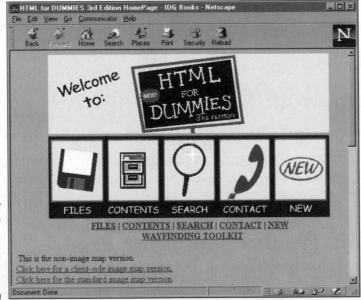

Figure 12-7:
HTML For Dummies home page using clickable images.

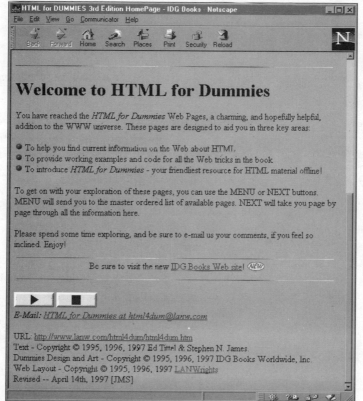

Figure 12-8:
HTML For Dummies home page without the images.

The HTML code for the *HTML For Dummies* home page is HTML 3.2 compliant. It shows some interesting tricks that you may find useful. The use of the ALT line after the "line.gif" shows a divider even when the browser doesn't load images automatically. Using "WIDTH=100%" in the "line.gif" tag displays the rainbow separator line across the whole width of the browser's page, regardless of the monitor type or window size. To get the equivalent of a "tab" in HTML, the "space.gif" file is used in several places. This is merely an image with either the same color as the background or a transparent background GIF file. When used with the appropriate width and height parameters, the "space.gif" holds the space to the left of either text or an image, simulating the "tab" key. It provides indentations without bullets like those list tags produce. You can also use the following code   with some browsers to get a single blank space:

```
<!DOCTYPE HTML PUBLIC "-//W3C//DTD HTML 3.2//EN">
<HTML>
<HEAD>
```

(continued)

(continued)

```
<META HTTP-EQUIV="Content-Type" CONTENT="text/html;
            charset=iso-8859-1">
<META NAME="GENERATOR" CONTENT="Mozilla/4.0b2 (Win95; I)
            [Netscape]">
<TITLE> HTML for DUMMIES 3rd Edition HomePage - IDG Books
            </TITLE>
</HEAD>
<BODY>
<A NAME="top"></A><IMG SRC="graphics/space.gif" ALT=""
HEIGHT=1 WIDTH=60 ALIGN=CENTER><A HREF="contents.htm">
<IMG SRC="graphics/ht4logoi.gif" ALT="HTML for Dummies Logo"
            BORDER=0 HEIGHT=140 WIDTH=500></A> 
<BR><IMG SRC="graphics/space.gif" ALT="" HEIGHT=1 WIDTH=
60 ALIGN=CENTER><A HREF="ftpstuff.htm"><IMG SRC="graphics/
ht4filei.gif" ALT="FILES" BORDER=0 HEIGHT=145 WIDTH=100>
</A><A HREF="contents.htm"><IMG SRC="graphics/ht4conti.gif"
ALT="CONTENTS" BORDER=0 HEIGHT=145 WIDTH=100></A>
<A HREF="search4d.htm"><IMG SRC="graphics/ht4seari.gif"
ALT="SEARCH" BORDER=0 HEIGHT=145 WIDTH=100></A>
<A HREF="contact.htm"><IMG SRC="graphics/ht4tacti.gif"
ALT="CONTACT" BORDER=0 HEIGHT=145 WIDTH=100></A>
<A HREF="whatsnew.htm"><IMG SRC="graphics/ht4newi.gif"
ALT="NEW" BORDER=0 HEIGHT=145 WIDTH=100></A> 
<BR><IMG SRC="graphics/space.gif" ALT="" HEIGHT=1 WIDTH=130
ALIGN=CENTER> <B><A HREF="ftpstuff.htm">FILES</A>
| <A HREF="contents.htm">CONTENTS</A> | <A
            HREF="search4d.htm">SEARCH</A>
| <A HREF="contact.htm">CONTACT</A> |
<A HREF="whatsnew.htm">NEW</A></B> 
<BR><IMG SRC="graphics/space.gif" ALT="" HEIGHT=1 WIDTH=
220 ALIGN=CENTER><B> <A HREF="wayfind.htm">WAYFINDING
TOOLKIT</A></B> <BR>
<BR> This is the non-image map version. 
<BR><A HREF="html4du2.htm">Click here for a client-side
            image map version.</A> 
<BR><A HREF="html4du3.htm">Click here for the standard image
map version</A>. <IMG SRC="graphics/
space.gif" ALT="" HEIGHT=1 WIDTH=160 ALIGN=CENTER> 
<!--<A HREF="registrn.htm">Click here to register online!
</A>--> <BR>
<BR><IMG SRC="graphics/line.gif" ALT="--==--==--==--==--==--"
            HEIGHT=1 WIDTH=567> 
<H1>Welcome to HTML for Dummies</H1>
```

```
You have reached the <I>HTML for Dummies</I> Web Pages,
a charming, and hopefully helpful, addition to the WWW
universe. These pages are designed to aid you in three key
         areas: <BR>
<BR><IMG SRC="graphics/dotred.gif" HEIGHT=14 WIDTH=14>
To help you find current information on the Web about
         HTML 
<BR><IMG SRC="graphics/dotred.gif" HEIGHT=14 WIDTH=14>
To provide working examples and code for all the Web tricks
         in the book <BR><IMG SRC="graphics/
dotred.gif" HEIGHT=14 WIDTH=14> To introduce <I>HTML for
         Dummies</I>
- your friendliest resource for HTML material
         offline! <BR>
<BR>To get on with your exploration of these pages, you can
use the MENU or NEXT buttons. MENU will send you to the
master ordered list of available pages. NEXT will take you
page by page through all the information here. 
<BR>
<BR>Please spend some time exploring, and be sure to e-mail
us your comments, if you feel so inclined. Enjoy! 
<BR> <IMG SRC="graphics/line.gif" ALT="--==--==--==--
         ==--==--" HEIGHT=1 WIDTH=567> 
<BR><IMG SRC="graphics/space.gif" ALT-"_" HEIGHT=1
         WIDTH=130> Be sure to visit the new
<A HREF="http://www.idgbooks.com/">IDG Books Web site
</A>! <IMG SRC="graphics/new.gif" HEIGHT=17 WIDTH=32
         ALIGN=TOP> 
<BR> <IMG SRC="graphics/line.gif" ALT="--==--==--==--
         ==--==--" HEIGHT=1 WIDTH=567> <BR>
<BR><A HREF="contents.htm"><IMG SRC="graphics/next.gif"
ALT="NEXT" BORDER=0 HEIGHT=27 WIDTH=72></A> 
<A HREF="search4d.htm#menu"><IMG SRC="graphics/menu.gif"
ALT="MENU" BORDER=0 HEIGHT=27 WIDTH=72></A> 
<ADDRESS>
E-Mail: <A HREF="mailto:html4dum@lanw.com">HTML for Dummies
at html4dum@lanw.com</A></ADDRESS><BR>URL: <A HREF="http://
www.lanw.com/html4dum/html4dum.htm">http://www.lanw.com/
html4dum/html4dum.htm</A> 
<BR>Text - Copyright &copy; 1995, 1996, 1997 Ed Tittel &amp;
Stephen N. James. 
<BR>Dummies Design and Art - Copyright &copy; 1995, 1996,
1997 IDG Books Worldwide, Inc.  .
<BR>Web Layout - Copyright &copy; 1995, 1996, 1997
```

(continued)

(continued)

```
<A HREF="http://www.lanw.com/">LANWrights</A> 
<BR>Revised--April 14th, 1997 [JMS] <BR>
</BODY>
</HTML>
```

As you can see, you don't have to use an image map to provide your users with nicely arranged, clickable images. The HTML code shows the lines necessary to display the "Welcome to HTML for Dummies" graphic and the Files, Contents, Search, Contact, and New graphics below it as clickable links to files. If you don't want to deal with image maps and don't mind going through some contortions to eliminate separation between the images, this kind of presentation is easier to implement than image maps on many sites.

However, if you really want to use either a client-side or a CGI image map, the following portions of HTML code show you how we did it:

Client-Side Image Map

```
<A NAME="top"></A>
<MAP NAME="h4dmap">
  <AREA COORDS="0,0,499,141" HREF="contents.htm">
  <AREA COORDS="0,142,98,285" HREF="ftpstuff.htm">
  <AREA COORDS="99,142,198,285" HREF="contents.htm">
  <AREA COORDS="199,142 298,285" HREF="search4d.htm">
  <AREA COORDS="299,142 398,285" HREF="contact.htm">
  <AREA COORDS="399,142 499,285" HREF="whatsnew.htm">
</MAP>
<IMG ALIGN=MIDDLE WIDTH=60 HEIGHT=0 SRC=graphics/space.gif
          ALT=" ">
<IMG BORDER=0 ALIGN=TOP SRC="graphics/ht4menum.gif"
ALT="Navigation Bar" USEMAP="#h4dmap"><BR>
```

CGI Image Map

```
<A NAME="top"></A>
<IMG ALIGN=MIDDLE WIDTH=60 HEIGHT=0 SRC=graphics/space.gif
          ALT=" ">
<A HREF="http://www.lanw.com//cgi-bin/ht4menum.map">
<IMG BORDER=0 ALIGN=TOP SRC="graphics/ht4menum.gif"
ALT="Navigation Bar" ISMAP></A><BR>
```

Chapter 13

Strictly Pro Forma: Using Forms for Feedback

● ●

In This Chapter

▶ Finding out what forms are for

▶ Dealing with browser and server limitations

▶ Understanding form tags

▶ Using form tags

▶ Forming good attitudes

▶ Formulating good layouts

● ●

*W*hen all the pieces come together properly, it's easy to see how the Web brings people or organizations together. At first glance, the Web can look pretty much like a one-way street — that is, an environment where Webmasters communicate aplenty with Web users, with not much interaction between the two. But it doesn't have to be that way.

What HTML Forms Are For

The essence of serving up useful information is relevancy and immediacy. But the best judge of the quality of your information is your audience. Wouldn't it be wonderful if your readers could give you feedback on your Web pages? Then they could tell you what parts they like, what they don't like, and what other things they'd like to see included in your site.

This is where HTML forms come into the picture. Up to this point in the book, we've talked about all of the basics — and even a few advanced techniques — for communicating with your audience. In this chapter, you find out how to turn the tables and create HTML text that lets your audience communicate with you!

As it turns out, HTML supports a rich variety of input capabilities to let you solicit feedback. In the pages that follow, you discover the tags to use, the controls and inputs they enable, along with some layout considerations for building forms. You also get to see some interesting example forms to help you understand what HTML forms look like and how they behave.

Living within Your Forms Limitations

HTML forms were established way back in the 2.0 DTD days. That's ancient history on the Web, but only a few years by our measurement of time. Since then, forms have changed very little and their foreseeable future promises the same level of radical alteration. Even though forms give users the ability to communicate with the Web developer, there are still some important limitations. You need to be aware of both the abilities and limitations of forms before you deploy them on your site.

Beware of browsers!

Although most of the "hot" browsers — Netscape Navigator/Communicator, Microsoft Internet Explorer, NCSA's Mosaic and its variants — already include forms support, other browsers may not. In fact, you won't know how well your favorite browser handles forms until you start testing your form tags against it. If you follow our suggestions and test your pages against multiple browsers, you'll immediately observe different levels of robustness and capability when it comes to form implementations.

The bottom line is that not all browsers support forms equally, but that support is pretty commonplace. Current or modern browser versions have no problem interacting with most form constructs. But don't be surprised if on older browsers, forms don't work that well or at all.

Assuming the information your form solicits is important to you, consider adding an FTP URL to your page to let users download a file containing a text-only version of the form's content. Then users can download the file and complete it by using any text editor. If you include an e-mail address inside the file, they can send it back to you and you'll get feedback, even from users who can't view your forms. That way nobody gets left out!

Sorry, servers . . .

Because the Web is a client/server environment, be aware that just because your browser supports forms doesn't automatically imply that the server installed at your site can handle them. Unfortunately, keeping up with HTML advancements means that Web servers have to change right along with the clients. In other words, your server may not support the input-handling programs necessary to process a form's input when it gets delivered.

However, there is a silver lining in this potentially dark cloud: The most common implementations of the *httpd* server (the http daemon — a publicly available "listener" program that waits for a form request to be made and responds as needed) come from NCSA and CERN and run in the UNIX environment. Both groups have standardized their forms-handling technology and offer useful, robust forms-handling capability.

These implementations are so common, in fact, that we assume your Web server works the way that they do. This means you may have to alter some of the approaches to CGI scripting and other programming that you might use to handle forms on your server. If you're not using UNIX and the NCSA or CERN implementations of httpd, investigate the particulars that your server's implementation requires and alter our instructions accordingly.

By this point in the evolution of the Web, it is extremely unlikely you'll run into a Web server that does not offer some sort of support for forms, either through CGI, a native scripting language, or some other proprietary solution.

What's in a Form?

When adding forms support to a Web page, you include special tags that let you solicit input from users. You surround these tags with text that prompts user responses. You also include tags that gather the input and ship it to your Web server or to other servers that might offer services — like Gopher or Archie — that your form knows how to query. Here's how the process works:

- ✔ On a particular Web page, you include tags to set up a form and to solicit input from users. Some of your users will work their way through this material and provide the information that you want. This essentially amounts to filling out the form that you've supplied.

- ✔ After users fill out your form, they can then direct their input to the program running on the Web server that delivered the form. In most cases, they need to select a particular control, called SUBMIT, that gathers the information and sends it to the proper destination on your Web server.

- ✔ Assuming that the program is available for use (installed and running properly, that is), it accepts the input information. Then the program decodes and interprets the contents for further action.

✔ After the input is received and interpreted, the program can do pretty much anything it wants. In practice, this boils down to recognizing key elements in a form's content and custom building an HTML document in response. Building a document isn't required, but it is a pretty commonplace capability within forms-handling programs.

✔ The custom-built document is then delivered to the user in response to the form's content. At this point, additional interaction can occur (if the "return page" includes another form), requested information can be delivered (in response to requests on the form), and so on.

The information collected from a form can be (1) written to a file; (2) submitted to a database such as Informix or Oracle; or (3) e-mailed to someone in particular. Forms also allow a user to participate in building a Web document such as on one Web site that allows users to dictate how a story is played out; in this case, the users collectively determine the outcome.

Thus, forms not only provide communication from users to servers, but also provide for ongoing interaction between users and servers. This is pretty powerful stuff and adds a lot of value to your Web pages.

Forms involve two-way communication

The input-catching programs on your server rely on an interface between Web browsers and servers called the *Common Gateway Interface* (CGI). This interface codifies how browsers can send information back to servers. It sets up the formatting for the user-supplied input information, so that forms-handling programs know what to expect and how to deal with what they receive.

The ACTION attribute in the <FORM> tag specifies a URL that indicates a specific CGI script or program that collects the form data that a user entered. Likewise, the METHOD attribute describes the way in which input data is delivered to a forms-handling program.

In this chapter, we concentrate on the input side of HTML forms — that is, you find out how to build forms. This is a pure exercise in building the front end of a form — that is, the part the users see. We cover how to build the back end — that is, how to build CGI or equivalent programs so your server can deal with forms input — in the "Extras" section of the CD-ROM. Not to worry, however — you have plenty of interesting front-end material to master here!

Tag! You're a form . . .

HTML includes several different classes of forms tags (for the details on syntax and usage, please consult Chapter 6). To begin with, all HTML forms occur within the <FORM>...</FORM> tags. The <FORM> tag also includes attributes that specify where and how to deliver input to the appropriate Web server.

Within the <FORM>...</FORM> tags, all other forms-related tags and text must appear. These tags include methods for

- ✔ Specifying input (the <INPUT> tag and its many attributes).
- ✔ Setting up text input areas (the <TEXTAREA>...</TEXTAREA> tags).
- ✔ Selecting values from a predefined set of possible inputs (the <SELECT>...</SELECT> tags).
- ✔ Managing the form's content (using the SUBMIT attribute for INPUT to deliver the content to the server, or the RESET attribute to clear its contents, and start over).

Forms input tags support multiple ways to interact with users, including

- ✔ Creating text input fields, where users can type in whatever they want.
- ✔ Generating pull-down menus, often called "pick lists" because they require making one or more selections from a set of predefined choices.
- ✔ Creating labeled check boxes or radio buttons on-screen, which users can select to indicate choices. Check boxes allow multiple selections and radio buttons allow just one selection.

This may not sound like much, but when you combine it with the ability to prompt users for input with surrounding text, it provides a surprisingly powerful way to ask for information right on a Web page. Thus, the real answer to the question at the head of this section: "What's in a form?" has to be: "Almost anything you want to put there!"

The remainder of this chapter steps you through all the details of building a form so you can use the capabilities that we just described.

Using Form Tags

To start out, you want to set up your <FORM> environment to build a form within a Web page. It's okay to add a form to an existing HTML document or to build a separate one just to contain your form. We recommend that you add shorter forms (half a screen or less) to existing documents but that you create new files for forms that are longer than half a screen.

Setting the <FORM> environment

The two key attributes within the <FORM> tag are METHOD and ACTION. Together, these attributes control how information is sent to the Web server and which input-handling program receives the form's contents.

There's no rhythm to METHOD

The METHOD indicates how the information is sent to the server when the form is submitted. METHOD can take one of two possible values: POST or GET.

Of these two methods, we prefer POST because it causes a form's contents to be parsed one element at a time. GET, on the other hand, concatenates all the field names and their associated values into one long string. Because UNIX (and most systems) have a limit on how long a single string can be (for UNIX, it's 255 characters), it's not hard to imagine that some of the information might get lost when its contents are truncated.

That's why you see us use POST as our only METHOD for submitting forms in this book. That's also why you should do the same, unless you're certain that the number of characters in a form will never, ever exceed 255.

Lights, camera . . . ACTION

ACTION supplies the URL for the CGI script or other input-handling program on the server that receives a form's input. The URL can be a full specification (absolute) or simply a relative reference. Either way, you need to make sure the URL points at the right program, in the right location, to do the job that's expected. You also need to make sure that the CGI script or program is executable and that it behaves properly. You hear a lot more about this in Chapter 16, which gets into the ins and outs of testing your HTML documents and their related CGI programs.

Let's make an assumption . . .

Because you won't have to worry about handling input until you try more advanced stuff, we follow two conventions for all the syntax in this chapter:

✔ In every `<FORM>` tag, `METHOD="POST"`.

✔ For every `ACTION`, `URL="/cgi-bin/form-name"` where we replace the placeholder *form-name* with the actual name of the form under discussion (that is, for the form named *get-inf.html*, `URL="/cgi-bin/get-inf"`).

These conventions make it easy to create sample HTML files to implement the forms in this chapter. (You can also find these examples on the CD-ROM that comes with this book.)

Knowing what's (in)coming: the <INPUT> tags

The `<INPUT>` tag defines a basic form element. This tag takes at least two attributes — namely `TYPE` and `NAME`. `TYPE` indicates what kind of element should appear on the form. `NAME` assigns a name to go with the input field or value that corresponds to the `<INPUT>` tag.

You use `NAME` to identify the contents of a field in the form information that is ultimately uploaded to the input-handling Web server. In fact, what the server receives is a series of name/value pairs. The name that identifies the value is the string supplied in the `NAME="string"` attribute, and the value is what the user enters or selects for that particular field. Read on — you can see an example in the next section that should make all this clear!

TYPE-casting still works!

The `TYPE` attribute can take any of the following values:

✔ **CHECKBOX:** Produces an on-screen check box for users to make multiple selections.

✔ **HIDDEN:** Produces no visible input area; use this to pass data needed for other uses through the form. For example, this might be an ongoing series of forms based on an earlier interaction during which the user identifies himself or herself — a `HIDDEN` field contains the `name-value` pair for that data but doesn't show it on the current form. (Some browsers display these fields at the bottom of a form, and each field has no accompanying label.)

✔ **IMAGE:** Lets you designate a graphic as a selectable item in a form. You can use this to include icons or other graphical symbols.

✔ **RADIO:** Creates a radio button for a range of selections, from which the user may select only one.

✔ **RESET:** Creates a button labeled "reset" in your form. Include this so that users can clear a form's contents and start over. Be sure to place it well away from other controls — you don't want them to clear the form by accident!

- SUBMIT: Creates a button labeled "submit" (by default, or whatever name you supply for the VALUE attribute for SUBMIT) in your form. The type SUBMIT tells the browser to bundle the form data and pass it all to the CGI script indicated by the ACTION attribute. In plain English (remember that??), SUBMIT is the button readers use to send in the filled-out form, so a form is useless without an <INPUT> field of type SUBMIT.

- TEXT: Provides a one-line area for text entry. Use this for short fields only (as in the example that is coming up). For longer text fields, use the <TEXTAREA>...</TEXTAREA> tags instead.

These TYPE attribute values provide a wide range of input displays and data types for form input. As you look at HTML forms on the Web and in this book with a new (and more trained) eye, you can see how effectively you can use these types.

Other <INPUT> attributes

Most remaining attributes exist to modify or qualify the <INPUT> attribute with TEXT type as the default. Following is a quick review to remind you of what we covered in Chapter 6:

- VALUE="value": Supplies a default value for a TEXT or HIDDEN element or supplies the corresponding value for a radio button or check box selection. You can use this to determine the label of a submit or a reset button, like VALUE="Submit to Admin" for a submit or VALUE="Clear Form" for a reset.

- SRC="URL": Provides a pointer to the graphic for an IMAGE.

- CHECKED: Makes sure that a certain radio button or check box is checked when the form is either visited for the first time or when it is reset. You can control default settings with the CHECKED attribute of <INPUT>.

- SIZE="number": Sets the number of characters that a TEXT element can display without scrolling.

- MAXLENGTH="number": Sets the maximum number of characters that a value in a TEXT element can contain.

- ALIGN=(TOP|MIDDLE|BOTTOM|LEFT|RIGHT): For IMAGE elements, determines how the graphic is aligned on the form, vis-à-vis the accompanying text.

A TEXT-oriented <INPUT> example

That's it for the <INPUT> tag. Following is a look at a relatively simple example of a survey form:

```
<HTML>
<HEAD>
<TITLE>Reader Contact Information</TITLE>
<!-- the name of this form is usr-inf.html -->
</HEAD>
<BODY>
<H3>Reader Contact Information</H3>
<P>Please fill out this form, so we'll know how to get in
touch with you. Thanks!
<FORM METHOD="POST" ACTION="/cgi-bin/usr-inf">
<P>Please enter your name:
<P>First name: <INPUT NAME="first" TYPE="TEXT" SIZE="12"
   MAXLENGTH="20">
MI: <INPUT NAME ="MI" TYPE="TEXT" SIZE="3" MAXLENGTH="3">
Surname(last name): <INPUT NAME="surname" TYPE="TEXT"
            SIZE="15"
   MAXLENGTH="25">
<P>
<P>Please give us your mailing address:
<P>Address 1: <INPUT NAME="adr1" TYPE="TEXT" SIZE="30"
   MAXLENGTH="45">
<P>Address 2: <INPUT NAME="adr2" TYPE="TEXT" SIZE="30"
   MAXLENGTH="45">
<P>City: <INPUT NAME="city" TYPE="TEXT" SIZE="15"
   MAXLENGTH="30">
<P>State: <INPUT NAME="state" TYPE="TEXT" SIZE="15"
            MAXLENGTH="15">
   ZIP&#47;Postal Code: <INPUT NAME="zip" TYPE="TEXT"
            SIZE="10"
   MAXLENGTH="10">
<P>Country: <INPUT NAME="country" TYPE="TEXT" SIZE="15"
   MAXLENGTH="15">
<P>
<P>Thank you! <INPUT TYPE="SUBMIT"> <INPUT TYPE="RESET">
</FORM>
<ADDRESS>
Sample form for <I>HTML for Dummies</I> Version 3.1<BR>
3/17/97 http://www.noplace.com/HTML4D/usr-inf.html
</ADDRESS>
</BODY></HTML>
```

Figure 13-1 shows this HTML form on Netscape. Note the positions of the one-line text boxes immediately after the field names and the ability to set these boxes on individual lines (as with Address1 and Address2) or together (as with First name, Middle initial (MI), and Last name (Surname)). These options makes it easy to build simple, usable forms.

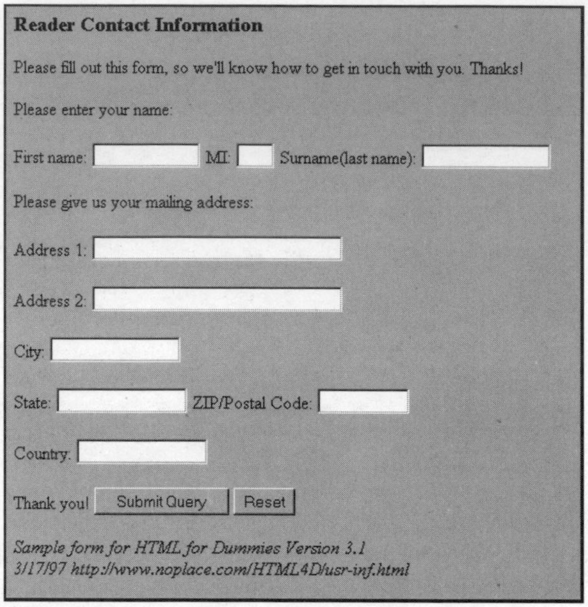

Reader Contact Information

Please fill out this form, so we'll know how to get in touch with you. Thanks!

Please enter your name:

First name: [ ]   MI: [ ]   Surname(last name): [ ]

Please give us your mailing address:

Address 1: [ ]

Address 2: [ ]

City: [ ]

State: [ ]   ZIP/Postal Code: [ ]

Country: [ ]

Thank you! [Submit Query] [Reset]

Sample form for HTML for Dummies Version 3.1
3/17/97 http://www.noplace.com/HTML4D/usr-inf.html

Figure 13-1: The "Reader Contact Information" form on-screen.

Being <SELECT>ive

The `<SELECT>...</SELECT>` pair works much like a list style, except that it builds a selectable list of `<OPTION>` elements, instead of the `<LI>` list items. Within the `<SELECT>` tag, the following attributes can occur:

- `NAME="text"`: Provides the name that is passed to the server as the identifying portion of the `name-value` pair for this element.
- `SIZE="number"`: Controls the number of elements that the pick list displays; even though you can still define more than this many elements, it keeps the size of the list more manageable on-screen.
- `MULTIPLE`: Indicates that multiple selections from a list are possible; if this flag isn't present in a `<SELECT>` statement, your users can select only a single element from the pick list.

Building a `<SELECT>` field for your form doesn't take much work. In the following example, you see how easy it is to construct a list of spices from which a user can select and order:

```
<HTML>
<HEAD>
<TITLE>&lt;SELECT&gt; Spices</TITLE>
   <!-- the name of this form is sel-spi.html -->
   </HEAD>
```

```
<BODY>
<H3>This Month's Spicy Selections!</H3>

<P>Spice up your life.  Order from this
   month's special selections.<BR> All items
   include 2 oz. of the finest condiments,
   packed in tinted glass bottles for best
   storage.


<HR>
   <FORM METHOD="POST" ACTION="/cgi/sel-spi">

<P>Pepper Selections:
   <SELECT NAME="pepper" SIZE="4" MULTIPLE>
   <OPTION>Plain-black
   <OPTION>Malabar
   <OPTION>Telicherry
   <OPTION>Green-dried
   <OPTION>Green-pickled
   <OPTION>Red
   <OPTION>White
   </SELECT>
   <P>
   Please pick a button to indicate how the pepper<BR>
   should be delivered:<BR>
   Ground <INPUT TYPE="RADIO" NAME="grind" VALUE="ground">
          <BR>
   Whole <INPUT TYPE="RADIO" NAME="grind" VALUE="whole">
          <BR>
   <P>
   <HR>
   <P>Imported and Domestic Oregano:
   <SELECT NAME="oregano" SIZE="4" MULTIPLE>
   <OPTION> Italian-whole
   <OPTION> Italian-crumbled
   <OPTION> Greek-whole
   <OPTION> Indian
   <OPTION> Mexican
   <OPTION> Organic-California
   </SELECT>
   <P>Thanks for your order! <INPUT TYPE="SUBMIT"
          VALUE="Send Order">
```

(continued)

(continued)

```
<INPUT TYPE="RESET">
    </FORM>
<ADDRESS>
Sample form for <I>HTML for Dummies</I> Version 3.1<BR>
3/17/97 http://www.noplace.com/HTML4D/usr-inf.html
</ADDRESS></BODY></HTML>
```

Figure 13-2 shows what nice results you can get from using `<SELECT>` elements to provide options for your users to pick from. Also, notice the radio buttons to specify whether they want whole or ground pepper. By giving both radio buttons the same `NAME`, we indicate that only one option can be chosen.

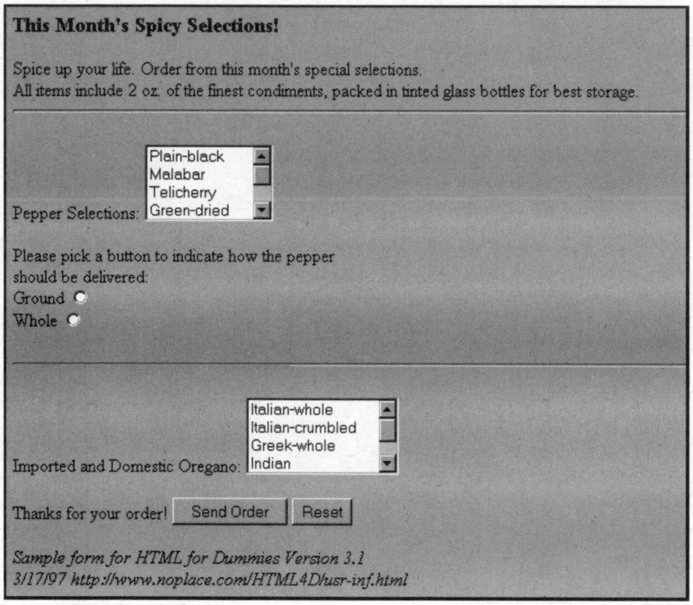

Figure 13-2:
The `<SELECT>` tag creates scrolling *pick lists* of choices for users to select.

> **This Month's Spicy Selections!**
>
> Spice up your life. Order from this month's special selections.
> All items include 2 oz. of the finest condiments, packed in tinted glass bottles for best storage.
>
> Pepper Selections: Plain-black / Malabar / Telicherry / Green-dried
>
> Please pick a button to indicate how the pepper should be delivered:
> Ground ○
> Whole ○
>
> Imported and Domestic Oregano: Italian-whole / Italian-crumbled / Greek-whole / Indian
>
> Thanks for your order! [Send Order] [Reset]
>
> *Sample form for HTML for Dummies Version 3.1*
> *3/17/97 http://www.noplace.com/HTML4D/usr-inf.html*

<TEXTAREA> lets users wax eloquent . . . or profane!

The `<TEXTAREA>...</TEXTAREA>` tags let you create input elements of more or less arbitrary size on a form. Any text that appears between the opening and closing tags is displayed within the text area on-screen (and if left unaltered, the text area supplies the default value delivered by the form).

<TEXTAREA> takes three important attributes:

- NAME="text": Provides the identifier part of the all-important name-value pair delivered to the server.
- ROWS="number": Specifies the number of lines of text that the text area will contain.
- COLS="number": Specifies the number of characters that can fit onto any one row of the text area; this value also sets the width of the text area on-screen.

The example that follows shows how you can use a text area to provide space for free-form feedback or information as part of a survey-style form:

```
<HTML>
<HEAD>
<TITLE>&lt;TEXTAREA&gt; On Display</TITLE>
   <!-- the name of this form is txt-ara.html -->
</HEAD>
   <BODY>
   <H3>The Widget Waffle Iron Survey</H3>
<P>Please fill out the following information so that we
   can register your new Widget Waffle Iron.
<HR>
   <FORM METHOD="POST" ACTION="/cgi/txt-ara">
<P>Model Number
   <SELECT NAME="mod-num" SIZE="3">
   <OPTION>102 (Single Belgian)
   <OPTION>103 (Double Belgian)
   <OPTION>104 (Single Heart-shaped)
   <OPTION>105 (Double Heart-shaped)
   <OPTION>204 (Restaurant Waffler)
   <OPTION>297 (Cone Waffler)
   </SELECT>
   <HR>
   <B>Please complete the following purchase information:
          </B><BR>
<P>Serial number: <INPUT NAME="snum" TYPE="TEXT" SIZE="10"
   MAXLENGTH="10">
   <P>Purchase Price: <INPUT NAME="price" TYPE="TEXT"
          SIZE="6"
   MAXLENGTH="10">
   <P>Location: <INPUT NAME="location" TYPE="TEXT" SIZE="15"
   MAXLENGTH="30">
```

(continued)

(continued)

```
    <HR>
    <B>Please tell us about yourself:</B>

<P>Male <INPUT NAME="sex" TYPE="CHECKBOX" VALUE="male">
    Female <INPUT NAME="sex" TYPE="CHECKBOX" VALUE="female">
    <P>Age:
    under 25 <INPUT NAME="age" TYPE="CHECKBOX" VALUE="lo">
    25-50 <INPUT NAME="age" TYPE="CHECKBOX" VALUE="med">
    over 50 <INPUT NAME="age" TYPE="CHECKBOX" VALUE="hi">
<P>
<HR>
    Please share your favorite waffle recipe with us. If we
            like it, we'll include it in our next Widget
            Waffler cookbook!
    Here's an example to inspire you.
<P><TEXTAREA NAME="recipe" ROWS="10" COLS="65">
    Banana Waffles
    Ingredients:
    2 c. waffle batter (see Widget Waffler cookbook for
            recipe)
    2 ripe bananas, peeled, sliced 1/4" thick
    1 tsp. cinnamon
    Preparation:
    Mix ingredients together.
    Preheat Widget Waffler (wait 'til light goes off).
    Pour 1/2 c. batter in Waffler (wait 'til light goes off).
    Keep browned waffles warm in oven until ready to serve.
    </TEXTAREA>
<P>Thank you! <INPUT TYPE="SUBMIT" VALUE="Register now">
<INPUT TYPE="RESET">
</FORM>
<ADDRESS>
Sample form for <I>HTML for Dummies</I> Version 3.1<BR>
3/17/97 http://www.noplace.com/HTML4D/usr-inf.html
</ADDRESS></BODY></HTML>
```

The screen that results from this HTML document is shown in part in Figure 13-3. Notice the use of check boxes for survey information, coupled with the text input area for recipes. Makes us wonder: "What time's breakfast?"

At this point, you've seen all the nifty little tricks — we like to call them widgets — that work within forms, but you can't really appreciate what forms can do until you've browsed the Web to look at the many examples out there. Our examples barely scratch the surface, so there's a lot more to see!

The Widget Waffle Iron Survey

Please fill out the following information so that we can register your new Widget Waffle Iron.

Model Number
```
102 (Single Belgian)
103 (Double Belgian)
104 (Single Heart-shaped)
```

Please complete the following purchase information:

Serial number:

Purchase Price:

Location:

Please tell us about yourself:

Male ☐ Female ☐

Age: under 25 ☐ 25-50 ☐ over 50 ☐

Please share your favorite waffle recipe with us. If we like it, we'll include it in our next Widget Waffler cookbook! Here's an example to inspire you.

```
Banana Waffles
Ingredients:
2 c. waffle batter (see Widget Waffler cookbook for recipe)
2 ripe bananas, peeled, sliced 1/4" thick
1 tsp. cinnamon
Preparation:
Mix ingredients together.
Preheat Widget Waffler (wait 'til light goes off).
Pour 1/2 c. batter in Waffler (wait 'til light goes off).
Keep browned waffles warm in oven until ready to serve.
```

Thank you! [Register now] [Reset]

Sample form for HTML for Dummies Version 3.1
3/17/97 http://www.noplace.com/HTML4D/usr-inf.html

Figure 13-3: Notice how you can supply example information for the text area in a form.

Formulating Good Attitudes

Whenever you create an HTML form, it's especially important to test it against as many browsers as you possibly can. Don't forget to work with character-mode browsers, like Lynx, as well as more exciting graphical browsers. Remember also that, although some browsers support some pretty keen extensions, the effort it takes to use them is wasted on those readers who pass through in other browsers that don't support them.

Ultimately, the HTML rules regarding layout versus content apply to forms: If you can create a clear, readable layout and make the form interesting to your users, you'll probably be a lot happier with the information returned than if you spend extra hours tuning and tweaking graphics elements and precise placement of type, widgets, and fields. Remember, too, that the form's just the front end for your user interaction or data collection. If you need more details on this subject, don't forget to check out our other books:

- ✓ *CGI Bible,* by Ed Tittel, Mark Gaither, Sebastian Hassinger, and Mike Erwin. IDG Books Worldwide, Inc., ISBN 0-7645-8016-7

- ✓ *Web Programming Secrets With HTML, CGI, and Perl,* by Ed Tittel, Mark Gaither, Sebastian Hassinger, and Mike Erwin. IDG Books Worldwide, Inc., ISBN 1-56884-848-X

In the next chapter, you see how to turn graphics into addressable on-screen selectors called clickable maps. These clickable maps add zest to forms and other HTML documents because they let users select links at different points within a graphic.

Chapter 14

The Map's the Thing!

In This Chapter

▶ Using clickable maps

▶ Finding out what it takes to present maps

▶ Carving up maps for use

▶ Knowing the limitations to map use

▶ Mapping your way to perfection

*Y*ou may have already found out how to insert graphics into your HTML documents by using the `<IMG>` tag. And you probably have even seen examples of using graphics as hypertext links within anchor tags (`<A HREF=...><IMG SRC=...></A>`). In this chapter, we show you how to take the next logical step and treat a graphic as a collection of selectable regions, each of which points to some kind of hypertext link or resource.

Where Are You? (Using Clickable Maps)

Geographically speaking, a map takes a land mass and divides it up along boundary lines into named regions: Typically, these can be countries, counties, or other kinds of territories. When it comes to using graphics in this way on the Web, the boundaries are obvious in the graphic that's displayed, and users simply select the portion of the graphic that attracts their interest. Users familiar with graphical interfaces have no trouble interacting with on-screen buttons, icons, and other kinds of interface controls. Graphical maps add this kind of capability to a single image displayed on a Web page.

In Web-speak, such graphical maps are usually called *image maps* or *clickable maps*. We prefer the latter term because it emphasizes the important aspects of this graphical element:

✔ Clickable maps break a graphic into discrete regions that function as a map of individual hyperlinks.

✔ Users can select regions by putting the cursor inside the desired region and clicking the mouse.

You should already have a clue about the fundamental limitation inherent in a clickable map: It absolutely requires a graphical browser. The image that represents the map and drives the selection process doesn't appear in a character-mode browser, period. Therefore, if you use clickable map elements, you must implement alternate methods for users with text-only browsers.

An example of a clickable map should lend some reality to this concept. Figure 14-1 shows the *HTML For Dummies* home page main graphic (named HT4MENUM.GIF in the /GRAPHICS subdirectory). This graphic features a set of buttons at the bottom, where each button contains a major access category for the *HTML For Dummies* pages. As part of a set of Web pages for this book, it acts as the gateway to a page, or set of pages, for each category or topic mentioned.

Figure 14-1:
The HTML For Dummies home page (server version) includes a row of buttons on the bottom.

FILES   CONTENTS   SEARCH   CONTACT   NEW

In this chapter, you see how to set up an image as a clickable map and how to use it to drive page navigation. Please note: The approach that we used to build the identical graphic for the pages on the CD-ROM (the one that comes with this book) breaks the image up into pieces. The top part of the graphic represents one piece (HT4LOGOI.GIF), and each button has its own associated icon file. We did this because a local HTML file cannot use an image map. This restriction exists because there's no server in the background to map the user's selection coordinates into a corresponding URL. Instead, each button's icon is directly linked to a URL, and clicking a graphical element automatically selects the right link.

Cosmic Cartography: What It Takes to Present Maps on the Web

Building a clickable map requires three ingredients:

- **Creating (or selecting) a usable image:** This can be an existing graphic or a custom-built one. Our *HTML For Dummies* button bar uses five custom-built icons, one for each button.

- **Creating the *map file:*** This requires a step-by-step investigation of the image file inside a graphics program that can give you the pixel addresses (coordinates) of each point on the boundary of the regions you want to create (or use of a map-building utility, like the one we mention later in the chapter).

Our icons are all about the same size, so working through this process is easy: The image starts in the upper-left corner of the button bar (at vertical location 142, or about the middle of this 285-pixel-high image) and is consistently 143 pixels high. The individual buttons vary slightly in width, producing the following set of coordinates:

```
( 0,142)--( 99,142)---(199,142)---(299,142)---(399,142)-(499,142)
|          |           |           |           |          |
|  button 1 | button 2 | button 3 | button 4 | button 5  |
|          |           |           |           |          |
( 0,285)--( 99,285)---(199,285)---(299,285)---(399,285)-(499,285)
```

Unfortunately, the only way to produce this collection of numbers is to view the graphic from within a graphics program capable of displaying pixel coordinates (we used PaintShop Pro 3.0, a widely available shareware graphics program for Windows), or to use an image-map construction program.

If you use an image map tool, it generates the map for you after you tell it what kind of shapes you're outlining. One example is Tom Boutell's excellent program, called *mapedit,* which builds map files for you on command. It's available for lots of computer types, including Mac, DOS/Windows, Window NT, and UNIX. To find a suitable version, use "mapedit" as the search string in your favorite Web search engine (a quick jump to Yahoo! turned up more than 40 sites that offer one or more versions of this program).

✔ **Establishing the right HTML information in your page:** You need to link the image, the map file, and a CGI script to handle decoding map coordinates and use that information to select the appropriate link to follow.

Here, we take you through the concepts of making this work in your HTML document. Later on, we show you how to build a complete back-end CGI script to translate the pixel coordinates for a user's map selection into a corresponding HTML link. In this chapter, we only cover the techniques and generalities needed to construct the image map and to create links between map regions and hypertext documents or resources.

By obtaining the information for the images and map files and establishing a convention to call the script that handles coordinate-to-link translation, you have most of what you need to know to set up a clickable map.

We suggest that you use the name of the image map as the name for its corresponding script file: Thus, if the image is named HT4MENUM.GIF, the script would be called HT4MENUM.MAP, or simply HT4MENUM. If your scripts are in a CGI directory one level down from your HTML files, the corresponding URL for this script would then be `/cgi-bin/ht4menum.map`.

Warning: different maps for different servers

Unfortunately, clickable maps are a topic where the two most popular *httpd* servers — NCSA and CERN — differ. You find format differences in defining image maps for one kind of server versus the other. You also find Web servers that don't support either format, especially if they're not running UNIX (Windows NT currently supports more than 30 different Web servers. Some Web servers use their own proprietary image map formats. The leading Macintosh Web server — WebSTAR — supports NCSA format).

To get your clickable map to work, you must work within the requirements of the server where the map resides. If you don't know what those requirements are, we strongly suggest that you contact your local Webmaster — or at least, the system administrator for your Web server.

He or she should be able to set you straight right away and can probably help you find some useful information about how to build clickable maps for your system, above and beyond what we tell you here.

Throughout the chapter, where differences between the CERN and NCSA requirements exist, we fill you in. If you're not using an *httpd* server of either variety, you may want to investigate its requirements immediately and adjust our examples and recommendations to meet those requirements!

Dealing with shapes in maps

You can use various ways to identify boundaries when assembling coordinates to build a clickable map. Both CERN and NCSA image map definitions recognize the following regions:

- **Circle:** (Specified by the coordinates for a point at the center and the number of pixels for the radius.) Use this to select a circular (or nearly circular) region within an image.

- **Rectangle:** (Specified by the coordinates for the upper-left and lower-right corners.) Use this to select a square or rectangular region in your image. (This is the one we use in our button bar map.)

- **Polygon:** (Specified by the coordinates for the point at the vertex of each edge.) Use this to outline the boundaries of regularly or irregularly shaped regions that aren't circular or rectangular. Although it takes more effort, the more points you pick to define the outline, the more the region behaves as the user expects it to when they're clicking.

- **Point:** (Specified by its x and y coordinates.) Use this only when a specific point is easy for a user to select. (A point is usually too small a region on-screen and requires exact control to select — we recommend surrounding a point with a small circle or square to give users a little room to be sloppy.) We've never actually used a point reference in an image map, except as the vertices for a polygon, rectangle, or center of a circle.

Selecting boundaries for map regions is what determines the selection of the corresponding links. Even though users see a nicely shaped graphic to click, what really drives the selection process are the areas that you've outlined on top of that graphic.

The better the map regions fit the figure layout, the more the map behaves like users expect it to! The moral of the story is: Take your time and, when in doubt, pick more points to outline something, rather than less. Even better, use a tool that follows your cursor movement to build the image map for you. We mentioned Tom Boutell's mapedit program earlier; you can find other alternatives galore on the Web. For example, an interactive, Web-based image map tool called *MapMaker* is available at:

```
http://www.tns.lcs.mit/cgi-bin/mapmaker
```

If you provide it with a URL for the graphics file you want to build a map for, it can guide you through the rest of the process using your very own Web browser!

Building and Linking to CERN Map Files

Map files for CERN *httpd* servers take a general form that looks something like this:

```
circle (x,y) r URL
rectangle (x1,y1) (x2,y2) URL
polygon (x1,y1) (x2,.y2) (x3,y3) ... (xn,yn) URL
point (x,y) URL
default URL
```

The shapes are pretty much self-evident, except for the polygon, which represents an attempt to trace a region's outline by connecting a series of points. If this sounds like connect-the-dots, you've definitely gotten the underlying concept!

Don't forget to close your polygons; make sure that the last segment fills the gap between your last point and your first.

The other entry that might seem mysterious is the default URL. This defines the default so that if a user clicks a location that's not defined in the map, they can still choose a fail-safe. The default can be a script that sends a message back to the user, saying, "Click within the lines!" or "You have selected an area of the image that is not defined. Please try again."

The menu bar map file

Thus, for our menu bar example, the CERN map would be

```
rectangle (0,142) (98,285) http://www.domain.com/html4dum/
          ftpstuff.htm
rectangle (99,142) (198,285) http://www.domain.com/html4dum/
          contents.htm
rectangle (199,142) (298,285) http://www.domain.com/
          html4dum/search4d.htm
rectangle (299,142) (398,285) http://www.domain.com/
          html4dum/contact.htm
rectangle (399,142) (499,285) http://www.domain.com/
          html4dum/whatsnew.htm
default http://www.domain.com/html4dum/contents.htm
```

Because the button bar is a collection of rectangles, filling in the coordinates is easy. (Why do you think we picked this example?) Then we provide a default link to the contents page if somebody insists on staying outside the nice little boxes that we gave them to play in! Notice, too, that we use absolute URLs. Using absolute URLs in map files makes the maps easier to debug and to relocate.

Using map files

To use a map file with the CERN *httpd,* your system must already have a program that handles image maps. The name of this program, which is included with the CERN distribution *httpd* materials, is *htimage.* You must have htimage installed if you plan to use image maps on your system. After it's available, you must also know how to invoke it on the server. For the purposes of this example, we assume it lives on the directory path /CGI-BIN/.

Building and Linking to NCSA Map Files

Map files for NCSA *httpd* servers look an awful lot like those for CERN servers, but there are some differences. They take a general form that looks something like this:

```
circle URL x,y r
rect URL x1,y1 x2,y2
poly URL x1,y1 x2,y2 x3,y3 ... xn,yn
point URL x,y
default URL
```

The shapes are the same as the CERN variety, and the same kinds of coordinates define them. But the names are shorter, and the URLs come first (instead of last) in the list of attributes. Here again, defaults work the same way: to provide a handler for people who click outside the image frame.

The button bar map file

For the *HTML For Dummies* home page main graphic, for example, the NCSA map would be

```
rect http://www.domain.com/html4dum/ftpstuff.htm (0,142)
          (98,285)
rect http://www.domain.com/html4dum/contents.htm (99,142)
          (198,285)
rect http://www.domain.com/html4dum/search4d.htm (199,142)
          (298,285)
rect http://www.domain.com/html4dum/contact.htm (299,142)
          (398,285)
rect http://www.domain.com/html4dum/whatsnew.htm (399,142)
          (499,285)
default http://www.domain.com/html4dum/contents.htm
```

Except for a slight change in the shape's name (rect instead of rectangle) and a reordering of the arguments (URL first, then coordinates), the map is pretty much identical to the CERN variety.

Using map files

Like CERN, in order to use a map file with the NCSA *httpd,* your system must already have a program that handles image maps. The name of this program, which comes with the NCSA distribution *httpd* materials, is *imagemap.* If it's not installed, you must have the imagemap installed in order to use image maps on your system. You also need to check that you have the latest version. You can check the version information at

`http://hoohoo.ncsa.uiuc.edu/docs/setup/admin/imagemap.txt`

against what's installed on your server. If the date is more recent at the NCSA server, download the file, rename it to `imagemag.c`, and recompile it. Throw the old version away and use your new one instead.

After you have *imagemap* available, you must also know how to invoke it on the server. For the purposes of this example, we assume it lives on the directory path /CGI-BIN/.

Final Touches

No matter which type of Web server you use to host your image maps, they all have a few things in common.

Creating and storing map files

You can create a map file with any plain text editor. Store the map file on the server in a special directory for your map definition files. Contact your system administrator or your Webmaster to find out where this is and if you have *write* permissions. If you don't, you need to enlist their help in getting those files installed. For these examples, we use the name, HT4MENUM.MAP, and store it in the `http://www.domain.com/cg-bin/` directory, along with all our other scripts.

Defining a clickable map in your HTML document

After you defined the map and stored it in the right location, you need to bring all three elements together in your HTML file. Here's how you do it:

```
<A HREF="http://www.outer.net/cgi-bin/ht4menum.map">
<IMG SRC="graphics/ht4menum.gif" ISMAP>
</A>
```

Here's what's going on in this series of statements:

✔ The opening anchor tag combines the *htimage* location, which handles the coordinate-to-URL translation, with the full specification for the map file. Even though there's no space between the name of the program (*htimage*) and the map file specification, the server still knows what to do.

✔ The IMG tag points to the button bar graphic, but adds the ISMAP attribute to indicate that it's a clickable map.

✔ The closing anchor tag </A> indicates that the graphic specified by IMG is the target for the map file specified in the opening anchor tag.

There you are! After you make sure that all the right pieces are in place on your CERN server, you can try this, too.

"The Map Is Not the Territory"

Although Alfred Korzybski wasn't thinking of clickable images when he uttered the title of this section, it's still a point worth pondering. Because not all users can see an image map, you need to be prepared to give them the same set of selections that your graphically enabled users get in visual form. How might you go about doing this?

Because what you're providing in the image map is an array of choices, you can also add an equivalent set of text-based links right below the image. Here's what the HTML for this would look like:

```
<A HREF="http://www.outer.net/cgi-bin/html4dum.map">
<IMG BORDER=0 ALIGN=TOP SRC="graphics/ht4menum.gif"
  ALT="Navigation Bar" ISMAP></A><P>
<IMG ALIGN=MIDDLE WIDTH=130 HEIGHT=0 SRC=graphics/space.gif
  ALT=" ">
<B><A HREF="ftpstuff.htm">FILES</A> &#32;&#124;
<A HREF="contents.htm">CONTENTS</A> &#32;&#124;
<A HREF="search4d.htm">SEARCH</A> &#32;&#124;
<A HREF="contact.htm">CONTACT</A> &#32;&#124;
<A HREF="whatsnew.htm">NEW</A><BR>
<IMG ALIGN=MIDDLE WIDTH=240 HEIGHT=0 SRC=graphics/space.gif
  ALT=" ">
<A HREF="navigate.htm">HOW TO NAVIGATE</A></B><P>
<A HREF="html4du2.htm">Click here for a non-imagemap
version</A>
```

As shown in Figure 14-2, this results in a text bar (right underneath the graphic) that offers the same choices that the graphic does. Users with graphical browsers won't be discommoded by this redundancy, and character-mode browsers will see a reasonable facsimile of what their graphically advantaged brethren see in living color. We call this *mastering the art of compromise!*

Figure 14-2:
A text-based alternative combined with the button bar keeps everybody in the know.

Of Clickable Maps and URLs

Image links can sometimes play hob with relative URL specifications within HTML documents. One unforeseen side effect of following the links through a map-reading script — to the map and back to the target page — can be a complete mangling of the context within which URLs are addressed. In English, this means it's a really, really, really good idea to use full URLs, instead of relative references, in HTML documents that also include clickable maps.

You would be wise to be cagey when using relative URL references in documents with clickable maps. You need to test this practice thoroughly to make sure everything works as it should, or use the <BASE> tag. Avoiding trouble is, in general, the best way to cure the URL relative reference blues!

Late-Breaking News! Client-Side Image Maps!

A client-side image map is a graphical navigation tool that exists solely on the client-side and does not require a server or a CGI map file to operate. Both Netscape and Microsoft's Web browsers support client-side image maps. Creating one of these guys is almost as easy as its server-side cousins.

Building a client-side image map involves:

- ✔ Defining the hot-spot areas of the image
- ✔ Embedding the coordinates in an HTML document

The possible area definitions are:

- ✔ Point — `<AREA SHAPE="point" COORDS="x,y" HREF="URL1">`
- ✔ Circle — `<AREA SHAPE="circle" COORDS="x,y,x2,y2" HREF="URL2">`
- ✔ Rectangle — `<AREA SHAPE="rect" COORDS="x,y,x2,y2" HREF="URL3">`
- ✔ Polygon — `<AREA SHAPE="poly" COORDS="x,y,x2,y2,x3,y3,…" HREF="URL4">`
- ✔ Default — `<AREA SHAPE="default" HREF="URL5">`

You probably recognize all of these area types except for circle. The circle area is defined by a central point then a point on the circle's edge (a method of defining its radius). Also note that the coordinates are grouped together and separated by commas.

Slam a group of `AREA` tags inside of a `MAP` tag associated with a properly labeled `IMG` tag, and you've got a client-side image map. Notice that we name the client-side image map with the `NAME` attribute of the `MAP` tag and reference it with the `USEMAP` attribute in the `IMG` tag. Here is an example:

```
<IMG SRC="HT4MEMU.GIF" USEMAP="#h4dmap">
<MAP NAME="h4dmap">
    <AREA SHAPE="rect" COORDS="0,142,98,285" HREF="http://
        www.domain.com/html4dum/ftpstuff.htm">
    <AREA SHAPE="rect" COORDS="99,142,198,285" HREF="http://
        www.domain.com/html4dum/contents.htm">
    <AREA SHAPE="rect" COORDS="199,142,298,285" HREF="http:
        //www.domain.com/html4dum/search4d.htm">
    <AREA SHAPE="rect" COORDS="299,142,398,285" HREF="http:
        //www.domain.com/html4dum/contact.htm">
    <AREA SHAPE="rect" COORDS="399,142,499,285" HREF="http:
        //www.domain.com/html4dum/whatsnew.htm">
    <AREA SHAPE="default" HREF="http://www.domain.com/
        html4dum/contents.htm">
</MAP>
```

If you can master the art of cut-and-paste, then you're sure to be able to use these simple map constructs in your own documents. Remember, client-side image maps don't need a map file (that information is included in the HTML) or a server (the client handles all the processing for the map). If you want to see one in action, load up the front page of the example Web site from the book's CD-ROM and select "client-side image map version."

Get ready for some real action in the next chapter, as you finally roll up your sleeves and get down and dirty on the back-end side of the Web environment. You get the lowdown on what happens with CGI scripts, input-handling programs for forms, search engines, and other tools that extend what the Web can do for your users. Better buckle up!

Chapter 15
Navigation Aids

• •

In This Chapter

▶ Searching for Web satisfaction

▶ Staying out of the maze

▶ Providing added document structure

▶ Doing things the database way

▶ Avoiding diminished returns

▶ Leading the search for good information

• •

*I*f you think that forms are where the fun is in HTML, be prepared to enjoy yourself further. In this chapter, you find out about additional widgets and techniques that you can use to make your documents searchable and your sites easier to surf so that users can find what they want quickly and easily. Some of these items are overkill for basic home pages, but they are wonderful for larger, more complex sites. (In fact, without searchable versions of the HTML DTDs, we probably couldn't have written this book.)

You need to help your potential readers find your Web site and then help them move around easily within your site after they get there. Although there are a variety of ways to do this, some of the best methods include

✔ Improving the information that search engines gather about your site (using the <META> tag)

✔ Working with intelligent robots (a.k.a. Web spiders)

✔ Adding a search engine to your site

✔ Adding a menu, a list of pages, an index, or a site map

✔ Creating a Wayfinding Toolkit

✔ Providing consistent navigation tools

You find out more about each of these techniques in the following sections.

The <META> Tag

The <META> tag is an HTML markup element that you can use within the head of a document to define information about the information contained in the document. That really sounds like a mouthful, but it's true. The <META> tag identifies meta-information or data about the content of a document. If you don't understand what we mean, take a peek at the examples in this section. Hopefully, they will help clarify this concept.

Browsers and Web automata (spiders, worms, wanderers, and so on) often use the <META> tag to gather information about a Web site. Browsers use this information to alter their displays, gather statistics, or even associate activities with commands. Much more common is for a search engine robot to read the <META> information and include the information in its database. When a user performs a search with a query that matches the <META> info, the results returned are much more likely to be accurate and informative. In other words, when you use <META> tags, you improve the odds that search engine users can find relevant information at your site.

Now that you know this secret, you may want to add <META> tags to your documents. As a general rule, only place <META> tags in your entry-point documents (that is, in those documents where most users — or robots — enter or access your site).

The NAME and HTTP-EQUIV values (other strings that automated Web wanderers search for) are not predetermined by the HTML DTDs, but rather can be fully customized. This means that every search engine can define its own unique sets of meta-data that it wants to collect and catalog. Nevertheless, we don't recommend that end users like you (yep, as a Webmaster, you're just an end user compared to those who manage search engines and Web tool sites) create any new or hitherto unused values for the <META> tag. In fact, you'd just be wasting your time because most search engines or other Web tools ignore any items they don't recognize.

In the examples that follow, we show some of the most common NAME and HTTP-EQUIV values. We recommend that you stick with these. If you find that a specific search engine or Web tool supports other strings, feel free to add those to your collection.

Rather than repeating the tag definition for <META> that appears in Chapter 6, we skip the formalities and show you a few great examples you use in your own Web documents. Remember, the <META> tag must appear within the <HEAD> tag pair.

✔ Use this construction to indicate the creation date of the document:

```
<META NAME="creation_date"
CONTENT="DDD, DD MMM YYYY HH:MM:SS GMT">
```

✔ Use this construction to indicate the date the content expires, which helps a search engine know when to remove stale documents from its database and to refresh this information:

```
<META HTTP-EQUIV="expires"
CONTENT="DDD, DD MMM YYYY HH:MM:SS GMT">
```

✔ Use this construction to supply keywords to search engines in addition to those found automatically by robots within the document itself:

```
<META NAME="keywords"
 CONTENT="keyword1 keyword2 keyword3">
```

✔ Use this construction to supply the e-mail address for the author or individual who's responsible for the document:

```
<META HTTP-EQUIV="reply-to"
CONTENT="username@email.domain.name">
```

✔ Use this construction to indicate the name of the author:

```
<META NAME="author" CONTENT="Name">
```

✔ Use this construction to indicate the document's resource type (common values include document, catalog, bibliography, and news release):

```
<META HTTP-EQUIV="resource-type" CONTENT="document">
```

✔ Use this construction to define a description that a search engine can use to support this tag:

```
<META NAME="description" CONTENT="text">
```

✔ Use this construction to indicate the scope or range of a document's distribution or application (common values include global, domestic, local, or private):

```
<META HTTP-EQUIV="distribution" CONTENT="scope">
```

✔ Use this construction to indicate the program used to generate a document, such as the name of the HTML editor used:

```
<META NAME="generator" CONTENT="program name">
```

✔ Use this construction to indicate a document's copyright holder and date:

```
<META HTTP-EQUIV="copyright" CONTENT="name -- date">
```

✔ Use this construction to force a document to be reloaded or a new document to be loaded after a specific number of seconds:

```
<META HTTP-EQUIV="REFRESH" CONTENT="value[; URL]">
```

Tada!! That's the `<META>` tag in a nutshell.

There's a Spider on the Web!

If you think of the Web as a vast, gossamer skein of interconnected documents all over the world, you're close to understanding its basic topology. But knowing how the strands are arranged is only half the picture. You must also understand a little about the denizens that inhabit this cyberspace realm.

Webcrawlers and search engines

In addition to the vast multitude of users who happily browse their way through the myriad links on the Web, there are cyberbeasts that frolic through these same documents as well. Some are computer programs called *robots* or *spiders* that do nothing but follow links around the Web (to see where they lead) and catalog and categorize what they find along the way.

The best known cyberbeasts lurk behind the scenes of popular search engine sites at

- Yahoo! Guide to the WWW

  `http://www.yahoo.com/`

- Infoseek Net Search

  `http://www.infoseek.com/`

- Lycos Search Engine

  `http://www.lycos.com/`

- WebCrawler Searching

  `http://www.webcrawler.com/`

We mention search engines elsewhere in this book. No matter whether you call them spiders, robots, Webcrawlers, or "Hey, you!", these tireless, automatic searchers use `<META>` tag info, document titles, headings, and the first paragraph of text within each document they visit to help them catalog and report on what they find. Search engines compile and manage the information that these spiders report. Then humans use the catalogs that the search engines build when they seek to locate Web sites of interest.

If your Web site appears in all major Web search databases, you'll be more likely to attract large numbers of users to your work. Because the number of Web sites surpassed 7 million in 1996, users have lots of variety to choose from! If yours is listed at a search site, this often increases the number of visitors because your site is more visible to the public.

Don't wait for the spider to come to you — register!

Most Web search engines offer methods to register your site, or at least to supply them with your site's URL. Make sure that you register or list your site at all possible locations. Such listings don't cost anything, and they don't take much time or effort, either. You may also elect to pay for listings at numerous online *malls* if you like their exposure and can afford their charges. These malls aren't used nearly as much as free search engines, but if you're in a specialized niche, one or more of these malls may be right up your alley (find them by searching for **mall** or **marketplace** by using any of the free search engines).

Keeping the Bugs Away

Just because a spider can find every document on the Web doesn't mean it should. All too often, the automated robots of the Internet find their way into areas of a Web site that the owner would rather not have indexed or linked to from outside sources. In such cases, the only way to prevent a robot from looking everywhere and anywhere is to tell it to stay away. Fortunately there are two ways to do this: First, you can use a special <META> tag to discourage robots; or second, you can create a robots.txt file to control robot activities at your site.

Complete details on both of these exclusion methods appear on the Web Robots Pages. We encourage you to figure out how to put these conventions into practice:

```
http://info.webcrawler.com/mak/projects/robots/
            robots.html
```

<META> CONTENT

The <META> tag markup defines how robots should deal with a specific document. For example, the following markup prevents robots from indexing or analyzing links that may appear therein:

```
<META NAME="ROBOTS" CONTENT="NOINDEX, NOFOLLOW">
```

By using various CONTENT values, you can specify a different level of activity for each document:

- INDEX — Index the document
- NOINDEX — Do not index the document
- FOLLOW — Analyze the links in the document
- NOFOLLOW — Do not analyze the links in the document
- ALL — INDEX, FOLLOW
- NONE — NOINDEX, NOFOLLOW

Note that such values pertain only to documents in which they appear. Adding a <META> tag construct to one document does not affect the activity of the robot for other documents. Note also that the <META> tag is not as widely supported as the Robot Exclusion Protocol that's covered in the next section.

Robots, go home!

The robots.txt file uses a scripting language called the Robots Exclusion Protocol (the complete details are available at the WebCrawler site mentioned earlier in this chapter). This protocol allows you to restrict all, or part, of your Web site from all or merely from specific robots. For example, a robots.txt file that contains the following code restricts all robots from visiting the CGI-BIN and TMP directories off the Web site's root:

```
User-agent: *
Disallow: /cgi-bin/
Disallow: /tmp/
```

This next example restricts all but one robot:

```
User-agent: WebCrawler
Disallow:
User-agent: *
Disallow: /
```

If you take the time to learn the syntax of the Robots Exclusion Protocol, it can provide a simple solution to the issues of robot control. Most robots are programmed to recognize and follow this protocol. We recommend using this technique to control their activities on your Web site.

Searching Documents for Details . . .

The latest versions of such Web robots and crawlers don't delve deeply into the contents of every document they find. In computer lingo, they search broadly (go everywhere and grab one or a few pages from each site), but not deeply (they don't catalog the entire contents for every site). They'll probably find your site, but you'll be lucky if you get more than your home page indexed and listed in their search engines. If your site contains large, complex documents, you may need to install a different kind of search tool locally to make it easier for serious researchers to find what they want.

The functionality that's required is like the electronic equivalent of an index for a book: A list of key words, topics, or phrases that provides pointers to their locations within your site's documents. Fortunately for you, this technology is easy to deploy because your documents are already in electronic formats and merely require a bit of extra massaging to accommodate such use.

As a budding Web author, you may wonder what you have to do to add this kind of capability to your documents. We can give you two kinds of answers to this question.

✔ **In nontechnical terms:** You have to create an index to your document and then figure out how to link that index to the actual content.

✔ **In technical terms:** You must do the following:

- Add the ⟨ISINDEX⟩ tag to your document's ⟨HEAD⟩ . . . ⟨/HEAD⟩ section.

- Use a database or some similar program to build an index of keywords and phrases for your document.

- Identify all the index words as anchors for hypertext links in your document (so that the index can take users to those words and phrases).

- Establish the anchors in your document.

- Create a CGI program to handle user requests for keywords or phrases; the program needs to build a list of links for each corresponding instance in the document.

Basically, the way this works is that you turn on the search capability in the user's browser (where available) by including an ⟨ISINDEX⟩ tag in your document's head section. Then you provide a URL for an input-handling CGI program that builds search responses for users with specific requests. This program uses the electronic equivalent of an index — a list of keywords and phrases with pointers to their locations in the document's text — to respond to queries. These responses consist of HTML documents with links to the locations in your document set where the requested keywords or phrases reside.

As programming problems go, this one is not too difficult. You do have to locate or build an indexing tool to prepare the data files that you search in response to user queries. These data files usually consist of alphabetized (or, ASCII-collated) lists of the keywords and phrases that your index recognizes. If you build your program so that it returns information for unsuccessful searches ("String not found" is good; a list of near-matches is even better), you can field some of the weird non sequiturs that bored users may sometimes be tempted to try on your indexing program.

Then you can use the CGI program that searches the list to build an HTML document that lists the *hits* in order of occurrence, with links to the various locations in your document where matches were found. This creates a hotlist of these locations that your users can select to find the information they're seeking.

We also suggest pulling some surrounding text from each part of the document where a hit occurs and writing that to your *return page* with your CGI program as well. Including surrounding text gives users some understanding of the context in which a hit occurs and helps them to decide which links they really want to follow.

For an outstanding example of what a well-organized index can offer, please investigate the searchable version of the HTML 2.0 specification available at the following URL:

```
http://hopf.math.nwu.edu:80/html2.0/dosearch.html
```

This document is the work of the HTML working group, Internet Engineering Task Force (IETF), focused on making HTML into an Internet RFC-level specification.

The Bigger Things Get, the Easier It Is to Get Lost!

If you're wondering why indexing tools are worthwhile, it's because finding your way around complex collections of information — like the HTML specifications and related DTDs — can get kind of hairy without computer-aided assistance. A good rule for deciding whether you need indexing is: If your site is comprised of more than 30 documents, it's time to think about indexing!

Indexing is also extremely valuable for sites that contain large documents that cover government rules or regulations. By their nature, these documents are best displayed in a single file, even though they may be hundreds of screens long. Readers of large documents greatly appreciate a searchable index for such documents.

If you're worried about how much work is involved, don't be. If your question is, "Do I have to get into heavy database programming and implement all the functionality mentioned in the preceding section, just to make my document searchable?" — the answer is (fortunately) "No."

In fact, by using the first type of search engine we mentioned at the beginning of this chapter — the kind that looks for documents based on titles — we were able to come up with a number of pointers to help you get started on making your site searchable. By using the following search query on the Yahoo! search engine

```
http://search.yahoo.com/bin/search?p=indexing
```

we came up with a number of tools and locations that we can recommend for further investigation.

- ✔ *Indexmaker* is a Perl script whose function is to produce an index for a virtual document consisting of a number of HTML files in a single directory. (This is the tool used to build the searchable HTML DTDs that helped us write this book.)

  ```
  http://hopf.math.nwu.edu/docs/utility.html#indexmaker
  ```

- ✔ For inclusion in an online searchable index at the MIT Artificial Intelligence Laboratory, try this URL:

  ```
  http://www.cs.indiana.edu/item-index/intro.html
  ```

- ✔ For local indexing and related services, please consult

  ```
  http://www.ai.mit.edu/tools/site-index.html
  ```

- ✔ *Harvest* is an integrated set of tools designed to gather, extract, organize, search, cache, and replicate relevant information on the Internet. (Harvest may be a bit too formal for documents not in need of wide distribution.)

  ```
  http://harvest.transarc.com/
  ```

- ✔ Finally, here's the URL for a whole page of information about indexing and related tools:

  ```
  http://union.ncsa.uiuc.edu/HyperNews/get/www/
           indexing.html
  ```

Rest assured that somewhere in the haystack of information that we just shared with you is the needle you may be seeking. Plus, it's no accident that the tool we admired most shows up first on the list! The Yahoo! search engine is a great magnet for finding that needling program in the cyberhaystack!

Documentary Integuments: Indexes, Jump Tables, and Internal Links

You probably have already heard this in several other chapters, but we feel compelled to remind you that as documents get bigger and more complicated, more structure is needed. That's one reason why we think indexes are such a great idea. But it's also why you need to make liberal and extensive use of internal links in your documents so that you can help your readers navigate without having to scroll, scroll, scroll.

Starting off a long document with a hyperlinked table of contents is a really good idea. A hyperlinked TOC can act like a "jump table" and provide an immediate way to get your readers from a list of topics to the real thing with the click of the mouse. Also, if you break long blocks of text into regular screens of information coupled with navigation controls (which range from *navigation bars* to full-blown clickable *image maps* with nice-looking 3-D buttons), you can help your users from getting lost in your Web. Explicit document navigation controls should never be more than one screen of information away. (Even better is always having a control in sight when it's needed.)

Searchable indexes can greatly help readers in search of specific information, which is why they're a natural complement to our recommended frequency of navigation controls. Searchable indexes may be more difficult to implement, but if your content is appropriate, so be it. Your users will show their appreciation by returning time and again to your Web site, and they will bring their friends.

Doing Things the Database Way

For really long and complex documents (governmental regulations, tax code, how to build your own aircraft carrier, and so on), the only good way to manage the information is with a database. Whether you decide to operate within the confines of a document management program or use Paradox to build your own set of HTML document controls, when the number of files you have to manage exceeds 100, you'll appreciate getting some mechanical help and organization. Plus, the ability to search files on keywords or specific text makes finding things surprisingly easier. (We won't even mention the other nice things a good database can do for you, such as search and replace, automatic update propagation. . . .)

This added level of structure and control costs you, to be sure, but it's worth considering because of the time and effort that it can save you and your users. If you don't believe us, try managing a huge, intertwined collection of files without computer assistance for even a brief time. You'll be singing a different tune after dealing with changes galore.

Stay Away from Diminishing Returns

On the other hand, you can go overboard when organizing your materials. The temptation may be nearly overwhelming to break your documents into perfectly formatted single screens of beautifully laid-out information for your user's enjoyment. Before you succumb to this impulse, remember the following "home truths" about the Web:

- ✔ All those beautiful graphics and on-screen controls aren't visible from character-mode browsers.

- ✔ What looks wonderful to you through your Super-Geewhiz 3-D VR Metaverse goggles looks pretty drab to the guy down the hall running the third version back of Cello or Mosaic on a plain VGA monitor.

- ✔ When aiming for perfection, the "last 10 percent" usually costs as much — and takes as much time to achieve — as the first 90 percent. Don't waste your time making the excellent look sublime; you have better ways of filling your days (we hope)! Concentrate on content if you really want to better your site.

As thrilling as the quest for the perfect page may be, this search is usually not worth the effort. And, if the people who pay the bills (and your salary) find out about your costly quest for the "holy WWW Grail," even being penitent may not help you escape their buzz-saw wrath. Remember the words of the mystic sage upon seeing the infinite majesty of the Universe: "Enough already!"

Virtual Compass

One revolutionary addition that you (and everyone else) should include in your Web site's navigational arsenal is the *Wayfinding Toolkit*. This little gem is a tutorial, a help file, and a set of navigation instructions all rolled into one handy set of pages on a site. Of course, we think highly of the Wayfinding Toolkit because we invented the concept. Even so, we think you and your users will find such a kit a worthwhile addition to most Web sites. And we cheerfully admit we stole the concept from the folks who build airports, amusement parks, and other venues where lots of people pass through and therefore need help finding their way around.

To see a Wayfinding Toolkit in action, visit our LANWrights, Inc. Web site at

```
http://www.lanw.com/
```

Click the cute little toolkit that's labeled "Wayfinding Toolkit" for more details.

We include a list of the major sections for our site and describe what each one contains. Furthermore, we display and explain every navigational control we use in the site. You needn't limit yourself to these two topics. Go ahead and include any relevant information or instructions that may help people find their way around your site. Anything you can do to simplify access, or to speed a user toward "the good stuff," will be rewarded.

You can view other Wayfinding Toolkits we've created by checking the pages we've included on the CD that accompanies this book — just follow the Wayfinding Toolkit link on one of the main pages. You can also visit one of these other sites for more examples of this genre:

```
http://www.lanw.com/myw/
http://www.lanw.com/ht96/
http://www.lanw.com/beh/
http://www.lanw.com/wpd/
```

To access any of these collections of pages, you need a frame-compatible browser. After you load the home page, click the Compass icon to visit the Wayfinding Toolkit.

Rack and Pinion Steering

There's nothing worse than trying to steer a car with a broken steering wheel — you really don't have much control over where the vehicle goes. What's worse is you can't get around quickly for fear of crashing. The same is true of Web sites that fail to provide reasonable navigation. Every site doesn't have to be controlled the same way; that's part of the beauty of the Web. But every site should be easy to get around. Don't force your visitors to guess where links are — make them obvious!

We don't care if you use text, icons, or imagemaps (or even Java or ActiveX, if you're so inclined and have spare time on your hands). Just make sure they're there. Here are a few rules regarding effective navigational aids:

✔ Be consistent.

✔ Use navigation controls to enhance your content.

✔ Let the content dictate the controls.

✔ Make things as simple as possible to maintain.

✔ If the controls are complicated, explain them in great detail.

If you need some examples, check out the Web site we include on the CD; it's got a nice set of controls. Also, check out some of these Web sites to see a few other possibilities:

```
http://www.lanw.com/
http://www.lanw.com/mh4d/
http://www.holodeck3.com/
http://www.unitedmedia.com/comics/dilbert/
```

Where's the Search Lead?

As the Web becomes more commonplace and its publishing model better understood, you can expect to see more tools to help add structure to your creations. Today, proper decorum suggests indexing larger, more complex documents with a linked table of contents or a searchable index.

In the not-too-distant future, you'll be able to orient users with animated tutorials and other amazing feats of technology. The trend is clear, though: more and better communications based on a shared model of what Web pages can deliver, along with shared toolsets to help realize those models.

With this metaphorical view through the cyberportal of tomorrow, however, we leave the tools and advanced capabilities of HTML and CGI behind, and dive back into the reality of Web publishing, as you move on to tackle the nitty-gritty details of testing your work. *Allez!*

Part IV
Publishing on the Web

The 5th Wave   By Rich Tennant

"What do you mean you're updating our Web Homepage?"

In this part . . .

We show you how to catch and kill potential bugs in your Web site. You'll also be armed with strategies to enlist user feedback, to help you effectively communicate online, and to avoid having to deal with too many problems once you've taken your work public. We also tell you what it takes to let the world know not just where your pages are, but why they're worth a visit.

Chapter 16

Testing, Testing, 1-2-3

. . . .

In This Chapter

▶ Discovering why it's important to test your Web pages

▶ Finding out whose opinions count

▶ Investigating what to test

▶ Testing your own Web pages

▶ Writing a test plan

. . . .

*O*f course, you want to get your wonderful Web creations on the Web ASAP. But — cliché warning — "You only get one chance to make a good first impression." Nobody has time to get it right the first time, but they can always make the time to fix it later. So why not take that little bit of extra time while you're creating your Web pages and run them through a few tests to check spelling and accuracy, to validate their HTML syntax, links, anchors, and so on, as well as to judge your target audience's acceptance? That ounce of prevention can be worth embarrassing pounds, hours, and maybe even dollars of cure later on!

Why Test Your Pages?

Do you want to read this on the `comp.infosystems.www.authoring.html` newsgroup and realize that you're the "Netclown"?

> "Did you see that mess of a home page Netclown put up yesterday?"

> "Yeah. What a rookie! He forgot to close a heading tag, and I got inch-high text for a zillion screens."

> "That was a bummer. Did you run into the missing links, too? I guess he's never heard of testing before publishing."

Get the picture?

The rest of this chapter discusses how you can effectively test your own Web pages along with HTML testing and validation procedures. Chapter 18 discusses how to get others to help you with your testing, how to obtain participant feedback, and what to do with it.

What You Think Doesn't Count

It doesn't matter what you think of your Web pages unless you're planning on being the only one who looks at them. Of course, you like your Web pages; you created them. They look great on your browser and your monitor, and you're proud of them. So you can keep'm on your computer for only you to view, you can print'm, frame'm and hang'm on your wall, or you can publish'm on the WWW. The choice is always yours.

You wanna publish'm, do ya? You want to share them with the WWW community and show them your creations? You want millions of Net surfers to visit your Web pages frequently and applaud your work? Now the tables have turned. No matter how much you like your Web pages, your users' likes and dislikes determine your Web's future.

The rest of this chapter assumes that, regardless of the content in your Web pages and regardless of your desired participant audience, you want to provide Web pages that please your participants and keep them coming back for more. The testing procedures discussed in the following paragraphs are aimed at helping you create and maintain an enjoyable and informative site for your target audience.

Rule number 1: Users rule.

Rule number 2: When in doubt, refer to Rule number 1.

There's that word again, "user." Today's Web surfers aren't sitting in front of their computers to be passive participants. They want to actively participate in your Web site. They want to experience it, get into it, and be players in the action. Involve them in your testing or they won't become involved in your site.

These rules do not mean that you must do everything every user asks of you. If your Web page is about earthquakes, you certainly don't want to include information on kite flying just because somebody requests it. However, if some of your readers request a different arrangement of earthquake information so that they can review it more easily, you would be well advised to accommodate their wishes. Change for the sake of change is upsetting to most folks, but change for the better, with valid reasons and advanced participant education, can be beneficial to everyone involved.

Expect (And Test for) the Unexpected

"I should test for WHAT?" You should test for every possible, impossible, logical, illogical, expected, and unexpected occurrence. "But I want to publish my pages this century." Okay, then make sure that you plan for the *somewhat* unexpected.

In particular, you want to test in the following three areas:

- **Predicted ranges and values:** Everything that you intentionally put into your Web pages and expect participants to access. This includes all links, images, `ALT="wording"`, forms input sections and expected values, clickable map areas, and so on.

- **Boundaries:** The edges of the envelope of the expected. More problems occur at the edges than in the middle of most computer programs, which is what your HTML-coded Web page actually is. Many programs work perfectly with expected values, correctly ignoring values outside their boundaries, but then fail on those values at the exact boundaries between the expected and the unexpected. For example, making the expected range from 1 to 100 and putting in an error-checking routine for values less than zero and more than 101 may work fine until someone puts in zero or 101. Make sure you try the boundary values, too!

- **Outside the boundaries:** Everything not included in the two preceding bullets. Of course, you can't click on every pixel on every page any more than you can enter every out-of-range value on every form. You can try a few out-of-bounds values and clicks to make sure you haven't missed the somewhat obvious. Many a mistake has been found in a program when the programmer sneezed, causing the programmer to click the mouse button with the cursor on a place where "no sane user would ever click."

Don't lose sleep over testing absolutely everything. Do approach testing as something that definitely benefits your Web pages if done logically, methodically, and repeatedly during your Web page development and maintenance.

In Vitro Vitrification: Alpha Testing Methods

Testing your Web pages is very much like testing any other computer program. You test it while you are in the midst of creating the page because you have to look at it with a browser or your HTML editor's browser view. If you are using a completely WYSIWYG HTML authoring environment, most of the developmental HTML syntax testing is done for you by the authoring program.

As you proceed with your development of a page, you tag and view, tag and view, and so on, until you decide that you like what you see. When you have coded all features that you want into the page, it's ready for more stringent testing.

The following steps generally guide you through what is called the alpha testing phase. Only you and a few trusted assistants need to make it through this phase. Hopefully, by the end of the alpha phase, you will have removed most of the big, ugly, and obvious problems. If you're developing your own home page and personal Web, you still need to go through the steps because if it's worth doing, it's worth doing right, isn't it?

1. **Run it through a spell checker.**

   And while you're at it, *correct* the spelling and double-check your grammar. Poor grammar is even worse than spelling errors.

2. **Test the page by itself on your own computer with local files and relative URLs.**

   Fix the problems and test again.

3. **Test the page in the Web of other pages on your own computer.**

   Fix the problems and test again.

4. **Test the page by itself on the Web server in your private area with relative or full URLs.**

   Fix the problems and test again.

5. **Submit the page's URL to an online HTML validation form for syntax checking.**

   Fix the problems and resubmit until it's clean. Hey, nobody produces perfect code the first time.

6. **Use a link tester and other programs to test the page with the other pages in your private Web on the Web server.**

   Fix the problems and test again.

7. **Enlist a few work associates or close friends to critique the page.**

   Otherwise, keep it private and get them to keep quiet about it. Fix the problems and test again.

8. **When you think the pages are ready, submit them to the HTML validation site one last time.**

   If it comes up clean, it's ready to beta test.

After iterations of comments and revisions until your alpha testers abandon you — or until they don't find anything else to nitpick — your page(s) may be ready for honest-to-goodness beta testing (where you actually ask other people to pick your page apart and tell you about it). We discuss beta testing in Chapter 18. The rest of this chapter explains some details of your alpha testing.

Webbuilder, test thine own Web thyself

The two strongest reasons for testing your Web pages with an HTML testing and validation program, link checker, and anchor checker prior to making them available to the WWW community are

✔ Your Web pages may contain HTML tag errors or nonstandard tags that would cause them to display improperly on your targeted browsers.

✔ Your Web pages may not contain either required or optional HTML tags that are important to search engines or spiders in the future. Without proper usage of the tags that crawlers search on, your pages may not be listed in future indexes and jump pages; therefore, it won't be easy for participants to find your Web.

If you haven't created your page on a strict HTML syntax-checking, authoring system, submit it to one of the online HTML syntax validation systems or use one or more of the programs found at the following sites.

Go to the following URL at Yahoo! and you find links to 22 — that's right, 22 — sites with HTML validation checkers, link testers, forms testers, syntax checkers, anchor checkers, and more. Using some of these sites is as simple as linking to the tester's site and entering the URL of the site you want to test (that is, your site) into their form. Other sites you must download and run on your own computer. Here are a few of our favorites:

```
http://www.yahoo.com/Computers_and_Internet/
Information_and_Documentation/Data_Formats/HTML/
Validation_Checkers/
```

Weblint is a Perl script that checks your HTML for errors over the Web through an HTML form, or you can download it, as follows:

```
http://www.cre.canon.co.uk/~neilb/weblint/lintform.html
http://www.cre.canon.co.uk/~neilb/weblint/index.html
```

Htmlchek version 4.1 is an HTML syntax and cross-reference checker that checks HTML documents for errors, creates a cross-reference, automatically expands entities (such as European characters) to their proper HTML form, and performs other useful services. You can find it via the Web at

```
http://uts.cc.utexas.edu/~churchh/htmlchek.html
```

Lvrfy is a simple, UNIX-based link-checking program that checks your pages for broken links. You can obtain Lvrfy from

```
http://www.cs.dartmouth.edu/~crow/lvrfy.html
```

You may want to check out Georgia Tech College of Computing HTML Validation Service at

```
http://www.cc.gatech.edu/grads/j/Kipp.Jones/HaLidation/
validation-form.html
```

HAL HTML Validation Service validates multiple versions of the HTML DTD and many different browsers at

```
http://www.webtechs.com/html-val-svc/index.html
```

HTML Form-Testing Home Page at

```
http://www.research.digital.com/nsl/formtest/
```

Or you can download a stand-alone UNIX HTML syntax checker from

```
http://www.webtechs.com/html-tk/
```

After you get the report from one of the syntax checkers, revise your Web page if necessary. Most of these syntax checkers check for the HTML 2.0 DTD and HTML 3.2 DTD, so any tags you use that don't conform may be marked as errors. If you want to continue to use tags that are specific for certain browsers, do it knowing that your page may not look the way you expect on other browsers.

WebCrawler may not pick up your Web page if you use the `<!DOCTYPE>` tag with a reference to HTML 3.2 until HTML 3.2 is officially approved.

Iteration, iteration, iteration

Creating your Web pages and assembling your Web is a repetitive, build-and-change process. After you have more than one page, changes on any single page can affect others. Unless you repeat the same tests each time you make a change, you may find out the hard way from your users that errors have crept into your pages. Among the many things that build-and-change requires — unless you have perfect recall — is that you write down your testing procedures and keep accurate records of your testing.

Type it or write it; then do it

You actually started the testing and validation of your Web pages when you sketched the layout of each page and your overall Web structure. These sketches are the first documents in your test plan (see — you've already finished something, and you didn't even know you'd started).

For your personal Web, your test plan may consist of only a copy of these layout sketches with a checklist of testing steps that you want to use on each page of your Web. This testing takes some of your valuable time, but the results will make you happy later.

If you're in a business or institutional environment, you are probably more accustomed to formalized, structured development and testing. Familiarity with this environment can help your undoubtedly more complex Web accomplish its goals.

The following section presents a generic alpha test plan. Those of you who need to produce this type of document for your organization or anyone who really wants to proceed with testing your Web pages in an extremely orderly fashion may modify it to suit your specific needs. And for the rest of you, it won't strain your brain to read over the plan, too. Remember, do it right the first time or you'll have to take the time to fix it later.

Alpha test plan

The following sections outline a plan for alpha testing your pages.

Purpose

Provide a comprehensive plan for testing the accuracy and completeness of the Web page at stages during the development cycle or prior to the release of a new version.

Scope

The test plan encompasses testing the user-level functionality of all features, the accuracy of the data generated, the agreement of the user-guide information with the Web page operation, the agreement of the normative data from the manuals and errata sheets with the Web page data, and the compatibility of the Web page with various hardware and software configurations.

Test overview

- Test all functions of the Web page under expected usage conditions with appropriate hardware and software.

- Test all functions under abnormal usage conditions, such as inappropriate hardware or software, incorrect or extreme data conditions, and operator errors.

- Test the accuracy of any data by comparing Web-page generated values with known values.

Goals

- Determine the level of functionality and performance of the Web page.

- Document all operational abnormalities and Web page errors in an efficient and flexible test-tracking system.

- Verify Web page and participant information correlation.

Schedule and resources

Testing begins on (date) and continues until you complete the test plan and there are no correctable errors found on the Web page. The Software Testing and Quality Assurance Department staff (you and your friends) provide full-time testing. Make sure that you draft only people close to you who can keep the location of your pages to themselves. You don't need the aggravation of unwanted testers at this point in your page development. When you recruit your helpers, you need to give them some instructions on what type of feedback you want. At the simplest, you can just ask them to e-mail you with any problems or suggestions they may have. This e-mail method works if they are conscientious, organized people, which is the only type you want for your alpha testers.

Tester form

Providing a simple text form that your testers can complete and e-mail back to you really helps both your testers and you. Request at least the following on your form:

- Tester's name and e-mail address
- Date problem was found
- Page title and URL
- Page version date/time
- Feature/function affected
- Formatting

- Text/data
- Link (URL)
- Image (URL)
- Form (URL)
- Description of problem
- How to duplicate problem
- Comments and suggestions for solutions

Tell your testers that it would be really helpful if they religiously filled in all of the information on a separate form for each different problem. When the forms start clogging up your e-mail in-box, you'll need a place to store them and a method of sorting them. Any reasonable method, from printing each and visually sorting them to importing them into a database program, will work. Use the easiest one that works for you. Keep in mind that you'll probably want to use the same method for the beta test feedback, so choose a method that can handle the number of messages you expect — then double that number to get ready for the unexpected!

System configurations

Testing is conducted by using the following system configurations as representative of systems in the field:

- **Browsers:** List all browsers to be tested. If possible, try all browsers that you think your target audience may use (or every one you know about, anyway).
- **Computers:** List all computer systems you want tested along with the above browsers. Many of the browsers work on more than one system (such as, PC with Windows, Macintosh, X-Windows, and so on).
- **Web servers:** List Web server software you want tested with CGI scripts and forms. You may be limited to your own Internet Service Provider or your business or institution's Web server, but test it thoroughly and completely.

Test method and evaluation

- Testers evaluate Web page functionality and performance primarily at the user level by performing operations with keyboard and mouse input and evaluating data that the Web page generates.
- Testers document Web page errors and operational abnormalities by recording the following information when they encounter a problem: feature/function affected, page version date/time, date problem found,

tester's name, description of problem, method of re-creation, and any other notes that may help the developer understand and resolve the problem. Priorities are assigned to the problems as they are received: priority 1 — system lockup or data corruption, priority 2 — cosmetics (spelling, wording, screens), priority 3 — inconvenient operation.

✔ The document containing Web page problems is updated as often as possible and is made available to the developers for resolution of the problems.

Performance and functionality testing

The following sections outline some areas to consider during the performance and functionality testing.

Screen appearance: Browse through your hard work

Inspect each screen looking for inaccuracies or omissions related to spelling, formatting, and layout. Download and install all the browsers that will run on your own computer and test with them first. Make a deal with Web friends who have different types of computers. Have them test your pages in return for your testing their Web pages with your computer. Turnabout is still fair play, and it can expose you (and them) to new ideas and materials!

Link operation and content

Verify that each link functions correctly and that each destination URL exists and presents the information named in the hyperlink text. Use one of the link testing programs you found on Yahoo! to help you.

Forms operation

Verify that each form correctly receives, processes, and records the participant's responses. Verify that the Web server properly stores the data and delivers it to the appropriate location in the desired format. Use one of the forms testing programs you find on Yahoo! to help you with this also.

Clickable map operation

Verify that clicking on each portion of the map displays the appropriate image or page. Verify what happens when you click other portions of the map and screen around it.

Limits and boundary checking

Test all limit and boundary conditions, such as high and low numerical values and text amounts in forms. Make sure you test the edges, not just outside the expected limits.

Chapter 17

Going Live with Your Web Site

● ●

In This Chapter

▶ Getting your creation ready for prime time

▶ The problems of relativity

▶ Getting spaced

▶ From local to remote, doing the FTP thing

▶ Déjà vu investigation

● ●

*N*ow that you've spent countless hours creating the ultimate Web site, you need to get onto a public Internet Web server so the world can benefit from your enlightened genius. This is both a simple and complex activity that you need to thoroughly understand.

This chapter walks you through the arduous process of final refinement to public scrutiny.

Prelaunch Checklist

Before you even think about posting to a public site, you've got a bit of work to do. First and foremost, you must make absolutely sure that you are not distributing federally protected documentation or instructions on how to build the ultimate weapon. The tall guys with the gray suits, dark hats, and earphones really hate it when you do that. Actually, long before you review your content one final time, you need to investigate a few other important aspects of your site, such as whether it really functions.

If you are reading this book and following the material sequentially, then you've already been through the previous chapter on testing your Web pages. However, in the interest of public safety and to prevent the cyber-equivalent of running with the scissors, we are going to walk you through the major points again.

First, double-check your tags. Many issues related to markup are absolutely essential to the proper operation of your site. These include

- ✔ Spelling the tag and the attributes correctly
- ✔ Using quotation marks when required
- ✔ Using the closing tag on all tag pairs
- ✔ Using the proper order of nested tags
- ✔ Using the correct tag for the job

Instead of abusing you by requiring you to recite this 12 times while riding a hippopotamus, we're going to assume that you've got this tag stuff down pat.

Second, double-check your navigation. This double-check both inspects the existence and proper sequencing of your navigation and proves, hopefully, that users can drill down into your site and still be able to get back out. A few things to look into:

- ✔ Does every page have navigation capabilities?
- ✔ Does the navigation control point or get the user to the proper pages?
- ✔ Does the navigation actually work?
- ✔ Is it clear and obvious how to use the navigation controls?
- ✔ Can you reach every document by using only the navigation controls?
- ✔ Have you provided a site map to orient visitors?

Great, now you and your visitors can travel in style with only minimal possibilities of getting lost in cyberspace. We've been lost before, and you wouldn't believe where you can end up — sometimes it is not pretty.

Third, you must have your ticket validated. If you didn't pick up on it before or haven't yet dug into Chapter 19, you need to validate your Web documents. Validation is the process of running an HTML syntax checker against your markup to determine if you followed all the construction and use rules the latest HTML DTD defines. This step ensures that your site is compatible with the widest range of browsers.

Finally, check your content for polyps. If we've said it a 100 times, we've said it a 1,000 — focus on your content. After you solve all the problems of construction, syntax, and navigation, you've only cleared the way to deal with the central most important part of your Web site — its content. Before you even consider placing your Web site into the public eye, you need to look again at your content and consider

- ✔ Is it relevant?
- ✔ Does anyone other than you care about this material?

✔ Is it arranged in bite-sized pieces?

✔ Does the multimedia (the graphics, sound, video, and animation) draw attention to or distract from the primary content?

✔ Does your site add any real value to the global collection of knowledge?

We're not aiming at bursting your egotistical bubble, but why should you waste valuable Internet bandwidth distributing worthless gibberish if someone else can use that same bandwidth to distribute information about the plight of the endangered red-toed horny lizard.

All in the Family

Now we are getting into something good! Remember the discussion about absolute and relative URLs in Chapter 13? If not, go back and reread it. Anyway, we repeat the important bits here if you stick around, but if you want to go flipping pages or scrutinizing the index, go ahead; we'll be waiting for you right here when you return.

You have two schools of thought on the use of URLs in Web sites. The first claims that using all absolute URLs is the most reliable method, and the second claims that relative URLs are the way to go. We lean toward the relative side of the fence, but we can sympathize with those on the wrong *cough* we mean, other side.

The use of all absolute URLs in a Web site offers you the solid and reassuring knowledge that every link points directly and only to the intended document or resource. Even if a user downloads one of your HTML documents, whenever they click a link, it will bring them back to your site. But using all absolutes has its problems. If you host your site from multiple Web servers or move it from one directory to another, you must recode every URL to match the new system name or the new path name. This recoding is a long, tedious, and easily messed-up task. If your site is stationary on a single server, however, absolute URLs may work perfectly for you.

If you use relative URLs in your Web site, you have similar but almost the opposite benefits and drawbacks of absolute URLs. Relative URLs give you the freedom to move your site from one server to another or from one directory to another without needing any significant recoding. However, if a user downloads one of your documents to their hard drive, they can't link back to your Web site when they attempt to activate a link — instead they get an error.

Ultimately, the type of URLs you use within the documents of your Web site doesn't matter as long as they function properly after you get your site situated on the Web server. But here is the kicker: If you tuned and tested your site on a local or test Web server and you used absolute URLs, you must change all of them to match the new location before transferring them to the new server. In our opinion, this is too much work. So we always use relative URLs in our sites when linking to our own documents and only use absolute URLs for linking to resources or other sites outside of our site. We have found this method to be the easiest to manage and troubleshoot. But if you have a different opinion, you are welcome to it (as long as you remember that you are wrong, we'll get along just fine).

So, the big action point for this section: If you use absolute URLs, you need to edit your URLs to match the new Web server location. If you are using relative URLs, you don't have to do much of anything.

If you are using CGI programs and other multimedia type enhancements, you may be using absolute URLs in the call and response parameters of these items. In these cases, you don't have any choice but to use absolute URLs. Therefore, keep a list of these "have to be absolute" URLs so you will remember to update and change them when you finally post your site to the public Web server.

Elbow Room

If this section isn't a bit obvious to you, then maybe Web site hosting is a bit outside of your grasp. In order to post your Web site so that the public can access it, you need to have space (that's hard drive space) on a Web server somewhere. Usually, an Internet Service Provider (ISP) gives or offers its users space for the posting of their own Web sites, but you must contact your ISP to find out the details of this hosting configuration.

If you don't already have an ISP, you need to get one. You can find the details on that process in the companion book *MORE HTML For Dummies.* Or if you are really brave, you can try to wing it.

Many Web server, storage space, and ISP configurations exist — way too many to even attempt to describe them all. Even if we did chronicle them all, only one or two of them would be of any use to you. So instead of getting long-winded (which we never do), we'll just talk about a few common setups and let you get the specifics (say that word ten times and you forget what it means) from your own ISP.

You need to inquire about three aspects of personal Web page server configuration: your personal URL, your storage space location (and how to access it), and the default document name.

Most of the common configurations result in a personal Web page URL of the following:

```
www.isp.com/~username
www.isp.com/username
www.isp.com/user/username
```

The Web server and the particular configuration of the ISP determine the actual syntax of the personal Web page URL. Also, you need to ask your ISP how to form your own URL to access your personal Web site.

The storage space an ISP grants to a user for the posting of personal Web pages can be located and arranged in a variety of ways. You need to ask your ISP the specifics. Usually, you find one of two setups for this — storage off of your home directory or storage located on a dedicated Web server machine.

You accomplish storage off of your home directory by creating a sub-directory with a specific name, such as "public-web" or "wwwhome." This specified name is programmed into the Web server so that when your URL is used, the server knows to pull your Web documents from that directory. The specified name is essentially your Web root, meaning users cannot access any data located outside this specified directory.

Storage on a dedicated Web server machine is a situation where the ISP creates a directory with your username on a remote hard drive. That directory is your Web root. When your URL is used, the Web server knows to go to that named directory to pull your Web documents.

There are at least two more hosting configurations, but they do involve quite a bit more cost and work to get functioning. One method is to acquire your own unique domain name. We discuss this process a bit more in-depth in the companion book *MORE HTML For Dummies.* But if you just can't wait, call your ISP and ask them to give you a hand at obtaining your own domain name. Just think, you can be the proud owner of www.myoldbackporch.com where cyber-rednecks from across the world can gather to spit and yap on about getting drunk and pinching waitresses. The second hosting configuration is co-locating your own Web server machine and getting a domain name. This option is way beyond the scope of this book *and* the companion book. However, we wrote another excellent book on the subject that may be of interest to you: *Building Windows NT Web Servers,* by Ed Tittel, Mary Madden, and David B. Smith (IDG Books Worldwide, Inc.).

Finally, you need to know about the default document name. All Web servers have a configuration option to define the name of the HTML document to load if one is not provided for in the invoked URL. The default document name can be anything, but the most common names are `index.html` and `default.html`. Be sure to check with your ISP to find out exactly which name is being used.

Why is this important? Well, if someone accesses your site but does not include a filename and you don't have a default document, they may get an error or a listing of your Web root's directory listing. Both of these occurrences are unacceptable. Instead, you need to set up your site so a document is always loaded into the user's browser whether or not they indicated a specific document. You can accomplish this in one of two ways:

✔ Name your front page, home page, or main document the same name as the default document name.

✔ Create a symbolic link between the default document name and the real front page, home page, or main document. This requires shell access into your Web directory, which not many ISPs offer. But if you do have this kind of access, the UNIX command to establish a symbolic link is: `ln -s yourdocumentname.html default.html`.

Throwing Caution to the Wind

At this point, you've prepared your site as much as you can (that is, if you've been doing what you are told). Now you need to get your Web site files from your local drive to the storage area of your Web server (wherever that might be). This process is going to be a bit difficult, but we'll try to take it slow so you won't get too confused.

To move files from your local hard drive to the storage area on your ISP, you must use an *FTP* utility. FTP stands for File Transfer Protocol, and it is the primary method of transporting files to and from machines on the Internet. FTP is like copying files to a floppy from your hard drive, but you use FTP to move files from your hard drive, over your modem connection, to the storage area on the ISP.

So, with that said, you need to get an FTP utility. There are two types of FTP utilities — command-line text only and GUI (that's graphical user interface for the acronym challenged). It doesn't matter which type you get as long as you can use it. The command-line versions require you to know a lot of ugly and obtuse commands to perform the file transfer, and GUI ones make the process much easier on the cerebral cortex. If you want to figure out the command-line type, go get yourself a good UNIX book, read the FTP FAQ (see URL below), or read the help file for the utility.

```
ftp://rtfm.mit.edu/pub/usenet/news.answers/ftp-list/faq
```

For the nonmasochistic out there, get a GUI FTP utility. Here are some great recommendations:

✔ For Windows: ipswitch's WS_FTP Pro:

```
http://www.ipswitch.com/
```

✔ For Macintosh: Dartmouth's Fetch:

```
http://www.dartmouth.edu/pages/softdev/fetch.html
```

Sorry, UNIX, there are so many variants of the UNIX OS that we can't give a general recommendation (or even a specific one) for a GUI FTP. Unless you can find one, you are probably stuck with command-line FTP (but if you were really afraid of command-line utilities, you wouldn't be using UNIX in the first place).

Both of the previous GUI FTP utilities are easy to use, and the Web sites (and the utilities themselves) have extensive documentation on their use. So take the time to read it.

No matter what type of FTP utility you use, you need to know some important pieces of information. You have to ask your ISP about many of these tidbits, but because you've probably already developed a great repartee with them, asking a few more questions shouldn't be a big deal.

You need to know

✔ The domain name or the IP address of the FTP-able machine — this may be the Web server, the user host, or some other machine in their network. Often it has a domain name, such as ftp.isp.com, but not always.

✔ The username and password to gain access — most often this is your standard username and password, but sometimes a unique name and/or password is required to gain FTP access so as to improve overall security. Remember, you probably (and most likely) will only have full control access (the ability to write and delete files) in your root/home directory.

✔ The name of the Web root directory and path into which you must place your Web documents. As we mentioned before, this could be a subdirectory off of your home directory with a name like "public-web" or a directory named with your username on a dedicated Web server storage area. Either way, you need to know the exact name and path so you can get to it.

Here are the general steps for uploading your Web files to your ISP-hosted personal Web directory (we are assuming you've already established a PPP communications link to the Internet, otherwise the following steps will not work):

1. **Launch your FTP utility.**

2. **Contact the FTP server by providing the domain name or IP address to the FTP utility.**

3. **When required, input the username and password needed to gain access.**

   Depending on your FTP utility, you either enter this information at the same time as the domain name or you enter it when prompted.

4. **After you acquire access, traverse the directory structure to locate the path and assigned Web root directory.**

5. **If the Web root directory does not yet exist, create it by using the proper naming convention that your ISP mandates.**

6. **If you are unable to create the directory or the directory does not already exist, contact your ISP for help.**

7. **Locate the Web files on your local hard drive.**

8. **Initiate transfer of the files.**

   If you did not use subdirectories in your site, no additional transfer configuration is needed.

   If you used subdirectories and an FTP utility that supports directory tree transfer, be sure to command the utility to transfer and maintain the directory tree structure.

   If you used subdirectories and an FTP utility that does not support directory tree transfer, you must manually create each subdirectory and transfer the contents of these directories one at a time.

9. **Close the FTP connection.**

10. **Close the FTP utility.**

As we discuss earlier in this chapter about the default document name, if you need to create a symbolic link to the main document of your site, do so at this time by telneting to the site and by using the "ln" command.

You may also need to perform similar steps to upload any CGI or special multimedia files that are not stored within the standard Web root. Contact your ISP to find out exactly how and where to post your CGI and enhancement files.

Chapter 18

What Do the Users Think?

In This Chapter

▶ Performing a beta test

▶ Finding the right testers

▶ Keeping your sanity

▶ Promoting feedback

▶ Learning from your users

▶ Wondering when to quit testing

Actively seeking the opinions of strangers about your Web pages seems masochistic, doesn't it? But because you don't want to keep your work to yourself, you need to know what your audience thinks. Additionally, you need to continue to receive feedback from your users as long as your pages remain available on the Web. Read on to see how to accomplish this and more. At the end of the chapter, we even tell you when to stop . . . testing, that is.

Beta Testing

You're not alone in your quest for the perfect Web site. Practically everyone on the WWW would like every single page they view to match their vision of perfection. In fact, millions of them will be more than happy to judge your work. The key is to get a few of them to help you make it better during the test phase called *beta testing*.

During beta testing, you enlist a larger (but still manageable) group of WWW users to help you make your Web pages the best thing since coffee and candy bars. They not only test the performance and functionality, but they generously advise you as to how stupid you were to put the image of the sparrow in with the finches and so on. They spot problems that you didn't even know existed. What? Things that you looked at every day but ignored can bother enough of your beta testers that you may decide to change them, the problems, that is — not the beta testers!

You can use the same basic technical form that you used during alpha testing for beta testing. However, you should add the following questions:

- ✔ Do the pages present the material in the best possible way?
- ✔ Do the pages get the right message across?
- ✔ Do the pages answer users' questions quickly and obviously?
- ✔ Do the pages do their job (make users want to buy a product, visit a location, make a phone call, and so on)?

Ask your beta testers to tell you their specific likes and dislikes, and your beta testers will oblige you; believe us, they really will!

Beta testers

We hope that you can find beta testers who are directly interested in the content that your Web pages present. You need feedback on their likes and dislikes, as well as their impressions of your Web's functionality, layout, and behavior. They are your primary audience, albeit a small portion thereof, so treat them well.

Find beta testers by posting an invitation in relevant newsgroups. Simply ask for people interested in helping you test your new Web page. Filter them by asking them to e-mail their names, addresses, phone numbers, backgrounds in your content area, and some reasons why they think that they would make good beta testers. E-mail immediate thank-you messages to everyone who replies with a noncommittal statement that you were overwhelmed by the response and will get back to them shortly.

If you decide not to use some respondents, which is unlikely, send each of them a nice e-mail thanking him or her profusely and saying that you ran out of your allotted testing spaces before getting to their names, or something equally friendly. Cliché warning — Do a good deed for someone and that person will tell three friends about it. Do something that makes someone mad and that person will tell 11 people what a jerk you are. You may not be able to make everyone happy, but try your best not to irritate your users!

E-mail each beta tester an announcement for each change cycle, with a list of revisions and a copy of the beta test report form you want them to complete and return. Thank each tester for each problem report. Make sure that you recognize those testers whose problem reports resulted in a revision. Take the time to make real friends out of your beta testers and you will benefit from it for a long, long time. Your beta testers are your users. Remember **Rule number 1**? (If you don't, see Chapter 16.)

Cycling ahead of the gremlins

No, a revision cycle isn't something you pedal backward. It's a method for handling problems and changes to your pages in an orderly fashion. Simply stated, you don't fix problems in the order in which you receive them. Sure, you're anxious to clean up your pages, but you must prioritize the problems that you (or others) find. If you don't prioritize, fixing changes can cost more time in the long run. You'll find that for a large, complex Web, a one-week revision cycle is probably the shortest period possible, with a two-week cycle less anxiety provoking.

Cycling revisions also helps you keep ahead of the insidious gremlins called *unexpected side effects.* These occur when a seemingly small change is made in one page without enough thought put into its effects and without any testing of the entire site afterward. One common example is changing an image that's linked to every page in your site, like an icon or navigation button. Suppose you put that image in the wrong directory. That image wouldn't show up at all and that would be easy to detect. But suppose you change the e-mail address for feedback and make an error. You may not find out about that error for quite a while, unless you use the new address to send yourself mail immediately upon installing the change. (Now that we think about it, this is a good testing technique, too — why don't you try it?)

By batch-processing prioritized problems, you can give everyone in your testing crew adequate time to thoroughly perform their validations. While they're testing your most recent set of revisions, you can be working on the next set. Be sure that you note your fixes on each problem form as completely as the problem itself was documented. Also, be careful to update the version number and revision date/time for each page that you change and include this information in the problem fix section of the form or database.

From a testing report database, make and keep an ongoing list of problems. Prioritize them in your own order. Then decide which problem or group of problems to fix. Consider not only the time it takes to revise HTML documents, but also the time you need to run the changed pages on the entire site completely through your test checklists on all appropriate browsers and platforms. With this time frame in mind, you'll probably decide that daily changes aren't possible.

Gamma Testing and Beyond?

Although we don't discuss a formal gamma test category, consider all users who view your Web pages as testers and potential assistants in ongoing page development. Of course, you understand that the Web is alive, don't you? And your Web pages are a living part of the WWW. Therefore, you must feed and nurture your site to keep it up to date; otherwise it loses its users and fades into oblivion. To prevent this, you must employ sound methods to request and encourage user feedback, right in your Web pages. Your e-mail address suffices as a bare minimum, but a nice form can do the job much better.

There's nothing crazy about a sanity check!

By now you're saying to yourself, "What's all this about two-week revision cycles, fancy forms, and testers all over the place? My pages aren't going to be as buggy as a stray dog." You're probably correct in that sentiment, but you now understand that without careful planning and cyclic testing, you may be the one who goes buggy.

To keep that buggy feeling at bay, take the following advice: Maintain two separate copies of your site on your own computer and on your Web server (if space is available). Perform all changes on the *working* copy while the *published* copy is in use. While you're testing, you can compare the performance and functionality of the working copy to the published copy and observe any changes.

When you've completed a revision cycle, copy the working files over the published files — after making a backup, of course. If you've used relative URLs properly, you won't need to change anything in the revised working files before copying them over the old published files. They'll be ready for users instantly.

Stick it to me: the importance of feedback

Ahhhh, users. Funny how they keep popping up here, there, and every-where. Funny how you feed them your Web pages and ask for their feedback. User feedback is the lifeblood of your site, but if you're not careful, it's as useful as the feedback from an amplifier with a microphone in front of the speaker. That is, it makes you sit up and take notice, but it won't give you enough useful information to solve any problems. If you like playing Sherlock Holmes, by all means, just put a little message at the bottom of your home page requesting feedback to an e-mail address.

However, your users may not know exactly how to phrase their wants and needs so that you can understand them. It's up to you to give them a hand with feedback forms, nicely worded requests, and warm e-mail thank-yous when they do respond (no matter what they say). You'll definitely get e-mail when things are broken or go awry; you'll also learn to appreciate the occasional pat on the back from your users.

Building a report card

If you aren't getting any feedback, you may need to give your users a better method to respond, such as a feedback form. There's nothing quite like giving folks a chance to "grade" you to bring out their likes and dislikes. One of the better ways to decide what kind of feedback form to use is to look around the Web for forms you like. Check out the HTML source to see how the author created them. If that author used a script that works on your Web server, create one like it for yourself. Your server's Webmaster can probably help you, if you ask nicely.

A simple text form on a page of its own for users to copy, fill in, and e-mail back to you is better than nothing. A real CGI form with questions and response boxes is much better. (You can find out more about these in Chapter 13.) Although you need to be specific in your requests for information, a detailed check box form with no place for general comments can miss valuable information. Give the users space to be creative after you've aroused their interest with your own specific questions or check boxes.

Serious feedback methods

If you really want information, ask about something specific. Tell them you're thinking of adding or changing something, and ask the users to tell you what they think about your ideas. Have a contest in which you give a prize to the person who submits the best or worst feature of your site and explains why they think this is so. Get your users involved in your site and its design, and you'll all benefit. Here are some specific methods to get more feedback, if your online traffic isn't telling you everything you want to know.

Hocus-pocus, focus groups

If you're serious about accomplishing a set of goals with your Web pages, you may want to try the focus group approach, which marketing and advertising companies use so successfully. Because you want to focus on your Web site, why not try an online focus group approach? This activity can be similar to beta testing, but with a very select group.

With the focus group approach, you can e-mail each group member a request to participate and provide the group member with a special URL to view the pages in question. To make this approach work well, you must plan carefully. A focus group can become more of a marketing exercise than Web page testing, but it can also be important to you and your enterprise. You may want to involve your marketing department or an advertising consultant in the planning process and in creating an appropriate questionnaire.

Make friends with movers and shakers

Don't just lurk in the newsgroups, PARTICIPATE! Make online friends with the folks who are in-the-know in your industry's newsgroup(s). If you know the addresses of the important folks in your field of interest, e-mail them an announcement about your Web's grand opening; invite them to drop in.

Keep them informed about your site, but don't make a pest of yourself. Ask them if they've been looking for some kind of information on the Net but can't seem to find it in your area. Then find it, provide it, and let them know about it while you thank them profusely for their suggestions.

Don't just listen, do something!

When your users lavish you with their feedback, thank them immediately via e-mail. Then use their feedback to better your site. The best thanks you can give users is to put their great ideas to work quickly, and let them know that you appreciate their support.

Be careful, though, in giving credit directly in your Web pages to folks whose feedback you use. A few people who don't like the change could blame the provider instead of you. You're the one who's trying to keep your audience happy, so you're the one who has to take the abuse from disgruntled users. It's usually better to thank users personally via e-mail and as a group on your Web pages, if you feel the need to do so publicly.

Knowing When to Quit (Testing)

Now that you're completely catatonic with fear about opening up your precious site to the prying eyes of the WWW masses, take solace in knowing that it's only a bunch of electrons running around in wires and silicon. You've nothing to fear from the WWW. No matter how carefully you plan, design, code, and test your Web pages, someone will find something they don't like. This is a function of the differences in outlook and perspective of the millions of users on the Web.

Cliché warning — You can't please everyone. You can try to please as many members of your intended audience as possible within your time and energy limits. Unless you have a deadline to meet that dictates when you open your site to the Net, you can be the sole judge of when it's ready for prime time. So open it up when you've tested it thoroughly and can't find any more "real" problems (but never quit testing!). And above all, SMILE; this is supposed to be fun!

Part V

It's Tool Time: HTML Development Tools and Environments

The 5th Wave · By Rich Tennant

©RICHTENNANT

"They're fruit flys, Rog. For gosh sake, how many applets have you written today?!"

In this part . . .

We show you many different tools available to help you build cool Web pages and manage those pages once they're built. We cover our favorite Web-related tools as well, and along the way, we reveal what HTML editors and related tools are available for UNIX, Macintosh, Windows, and other computing platforms.

Chapter 19

Tools of the Trade: HTML and Web Publishing Tools

• •

In This Chapter

▶ A Web is more than HTML

▶ Web publishing tools

▶ Web checking and validation tools

▶ Web management tools

• •

*W*eb pages are made with HTML, but Web sites are made with much more than that. Web site publishing involves creating HTML, checking and validating your HTML after it is written, document coordination, and site management. When the first Web sites came online, pioneer Webmasters had to perform all of these activities manually — not a fun job even for the most compulsive person on the planet!

The need for a comprehensive set of tools for Webmasters emerged soon after the Web did. Since then, many software developers have sought to meet that need. Their efforts have produced a great many tools and utilities that aid Webmasters in creating and maintaining their Web sites. Thus, after you've gotten HTML under control, you need to gather those publishing and administration tools that work best for both you and your platform, and tackle the real work of Webmastery — namely, maintenance!

In this chapter, we talk about what kind of tools you should look out for. In following chapters, we begin by explaining how we do this Web thang ourselves, and then we cover platform-specific tools for the PC, Macintosh, and UNIX platforms. After you've worked your way through an entire section and spent some time testing and playing with the available tools, you will be well on your way to constructing a useful and powerful Webmaster's toolkit of your very own.

Making Coding Easier: HTML Editors

Stone-age HTML was created by using only simple text editors, with each and every tag composed by hand. Today, a mere seven years later, hand-coding HTML is no longer the only way to do it, although it's still the preferred method for some authors. A new generation of HTML editors declares that you can create HTML pages without knowing HTML. Amazing . . . or maybe not.

HTML editors are intended to make Web page creation easier, but editors that claim to do "all the work for you" make us more than a little nervous. Imagine a word processor that claims to know English grammar and will write your documents for you. Newfangled HTML editors fall just short of a similar declaration, but it's still kind of scary. Before we go on to discuss these editors, let us digress for a moment and make a case for why you should know HTML, whether the editor gets involved in the process of creation or not.

Why you should know HTML

There's a boat-load of reasons why you should know HTML, despite what any HTML editor marketing weasel may tell you. We could write an entire book about this, but that's not why we're here. Here's a brief point-by-point rundown of our arguments instead:

- **You need to know what HTML can and can't do.** HTML has many capabilities, but it has just as many limitations. If you don't know HTML, you won't be completely aware of either side of the puzzle. For instance, even with the latest Cougar additions, you can't be sure that your complicated table, image, or text formatting will render exactly as you expect. There are too many variables to contend with — different browser types and versions, user preferences, and more. On the flip side, if your editor doesn't support the latest table attributes, you wouldn't know the first thing about them, much less be able to use them in your page design. Generally, ignorance is a bad thing. This rule is doubly true for HTML.

- **You need to know HTML to identify problems and fix them.** To figure out what's wrong on a page, you have to know what's right. Your pages may look great in an editor or even in your browser of choice, but chances are they won't always stay that way. Broken links, corrupted files, and new tags and interpretations can all change the way your HTML looks. If you can't identify errors or changes because you can't recognize them for what they are, then you'll never be able to troubleshoot your pages without the help of a professional, and we don't come cheap (but we can be had!).

✔ **You need to know HTML to know what tags to use.** What's the difference between `<STRONG>` and `<BOLD>`? They look the same, but one is logical and the other is physical. One conveys meaning while the other creates only a textual effect. If you don't know HTML, all you'll see is boldface text. Another, more extreme, example is using `<PRE>` to create columnar data instead of the `<TABLE>` tag because you don't know about table markup. Although you can build a page in a variety of ways, usually there's only one best way. If you know HTML, you can figure out the best way.

✔ **You need to know HTML to implement the latest cool stuff.** That HTML editor you invested so much time and money in may not support frames, but what if you want frames on your pages? If you know HTML, the solution is simple: Dust off your old text editor and code them by hand. If you don't know HTML, you must wait until a new version of your editor — presumably, one that supports tables — is released. In short, if you don't know the HTML tags you can implement on, your pages will be limited to those your editor supports.

We hope that you bought this book because you are interested in learning HTML and therefore won't fall prey to the attractive promises of the many editors out there and give up on learning HTML because you don't think you need to. Take it from us — you need to.

Making an editor work for you

Despite our lecture on why you should know HTML, we don't want you to think that editors are the spawn of the devil and should be avoided at all costs. Rather, we want you to understand that they are tools like any other tool you use in the development of HTML. Editors have a definite role in page creation. Most of them support drag-and-drop technologies, file linking, site mapping, and more. We use editors for preliminary design and prototyping. After all, it's much easier to drag-and-drop an image than it is to manually alter the HTML and reload the page in a browser to see if right-justified is better than centered. It's also about a thousand times easier to sit back and have a drink while an editor creates a site outline than it is to code it by hand (we know this from firsthand experience).

Because HTML editors seem to have multiplied as quickly as rabbits, we'd like to give you a few tips on how to choose a good one. Keep in mind that shareware editors aren't as multifunctional as those that cost real money. If you're going to write a lot of HTML and manage a large site (or more than one site), you may find it best to invest in an editor that can handle many different tasks. At the very least, your editor should

✔ Have a friendly interface that is easy to understand and work with

✔ Provide accurate HTML previews without using an external browser

- ✔ Be HTML 3.2 compatible
- ✔ Be committed to continuous upgrades as HTML changes
- ✔ Support image map creation
- ✔ Check local links for accuracy
- ✔ Support HTML validation and spell checking
- ✔ Allow you to see and tweak your HTML code directly

An exceptional (but expensive) editor will also

- ✔ Provide site map information
- ✔ Check external links for accuracy
- ✔ Provide pixel-level control over object and text placement
- ✔ Accommodate CGI scripts, Java applets, and scripting

All of the major players have jumped into the HTML editor fray, making it difficult to choose an editor for your toolbox. The March 1997 issue of *Internet World* features a great review of the major HTML editors available today. We agree with their overall assessments of each editor, and the article is a great place to start evaluating an HTML editor for your own use. You can reach *Internet World* online at

```
http://www.iw.com/
```

While you're there, perform a search for "Under Construction" and choose the "Internet World March 1997 – Live Pages" entry — then you can read the article for yourself online!

After you select an HTML editor, you may find that it performs many of the other functions we discuss in the chapter. If so, good for you (although maybe not for your wallet). But if not, don't worry; you don't need a fancy-schmanzy editor to manage your site. A lot of other tools are available to help you out.

The Doctor Is In: Page Checkups

So you've written a bunch of HTML, and you think you're done. Not by a long shot — at least, not if you want to avoid being the laughing stock of the Web. Before all these great tools were available, an occasional misspelled word or broken link was acceptable, but now you have no excuse for those boo-boos. Before you post your pages for public display, you must perform three important checks: HTML, spelling, and links. Many different tools can do one or more of these jobs, many of which are available for free on the

Web. You can find a number of stand-alone utilities as well, not to mention those already embedded in HTML editors. As we said, you no longer have a valid excuse for mistakes.

HTML validation: bad code is bad news

A majority of the browsers out there are forgiving of markup errors. Most don't even require an <HTML> tag to identify an HTML page, instead looking only for an .html or .htm suffix to identify a document as a Web page. Just because the real world is that way doesn't make it right. There may come a day when browsers can't afford to be so forgiving, and that day is drawing closer as HTML becomes more complicated and precise. It's better to get it right from the beginning and save yourself a bunch of trouble later on.

What browsers forgive, a validator may not!

Validators are a type of software program that performs basic quality control on your HTML documents. Validators check the syntax and structure of a document against a model for what the syntax and structure should be in order to help developers find and fix errors, omissions, and other gotchas.

Where HTML is concerned, such programs are sometimes called *HTML validators*. The ultimate HTML validator comes from — who else? — the World Wide Web Consortium, fondly abbreviated as the W3C. The name of their program is the HTML Validator Service, and you can use it through the Web page as a validator.w3.org to check out your own HTML documents free of charge.

The interesting thing about going through the validator is that you discover that what a Web browser happily lets you get away with, the validator finds fault with — loudly and vociferously. In other words, most Web browsers are quite indifferent to the requirements built into HTML and cheerfully display so-called HTML documents that aren't worthy of the name!

Today, this is no big deal, because HTML itself doesn't follow a truly strict or regular syntax. (And we're not talking about a tax on booze or cigarettes here; we're talking about a regular, predictable way to describe what HTML markup is and how it works.) In fact, some of what HTML allows is hard for computers to check at all! But the W3C is busily engaged in building a next-generation HTML that will be more rigorously defined and extremely well-suited to mechanical validation. When that happens, all bets on current-generation pages will be off. Don't ever say we didn't warn you.

Computer geeks like to talk about code as being valid, which means that it passes through a validator program well-formed with no errors showing, following all the syntax rules for those elements that must be present in a program, as well as adhering to the rules whenever optional elements appear. Someday soon, you'll be able to apply the same standards to HTML, so why not start now?

A Kinder, Gentler HTML Validator

An easy validator you can use is the "Kinder, Gentler, HTML Validator." As shown in Figure 19-1, you must enter the URL to be checked, make a couple of choices about what kind of information you want returned, and then wait for the results.

Figure 19-1:
The Kinder, Gentler HTML Validator is easy to use and understand.

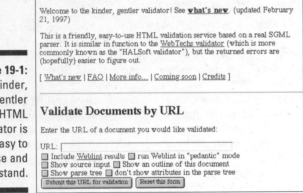

When we submit a Web page to this validator, we received not only an explanation of what was wrong but why. For instance, the page didn't include a <DOCTYPE> definition, and the validator provided us with a solid discussion of why the page needed to have this often-overlooked tag. The error output is easy to read as well, as Figure 19-2 indicates.

Granted, it takes a bit longer to get through this output, and you have no control over the DTD that your HTML is checked against. But if you've never worked with validator output, this is a good place to start.

Figure 19-2:
Kinder,
Gentler
HTML
Validator
output looks
more like
English.

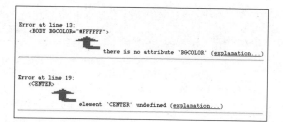

```
Error at line 13:
    <BODY BGCOLOR="#FFFFFF">

                  there is no attribute `BGCOLOR' (explanation...)


Error at line 19:
    <CENTER>

            element `CENTER' undefined (explanation...)
```

Regardless of what kind of validator you use, you must check each and every one of your HTML pages for accuracy. The more accurate your HTML, the better the chance that your pages will look as you intend them to on a variety of browsers.

Of course you can spel: spell check your pages!

What is the biggest problem with checking HTML pages for spelling errors? The tags themselves are misspellings, according to Webster's and most other dictionaries. Sitting and clicking the ignore key for each and every new tag can make spell checking tedious. After your eyes glaze over, you're more apt to miss real misspellings. Once again, many editors include HTML-aware spell checkers that skip markup and check just the text. Because so many editors support this option, few stand-alone utilities are available, or any dedicated online spell checkers that we could find.

Dr. HTML is an HTML checking tool that performs several different checks, including spell checks, on any HTML document or on an entire site. To investigate this utility and try its analytical skills, please visit this Web site:

```
http://www2.imagiware.com/RxHTML/
```

Regardless of how you do it, even if it means cutting and pasting text from a browser to a word processor, you must check your pages for spelling errors. Good spelling is often considered to be an indicator of intelligence and abilities, and we wouldn't want anyone to underestimate you.

Don't lose the connection: link checking

If you think spelling errors are embarrassing, here's something that's even worse: broken hyperlinks. Hyperlinks make the Web what it is; if you have broken links on your site, that's borderline blasphemy. Seriously, if your text promises a link to a great resource or page but produces the dreaded "404 Object Not Found" error when that link is clicked, users will be disappointed and may not ever revisit your site. The worst broken link is one that points to a resource in your own pages. You can't be held responsible for what others do to their sites, but you are 100 percent accountable for your own site. Don't let this happen to you!

As with the other two checks, many HTML editors include built-in local link checkers, and some editors even traverse the Web for you and check external links. In addition, the large majority of Web servers also offer this feature. Checking external links isn't as simple as it sounds because there's a program involved that must work over an active Internet connection to query each link. This can be processor intensive, and you should check external links only during off-peak hours, like early morning, to avoid tying up other Web servers as well. A number of scripts and utilities are available on the Web to help you test your links. In the following sections, we explore some of our favorites.

MOMSpider

MOMSpider was one of the first link checkers available to Web authors. This link checker is written in Perl and runs on virtually any UNIX machine. The nice thing about MOMSpider is that it needn't reside on the same computer as the site it's checking, so even if you don't serve your Web from a UNIX box, you can still check your links by using MOMSpider and a remote system.

Anyone who has some knowledge of Perl can easily configure MOMSpider to create custom output and to check both internal and external links on a site. Don't fret; if you don't know Perl, you can easily find a programmer who can adjust a MOMSpider in his or her sleep for a nominal fee. Many ISPs will run a MOMSpider on your site for a low monthly fee and will cheerfully handle the configuration and implementation for you.

To find out more about MOMSpider, visit the official site at

```
http://www.ics.uci.edu/pub/websoft/MOMspider/
```

WebWalker

WebWalker is a simpler, annotated version of MOMSpider that non-Perl users can implement themselves with just a little study. Once again, it must be run on a UNIX server with Perl installed, but the program itself is heavily commented to help you configure it without calling in a programmer. If you're feeling adventurous and want to try your hand at a little programming, give WebWalker a shot.

Point your browser at the WebWalker page for more information:

```
http://www.mcp.com/softlib/Internet/WebWalker/
```

CheckBot

CheckBot is yet another Perl script based on the work of Roy Fielding, the programmer who created MOMSpider, and is similar to WebWalker in that it is a simpler, more annotated version of MOMSpider. CheckBot runs on any server with Perl installed and you can configure it without too much hassle if you're willing to do a little reading.

To find out more about CheckBot, take a look at its Web page at

```
http://dutifp.twi.tudelft.nl:8000/checkbot/
```

You've probably noticed that all the link checkers we mention are scripts (Perl scripts to be specific). Let this be your first clue that link checking is not a quick and easy task, but an essential jog all the same. We recommend you check all links on your site once a week. If you can't manage that, then check them at least once a month. If not, you'll have dead links and eventually a dead site.

We've only highlighted a few of the many different validation and checking utilities available on the Web. There are numerous others and more are sure to be created soon. For a complete, up-to-date list of these tools, visit the Yahoo! Validation/Checkers page at

```
http://www.yahoo.com/Computers_and_Internet
          /Information_and_Documentation/Data_Formats
          /HTML/Validation_Checkers/
```

Keeper of the Zoo: Tools for Managing Your Site

You've created your pages, checked them twice, and amassed a nice collection of documents that have become a site. Now what? Your site will require constant care and feeding, sort of like houseplants but more like children. That's where so-called "site management tools" come into play.

All the tools we discuss earlier are part of site management because they affect the documents that make up a site, albeit for only one document at a time. Site management tools help you control your site as a whole, as a coherent collection of documents. Many site management tools perform some of the same functions as HTML editors, such as link and spell checking, and they may even feature their own built-in HTML editors. But these are not the most important functions of a site management tool.

In short, site management utilities have a larger focus. They give you a bird's-eye view of a site and help you to visualize it and work with it as a whole, rather than on a per-document basis. Any site management tool worth its salt will do the following:

✔ Create a current site map and/or outline

✔ Automatically change links in all pages when you rename or move a local document

✔ Analyze log files and other data to provide feedback about a site

As an extra bonus, most site management tools can help you create search information for your pages and make the integration of a search engine quick and painless. Many site management tools available today (there's no shareware in this category, alas) also offer visual site maps and manipulation tools, support drag-and-drop site operations, and can tell you more about your site than you ever wanted to know. To get you started on a site management tool search, we offer five good product names and their associated URLs:

- Cyber Pilot Pro:

  ```
  http://www.netcarta.com
  ```

- SiteMill:

  ```
  http://www.adobe.com/Apps/SiteMill/
  ```

- Front Page:

  ```
  http://www.microsoft.com/Apps/SiteMill/
  ```

- O'Reilly WebSite:

  ```
  http://www.ora.com/
  ```

- NetCarta:

  ```
  http://www.netcarta.com/
  ```

There's nothing we can tell you about these products that isn't on their Web pages, and the developers know their products far better than we do. Your best bet is to download demos or trial versions of any package that sounds appealing, and test it out on your site. After you find a package that works for you, invest in a legal version so you can remain eligible for free or reduced-cost upgrades. With HTML changing as much as it is, you'll want to keep your site management tools as current as possible.

A good site management tool will round out your Web publishing toolkit and give you a solid group of utilities to use. HTML editors, site management tools, and even servers often offer overlapping features and capabilities. But after a little experimentation, you can master those aspects of each one that works best for you.

Chapter 20

Using UNIX Uniformly

In This Chapter

▶ Surveying the UNIX HTML authoring tools

▶ Investigating stand-alone editors

▶ Wondering about EMACS modes?

▶ Pouring through filters and file converters

▶ Skimming through the UNIX Web servers

*W*onderful new HTML authoring tools for UNIX-based systems have sprung up in recent months. Many are still undergoing testing, but they all look quite promising to UNIX users tired of text-only systems. And for those of you who happen to like text-only, the old EMACS standby is alive and well, with a few added HTML modes to liven it up. To top it off, you can convert or filter almost any file type into or out of HTML using one of the myriad HTML utility programs available for UNIX.

The UNIX mystique is one of sharing resources; so practically all of the UNIX-based HTML authoring systems are freeware. Even commercial UNIX packages typically offer a freeware version for downloading.

But free and shareware UNIX HTML authoring tools aren't supported in the same manner as recently released commercial products are. Thankfully, they don't cost much, either. These tools are usually easy to figure out because they use familiar text editor metaphors or they act as add-ins to your own UNIX text editors. Either way, if you've ever used any kind of editor, you can learn one of these HTML tools easily.

Diving for Treasure in the UNIX HTML Tools Sea

The sections that follow describe some of the currently popular UNIX-based HTML authoring tools and give you important facts about each one of them. These tools vary in their scope and functionality, but all of them are designed to help you create HTML documents more easily. Check out the URLs that follow for complete information on these tools, and many more.

Some tools are stand-alone UNIX programs that provide structure and error checking while they guide you through the creation of your Web pages. Some tools simply and elegantly provide you with quicker ways of inserting the requisite HTML tags into plain-text documents. Others are comprised of groups of macros for HTML editing for use by existing UNIX text editors, such as EMACS. File conversion tools take a different approach and change existing text files into HTML-tagged documents.

No matter which kind of tool you choose to try first, remember that the ultimate objective is to create eye-catching, informative Web pages that function on everybody's browser. If the tool you try doesn't help you meet this objective, try another tool. Rest assured: There's one out there that can do the job for you!

More information on the latest and greatest UNIX authoring tools is readily available starting at the following WWW sites:

```
http://www.utoronto.ca/webdocs/HTMLdocs/unix_tools.html
http://union.ncsa.uiuc.edu/HyperNews/get/www/html/
          editors.html
http://www.w3.org/hypertext/WWW/Tools/Overview.html
```

Standing Alone Amidst the UNIX HTML Editors

Stand-alone HTML tools come in flavors that range from plain-text editors to complete WYSIWYG (What You See Is What You Get) authoring systems with more bells and whistles than an AMTRAK station. The following examples start simple and proceed upward in functionality and cost from there.

The stand-alone, plain-text HTML editors for UNIX, such as A.S.H.E (A Simple HTML Editor) give you a screen that you type your text into. They also provide buttons or menu options from which you select HTML tags, which you must then insert at the proper places in the text. The emphasis in A.S.H.E. is Simple. If you understand the UNIX environment, you can learn A.S.H.E. fairly quickly.

A.S.H.E.

A.S.H.E. was written using C language, Motif, and NCSA HTML Widgets. It is a stand-alone, unchecked, plain-text HTML editor. A.S.H.E. provides active hyperlinks, supports multiple windows, prints text or postscript, and offers automatic file backup. The menu bar is well designed with File, Edit, HTML, Styles, and Lists menus. It provides a unique user Message Area while displaying the HTML code in a browser screen view (see Figure 20-1). Unfortunately, it only works under Motif on Sun workstations and requires the NCSA HTML Widget library. A.S.H.E provides simple but adequate HTML assistance for users of Motif. If that sounds like it's up your alley, please give it a try!

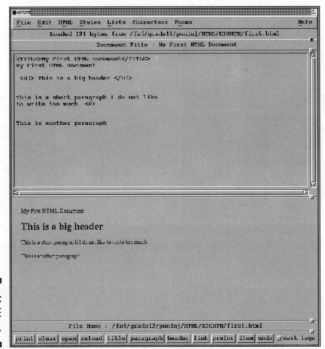

Figure 20-1:
The A.S.H.E
screen.

The A.S.H.E. beta version was created by John R. Punin, Dept. of Comp. Sci. RPI, Troy, NY 12180, E-mail: puninj@cs.rpi.edu. You can download it from

```
ftp://ftp.cs.rpi.edu/pub/puninj/ASHE
```

Several other programs are semi-WYSIWYG in that they provide you with a somewhat standard text-editing screen into which you type your text. The editor then helps you place the appropriate HTML tags in your text and keeps you from making errors in HTML syntax. These editors also help you with the creation of more complex HTML links and references. HoTMetaL is one example of this type of system.

Phoenix

Phoenix (Alpha 0.1.8), an X-Windows-based HTML Editor, is freeware from Lee Newberg, Biological Sciences Division, Office of Academic Computing, The University of Chicago, 924 E. 57th St., Chicago, IL 60637-5415. Phoenix offers true WYSIWYG HTML creation with a built-in browser. It copies and pastes plain, heading, anchor, and/or styled text with the attributes retained. Phoenix also provides easy anchor (<A>) editing with no need to type the URL in most cases. It supports full forms-browsing, and it copies and pastes images and ISMAPS from Web pages. A couple of negatives to remember are that you must register to get into The University of Chicago's system and that Phoenix is an academic endeavor in an alpha version that will be developed at an academic pace. So if you're in a hurry for additional features, you'd better try another program. You can download the source directly via anonymous FTP from

```
http://www.bsd.uchicago.edu/ftp/pub/phoenix/
```

Other editors, such as HoTMetaL and NaviPress, are complete WYSIWYG HTML authoring systems that let you type your text and format it as it will be displayed by a browser (sometimes yours, sometimes theirs). Then the system not only produces the appropriate HTML-formatted document, it lets you cut and paste from other HTML documents and carries the tags with the copied text. These systems also check your HTML syntax for proper usage. They are the most comprehensive of the HTML authoring systems available for UNIX.

HoTMetaL Pro

HoTMetaL Pro is SoftQuad's commercial HTML editor (see Figure 20-2). A UNIX version for Sun computers is available for free download at various sites. HoTMetaL requires you to edit a document with its embedded HTML codes visible, and then it hands the code off to your browser for viewing.

It supports all of the HTML 3.2 tags and selected 3.0 and Netscape extensions. HoTMetaL can open many document formats — Lotus Ami Pro; Microsoft Word for Macintosh, Windows, and DOS; RTF (Rich Text Format); and WordPerfect for DOS, Windows, and Macintosh — and convert them to HTML.

HoTMetaL performs both syntax checking and HTML validation. With syntax (rules) checking turned on, HoTMetaL helps you enter only valid HTML. If you select HTML validation, it checks your document for conformance to the HTML 2.0 specification. It also provides a list of all HTML 3.0 and Netscape extension tags in your document to alert you to possible incompatibilities with browsers that don't support those codes.

The HTML validation and format conversions are quite useful, but they don't allow you to create image maps nor do they let you see what your images will look like on the page. You can download the free version from a site on SoftQuad's download site list at

http://www.sq.com/products/hotmetal/hm-ftp.htm

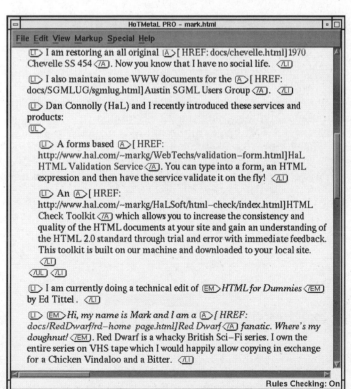

Figure 20-2:
The
HoTMetaL
screen.

AOLPress

AOLPress is part of America Online's AOLService, or not, if you don't want the service. Confusing? Yes, it is. The overall service, should you agree to subscribe to it, leads you step-by-step through the Web site creation and maintenance for just a little bit (or more) a month. You may want to look into AOLPress if what you want is a Web site that doesn't require much effort and if money isn't a limiting factor.

In any case, AOLPress is a good stand-alone HTML editor. AOLPress's WYSIWYG authoring produces Web pages compliant with the proposed HTML 3.0 standard and specifications. It contains embedded support and friendly interfaces for authoring forms, image maps, all standard HTML elements and formats, and many nonstandard HTML elements. It supports nonstandard HTML extensions via the Special Tag command. AOLPress has embedded interfaces for authoring HTML pages, including tables.

It allows you to create pages, view them, and edit them graphically — all within the same program and without typing a single HTML tag. Very impressive. AOLPress's editing window displays your HTML in close-to-Netscape quality and lets you insert and delete GIF and JPEG graphics directly. AOLPress's point-and-click dialog box for table creation works very well. Also, you can click the AOLPress's color wheels to select background and text colors.

Image map creation is a snap, as long as you only want rectangular hot spots. AOLPress does simple syntax checking but doesn't import any document file formats. AOLPress includes a few megabytes of clip art, such as colored bullets, arrows, icons, and backgrounds with the software. Also, AOLPress can save HTML pages and other files directly to an AOLService account, to AOLServers, or to any Web server that accepts the HTTP PUT protocol, which saves you the trouble of FTPing them yourself. AOLPress works with AOL's AOLService and other Internet Service Providers.

AOLPress is available for Motif (SunOS), Windows 3.1/3.11/Win95/NT, and Macintosh. The Windows version is 16-bit, but it runs under both Windows 95 and Windows NT. For more information, please visit

    http://www.aolserver.com/server/download.html

EMACS modes and templates

The old tried-and-true UNIX EMACS editor has several add-in macro systems (modes) available to help you create HTML documents. These modes vary in their features but generally are basic in their approach. They save you from typing each tag in its entirety and show you a list from which to choose.

(EMACS users will understand this section, and everyone else will think it's written in E-Greek. But then EMACS is a foreign language to most non-UNIX computer users.)

Various EMACS macro packages are available for editing HTML documents. The first and oldest is Marc Andreesen's *html-mode.el* (see Figure 20-3). It was written while he was at the University of Illinois. (Marc is the primary designer of Mosaic and Netscape.) Heiko Muenkel of the University of Hannover, Germany, added pull-down menus (*hm-html-menus.el*) and template handling (*tmpl-minor-mode.el*), which is up to version 4.15.

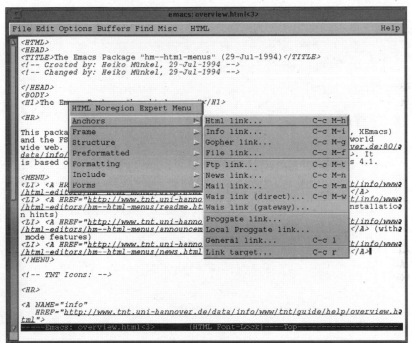

Figure 20-3:
The hm-html-menus.el screen.

Nelson Minar of The Santa Fe Institute wrote and continues to improve *html-helper-mode.el*, which supports Lucid EMACS menu bar and font-lock capabilities and runs under GNU EMACS v18 and v19, Epoch, and Lucid EMACS.

Generally speaking, the various iterations of HTML mode display text and HTML tags alike in fixed-size fonts. By using the *hilit.el* package, tags and references can be colored differently than text. The HTML modes do not support in-line display of graphics. The more recent versions of HTML mode can call a Mosaic process to display pages in browser view.

All of the HTML modes work primarily from direct keyboard commands that create paired begin/end HTML tags with an entry point available between the tags. It is possible to select a segment of text, and the tags will be inserted around it. None of the modes check the validity of tags or suggest possible tag usage. However, *html-helper-mode* and *tmpl-minor-mode* provide templates for entering multiple fields inside link tags.

For EMACS users, these modes may be just the thing for creating HTML documents. Using them should make HTML tagging easier and less prone to error than manually typing in complete tags. You must still know what tags to use and where to use them. You can obtain information and copies of Muenkel's and Minar's packages, respectively, at

```
http://www.tnt.uni-hannover.de/~muenkel/software
            /own/hm--html-menus/overview.html
http://www.santafe.edu/%7Enelson/tools/
```

Filtering and Converting Your UNIX Files

Because so many different file types are used on UNIX systems, a long list of HTML filters and converters has accumulated over the past few years. URLs to these lists are given at the end of this section. These programs transform text, RTF, FrameMaker, or other file types into an HTML-tagged file based on the original file's formatting. Of course, these converters are only as good as their HTML rule sets, and their authors' abilities to guess what you really want. In general, they give you a head start on converting existing files to HTML documents. WebMaker and WebWorks Publisher are two especially promising new entries into the FrameMaker conversion arena.

WebMaker

WebMaker from The Harlequin Group Limited is a new and promising FrameMaker converter (see Figure 20-4). WebMaker is a powerful, easy-to-use Web publishing program for the creation of Web pages from FrameMaker documents. Its conversion capabilities convert FrameMaker documents and books to HTML, complete with graphics, tables, and equations.

WebMaker takes advantage of the layout styles applied in FrameMaker to let you define specialized layout styles for Web publishing. Customization and hyperlinking are automated. After you complete the conversion, the conversion template you create can be used again to automatically convert documents to HTML in the format you've specified.

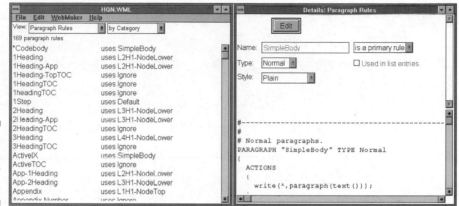

Figure 20-4:
Sample
WebMaker
screens.

WebMaker is available on several versions of UNIX, as well as Windows and Macintosh platforms at

```
http://www.harlequin.com/webmaker/2.0/Welcome.html
```

WebWorks Publisher

WebWorks Publisher from Quadralay was designed to be used with FrameMaker. WebWorks Publisher is an easy-to-use, full-featured system for the creation and maintenance of Web pages and hypermedia documents. It lets you design and maintain your complete documentation base in one single master version and then produces both print media and electronic hypermedia tailored to Web distribution, or even online help.

WebWorks Publisher can handle complex text, graphics, and hyperlinks. It makes full use of the layout and style information embedded in your original documents to automatically produce HTML documents. When you use WebWorks Publisher in conjunction with FrameMaker, you can convert documents from file formats including Microsoft Word and WordPerfect. It is available for HP-UX 9.*x*, MacOS 7.1, SunOS 4.1, Sun Solaris 2.3, and Windows 3.1 or NT.

You may obtain more information and download an evaluation copy from

```
http://www.quadralay.com/
```

Lists of UNIX helper and filter programs are available at

```
http://www.utirc.utoronto.ca/HTMLdocs/UNIXTOOLS/
          unix_doc_man.html
http://www.w3.org/hypertext/WWW/Tools/Word_proc_filters.html
```

UNIX Web Server Search

A WWW (or HTTP) server is a daemon program constantly running on an Internet-attached computer that responds to an incoming TCP connection and provides a service to the caller. The vast majority of WWW servers (about 83 percent) run on UNIX platforms around the world. And as everyone knows, there are more flavors of UNIX than ice cream at Baskin-Robbins. Consequently, you also can find many different kinds of WWW servers on those UNIX platforms.

Big surprise — free servers are the most popular with 82 percent of the servers being free or proprietary. Most of these run on UNIX, but not all do. About 45 percent of the world's Web sites use the NCSA HTTPD, with the CERN server as the second most used at about 15 percent, and Apache is third with about 5 percent. Several commercial servers are rapidly gaining popularity, due primarily to their ease of use and support for secure transactions. The major commercial player in the UNIX market is Netscape with about 7 percent of the sites worldwide. For the most recent information on UNIX-based WWW (HTTP) servers, check out these sites and follow their links:

```
http://webcompare.iworld.com/
http://www.w3.org/hypertext/WWW/Servers.html
http://www.yahoo.com/Computers_and_Internet/Software/
          Internet/World_Wide_Web/Servers/Unix/
```

This chapter has provided you with a brief overview of the major UNIX-based HTML authoring systems, as well as some of the ancillary packages. The Web itself is the best place to obtain the latest and greatest UNIX Web tools so, "The Web's up. Let's go surfin' now." In the next chapter, we drop UNIX like a hot potato and get tight with the Macintosh.

Chapter 21

More Macintosh Madness

In This Chapter

▶ Sampling the Mac varieties

▶ Evolving stand-alone editors

▶ Leaning toward BBEdit extensions

▶ Flowing through filters and file converters

▶ Perusing Web servers

A plethora of excellent HTML authoring tools for the Macintosh is available for downloading from numerous online sites. All but a couple of these tools are freeware or shareware, and most of them are appropriate for beginning to advanced HTML authors. Because of their low- or no-cost status, these freeware/shareware tools don't offer the kind of hand-holding you might expect from commercial products. But then, they don't weigh down the bottom line much, either. Most of these Macintosh products ship with very good to pretty good documentation, and some even have online or "balloon" help. Thankfully, these tools are easy to learn because they use familiar Macintosh word-processing or text-editor models and the Macintosh menuing system.

Surveying the Orchard: Macintosh HTML Tools

In the subsections that follow, you encounter information on several types of Macintosh HTML authoring tools that are available to help you create Web pages. These tools vary in their scope and functionality, but all of them can provide solid HTML assistance.

Many Macintosh HTML authoring tools are able to display a WYSIWYG or semi-WYSIWYG view of HTML documents. Along with this capability comes a certain amount of error checking, because these programs' internal display mechanisms can simulate a browser and recognize HTML tags. The best tools let you see both WYSIWYG and tagged views of documents, and all of the truly complete implementations provide balloon help as well.

Several stand-alone WYSIWYG programs let you check your HTML code and keep you from making syntax or placement errors. Some of these tools add to the functionality of existing word-processing and text editors, thereby giving them the capability to handle HTML tags. Some even go so far as converting existing files from normal formats to HTML, and vice versa.

While you're trying out one or more of these tools, ask yourself, "Does this program make writing HTML easier?" If your answer is "No," try another tool. Regardless of the kind of tool you choose, you can reasonably expect it to make your HTML creation job easier, not harder.

You can find the most up-to-date information on Macintosh HTML tools at these sites:

```
http://www.comvista.com/net/www/htmleditor.html
http://www.yahoo.com/Computers_and_Internet/Software/
        Internet/World_Wide_Web/HTML_Editors/Macintosh/
http://www.w3.org/hypertext/WWW/Tools/Overview.html
```

Biting into Stand-Alone HTML Editors for Macintosh

Stand-alone authoring tools for the Macintosh range in complexity from the Simple HTML Editor (SHE) to complete Web creation environments such as PageMill and NaviPress. The simple, generally plain-text HTML editors like HTML Editor, HTML.edit, and Simple HTML Editor (SHE) basically let you enter your text and supply buttons or menu options to select tags at appropriate insertion points. These are being superseded by completely WYSIWYG environments, such as the freeware Webtor, and partially WYSIWYG shareware, such as HTML Pro. The packages we discuss in the following sections are the most popular — and perhaps the easiest to use — of the myriad of stand-alone Macintosh HTML creation tools.

Webtor

Jochen Schales at the Fraunhofer Institute for Computer Graphics in Darmstadt, Germany, created this outstanding freeware package. Webtor displays inline graphics and provides a full WYSIWYG environment for editing multiple documents with no tags showing. You can send your documents to a browser to test them or to a text editor to see the HTML tags.

Making an HTML mistake is virtually impossible when using Webtor because it performs HTML DTD checking of all text. Webtor also includes a configurable DTD that lets you use HTML extensions, and it also includes a document outliner. Webtor is a winner for novice to intermediate Web makers. You may download it from

```
http://www.informatik.th-darmstadt.de/~neuss/webtor/
                webtor.html
```

HTML Pro

HTML Pro is a Macintosh product from Niklas Frykholm. In this beginner-oriented program, you edit HTML-coded text in one window with another window with a near-WYSIWYG display simultaneously visible. You can edit the document in both windows and all menu options — such as copying, pasting, and formatting text — apply in both windows. To switch between the two windows, use the View menu or simply click the window. You can click or type your codes and then get an instant look at the results in the other window. HTML only edits one 32K document at a time. Download a copy of this ($5) shareware program from

```
http://www.ts.umu.se:80/~r2d2/package/htmlpro_help.html
```

Claris Home Page

The Claris Home Page site designer is for novice and expert Web authors alike. It permits its users to create dynamic Web pages without having to know everything about programming. The package has lots of automatic programming features that perform all the complicated HTML work behind the scenes. Plus, Claris Home Page has many advanced features, such as support for Java applets, multimedia plug-ins, and forms. And, after you complete construction, Home Page can publish your finished product to any designated Web server. Go check it out at

```
http://www.claris.com/products/claris/clarispage/
                clarispage.html
```

NetObjects Fusion

Unlike other Web-building tools, NetObjects Fusion is more than a word processor that supports HTML. It is a fully integrated site creation and publishing application for dynamic Web sites. With Fusion, you can create complicated multipage structure, centrally control all of your navigation controls, icons, and banners, pull data from databases, and drag-and-drop multimedia into the familiar WYSIWYG processing interface. This high-tech tool is a breeze to use for both programmers and newbies. Get a trial version from

```
http://www.netobjects.com/
```

PageMill

PageMill from Adobe is hot, hot, hot! It provides an easy-to-understand word processing environment where you don't type HTML tags or look at them. Can you spell WYSIWYG? Your Web pages look like they would appear in a browser, except their contents are editable and PageMill writes the HTML code for you (see Figure 21-1).

PageMill makes good use of Macintosh drag-and-drop to paste in links, text snippets, and graphics. You can drag links directly from your Netscape browser and drop them into your own pages. It also converts from JPEG or PICT to GIF graphics and creates imagemaps directly in the page. Of course, you expect and receive only the best in graphics manipulation from Adobe in PageMill.

Take a look for yourself at their Web site. They even have screen shots like the one in Figure 21-1 on the site. When you graduate from novice to Webspert, Adobe also offers SiteMill as an upgrade from PageMill.

```
http://www.adobe.com/prodindex/pagemill/
```

HoTMetaL Pro

HoTMetaL Pro is SoftQuad's commercial HTML editor (see Figure 21-2). A Macintosh version is available for free downloading at various sites. HoTMetaL requires you to edit a document with the embedded HTML codes visible; then it hands the code off to your own browser for viewing. HoTMetaL Pro provides all of the HTML DTD tags and selected Internet

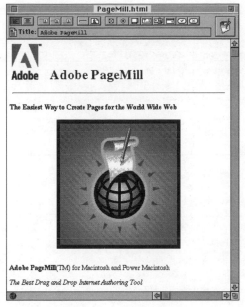

Figure 21-1:
The
PageMill
edit screen.

Explorer and Netscape extensions. It can open many document formats — Lotus Ami Pro; Microsoft Word for Macintosh, Windows, and DOS; RTF (Rich Text Format); and WordPerfect for DOS, Windows, and Macintosh — and convert them to HTML.

HoTMetaL does both syntax checking and HTML validation. With syntax (rules) checking turned on, HoTMetaL helps you enter only valid HTML. If you select HTML validation, it checks your document for conformance to an HTML specification. It also provides a list of all non-DTD, IE, and Netscape extension tags in your document to alert you to possible incompatibilities with browsers that don't support those codes.

The HTML validation and format conversions are quite useful, but this editor doesn't allow you to create image maps nor does it let you see what your images will look like on the page. You can download the free version from any site on SoftQuad's download site list:

```
http://www.sq.com/products/hotmetal/hm-ftp.htm
```

AOLPress

AOLPress is part of America Online's Web Service. The overall service, should you agree to subscribe to it, will lead you step-by-step through the

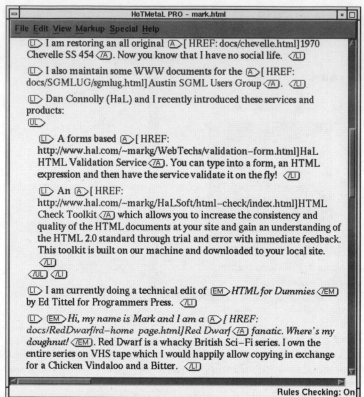

LI> I am restoring an all original A>[HREF: docs/chevelle.html]1970 Chevelle SS 454 /A>. Now you know that I have no social life. /LI>

LI> I also maintain some WWW documents for the A>[HREF: docs/SGMLUG/sgmlug.html] Austin SGML Users Group /A>. /LI>

LI> Dan Connolly (HaL) and I recently introduced these services and products:
UL>

LI> A forms based A>[HREF: http://www.hal.com/~markg/WebTechs/validation–form.html]HaL HTML Validation Service /A>. You can type into a form, an HTML expression and then have the service validate it on the fly! /LI>

LI> An A>[HREF: http://www.hal.com/~markg/HaLSoft/html–check/index.html]HTML Check Toolkit /A> which allows you to increase the consistency and quality of the HTML documents at your site and gain an understanding of the HTML 2.0 standard through trial and error with immediate feedback. This toolkit is built on our machine and downloaded to your local site. /LI>
/UL> /LI>

LI> I am currently doing a technical edit of EM>*HTML for Dummies* /EM> by Ed Tittel for Programmers Press. /LI>

LI> EM>*Hi, my name is Mark and I am a* A>*[HREF: docs/RedDwarf/rd–home page.html]Red Dwarf* /A> *fanatic. Where's my doughnut!* /EM>. Red Dwarf is a whacky British Sci–Fi series. I own the entire series on VHS tape which I would happily allow copying in exchange for a Chicken Vindaloo and a Bitter. /LI>

Rules Checking: On

Figure 21-2:
The HoTMetaL screen.

Web site creation and maintenance for just a little bit (or more) a month. You may want to look into AOLPress if you want a Web site without much effort and money isn't a limiting factor.

In any case, the AOLPress program is a good stand-alone HTML editor. AOLPress's WYSIWYG authoring produces Web pages compliant with the proposed HTML DTDs standard and specifications. It contains embedded support and friendly interfaces for authoring forms, image maps, all standard HTML elements and formats, and many new elements and extensions. It supports nonstandard HTML extensions via the Special Tag command. AOLPress 1.1 has embedded interfaces for authoring HTML 3.0 pages, including tables.

AOLPress allows you to create pages, view them, and edit them graphically — all within the same program and without typing a single HTML tag. Very impressive. AOLPress's editing window displays your HTML in close-to-Netscape quality and lets you insert and delete GIF and JPEG graphics directly. AOLPress's point-and-click dialog box for table creation works well. Also, you can click the AOLPress's color wheels to select background and text colors.

Image map creation is a snap, as long as you only want rectangular hot spots. AOLPress does simple syntax checking but doesn't import any document file formats. AOLPress includes a few megabytes of clip art, such as colored bullets, arrows, icons, and backgrounds with the software. AOLPress can save HTML pages and other files directly to a NaviService account, to NaviServers, or to any Web server that accepts the HTTP PUT protocol to save you the trouble of FTPing them yourself. AOLPress works with AOL's NaviService and other Internet Service Providers. AOLPress is available for the Macintosh System 7 and up at

```
http://www.aolserver.com/index.html
```

Netscape Navigator Gold

Netscape's take-the-world-by-storm browser has a few new tricks — HTML editing. Now you can use the interface you are already familiar with to create your own Web documents. Navigator Gold is fully WYSIWYG and lets you drag and drop elements right where you want them. A few deft clicks here and there are all the work you have to do — Navigator Gold will write all the code and spit out a fully working document. You've got to see it to believe it, so go get it and try it:

```
http://home.netscape.com/comprod/products/navigator/gold/
index.html
```

Tackling Text Editor Extensions and Templates

Editor or word-processing add-in functions are templates and programs that are installed into your existing editor or word-processing program. These extensions appear in the editor's menus as HTML functions that insert tags, create forms, and the like. Some extensions give the program the capability to open and save HTML-tagged documents.

The HTML add-ins for BBEdit and BBEditLite are quite extensive and provide a well-rounded HTML authoring system. Tools of this kind can cause the editor to open a standard text file and save it with HTML tags automatically. To use these add-ins, you must first have the editor or word-processing software on your computer that the add-in requires.

If you use BBEdit, two excellent sets of add-ins for HTML editing are available. They are BBEdit HTML Extensions by Carles Bellver and BBEdit HTML Tools by Lindsay Davies. We discuss them together here because they are so similar in form and function.

Using either of these add-ins with BBEdit or BBEditLite gives you access to most, if not all, of the HTML authoring functions you probably need for all but the most complex Web pages. Because you probably already use BBEdit or BBEditLite, you may be able to get going very quickly with these add-ins. It won't take you much time to try one of these and see if you like it.

BBEdit

Even without its available add-ons, extensions, and tools, the newest version of BBEdit is fully HTML-aware and can be the most powerful HTML authoring tool in your arsenal. If you're already using this program, there's little we can say that you don't already know. If you're not already an aficionado of this outstanding tool, BBEdit has powers that are heretofore unknown in this universe. If you haven't tried BBEdit, or are using an old version, go get the latest info and trial version from

```
http://www.barebones.com/
```

BBEdit HTML extensions

Carles Bellver's extensions work well with BBEdit and are distributed along with many packages, including BBEdit and some of Apple CD's. They are freeware. Download them from

```
http://www.uji.es/bbedit-html-extensions.html
```

BBEdit HTML tools

Lindsay Davies's extensions (with BBEdit 3.1.x) provide a good method for creating HTML documents for current BBEdit users. The tools are quite complete, and include their own balloon help inside the program's dialog boxes. Davies's extensions can help you create templates, check HTML syntax, translate special characters in both directions, and more. These tools also help with includes and create special insertion tags to make updating pages quick and easy. You can download the freeware files from

```
http://www.york.ac.uk/~ld11/BBEditTools.html
```

Magnificent Miscellaneous Mac Tools

Numerous tools to assist in creation of maps, forms, CGI applications, and more are readily available for the Macintosh. An extensive list of such tools is available at the following site:

```
http://www.comvista.com/net/www/WWWDirectory.html
```

Web Server Primer

A WWW or HTTP server is a program constantly running on a computer that responds to incoming TCP connections and provides services to all clients. Several varieties of HTTP server software are available for the Macintosh. The most popular is WebStar, although it only represents a few percent of the overall HTTP servers in use on the WWW. Of course, most HTTP servers are UNIX based (more than 65 percent).

Here's a brief look at some Macintosh Web server software, which you may not yet be ready to tackle. We just want to help you broaden your Web horizons a bit. You can find more information on servers by starting at the ComVista or Yahoo! sites:

```
http://www.comvista.com/net/www/server.html
http://www.yahoo.com/Computers_and_Internet/Software/
           Internet/World_Wide_Web/Servers/Macintosh/
```

WebSTAR / MacHTTP Web server

WebSTAR, from StarNine Technologies, is the commercial successor to MacHTTP, building on the same code base with the same great programming by Chuck Shotton. The latest release of WebSTAR is several times faster than MacHTTP and has the same features as commercial servers on other platforms.

MacHTTP, by Chuck Shotton of BIAP Systems, was the first HTTP server for Macintosh computers. It is still a full-featured server and is currently sold by StarNine Technologies, a division of Quarterdeck Corporation.

Quarterdeck has announced two add-ons for WebSTAR: the Commerce Kit and the Security Kit. The Commerce Kit provides the capability to accept online payments for products or services (via a link to FirstVirtual) by using either credit cards or a custom commerce interface. The Security Kit provides secure transmission of data between client and server using the Secure Sockets Layer (SSL) protocol. Have a look at more information at

```
http://www.starnine.com/webstar/webstar.html
```

Netwings

NetWings is a full-featured HTTP server for Macintosh built on the 4D database system. NetWings Corp. released NetWings in 1995. It uses the HTTP 1.0 standard, supports CGI applications through AppleEvents, has site protection, can load documents from any drive on the network, and can serve either documents and files or pages built on the fly from information in its 4D databases. The software is available now and a demo version should also be available. Have a look for yourself at

```
http://netwings.com/
```

httpd4Mac

Bill Melotti's httpd4Mac is a free, minimal functionality, HTTP server. It runs as a background application and has been tested under System 7.1. You can download it from

```
http://sodium.ch.man.ac.uk/pages/httpd4Mac/home.html
```

Isn't your head about to explode with all of this information? Congratulations — you must be really stuck on the Web. Grab one of these editors and get cracking on your own super Web, or dive into a server, and see what it can do. If you're game, you can find the scoop on Windows Web editors and servers in the next chapter!

Chapter 22

Webbing Up Windows

• •

In This Chapter

▶ Picking your Windows HTML authoring tools

▶ Choosing the best HTML editors

▶ Hiding HTML with a WYSIWYG Web document creator

▶ Using your word processor for Web development

▶ Slipping through file converters

• •

A mazing, new, richly featured, and easy-to-use HTML authoring tools for Windows-based systems have finally arrived. Many are the latest and greatest version of shareware HTML editors. All of the really good programs are the culmination of a couple of years of refinement and make use of the latest features that Windows 95 has to offer. Some even make use of the Windows 95 user interface.

You now have your choice of HTML editors that let you work directly with the HTML code, and WYSIWYG Web creators that hide the HTML code and let you create your Web documents directly on-screen by clicking buttons and dragging and dropping elements. In addition, you can convert or filter almost any file type into or out of HTML by using one of the latest word processors with an HTML output or by using one of the myriad HTML utility programs available for Windows.

Many of the Windows-based HTML authoring systems are shareware. Most of the commercial Windows HTML authoring packages offer a freeware version for downloading and many are relatively inexpensive anyway (under $50). Keep in mind that the free and shareware Windows HTML authoring tools aren't supported in the same manner as the commercial products. But then, they don't cost you much either. Thankfully, these tools are usually easy to learn because they use familiar text editor metaphors. In any case, if you've ever used a Windows-based word processor, you can figure out one of these HTML tools easily.

Surveying the Field of HTML Software Tools

The sections that follow describe where to find some of the currently popular Windows-based HTML authoring tools and give you important facts about each of them. These tools vary in their scope and functionality; however, all of them are designed to help you create HTML documents with greater ease. Check out the URLs that follow for complete information on these tools and many more.

We separate the tools into four major categories: WYSIWYG HTML authoring tools, HTML code editors, word-processing programs, and HTML file converters.

No matter which kind of tool you choose to try first, remember that the objective is to create eye-catching, informative Web pages quickly that can also function on your targeted browsers. If the tool you try doesn't help you meet this objective, try another tool. You can find one out there that will do the job for you.

More information on the latest and greatest Windows HTML authoring tools is readily available on many WWW sites. You may use your favorite search site (Yahoo!, Excite, Lycos, Netscape, and so on) and search for "HTML editor." Or you may go directly to one of these URLs:

```
http://union.ncsa.uiuc.edu/HyperNews/get/www/html/
            editors.html
http://www.yahoo.com/Computers_and_Internet/Software/
            Internet/World_Wide_Web/HTML_Editors/MS_Windows/
http://cws.iworld.com/
http://futuris.net/nickp/html/
```

WYSIWYG Web Authoring Systems

It seems like every programmer and company is trying to produce a better mousetrap for Windows-based Web authoring. Some of them we surveyed appear to be well-constructed and low on bugs, but we decided it would be more fun to cover the cheesy, buggy ones instead. (If you believe that, we have a deal for you on some swamp land in . . . never mind.) We wouldn't waste your time or ours by discussing anything but the best we could find. The following sections describe the (most widely acknowledged) best in this category.

FrontPage 97

FrontPage 97 with Bonus Pack ($149) is Microsoft's commercial Web authoring system for Windows 95 and NT. Since Microsoft bought FrontPage from Vermeer Technologies, Inc. in January 1996, Microsoft has made FrontPage the premier personal Web authoring, publishing, and maintenance tool for Windows systems. With Microsoft behind it, this product undoubtedly will become the most widely used tool of its kind in the Internet in the near future.

As Microsoft states in its promotional literature, "...with the WYSIWYG FrontPage Editor, there's no need to know HTML!" See for yourself in Figure 22-1. You have at your disposal more than 30 built-in templates and wizards to help you build Web documents *and* your entire Web site. You may copy one of the existing templates and then replace the content with your own words, images, and ideas to help you generate your Web site. Or you can select a Wizard, answer a few questions, and let the Wizard do the rest.

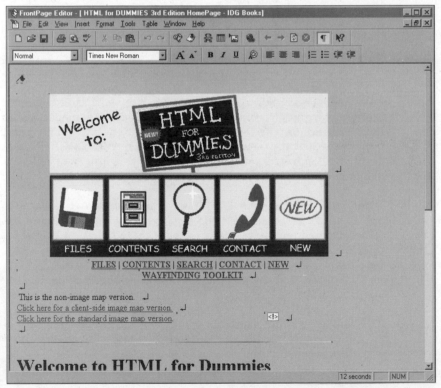

Figure 22-1:
The
FrontPage
WYSIWYG
editor
screen.

Each Web site is in its own project folder so you can develop and manage multiple sites, as shown in Figure 22-2.

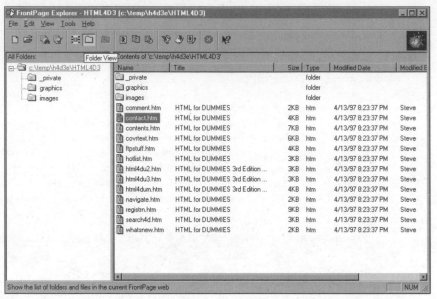

Figure 22-2:
The
FrontPage
project
folder
screen.

Enhanced drag-and-drop features let you drag Microsoft Office files into the FrontPage Explorer or move hyperlinks, tables, and images within the FrontPage Editor. The "Verify all links" feature automatically verifies that all hyperlinks are valid — within and outside your Web site. This feature even corrects all link errors within your site for you. You can easily see the links in Figure 22-3.

FrontPage 97 also supports database connectivity, ActiveX control, Java applet usage (not creation), VBScript and JavaScript creation and insertion, tables, frames, and most Microsoft Internet Explorer and Netscape Navigator plug-ins.

As if all of this isn't enough, the FrontPage Bonus Pack includes the following programs:

✔ **The Image Composer** lets you create and edit graphics for your Web documents. It includes more than 500 tools and effects and works with PhotoShop-compatible plug-in products, such as Kai's Power Tools from MetaTools, Inc. Image Composer includes more than 600 royalty-free Web-ready images. You may also download the free Microsoft GIF Animator to animate your own Image Composer images and make your Web site really jump on the screen.

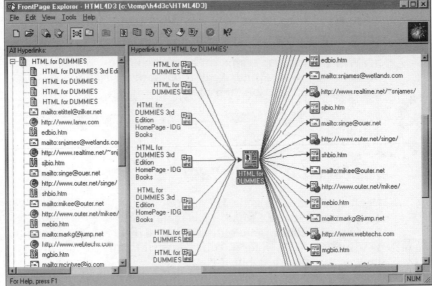

Figure 22-3:
The
FrontPage
hyperlink
screen.

✔ **The Personal Web Server** lets you host your Web sites on your own PC. This program is the Windows 95 version of the Microsoft Internet Information Server. The Personal Web Server gives you performance and management features to make administering your Internet or intranet site relatively easy (with the emphasis on the relatively because administering your Web site is still somewhat complex).

✔ **The Web Publishing Wizard** makes it relatively (again not really easy) straightforward to post your Web site (send your HTML files) to most Web servers (at your ISP). The Web Publishing Wizard gives you step-by-step guidance, as long as you know your Web server directory at your ISP and have upload clearance. You can get this information from your ISP.

✔ **Microsoft's Internet Explorer** is included in the FrontPage Bonus Pack. Internet Explorer's features undoubtedly will change monthly, but at the least, the next version will probably include browser, e-mail, newsgroup, and FTP functions.

The FrontPage 97 with Bonus Pack interface also allows you to use any document created with Microsoft Office 97 because it works like other Office 97 applications. FrontPage 97 uses the shared spelling checker, global Find and Replace, and the Microsoft Thesaurus.

Now you can't quite say, "Use FrontPage to create my Web site" into your PC's microphone, walk off, have an espresso, and come back to view the finished work. But if you apply the knowledge of planning and preparation from earlier chapters in this book, you should be able to have an outstanding Web site created, tested, and running on your ISP's Web server in very little time by using FrontPage 97. For more information about FrontPage 97, check out the Microsoft Web site:

```
http://www.microsoft.com/frontpage/
```

Netscape Composer

Netscape Composer is the HTML creation portion of the Netscape Communicator Internet Suite. From the Netscape Browser, you simply open an HTML file with the Editor radio button selected. Figure 22-4 shows the Composer's WYSIWYG editing window. You can use it to directly manipulate the text and images that you see while it composes the HTML for you.

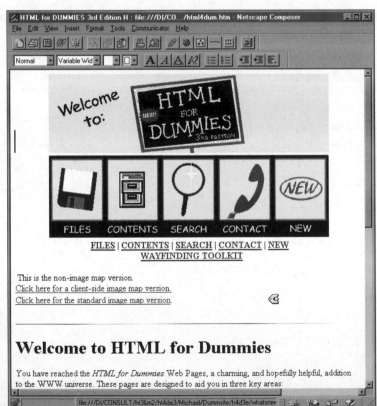

Figure 22-4:
The Netscape composer screen.

For those aspects of Web creation that can't be handled directly, Netscape Composer contains a very functional toolbar. This toolbar assists you with links, tables, frames, and other necessary Web development functions. Because Composer is a part of Netscape Communicator, you may want to give it a try and see if it performs to your expectations. Composer isn't as full-featured as FrontPage or HomeSite, but it can help you create all but the most complex Web documents. You can find it at the following URL:

```
http://www.netscape.com
```

HTML Code Editors

One HTML code editor has risen to the top of the heap as the all-around best available today. That code editor is HomeSite by Nick Bradbury. He recently chose Allaire Corporation to market HomeSite 2.5 and future versions.

HomeSite 2.5

HomeSite 2.5 (pre-release) ($39.95) is available on the Allaire Web site for evaluation and purchase. HomeSite is an extremely feature-rich HTML editor for both the beginner and the professional. You edit the HTML directly but can instantly get a browser view by clicking a tab (see Figure 22-5).

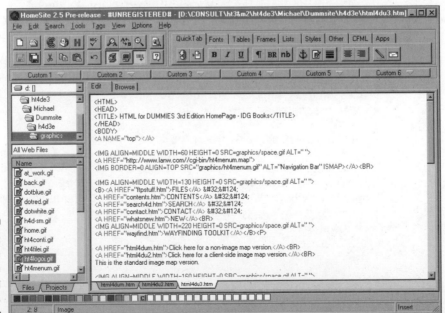

Figure 22-5: The HomeSite editing screen.

HomeSite color-codes the HTML to help you in your editing. It uses drag-and-drop and right-mouse click menus. The integrated spell checker and global search and replace can check your spelling and update entire projects, folders, and files simultaneously. You can use the image and thumbnail viewers to browse image libraries directly in your editor.

HomeSite even has customizable toolbars and menus. Add to that an extensive online help system to access documentation on HTML and other popular scripting languages, and you have an impressive system. But there's even more. HomeSite helps you with your project management, provides for link verification, internally validates your HTML, and opens and uploads your files to your remote Web server.

HomeSite contains Code Wizards to help you build frames and tables, and it creates JavaScript client-side scripts. It also contains Cold Fusion and Active Server Toolbars to help you add scripts and tags from these popular Web application development tools.

HomeSite supports custom style sheets, HTML 3.2, Netscape and Microsoft HTML extensions, embedded multimedia, and ActiveX and Java controls.

```
http://www.dexnet.com/homesite.html
```

Word Processors as HTML Editors

If you're joined at the hip to Microsoft Word 97 for Windows, Corel WordPerfect 7.0 for Windows, or Lotus Word Pro 97 for Windows, you may be interested in trying their built-in HTML editing and site management features. These features provide adequate HTML assistance but aren't really in the same ballpark with the better stand-alone WYSIWYG Web development and HTML editing systems. If you already own one of these word-processing programs, the Web functionality is free. So for now, you may want to use your favorite of the three for text and for Web development.

As an example of these, Word 97 for Windows has a nice WYSIWYG editing window with a good number of functions in its toolbar. This program's functionality is adequate for a word processor-turned-Web document editor. However, who knows what Microsoft will do in the long term with its problem of having both Word 97 and FrontPage as Web document development systems. But why worry about that now? If you own it, give it a try for your Web development.

See the following sites for their respective information on Microsoft Word 97 for Windows, Corel WordPerfect 7.0 for Windows, and Lotus Word Pro 97 for Windows:

```
http://www.microsoft.com/msoffice/office97/
http://wp.novell.com/products/wordperfect/cwps7/
http://www2.lotus.com/wordpro.nsf
```

Filters and File Converters

Automatically converting existing text documents into HTML is supported by several of the current crop of HTML editors, word processors, and the stand-alone converters, such as HTML Transit and WebMaker. They work quickly and easily. For example, if you use Word 97 for Windows, simply open a standard Word document and then save the file in HTML format via the Save As command, and it's converted. Most of the text formatting that really counts, including headings, is converted.

The following two stand-alone converters are examples of the numerous converters available on every conceivable computer platform to convert virtually every file format to HTML and sometimes back again. HTML Transit imports and converts a large number of file formats, whereas WebMaker is designed specifically to convert FrameMaker files. If you have many highly formatted files that you want to convert to HTML for Web display, check into these two systems and the other you can find at the URLs listed at the end of this section.

HTML Transit

HTML Transit, from InfoAccess, Inc., reads the structure of the source document, recognizing elements such as headings, subheads, bullets, images, and so on. HTML Transit then creates a default template based on this structure that becomes the foundation for one-button generation of HTML documents. HTML Transit offers direct translation of all major word processing formats and all major graphics formats.

With a well-formatted word processor or page layout file and HTML Transit, you may not need an HTML "editor" at all. Although HTML Transit is a bit expensive ($495), it may just be what you're looking for. Have a look for yourself at

```
http://www.infoaccess.com/
```

WebMaker 3.0

WebMaker 3.0 from The Harlequin Group Limited is a new and promising FrameMaker converter, and at $99, it's quite a deal for FrameMaker users. WebMaker is a powerful, easy-to-use Web publishing solution for the creation of full-featured Web pages from FrameMaker documents. WebMaker's conversion capabilities convert FrameMaker documents and books to HTML complete with graphics, tables, and equations.

WebMaker takes full advantage of the layout styles you apply in FrameMaker to let you define specialized layout styles for Web publishing. Customization and hyperlinking are accomplished and automated easily and produce fast, predictable results. After you complete the conversion, the conversion template you create can be used over and over again to automatically convert documents to HTML in the format you've specified. No additional work is required no matter how many pages, documents, or books you decide to convert.

WebMaker is available for Windows at

```
http://www.harlequin.com/webmaker/Welcome.html
```

For a look at the myriad of other HTML converters and filters, start your surfing at these sites:

```
http://union.ncsa.uiuc.edu/HyperNews/get/www/html/
          converters.html
http://www.w3.org/pub/WWW/Tools/Filters.html
http://www.yahoo.com/Computers_and_Internet/Software/
          Internet/World_Wide_Web/HTML_Converters/
http://www.yahoo.com/Computers_and_Internet/Software/
          Internet/World_Wide_Web/HTML_Converters/
          Commercial_Products/
```

You sure are a glutton for information if you've read this far! Congratulations, you must be *really* stuck on the Web. Grab one of these HTML editors or authoring systems and get cracking on your own super Web. See ya on the Web.

Part VI
The Part of Tens

The 5th Wave   By Rich Tennant

Andy soon began to think he shouldn't have opted for the cut-rate Web hookup after all.

©RICHTENNANT

In this part . . .

Here, we cover the dos and don'ts for HTML markup, help you rethink your views on document design, and help you catch potential bugs and errors in your pages. Finally, we help you decide whether your pages should reside on an Internet provider's Web server or whether you should build a Web server of your own.

Chapter 23

The Top Ten HTML Dos and Don'ts

In This Chapter

▶ Remembering your content

▶ Structuring your documents

▶ Keeping track of tags

▶ Making the most from the least

▶ Building attractive pages

▶ Avoiding browser dependencies

▶ Eliminating distractions

▶ Navigating your wild and woolly Web

▶ Beating the two-dimensional text trap

▶ Overcoming inertia takes constant vigilance

*B*y itself, HTML is neither excessively complex nor overwhelmingly difficult. As better wags than we have put it, "This ain't rocket science!" Nevertheless, having a set of guidelines is a good idea. These guidelines can help you make the most out of HTML without stepping away from your need to communicate effectively with your users.

This chapter attempts to underscore the fundamental points that we've made throughout this book regarding proper and improper use of HTML. We hope that you adhere to the prescriptions and avoid the maledictions. But hey, they're your pages, and you can do what you want with them. The users will decide the ultimate outcome. (Just don't make us say, "We *told* you so!")

Remembering Your Content!

Darrell Royal, the legendary coach of the University of Texas Longhorns football team in the '60s and '70s, is rumored to have said to his players, "Dance with who brung ya." In normal English, we think this means that you should stick to the people who've supported you all along and give your loyalty to those who've given it to you.

We're not sure what this means for football, but for Web pages, it means keeping the content paramount. If you don't have strong, solid, informative content, users will quickly realize that your Web pages are relatively content-free. Then they'll be off elsewhere on the Web looking for the content your pages may have lacked.

Above all, this means placing your most important content on the site's major pages, and frills and supplementary materials on secondary pages. The short statement of this principle for HTML is "Tags are important, but what's between the tags — the content — is what really counts." Make your content the best it can possibly be!

Structuring Your Documents

Providing users with a clear road map and guiding them through your content is as important for a home page as it is for an online encyclopedia. But the longer or more complex the document, the more important a road map becomes. This map ideally takes the form of a flow chart showing page organization, or it can even appear as a graphic for inclusion on an orientation page for your site.

We're strong advocates of top-down page design. Start the construction of any HTML document or collection of documents with a paper and pencil (or whatever modeling tool you like best). Sketch out the relationships within the content and the relationships among your pages. Don't start writing content or placing tags until you understand what you want to say and how you want to organize your materials.

Good content flows from good organization. Strong organization helps you stay on track during page design, testing, delivery, and maintenance, and it helps your users find their way through your site. Need we say more?

Keeping Track of Tags

While you're building documents, you can easily forget to use closing tags where they're required (for example, the ⟨/A⟩ that closes the opening anchor tag ⟨A⟩). Even when you're testing your pages, some browsers are so forgiving that they compensate for your lack of correctness, leading you into possible problems from other browsers that aren't quite so understanding (or lax, as the case may be).

We can say a lot about this subject, but we'll try to stick to the ones that really count:

- ✔ Keep track of yourself while you're writing or editing HTML. If you open an anchor, or text area, or whatever, go back through and find the closing tag for each opening one.

- ✔ Use a syntax-checker to validate your work as part of the testing process. These checkers are mindless, automatic tools that find missing tags and also find other ways to drive you crazy along the way!

- ✔ Here's a URL that's a jump page for HTML validation tools:

```
http://www.charm.net/~web/Vlib/Providers/Validation.html
```

- ✔ Try to obtain and use as many browsers as you possibly can when testing your pages. This not only alerts you to the "missing tag" problem; it also points out potential design flaws and reminds you of the importance of providing alternate text information.

- ✔ Always follow the rules of HTML document syntax and layout. Just because most browsers don't require structure tags like <HTML>, <HEAD>, and <BODY> doesn't mean it's okay to leave them out; it just means that the browsers don't care if you do. Your users may care, and we certainly don't want you writing any improperly structured HTML, either!

Although HTML isn't exactly a programming language, it still makes sense to treat it like one. Therefore, following formats and syntax helps avoid trouble, and careful testing and rechecking of your work ensures a high degree of quality and standards compliance.

Making the Most from the Least

More is not always better, especially when it comes to Web pages. Try to design and build your pages using a simple layout and the least amount of ornament possible; don't overload pages with lots of graphics, as many heading levels as you can cram in, and links in every possible description.

Structure exists to highlight the content. The more structure dominates, the more it takes away from content. Therefore, use structure sparingly, wisely, and as carefully as possible. Anything more becomes an obstacle to delivering your content. This means stay away from excessive use of graphics, links, and layout tags!

Building Attractive Pages

Working within a consistent framework enables users to figure out how to view and navigate your pages. Making them easy to navigate only adds to their appeal. If you're in need of inspiration, cruise the Web and look for layouts and graphics that work for you. If you take the time to analyze what you like about them, you can work from other people's design principles without having to steal the details of their layout and look.

When designing Web documents, start with a fundamental layout for your pages. Pick a small but interesting set of graphical symbols or icons and adopt a consistent navigation style. Use graphics sparingly and make them as small as possible (by reducing size, number of colors, shading, and so on) while still retaining their "eye-candy" appeal. Use simple, consistent navigation tools throughout. You can make your pages both appealing and informative if you're willing to invest the time and effort.

Avoiding Browser Dependencies

When building Web pages, viewing your Web with your favorite browser is nearly irresistible. That's why you should always remember that users view the Web in general and your pages in particular, from many different perspectives and through many different browsers.

During the design and writing phase, it's common to ping-pong between HTML and a browser's eye-view of that text. At this early point in the process, we recommend switching among a group of browsers, including at least one character-mode browser. This switching helps balance your viewpoint on your pages and usually helps to maintain a focus on the content.

During testing and maintenance, browsing your pages through as many different viewpoints as you can is even more important. Make sure to work from multiple platforms and to try both graphical and character-mode browsers on each. Such testing takes time but repays itself with pages that are easy for everyone to read and follow. It also helps those viewers who come at your materials from a different platform than your own native one, and helps your pages achieve true platform (as well as browser) independence.

Evolution, Not Revolution

Over time, Web pages change and grow. Keep looking at your work with a fresh eye (or keep recruiting fresh eyes from the ranks of those who haven't seen your pages before) in order to avoid the process we call "organic acceptance."

We can best explain this organic acceptance by using the analogy of your face and the mirror: You see your face every day, and you know it intimately, so you may not be as sensitive to the impact of change over time as someone else. Then you see yourself on videotape, in a photograph, or through the eyes of an old friend. At that point, changes obvious to the entire world become obvious to you: "My hairline's really receded," or "I've gone completely gray," or "My spare tire could mount on a semi!"

Just as with the rest of life, changes to your Web pages are evolutionary, not revolutionary. They usually proceed in small daily steps, not big radical ones. Nevertheless, you need to remain sensitive to the supporting infrastructure and readability of your content as your pages evolve. Maybe the lack of on-screen links to each section of the Product Catalog didn't matter when you only had three products; now that you have 25, it's a different story. Over time, structure needs to adapt to follow the content. If you regularly reevaluate your site's effectiveness at communicating its content, you'll know when it's time to make changes, both large and small.

This is where user feedback is absolutely crucial. If you don't get feedback through forms or other means of communication, you should go out and aggressively solicit from your users. "If you don't ask," goes the common wisdom, "you can't tell how you're doing!"

Navigating Your Wild and Woolly Web

A key ingredient for building quality Web pages is the inclusion of navigational aids. In Chapter 15, we introduce the concept of a *navigation bar* that provides users with a method to avoid or minimize scrolling. With the judicious use of links and the careful observation of what constitutes a "screenful" of text, text anchors can make moving to the "previous," "next," "top," "index," and "bottom" of a document easy.

We believe pretty strongly in the *low scroll* rule: That is, users should have to scroll *no more than one* screenful in either direction from a point of focus or entry without encountering a navigation aid to let them jump (not scroll) to the next point of interest.

We don't believe that navigation bars are required or that the names of controls should always be the same. We do believe that the more control you give users over their reading, the better they like it (and the more traffic your Web pages get). The longer any particular document gets, the more important such controls become. We find that controls work best if they occur about every 20 lines in longer documents (or in a separate, always viewable frame, if you're inclined to use advanced HTML techniques).

Beating the Two-Dimensional Text Trap

Conditioned by centuries of printed material and the linear nature of books, our mindsets about hypertext can always use some adjustment. When building documents, remember that hypermedia should add interest, expand on the content, or make a serious impact on the user. Within these constraints, this kind of material can vastly improve any user's experience of your site.

If you avoid old-fashioned linear thinking, you may not only succeed in improving your users' experience, you may even make your information more readily available to your audience. That's why we encourage careful consideration of document indexes, cross-references, links to related documents, and other tools to help users navigate within your site. Keep thinking about the impact of links and looking at other people's materials, and you may yet shake free of the linear trap imposed by Gutenberg's great legacy (the printing press)! If you're looking for a model for your site's behavior, don't think about your great new trifold four-color brochure; instead think about how your customer service people interact with new customers on the telephone ("What can I do to help you today?").

Overcoming Inertia Takes Constant Vigilance

Finally, when dealing with your Web materials post-publication, remember that your tendency is to come to rest regarding future efforts. Maintenance is nowhere near as heroic, inspiring, or remarkable as creation, yet it represents the bulk of activity needed to keep a living document alive and well.

Make maintenance a positive term and look for ways to improve its perception. If you start with something valuable and keep adding value, your materials appreciate over time. If you start with something valuable and leave it alone, your materials become stale and lose value.

Chapter 24
Ten Design Desiderata

In This Chapter

▶ Creating page layouts

▶ Building a graphical vocabulary

▶ Using white space

▶ Formatting for impact

▶ Enhancing content

▶ Making effective use of graphics

▶ Aiding navigation

▶ Forming good opinions

▶ Knowing when to split

▶ Adding value for value

*W*hen building a Web site, it's essential to know what you're trying to communicate. The content must always remain king. Nevertheless, we'd like to suggest a bevy of design desiderata to consider when assembling the frames and devices for your pages.

Creating Page Layouts

The first thing to decide upon is a common layout (template) for your Web pages. Layout involves deciding whether to use text links or graphical controls, and layout also involves setting a style for page headings and footers. It may even involve establishing a set of "framing rules" to lay out common page areas and elements.

Headings can incorporate text navigation bars or other information that you want to make consistent for your users. Footers need to include contact information and the original URL for reference, possibly preceded by a horizontal rule.

Some organizations have gone so far as to lay down a border for each page, with the area above the frame used as the header and the area below as the footer. Whatever layout you choose, make it as attractive as you can (without making it distracting) and use it consistently. Doing this helps to create a welcome feeling of familiarity across your pages that, in turn, helps users find their way around your site. The cⅠnet site (at `www.cnet.com`) is an example of a good-looking, consistent site layout.

Building a Graphical Vocabulary

If you decide to use graphics for navigation, keep the icons or buttons as small and simple as possible. Using small, simple graphics reduces transfer time and makes them faster for browsers to render.

Building a small, consistent set of graphical symbols (what we call a *vocabulary*) also improves browser efficiency: Most browsers cache graphics so that they don't have to be downloaded after they first appear. Reusing an existing graphic is much faster than referencing a new one. That's why we advocate a fairly limited graphics vocabulary.

Remember to supply ALT text definitions for such elements when you reference them. This keeps users with character-mode browsers from being left in the lurch. Such graphical elements should be simple enough that a single word or short phrase can substitute for them and still deliver the same meaning and impact.

Using White Space

Although content may be king in Web pages, it's still possible to have too much of a good thing. Don't try to limit the amount of scrolling by eliminating headings and paragraph breaks.

White space is the term page designers use to describe the space on a page that's unoccupied by other things like graphics and type. A certain amount of white space is critical for the human eye. In general, the more complex or convoluted the images or content, the more positive the effect of white space on a page.

Be sure to give your content and images room to breathe by leaving at least 20 percent of any screen unoccupied. You can build white space into your documents with extra paragraph tags, by using alignment attributes on graphics, or by using headings to separate regions of text and graphics. Whatever method you use, be sure to give readers enough room to follow your lead through your pages!

Formatting for Impact

HTML includes a variety of descriptive (<EM>, <STRONG>, <CITE>, and so on) and physical (<I>, <B>, <TT>, and so on) character tags. It also employs larger fonts and text styles to set headings off from ordinary text. When you're using these controls, remember that emphasis and impact are relative terms. In fact, the less you use these types of tags, the more impact they have.

Overuse of character handling, whether descriptive or physical, can blunt your document's overall impact. Be sure to use such controls only where impact is critical.

When trying to decide whether to use a descriptive or physical character tag, be aware that certain browsers may provide wider latitudes in rendering descriptive tags. Physical tags are often associated with certain fonts (for example, a monospaced Courier font is typical for the typewriter tag <TT>). Descriptive tags can be associated with the same characteristics, but they can also be represented through other fonts or text colors, especially for graphical browsers. Thus, it's important to consider whether the rendering or the emphasis is important: If it's the rendering, use a physical style; if it's the emphasis, use a logical one.

Enhancing Content

If a picture is worth a thousand words, are a thousand words worth a picture? When combining text and graphics in Web pages, be sure to emphasize the relationship between the two in the content. Graphics can be especially useful in diagramming complex ideas, in representing physical objects or other tangible phenomena, and in compressing large amounts of content into a small space.

Yet the surrounding text also needs to take cognizance of the graphics, to use them as a point of reference, and to refer back to key elements or components as they're being discussed. This makes labels, captions, and other methods for identifying particular elements on a graphic almost as important as a graphic itself. Careful integration of text and graphics enhances the content of a page.

The same is true for other hypermedia within Web pages. Beyond the novelty of including sounds or music, animation or video, the content of these other media types needs to be integrated with the text to create the greatest impact.

Rather than explaining a leitmotif only in words, it becomes possible to define and then discuss a leitmotif around a musical phrase from a symphony or string quartet. Likewise, you can amplify a discussion of film-editing techniques, like dissolves, with examples taken from the work of classic directors.

Whatever materials appear in or through your Web pages, they need to be solidly integrated and share a common focus. This applies as strongly to hypermedia as it does to text, but you should never overlook the possibilities for enhancing content.

Making Effective Use of Hypermedia

Strong integration of hypermedia with other content on a page is the most important ingredient for effective use. It's also necessary to understand the potential bottlenecks that some users face.

Effective use of hypermedia, therefore, implies asking your users for informed consent before inflicting such materials on them. For graphics, this means preparing thumbnails of large images, labeling them with file sizes, and using them as clickable maps to let users request a download of the full-sized image. In other words, a user who decides to pull down a full-color image of *The Last Supper* cannot be dismayed when he or she already knows that it's a 1.2MB file that may take several minutes to download. By the same token, including such an image right on a Web page may irritate people who were merely looking for information.

This principle applies equally to sounds, video, and other kinds of hypermedia. Remember to ask for informed consent from your users, and you can be sure that only those individuals who are willing to wait are subjected to delivery delays.

Aiding Navigation

By including outlines, tables of contents, indexes, or search engines within your Web documents, you make it easier for users to find their way around your materials. So why not do it?

Forming Good Opinions

We think that no Web site is complete without an interactive HTML form to ask users for their feedback. Their feedback not only gives you a chance to see your work from somebody else's perspective, but it also serves as a valuable source of input and ideas to enhance and improve your content. Remember, "If you don't ask, they won't tell you!"

Knowing When to Split

As pages get larger and larger, or as your content shows itself to be more complex than you originally thought, you may come to a point where a single, long document would function better as a collection of smaller documents.

How can you decide when it's time to split things up? By trading off convenience against impatience. A single, long document takes longer to download and read than any individual smaller one, but each time a user requests an individual document, it may have to be downloaded on the spot. The question then becomes "One long wait, or several short ones?"

The answer lies in the content. If your document is something that's touched quickly and then exited immediately, delivering information in small chunks makes sense. The only people who have to pay a delay penalty are those who choose to read through many pages; in-and-outers don't have to pay much at all. If your document is something that's downloaded and perused in detail, it may make sense to keep large amounts of information within a single document.

By using your materials frequently yourself (make sure to use them over a slow link as well as a fast one), and by asking users for feedback, you can strike the happy medium between these extremes, as soon as one wanders by!

Adding Value for Value

Obtaining feedback from users is incredibly valuable and makes HTML forms all the more worthwhile. But responding to that feedback in a visible, obvious way can make the experience as good for the respondents as it should be for you.

Publicly acknowledging feedback that resulted in you changing your pages — whether for reasons good or ill — is always a smart idea. The "What's New" page that links to many home pages (and maybe on yours, too) is an excellent place to make such acknowledgments. We also believe in acknowledging strong opinions by e-mail or letter to let respondents know that you heard what they said and to thank them for their input.

If you can develop your users as allies and confederates, they can help you improve and enhance your content. These improvements, in turn, can lead to improved business or maybe just to improved communications. Either way, by giving valuable information and acknowledging the value of other people's contributions, you've added to the total value of the Web itself!

Chapter 25

Almost Ten Ways to Exterminate Web Bugs

● ●

In This Chapter

▶ Making a list and checking it twice

▶ Mastering the mechanics of text

▶ Lacking live links leaves loathsome legacies

▶ Looking for trouble in all the right places

▶ Covering all the bases

▶ Tools of the testing trade

▶ Fostering feedback

▶ Making the most of your audience

● ●

*W*hen you've put the finishing touches on a set of pages, it's time to put them through their paces. Testing is a key ingredient to help control the quality of your content. It should include a thorough content review, a complete check of your HTML syntax and semantics, investigations of every possible link, and a series of sanity checks to make doubly and triply sure that what you've wound up with is what you really wanted to build. Read on for some gems of testing wisdom that can help you rid your Web pages of bugs, errors, and other undesirable elements.

Making a List and Checking It Twice

Your document design should include a road map for all individual HTML documents in your site and the relationships among them. If you're smart, you kept this up to date as you moved from design to implementation (and in our experience, things always change when you go down this path). If you're not smart, don't berate yourself — go out and update this map now. Be sure to include all intradocument *and* interdocument links.

This road map can serve as the foundation for a testing plan, wherein you systematically investigate and check every page and every link. You want to make sure that everything works as you think it does and that what you've built has some relationship, however surprising, to what you designed. This road map becomes your list of things to check, and as you go through the testing process, you'll be checking it (at least) twice.

Mastering the Mechanics of Text

By the time any collection of Web pages comes together, you're typically looking at thousands of words, if not more. Yet the number of Web pages that are published without even a cursory spelling check is astonishing. That's why we suggest — no, demand — that you include a spelling check as a step in testing and checking your materials.

You can use your favorite word processor to spell-check your pages. Before you check them, add HTML markup to your custom dictionary, and pretty soon, the program pukes only on URLs and other strange strings that occur from time to time in HTML files.

Or, if you'd prefer, you can try out one of the several HTML-based spell-checking services that are now available on the Web. We like the one you can find at

```
http://imagiware.com/RxHTML.cgi
```

If this spell checker doesn't work for you, visit one of the search engines that we mention in Chapter 15, and use *spell check* as a search string. For us, a recent visit to Yahoo! turned up more than a half dozen likely-looking candidates. Nevertheless, you must persist and root out all real typos and misspellings. Your users may not thank you, but they'll have a higher opinion of your pages if they don't find them full of errors!

Lacking Live Links Leaves Loathsome Legacies

Nothing is more irritating to users that a link to some Web resource on a page that they're dying to follow, only to get the dreaded 404 Server not found error. Our admittedly unscientific and random sampling of users shows us that users' impressions of a set of pages is strongly proportional to the number of working links they contain.

The moral of this story is: Always check your links. This dictum is as true after you've published your pages as it is before they've been subjected to the limelight of public scrutiny. Checking links is as important for page maintenance as it is for testing initial pages for release. If you're smart, you'll hire a robot to do the job for you: They work incredibly long hours, don't charge much, and faithfully check every last link in your site (or beyond, if you let them loose). We're rather fond of a robot named MOMspider, created by Roy Fielding of the W3C. Visit MOMspider's home page at

```
http://www.ics.uci.edu/WebSoft/MOMspider
```

This spider takes a bit of work to use, but you can set it to check only local links so that it can do a bang-up job of catching stale links before users do. If you don't like this tool, try a search engine with "robot" or "spider" as your search term. There are lots to choose from! The best thing about robots is that you can schedule them to do their jobs at regular intervals: They always show up on time, always do a thorough job, and never complain.

Another hint: Just because a URL has a pointer to the real content's location doesn't mean that it's okay to leave the original link alone. If your link-checking shows a situation like this, do yourself and your users a favor by updating the URL to a current location. You can save users time and lower the number of bogus packets on the Internet, too.

Looking for Trouble in All the Right Places

When it comes to beta-testing your pages, you want to bring in as rowdy and refractory a crowd as you possibly find. If you have customers or colleagues who are picky, opinionated, pushy, or argumentative, be comforted to know that such people make ideal beta testers.

They use your pages in ways you never imagined possible. They interpret your content to mean things that you never intended in a million years. They drive you crazy and crawl all over your most cherished beliefs and principles.

These colleagues also find gotchas, big and small, that you never knew were there. They can catch typos that the word processors couldn't. They can tell you things you left out and things that you should have omitted. They can even give you a whole new perspective on your Web pages, and they can help you to see them from extreme points of view.

The results of all this suffering, believe it or not, are positive. Your pages emerge clearer, more direct, and more correct than they would have if you'd tried to do all the testing yourself. If you don't believe us, try skipping this step and see what happens when the real users start banging on your materials! Beta testing is a must for a well-rounded Web site, especially one intended for business use.

Covering All the Bases

If you're an individual user with a simple home page or a collection of facts and figures on your private obsession, this step may not apply. But go ahead and read along anyway — you just may discover something.

If your pages represent the views and content of an organization, chances are 100 percent that you want to subject your pages to some kind of peer and management review before publishing them to the world. In fact, we'd recommend that you build reviews into each step along the way toward building your pages — starting with overall design, to writing copy for each page, to reviewing the final assembly of pages. These reviews help you to avoid hitting any potential stumbling blocks. If you've got any doubts about copyright protection (or violation), references, logo usage, or other such important details, you may want to get the legal department involved (if you have one, that is).

It may even be a good idea to build some kind of sign-off process into reviews so that you can prove that responsible parties reviewed and approved your materials. We hope you don't have to be that formal about publishing your Web pages, but it's far, far better to be safe than sorry. Is this covering the bases or covering something else? You decide.

Tools of the Testing Trade

When you're grinding through your Web pages, checking your links and your HTML, remember that automated help is available. If you check the validation tools in Chapter 19, you'll be well on your way to finding some computerized assistance in making sure your HTML is as clean and standards-compliant as the freshly driven snow. (Do we know how to mix a metaphor, or what?)

Likewise, it's a good idea to investigate the Web spiders that we cover in Chapter 15 and use them regularly to check the links in your pages. The spiders get back to you if something isn't current, so you'll know where to start looking for the links that you need. And while you're at it, remember to make link-checking part of your maintenance routine. In other words, schedule and use a spider at regular intervals!

Fostering Feedback

You may not think of user feedback as a form (or consequence) of testing, but it represents some of the best reality checks that your Web pages are ever likely to get. That's why it's a good idea to do everything that you can — including prizes or other tangible inducements — to get users to fill out HTML forms on your Web site.

That's also why it's even better to read all feedback that you do get. Go out and solicit as much as you can handle (or more). But the best idea of all is to carefully consider the feedback that you read and then implement the ideas that improve your Web offerings.

Making the Most of Your Audience

Asking for feedback is an important step toward developing a relationship with your users. Even the most finicky and picky of your users can be an incredible asset: Who better to pick over your newest pages and to point out those small, subtle errors or flaws that they revel upon finding? Working with your users can mean that over time, some become more involved in your work and in helping guide the content of your Web pages (if not the rest of your professional or obsessional life). Who could ask for more?

Chapter 26

Ten "Build or Buy" Tips for Web Services

. . . .

In This Chapter

▶ Understanding objectives

▶ Counting your pennies

▶ Projecting traffic

▶ How much is too much?

▶ Managing volatility

▶ Communicating corporately

▶ Reaching your audience

▶ "Web-ifying" commerce

▶ Understanding your options

▶ Overcoming success

. . . .

*W*hen the time comes to publish your Web pages, one of the toughest and most important decisions you have to face is where those pages should live. Should you set up your own server and handle this yourself? Or should you find a friendly national, regional, or local Internet Service Provider (ISP) and let them do it for you?

These are good questions, indeed. Answering them will tell you whether you want to buy or build, or perhaps buy now and build later (or even build now and buy later). Stick with us as we take you through the numbers and the reasons why you might choose to roll your own or to get underneath somebody else's Web umbrella.

Understanding Objectives

The most important thing to understand is your overall objectives. If your organization is planning on staking a major presence on the Internet or views the Web as a key ingredient to its future success and well-being, then building your own server might be a natural extension of other plans.

If your organization simply views the Web as yet another way to disseminate news and information along with existing media and techniques, your own Web server might not add strategic value. At that point, you could perform some simple analyses and figure out whether building or buying makes more sense.

Point 1: If the Web is a paramount method for communicating with your audience, your own server helps to establish your organization as a legitimate, full-time Web presence.

Counting Your Pennies

For a detailed analysis of the costs and considerations, please refer back to Chapter 17. A quick and dirty formula goes like this: If Web-related costs from a provider average $1,000 a month or more, it's worth considering a server of your own. If average costs are less than $1,000 a month, it's probably not worthwhile unless other compelling factors exist. For example, an Internet Service Provider may not use its Web server as heavily as its clients, yet they'd look kind of lame if they didn't have one!

When calculating costs, figure at least one-fourth of a system administrator's time is required to run a Web server. Remember also that costs include monthly communications fees, Internet access charges, and maintenance-related costs, plus amortizing hardware and software costs to set up the system. It's not at all unusual for after-purchase costs to add up to ten (or more) times initial costs over the life of a system.

Point 2: At $1,000 per month or more for Web services, it's reasonable to start thinking about building, rather than buying, a Web server.

Projecting and Monitoring Traffic

One key element in determining Web service costs is figuring download fees that ISPs usually assess. Normally, such costs run from two to ten cents per megabyte of data downloaded. This might not sound like much, but stop to crunch some numbers: If your pages are 2MB in size and you average 30 users per day, that translates into $36.50 to $182.50 for an average month. Raise the amount of data to 5MB, and the costs go from $91.25 to $456.25 for an average month.

None of these costs is prohibitive, though, nor would they add up to enough, including telephone or access line costs, and monthly account fees, to exceed the $1,000 monthly ceiling. Things get expensive, though, when hundreds to thousands of users a day start downloading data. At that point, multiplying costs three- to thirtyfold can be prohibitive. That's why initial testing and an audience survey are important when making projections.

Point 3: If you're expecting (or even hoping for) lots of traffic, you're better off building your own server instead of buying space on somebody else's. Don't forget to hire an experienced Webmaster or to train somebody in-house right away!

How Much Is Too Much?

The principle of parsimony argues that you'd better try to limit the amount of data you publish on your Web pages, especially if you're paying by the megabyte for data transferred from your server. It's important to keep an eye on the amount and kind of data that your Web server offers.

If you've got numerous large files or images that some, but not all, users find interesting, consider making them available through other means. This could include finding an anonymous FTP site on the Internet and directing users to pick up large files there, or it could mean setting up an e-mail-based file delivery system like *listserv* or *majordomo*.

Point 4: Keep an eye on the data that users download and try to make large, infrequently accessed files or documents available by other means.

Managing Volatility

The Web is an ever-changing galaxy of information. Keeping up with change means regular effort and a fair amount of volatility in your Web page offerings. Many providers charge extra when you change materials, but even if they don't, the effort of making and testing changes has associated — and inescapable — costs.

We recommend that you manage and schedule changes on your server. Plan on regular updates and stick to the plan. Gather up incremental and incidental changes in the meantime and apply them when the schedule or external factors say it's the right time. While you're at it, keep tabs on your materials' freshness, and regularly check your off-server links to other pages and locations for currency and correctness.

If you have loads of content that changes frequently, you may want the extra control over a server that you get with building your own. Convenience and access to your data have value, too, and may influence you to build your own server even if your costs hover below the $1,000 monthly cutoff.

Point 5: Constant, unceasing change is more expensive than planned change. Whether you build or buy your Web server, you still have to manage change, or it will manage you! Where change is frequent and regular, the convenience of access to your own server can have significant value.

Communicating Corporately

If your organization has a well-planned communications strategy, effective use of the Web can complement other channels of communication — like the trade press, the news media, and the industry analysts and pundits who follow your industry. In this kind of environment, Web documents reflect and coordinate with documents of many other kinds, including advertisements, collateral, and a range of other corporate publications.

In environments where tight controls over corporate or organizational communications must be maintained, it's pretty normal to find Web servers under the purview of a public relations or corporate communications department. Likewise, in environments where internal and external communications are formal and carefully managed, you might even find one set of servers for internal materials (not available to the public) and another set of servers for external materials.

Point 6: In tightly managed organizations, especially those with carefully orchestrated communications, control over the Web server may be an absolute requirement, irrespective of other considerations.

Reaching Your Audience

If you decide to build your own server and connect up to the Internet via a 28.8 Kbps modem through a provider, you've limited the number of users who can access your Web pages at any given time (probably to one to three users for each such connection). If, on the other hand, you attach a full 1.44 Mbps T-1 link to your server, you've increased the size (and the cost) of your pipe significantly, but you'll still be limited to under 100 simultaneous users.

Projecting traffic, as it turns out, is not only important to understanding costs; it's also important to matching the size of the Web server pipe against the number of potential users. Using a large pipe for low-traffic situations is wasteful, but providing a small-to-medium pipe when a tsunami of interest is heading your way can be catastrophic. Frustrate your users long enough, and they may decide to meet their interests elsewhere.

Monitoring usage and demand is the only way to cope with this phenomenon, but you'll be far better off if you start out with extra, unused capacity than if your pipes are clogged from the word "Go!" Because operating your own server gives you the flexibility to negotiate the right-sized pipe to the Internet with a telecommunications company and an ISP, many large-volume operations prefer to do it themselves. Even though these costs can be high, they're generally lower than if you paid someone else to provide them. Just don't expect to be able to add or expand pipes at a moment's notice, and you'll avoid getting too frustrated when it's time to add more capacity.

Point 7: Make it easy for the audience to browse your materials, and they'll do just that. Make it difficult or impossible, and they'll go away . . . forever!

"Web-ifying" Commerce

Companies of many stripes are hungrily eyeing the "millions" of Internet users as another customer base, ripe for electronic commerce. Today, you can conduct commercial transactions over the Internet in several ways, ranging from so-called *digital cash* to a variety of secure credit-card handling operations.

We don't want to take on the responsibility of recommending a particular approach. We'll just say that electronic commerce via the Web is a trendy phenomenon whose potential still vastly outweighs its current use.

But if your company is thinking seriously about adding electronic commerce to its existing sales channels, you'll probably want to consider building your own Web server. Issues of control, access to customer information, and managing the details of financial transactions all argue that the best hands on your Web server are your own!

Although electronic commerce is beyond the scope of this book, we recommend the following tome if you'd like to generate some cash from your site: *Building Web Commerce Sites,* by Ed Tittel, Charlie Scott, Paul Wolfe, and Mike Erwin (IDG Books Worldwide, Inc., 1997).

Point 8: If you're thinking about doing business via the Web, you'll probably want to control your own server for a variety of good business reasons.

Understanding Your Options

Whether you're building or buying Web services, you must clearly understand how your pages operate. This is especially true for forms-handling or other Common Gateway Interface-related programs that run on servers and handle user information requests or submissions.

It's imperative that the server that runs your pages be compatible with the services that you want to provide and the programs that you want to run on your users' behalf. This means specifying the kind of *httpd* implementation you need, and also means understanding the names and versions of surrounding standard services that CGI programs may call on (like the differing clickable image map implementations on the NCSA and CERN implementations of *httpd*, for example).

Point 9: When selecting a Web server, compatibility with CGI programs, related libraries, and other collections of widgets and data is a must. Don't build or buy the wrong server!

Overcoming Success

Finally, you may have to cope with what many people would consider an enviable problem: What happens if your Web pages become the latest rage, and your server gets completely inundated by users trying to avail themselves of your magnificent content?

If that happens, you'll want to make arrangements for fallback services. In this extreme case, working with a national Internet Service Provider — like ANS, PSI, BBN Planet, and so on — is an absolute must. If you can afford what these companies offer, you can buy as much capacity from them as you can stand to pay for.

Point 10: If you're smitten with boundless success, be prepared to suffer (especially in the checkbook) for your fame, but make alternative arrangements with a national provider to avoid the perils of Point 7.

Appendix

About the CD

• •

*I*n this section of the book, we explain what you find on the *HTML For Dummies,* 3rd Edition, CD-ROM. In a nutshell it contains the following goodies:

- ✔ A collection of Web documents built just to help you find your way around the book's materials
- ✔ A hotlist of all the URLs mentioned in the book to make it easy for you to access any of the Web resources we've mentioned
- ✔ An online version of the book's glossary, to help you look up all the strange and bizarre terminology that Webheads are prone to use from time to time
- ✔ Copies of all the HTML examples, easily accessible by chapter and heading, along with any graphics they use
- ✔ A hyperlinked table of contents for the book to help you find your way around its many topics and treasures
- ✔ Extra information on cool Web technologies like frames, nonstandard extensions to HTML, style sheets, CGI programming, and more.
- ✔ A collection of Common Gateway Interface (CGI) programs, built especially for you, to help add functionality to your own Web server (and to provide what we hope are sterling examples of the art of CGI programming)

How to Use the Web Pages and Examples

Regardless of what platform and operating system you are running you can view all of the material straight from the CD. To do so, you must have a Web browser installed on your system. We did not include browser software on the CD, but you can download evaluation versions of Netscape Navigator at http://www.netscape.com/ or Internet Explorer at http://www. microsoft.com/. To browse the CD contents, just do the following:

1. Launch your Web browser

2. Using the Open File command in your browser's File menu, open the file HTML4DUM\H4D3E\HTML4DUM.HTM from the CD.

This page serves as the "Home Page" for the CD and will connect you to all other files.

You won't be able to edit any of the files on the CD. To make changes and save them, you need to move the examples and templates to your local drive. To do so, simply copy the H4D3E folder to your hard drive. This will transfer the entire directory structure from the CD to your computer.

The HTML For Dummies Files

The *HTML For Dummies* CD directories, located in the HTML4DUM top level directory, are arranged in the following way:

Figure A-1:
The *HTML*
For
Dummies
CD-ROM
Directory
Structure.

Html4dum
Software
License.txt
Readme.txt

To give you an idea of what's there, we cover the files according to their home directory — and subdirectory when necessary (assuming, of course, that you've accepted the installation defaults and the files live where we say they do).

CGI

The CGI directory contains three subdirectories, one for each of the programming languages we used. Here's the annotated list of CGI files you find in the CGI directory, divided into those subdirectories:

APPLESCRIPT Subdirectory	
Script	**Description**
COUNTCGI.TXT	readme for counter script
RIGHT.HTML	text page for ismapper script

Script	*Description*
MAP_DEFAULT.HTML	test page for ismapper script
MAP.GIF	test image for ismapper script
LEFT.HTML	test image for ismapper script
ISMAP-TEST.HTML	test page for ismapper.script
ISMAPPER-AS.CGI.HQX	ismapper script
COUNTER.ACGI.HQX	counter script
TIME-AS.CGI.HQX	current time script

C Subdirectory

Script	*Description*
COUNTER-CGI.C	counter script
TIME_NOW	compiled current time script
ISMAPPER.C	ismapper script
ISMAPPER	compiled ismapper script
TIME-CGI.C	current time script

Perl Subdirectory

Script	*Description*
COUNTER.FORM.HTML	test page for counter script
RIGHT.HTML	text page for ismapper script
MAP_DEFAULT.HTML	test page for ismapper script
MAP.GIF	test image for ismapper script
LEFT.HTML	test image for ismapper script
ISMAP-TEST.HTML	test page for ismapper.script
ISMAPPER-CGI.PL	ismapper script
ISMAPPER.LOG	ismapper log file
ISMAPPER.CONF	ismapper conf file
COUNTER-CGI.PL	counter script
COUNTER.LOG	counter log file
TIME-CGI.PL	current time script

H4D3E

This directory contains the majority of the *HTML For Dummies* files. Nearly every file in this directory ends with the extension .HTM, indicating that it is an HTML document.

All in all, the best way to explore the *HTML For Dummies* Web pages is to fire up your browser and point it at the file named Html4dum.htm, the home page for the whole collection. As an initial run-through, if you simply select the NEXT link (the right-hand pointing arrow) at the bottom of each page, you can take a guided tour of the whole shebang and get a pretty good idea of what's available and how you might use it.

The majority of files in this directory fall into five categories:

✔ Those named Cont-nn.htm, where *n* is a digit between 0 and 9, are keyed to the chapters of the book and contain a listing of the chapter's contents. Thus, Cont-08.htm indicates that the file holds the contents of Chapter 8.

✔ Those files named Ex-nn.htm, where *n* is a digit between 0 and 9, are keyed to the chapters of the book and contain listings of the HTMLized versions of the markup examples shown in the chapters. These link to individual documents in the EXAMPLES folder. Unlike the contents pages, not every chapter has an equivalent example page. Only those that contain HTML markup will have an Ex HTML file.

✔ Glossary terms are divided by letter and contained in files name Glos-n.htm where *n* is a letter from A to Z.

✔ Those files name URL-nn.htm, where *n* is a digit between 0 and 9, are keyed to the chapters of the book and contain linked hotlists of all the URLs from that chapter. As with the example chapters, not every chapter has an equivalent URL page — only those that list URLs in the text.

✔ Those files that begin with something other than the strings listed above are HTML documents that belong to a collection of *HTML For Dummies* sample pages that we've constructed as a teaching aid and as a navigational tool to help you find your way around the materials we've assembled for the book. The next few pages show you a listing of what's what.

The H4D3E Directory File Listing

File	Description
CONT-01.HTM	Content for Chapter 1
...	Content for Chapters 2 through 30

File	Description
CONTACT.HTM	Listing of e-mail, home page, and bio page links for the authors and related people
CONTBLAH.HTM	Non-table version of contents page
CONTENTS.HTM	Contents page laid out using a table
EDBIO.HTM	Ed Tittel's bio page
EX-04.HTM	Listing of HTML examples for Chapter 4
…	Listing of HTML examples for Chapters 5-18
FTPBLAH.HTM	Non-table version of FTP information page
FTPSTUFF.HTM	Listing of and links to all CD FTP resources
GLOS-A.HTM	Glossary words *a*
…	Glossary words *b* through *x*
GLOSINDX.HTM	Index page for glossary terms listed by letter
HTML4DU2.HTM	Client-side imagemap version of the homepage
HTML4DU3	Standard imagemap version of the homepage
HTML4DUM	Non-imagemap version of the homepage
ISOLATIN.TXT	Plain-text listing of the ISO-LATIN character set
JMSBIO.HTM	James Michael Stewart's bio page
MEBIO.HTM	Mike Erwin's bio page
MGBIO.HTM	Mark Gaither's bio page
REGISTRN.HTM	Online registration page
SEARCH4D.HTM	List of main pages and online search utility
SHBIO.HTM	Sebastian Hassinger's bio page
SJBIO.HTM	Steve James' bio page
TEMPLATE.HTM	Jump page to the templates
URLS-01.HTM	Chapter 1 URLs
…	URLs for other chapters, by number
WAYFIND.HTM	HTML navigation information
WHATSNEW.HTM	Lists all alterations and changes made to the Web pages

H4D3E/CGI-BIN

The single file in this directory, HT4MENUM.MAP, contains the CGI map file for the homepage imagemap.

H4D3E/EXAMPLES

The folders in this directory contain the individual HTML example documents referenced by the Ex-nn.htm files in the main H4D3E directory. The following listing shows the folder name and corresponding chapter number, followed by a listing of the files in the folder and the HTML tag demonstrated in each one. Due to some last minute changes, some of the chapter numbers may not jive with our naming scheme, so be sure to check the chapter listed in parentheses for the exact match.

HTML Examples

Folder Name (Chapter Number)	Example File Name	Markup
CH04 (Chapter 4)	EX-04-01.HTM	A basic HTML page
	EX-04-02.HTM	A full-blown HTML page
CH05 (Chapter 5)	EX-05-01.HTM	Using a markup language to give form and structure to content
CH06 (Chapter 6)	A.HTM	The anchor tag
	ADDRESS.HTM	The document address tag
	APPLET.HTM	The Java applet tag
	AREA.HTM	The imagemap area tag
	B.HTM	The boldface text tag
	BASE.HTM	The document base tag
	BASEFONT.HTM	The base font tag
	BIG.HTM	The bigger text tag
	BLOCKQUO.HTM	The blockquote style tag
	BODY.HTM	The document body tag
	BR.HTM	The line break tag
	BUTTON.HTM	The form button tag
	CAPTION.HTM	The table and form caption tag
	CENTER.HTM	The center text tag
	CITE.HTM	The citation text tag
	CODE.HTM	The code text tag
	COL.HTM	The table column tag
	COLGROUP.HTM	The table column group tag
	DD.HTM	The definition list data tag

Folder Name (Chapter Number)	Example File Name	Markup
	DFN.HTM	The definition text tag
	DIR.HTM	The directory list tag
	DIV.HTM	The document division tag
	DL.HTM	The definition list tag
	DT.HTM	The definition list data term tag
	EM.HTM	The emphasis text tag
	FONT.HTM	The font style tag
	FORM.HTM	The form tag
	H.HTM	The heading tags
	HEAD.HTM	The body heading tag
	HR.HTM	The hard rule tag
	HTML.HTM	The HTML document tag
	I.HTM	The italics text tag
	IMG.HTM	The insert image tag
	INPUT.HTM	The form input tag
	ISINDEX.HTM	The document index tag
	KBD.HTM	The keyboard text tag
	LI.HTM	The list item tag
	LINK.HTM	The document link tag
	MAP.HTM	The imagemap coordinates tag
	MENU.HTM	The menu list tag
	META.HTM	The document information tag
	OL.HTM	The ordered list tag
	OPTION.HTM	The form option tag
	P.HTM	The paragraph tag
	PARAM.HTM	The Java applet parameter tag
	PRE.HTM	The preformatted text tag
	S.HTM	The strikethrough text tag
	SAMP.HTM	The sample text tag
	SCRIPT.HTM	The inline script tag
	SELECT.HTM	The form selection tag

(continued)

HTML Examples *(continued)*

Folder Name (Chapter Number)	Example File Name	Markup
	SMALL.HTM	The small text tag
	SPAN.HTM	The style span tag
	STRONG.HTM	The strong text tag
	STYLE.HTM	The style format tag
	SUB.HTM	The subscript text tag
	SUP.HTM	The superscript text tag
	TABLE.HTM	The table tag
	TBODY.HTM	The table body tag
	TD.HTM	The table cell data tag
	TEXTAREA.HTM	The form text area tag
	TFOOT.HTM	The table footer tag
	TH.HTM	The table column header tag
	THEAD.HTM	The table header tag
	TITLE.HTM	The document title tag
	TR.HTM	The table row tag
	TT.HTM	The teletype text tag
	U.HTM	The underline tag
	UL.HTM	The unordered list tag
	VAR.HTM	The variable text tag
	XMP.HTM	The example text tag
CH07 (Chapter 7)	EX-07-01.HTM	Correct use of HTML entities
CH09 (Chapter 9)	EX-09-01.HTM	A basic table
	EX-09-02.HTM	Table row spanning
CH12 (Chapter 10)	EX-12-01.HTM	A basic HTML document template
	EX-12-02.HTM	A sample unordered (bulleted) list
	EX-12-02.HTM	Using an unordered list with text
CH13 (Chapter 11)	EX-13-01.HTM	Recycling images in an HTML document

Folder Name (Chapter Number)	Example File Name	Markup
	EX-13-02.HTM	Using icons for page navigation
	EX-13-03.HTM	Using icons as hyperlinks
	EX-13-04.HTM	Web page footer elements
CH14 (Chapter 12)	EX-14-01.HTM	Using hyperlinks within a single document
	EX-14-02.HTM	Hyperlinks to outside sources
	EX-14-03.HTM	Using the `<LINK NAME=>` tag to provide an anchor from other locations
	EX-14-04.HTM	Example of nesting lists within lists
	EX-14-05.HTM	The syntax of nesting lists within lists
	EX-14-06.HTM	A sophisticated page
	EX-14-07.HTM	A client-side image map
	EX-14-08.HTM	A CGI image map
CH15 (Chapter 13)	EX-15-01.HTM	Sample form 1
	EX-15-02.HTM	Sample form 2
	EX-15-03.HTM	Sample form 3

H4D3E/EXTRAS

This folder contains information on several HTML related topics that we think you will find interesting and useful. The file HTMLCH.HTM serves as a table of contents for these pages. The topics and their related first pages are as follows:

The Extras

File	Topic
CH7HTML.HTM	The HTML entities table
CH8HTML.HTM	HTML extensions
CH10HTML.HTM	HTML frames
CH11HTML.HTM	HTML style
CH18HTML.HTM	CGIs and other scripting alternatives
CH23HTML.HTM	A Webmaster's Toolbox
HTMLGLOS.HTM	The glossary (again!)

H4D3E/GRAPHICS

This is the graphics subdirectory for the graphics used in the HTML documents for the *HTML For Dummies* pages themselves. As its name implies, this is where all the .GIF (Graphics Information Files) files for images in our sample HTML documents reside. If we used it in an example (or on the *HTML For Dummies* Web pages) you can find it here. All we can say further is "Help yourself!"

H4D3E/H4D2e

In this directory are the files from the 2nd edition of *HTML For Dummies*. You will find contents, URL, and example pages similar to the ones on this CD, all of which reference the 2nd edition. The most notable resource in the 2nd edition materials (and the main reason we included them) is the HTML tag information. To access this info, open the file H4D3E/H4D2E/TAGINDEX.HTM.

H4D3E/H4D3EFTP

To make transferring our file collections easier we've included compressed versions of the CGI, H4D3E, and TEMPLATE folders. Each one is available as a .zip (PC), .sea.hqx (Macintosh), and .tar (UNIX) archive to make them accessible regardless of what operating system you are using.

H4D3E/TEMPLATE

For your pleasure and convenience, we've included a few simple templates to get you started on your HTML authoring adventures. For a complete rundown on how to use these templates, consult the READ_ME.TXT file.

H4D3E/TEMPLATE/GRAPHICS

These are the graphics files used in the templates (as distinct from the graphics used in the *HTML For Dummies* Web pages we discussed earlier). You should spend some time exploring here, too, because you'll find some useful goodies.

The Software

In addition to the nifty files, examples, and scripts described above, we've added a small software collection to the CD as well. It is our hope that you will find among these evaluation and shareware versions of products a set of Webmaster tools that fit your needs. Because the CD is in a multi-platform, hybrid format, you only have access to those packages that can run on the platform you are currently using. To see the other tools, you must load the CD in a computer that uses a different OS. Each "side" of the hybrid disk contains a README.TXT text file that describes each package. Refer to this document for complete installation instructions.

Index

• Symbols and Numbers •

\# (pound sign) in entities, 164
& (ampersand)
  before character entities, 75
  in entities, 164
  HTML control character, 64
&#176, 163
&lt, 163
&r (and/or) metacharacter, 75
; (semicolon) in entities, 164
<> (angle brackets) in HTML, 63
< (left bracket), 63
> (right bracket), 63
<!--...--> string, enclosing comments, 78, 84, 220
... (ellipsis) metacharacter, 76
() (parentheses) metacharacter, 75
[] (square brackets) metacharacter, 75
/ (slash) in closing tags, 56
©, displaying, 218
\\ (backslashes) metacharacter, 75
{} metacharacter, 76
| (vertical bar) metacharacter, 75
8-bit ASCII, 62
"404 Object Not Found" error, 316
404 Server not found error, 366

• A •

<A>...</A> (Anchor) tags, 71, 80, 90–92
A.S.H.E. (A Simple HTML Editor), 323–324
"About this site" page, 45
absolute URLs
  in map files, 260
  versus relative URLs, 295–296
access rights, 11
acronyms, 10, 65
ACTION attribute in forms, 244, 245
active (linked) area, 28

<ADDRESS>...</ADDRESS> (Attribution info) tags, 81, 93, 219
Adobe PageMill, 334, 335
agent program, linking to, 47
ALIGN attribute
  with image tags, 74
  with table tags, 183
alpha test plan, generic, 289–292
alpha testers, 290–291
alpha testing, steps for, 286
ALT (alternate text) attribute, 74, 210, 211
ALT text definitions, supplying for graphical symbols, 360
ampersand (&)
  before character entities, 75
  in entities, 164
  HTML control character, 64
anchor tags, 71
anchors, 18, 46, 90–92
  internal, 28
  linking to, 47
and (logical and) metacharacter, 75
and/or (&r) metacharacter, 75
Andreesen, Marc, 15, 327
angle brackets (<>), 46, 63, 75
AOLPress HTML editor, 326, 335–337
Apache, 330
<APPLET>...</APPLET> (Java Applet) tags, 80, 93–95
applets. *See* Java applets
applications, hypertext, 30–31
<AREA> (Hotzone) tag, 82, 95–96
ASCII 7-bit character set (ISO 646), 62
ASCII characters, higher-order, 62, 163
attributes, 46
  common, 87
  defaults for, 78
  extended, proposed as standards, 176–177
  forms of, 86–87
  implied values for, 87
  in tags, 63–64, 74

attribution information, enclosing, 93
AU format, 32
audience. *See also* users
  designing for a multiple, 50
  getting to know your, 41
  grabbing their attention, 44
  memory abilities of, 45
  reaching, 374–375
audio files, size of, 36–37
audio formats, 32
author, indicating the name of, 269
authoring interface, 51
AVI (Audio Video Interleaved) format, 32

• *B* •

<B>...</B> (Bold style) tags, 83, 96–97
backslashes (\\) metacharacter, 75
Backus-Naur Form, 75
bandwidth, 26
<BASE> (Basis for relative addressing) tag,
  80, 97–98
<BASEFONT> (Base font) tag, 81, 98
BBEdit HTML authoring tool, 338–339
Bellver, Carles, 338
Berners-Lee, Tim, 9, 10, 48
beta testers, selecting, 302, 367–368
beta testing, 301–302
<BIG>...</BIG> (Big text) tags, 84, 98–99
bits per pixel, reducing for graphics
  files, 214
blanks in tags, 77
<BLOCKQUOTE>...</BLOCKQUOTE>
  (Quote style) tags, 81, 99
BNF grammar, 75
bodies of Web pages, 193–195
<BODY>...</BODY> (Mark off HTML
  document body) tags, 71, 80, 100–101
body section of an HTML document, 70, 71
boldfaced text, enclosing, 96–97
bookmark section, collecting titles in, 191
books about TCP/IP, 22
BORDER attribute in the <TABLE> tag, 183
borders, defining for tables, 147
boundaries, testing, 285

Boutell, Tom, 257

 (Force line break) tag, 81, 101–102
Bradbury, Nick, 347
broken hyperlinks, 316
browsers, 14, 65
  avoiding dependency on a favorite, 356
  character-mode, 35
  evolving standards for, 174
  forms implementation on, 240
  gathering information from <META>
    tags, 268
  home pages predefined in, 19
  inconsistencies among, 174
  opening HTML files, 55
  testing, 291
  testing with as many as possible, 355
build or buy tips for Web services,
  371–376
bulleted lists, 161, 196–198
<BUTTON>...</BUTTON> tags, 81
buttons (next.gif and menu.gif), 205–207

• *C* •

C|Net
  example of consistent site layout, 360
  tables in, 186
<CAPTION>...</CAPTION> (Table caption)
  tags, 83, 102–103, 181, 182
categories of HTML tags, 80–86
CD (with this book)
  building CGI or equivalent programs, 242
  example code for tags, 89
  list of non-standard tags on, 177
  separate page button icon files, 256
  /Template directory, 57
  template files included on, 57–58
  Wayfinding Toolkits on, 278
  Web site included on, 279
cells, padding in tables, 183
CELLSPACING attribute within the
  <TABLE> tag, 183
<CENTER>...</CENTER> (Center text) tags,
  81, 103

CERN, (European Laboratory for Particle Physics), 9
CERN httpd servers, map files for, 260–261
CERN server, 330
CGI, 242
CGI Image Map, code for, 238
CGI programs
 absolute URLs with, 296
 for searching index lists, 274
CGI script, 242
character entities, 64, 164, 166
 case sensitivity of, 165
 using and misusing, 165
character-mode browser, 35
check box in forms, 245
CheckBot link checker, 318
checklist of testing procedures, 293–295
circle region in clickable maps, 259
citations, highlighting, 103–104
<CITE>...</CITE> (Citation markup) tags, 84, 103–104
Claris Home Page site designer, 333
CLASS="text" attribute, 87
clickable image maps, 276
clickable maps, 255–256
 building, 257–259
 defining, 85, 263
 graphical browser required, 256
 shapes in, 259
 testing, 292
 URLs and, 255–256, 264–265
client, 20
client/server computing, 20
client-side image maps, 129–130, 265–266
 code for, 238
 defining hotzones in, 95–96
close message type, 23
closing tags
 forward slash (/) in, 64
 tracking, 354–355
<CODE>...</CODE> (Program code text) tags, 84, 104–105
<COL> (Column) tag, 83, 105–106
<COLGROUP> (A Column Group) tag, 83, 106–107

colored dots, 208
colored ruler lines, 207
colors
 adding splashes of, 204
 reducing the number in a graphic, 214
COLSPAN attribute in table cells, 184
column header information, defining, 156–158
columns
 defining, 106–107
 defining the settings for a group of, 105–106
command-line text only FTP utility, 298
comment lines, format of, 220
comment tags <!--...-->, placing around scripts, 141
comments
 adding to HTML documents, 220
 in HTML markup, 78
comments category of tags, 84, 86
commerce, electronic, 375
Commerce Kit for WebSTAR, 340
commercial transactions, conducting over the Internet, 375
common attributes, 87
common controls for screens, 43
Common Gateway Interface (CGI). *See* CGI
complex metacharacters, 76
computer systems, testing, 291
Connecting to HTTP Server status message, 23
connection message type, 23
Connection timed out message, 23
content
 double-checking, 294–295
 enhancing, 361–362
 expiration date, 269
 of HTML files, 25, 39
 keeping paramount, 353–354
 text, 24
CONTENT values in the <META> tag, 272
control information in HTML files, 24, 39
copyright holder and date, indicating, 269
copyright law, Web and, 218
copyright notices, 217, 218

copyright symbol (©), displaying, 218
Corel WordPerfect 7.0 for Windows, 348–349
Cougar code name, 69
Cougar DTD, listing of tags in, 90–162
creation date of documents, 268
cross-platform protocol, 11
Cyber Pilot Pro site management tool, 319

• D •

daemon program, 330
Dartmouth's Fetch FTP utility, 299
data cells, defining within tables, 149–151
databases for really long documents, 276–277
dates, formatting in footers, 218
Davies, Lindsay, 338–339
<DD> (Definition description) tag, 82, 108
dedicated Web server machine, storage on, 297
default document name, 297–298
defaults for attributes, 78
definition entries, descriptive part of, 111–112
definition items, enclosing a collection of, 110–111
definition list elements, descriptive part of, 108
Department of Defense (DoD), adoption of SGML, 66
description, defining for search engines, 269
descriptive markup language, 61–62
descriptive tags, compared to physical tags, 361
design
  desiderata for building Web sites, 359–364
  elements of Web pages, 45–51
  principles, 42–44
<DFN>...</DFN> (Definition) tags, 84, 108–109
digital cash, 375
Digital Video Interactive. *See* DVI

Dilbert Zone, tables in, 186
diminishing returns, avoiding, 277
DIR="(LTR | RTL)" attribute, 87
<DIR>...</DIR> (Directory list) tags, 82, 109
directories, navigating, 11
directory path in URLs, 17
disclaimers, using on the Web, 217
<DIV>...</DIV> (Logical division) tags, 81, 109–110
<DL>...</DL> (Definition list) tags, 82, 110–111
<!DOCTYPE> tag, WebCrawler and, 288
DOCTYPE statement, 70
document head. *See* head
document headings category of tags, 82, 85
document reference, 46
document structure category of tags, 80, 84
document titles, flagging, 70
Document Type Definition (DTD), 65
document type prolog, 70
documents
  adding structure to long, 276
  annotating, 86
  applying localized formatting to, 143–144
  attribution information about, 93
  copyright holder and date of, 269
  creation date of, 268
  delimiting the body of, 100–101
  enclosing titles of, 158
  generating program, 269
  identifying a term's first appearance within, 108–109
  indexing, 273
  jumping across, 29–30
  jumping around inside, 28–29
  layout of, 40
  linking between, 226
  linking to other, 128–129
  linking within the same, 226
  living, 51
  making searchable, 275
  parts of HTML, 70
  resource type of, 269

scope or range of, 269
setting the base font for, 98
splitting long, 363
structuring, 354
superstructure of, 43–44
domain name
acquiring a unique, 297
for searching FTP files, 299
in URLs, 17
dotred.gif (red dot), adding, 204–205
Dr. HTML checking tool, 316
<DT> (Definition term) tag, 82, 110, 111–112
DTD (Document Type Definition), 65
"DTD speak", 313
dumb terminals, Web functionality for, 14
DVI format, 33

• E •

editor extensions, 337–339
Edit-Review cycle for building HTML files, 54–57
electronic commerce, 375
electronic mail. *See* e-mail
ellipsis (...), indicating multiple attributes in tags, 64
<EM>...</EM> (Emphasis) tags, 84, 112
EMACS editor, 326–328
e-mail, 12
address, supplying, 269
link for feedback, 219
embedded blanks in tags, 77
embedded objects, specifying parameter settings for, 137
emphasis
providing, 112
providing strong, 144
versus rendering, 361
encoded files, converting, 25
enhancements to standards, 175
entities, 164
European Laboratory for Particle Physics (CERN), 9

extended attributes, proposed as standards, 176–177
extensions, 176–177
external links, checking, 317

• F •

fallback services, arrangements for, 376
feedback, 219, 304–306, 363–364
feedback forms, 305
Fetch FTP utility, 299
Fielding, Roy, 318
fields, grouping related, in forms, 113
<FIELDSET>...</FIELDSET> (Form field set) tags, 83, 113
file:// in URLs, 17
File Transfer Protocol. *See* FTP
Find-Replace utility, 172
fixed-width font, 129, 137–138, 162
FLI (Flick) format, 33
focus group approach to feedback, 305
<FONT>...</FONT> (Font settings) tags, 81, 113–114
fonts, defining, 113–114
footer section of an HTML document, 70, 71–72
footers, 215–219
for business-style home pages, 217
differentiating information in, 154–155
for government agency Web pages, 217
revision numbers in, 218
suggested elements of, 215–217
time in, 218
URL line in, 217
version numbers in, 218
<FORM>...</FORM> (User input form) tags, 83, 114–116, 243
setting the environment, 244
form fields, adding a label to, 126–127
form for alpha testers, 290–291
formal syntax, 74–76
formatting
applying localized, 143–144
for impact, 361

forms
  adding to Web pages, 241–243
  caption information for, 102
  for feedback, 305
  grouping related fields in, 113
  interactive, 363
  limitations of, 240–241
  managing the content of, 243
  multi-line input fields in, 151–153
  producing no visible input area, 245
  testing the operation of, 292
forms category of tags, 83, 85
forms tags, classes of, 243
forward relationship type, specifying, 128
forward slash (/), in closing tags, 64, 75
FrameMaker
  converter, 328–329, 350
  documents, creating Web pages from,
    328–329
  hypertext aspects of, 31
frames, 179
Front Page site management tool, 319
FrontPage 97, 343–346
Frykholm, Niklas, 333
FTP FAQ, URL for, 298
FTP (File Transfer Protocol), 11, 12, 298
FTP URL, adding for forms feedback, 240
FTP utilities, 298
ftp:// in URLs, 17
full links, 198, 199
full URLs, examples of, 205
full-featured graphical browsers, 15

• *G* •

generalized markup, 67
generic form for HTML tags, 63–64
Georgia Tech College of Computing HTML
    Validation Service, 288
GET value in the METHOD attribute, 244
GhostScript, 35
GhostView for Windows, 35
GIF format, 32, 213
GIF89a graphics, 213

GifConverter, 213
GIFs, searching for on the Web, 207
giftrans program for UNIX and DOS, 213
glossary, 44
GML (General Markup Language), 66
Goldfarb, Charles, 66, 67
Gopher protocol, 11
gopher:// in URLs, 17
government agency Web pages
  bodies of, 194
  footers for, 217
graphic images, selecting for clickable
    maps, 257
graphical browser
  full-featured, 15
  required by a clickable map, 256
graphical symbols, building a set of, 360
graphical Web browsers, 14
graphics. *See also* images
  adding to Web pages, 204
  compressing, 36
  designating as selectable items in
    forms, 245
  as hyperlinks, 210–211
  keeping small, 36
  keeping to a minimum, 36
  placing on a page, 120–121
  recycling, 205–207
  rules for using, 36
  size of files, 35
  switching off, 35
  thumbnail versions of, 36
  in Web pages, 35–36
  Web site about, 33
graphics category of tags, 82, 85
graphics files
  reducing bits per pixel, 214
  size and complexity of, 212
graphics images, rules for designing,
    214–215
Graphics Interchange Format. *See* GIF
    format
graphics program
  displaying pixel coordinates, 257
  selecting, 212–213

Graphics WorkShop, 212
GUI FTP utility, 298–299

• H •

<H*>...</H*> (Header levels 1 through 6)
    tags, 82, 116–117
HAL HTML Validation Service, 288
Harvest tools, 275
<HEAD>...</HEAD> (Document head block)
    tags, 71, 80, 117
head block in documents, 117
head section of an HTML document, 70
headers
  differentiating information in, 155–156
  inserting, 116–117
headings, 85, 192–193
helper applications, 33–35
hierarchical structure for Web pages, 222
hierarchies, modeling in HTML, 49
higher-order ASCII characters
  defining character entities for, 68
  representing, 163
hilit.el macro package, 327
hits
  listing in order of occurrence, 274
  logging of, 20
hm-html-menus.el macro package, 327
Holodeck 3, tables in, 186
home directory, ISP storage off of, 297
home page file, naming, 216
home pages
  linking to itself in the URL line, 216
  planning yours, 225
  predefined in browsers, 19
  selecting hyperlinks for, 200
  single screen, 189–191
HomeSite 2.5 code editor, 347–348
horizontal design element in HTML
    pages, 85
horizontal rule <HR>
  across the page, 117–118
  advantages of, 208
  compared to rainbow lines, 207
  drawing, 117–118

hot keys, defining for form fields, 126
hotlist section, collecting titles in, 191
hotlists, 18, 51
  titles in, 46
HoTMetaL Pro HTML editor, 324–325
  Macintosh version, 334–335
hotzones, defining in client-side image
    maps, 95–96
<HR> (Horizontal rule) tag, 81,
    117–118, 208
HREF="URL" attribute, 226
htimage program, 261
HTML, 9, 24
  angle brackets (<>) in, 63
  basics of, 27–28
  characteristics of, 68
  code, viewing, 20
  comments, 78
  converting existing documents, 349–350
  exploiting the hypertext capabilities of,
    48–51
  following rules of syntax and layout, 355
  future versions of, 175
  hierarchies in, 49
  links available in, 47–48
  nonstandard extensions, 176–177
  properties of, 77–79
  relationship to SGML, 67–68
  standardization levels of, 69
  URL for checking DTDs and
    terminology, 176
  URLs for checking new
    developments, 177
  validators, 313–316
  Web site for the latest information on, 86
  why you should know, 310–311
<HTML>...</HTML> (Main document head)
    tags, 70, 80, 119
HTML 2.0 specification, the searchable
    version of, 274
HTML 3.2 compliant code, tricks with, 235
HTML add-ins for BBEdit and
    BBEditLIte, 338
HTML anchor. *See* anchors

HTML authoring tools
  for the Macintosh, 331–337
  for UNIX-based systems, 321–330
  for Windows-based systems, 341–347
HTML-aware spell checkers, 316
HTML-based spell-checking services, 366
HTML character entities. *See*
    character entities
HTML code editors for Windows, 347–348
HTML converters and filters, URLs for, 350
HTML documents. *See also* Web pages
  basic template for, 188–189
  comments on, 220
  defining clickable maps in, 263
  delimiting the body of, 100–101
  enclosing entire, 119
  labels in, 47
  moving to a Web server, 58
  parts of, 70
  tags providing structure for, 84
  titles of, 46–47
HTML.edit, 332
HTML Editor, 332
HTML editors, 310
  selecting one, 311–312
  word processors as, 348–349
.html extension, 199
HTML files, 54–57
HTML For Dummies home page
  analyzing, 233–238
  footer of, 217
HTML forms. *See* forms
HTML Form-Testing Home Page, 288
html-helper-mode.el macro package,
    327, 328
HTML links. *See* links
html-mode.el macro package, 327
HTML pages, setting the base font for, 98
HTML Pro HTML editor, 333
HTML syntax, 62
  elements of, 63–64
  metacharacter set, 75–76
  validation systems, 287
HTML syntax checker, running, 294
HTML tags. *See* tags

HTML testing and validation program,
    testing Web pages with, 287
HTML Transit file converter, 349
HTML validation tools, jump page for, 355
Htmlchek version 4.1, 287
HTTP, 21, 23
http daemon, 241
HTTP-EQUIV values in <META> tags, 268
HTTP response header, binding elements
    to, 131
HTTP server, 330
HTTP server software for the Macintosh,
    339–340
http:// in URLs, 16
httpd implementation, specifying the kind
    of, 376
httpd server, 241
httpd4Mac HTTP server, 340
HyperCard, 30
hyperlinked table of contents (TOC), 276
hyperlinks
  broken, 316
  defining hot keys for, 90
  logos and graphics as, 209–211
  selecting, 200
  verifying in FrontPage 97, 344, 345
hypermedia, effective use of, 362
hypertext, 68
  exploiting the capabilities of, 48–51
  key advantage of, 29
hypertext applications, 30–31
hypertext concept, 28
hypertext links
  creating within a text paragraph, 228
  to outside resources, 229–230
HyperText Markup Language. *See* HTML
HyperText Transfer Protocol. *See* HTTP

<I>...</I> (Italicize text) tags, 84, 119–120
icons
  adding to Web pages, 209
  in this book, 5–6

ID="name" attribute, 87
identification tags, 70
IE. *See* Internet Explorer (IE)
Image Composer, 344
image map tools, 257, 259
image maps. *See also* clickable maps
  adding text-based links below, 263–264
  client-side, 265
  naming the script files for, 258
imagemap program, 262
images. *See also* graphics
  aligning with <BR> tags, 101
  in tabular form, 179
<IMG> command, printing to graphics
    sources, 85
<IMG> (Inline image) tag, 82, 120–121
  adding images with, 204
  attributes of, 74
  ISMAP attribute, 263
implied values for attributes, 87
indexes
  indicating searchable, 124–125
  replacing, 43
indexing, 273–275
indexing search engines, 191
Indexmaker Pcrl script, 275
Infoseek Net Search, URL for, 270
in-line graphics, placing on a page,
    120–121
<INPUT> attributes, used in forms, 246
<INPUT> (Input object) tag, 83, 122–124
  example in a survey form, 246–248
  specifying input in forms, 243, 245–248
input forms, defining a text input area for,
    151–153
input objects, defining, 122–124
integer metacharacter, 75
interactive forms, 363
interdocument linking, 47, 226
interlaced GIFs, 213, 214
internal anchors, 28
International Standards Organization.
    See ISO
Internet, attaching to, 25
Internet Architecture Board (IAB), 22

Internet Engineering Task Force (IETF), 22
Internet Explorer (IE), 16, 176, 345
Internet file formats, Web site on, 33
Internet navigation tools, prior to the
    Web, 11–14
Internet Official Protocol Standards, 22
Internet Service Provider. *See* ISP
Internet World online, URL for, 312
intradocument linking, 47, 226
IP address for searching FTP files, 299
<ISINDEX> (Document is indexed) tag, 80,
    124–125, 273
ISMAP attribute in the <IMG> tag, 74, 263
ISO 8879 standard (for SGML), 66
ISO standards, numeric tags for, 166
ISO-Latin-1 character set, 68, 166
  listing of, 166–171
ISP (Internet Service Provider), 25
  download fees of, 372–373
  securing hard drive space from, 296–298
  transferring Web pages to, 58, 298
italics, providing emphasis with, 112

Java Applets, 37
  alternative text for, 153
  embedding, 93–95
  specifying parameter settings for, 137
JavaScript script, inserting, 140–141
JPEG format, 32, 213
JPEGs, searching for on the Web, 207
JPG format, 32
jump pages, 51, 230. *See also* hotlists
jumped-in users, navigational clues
    for, 223

• *K* •

<KBD>...</KBD> (Keyboard text style)
    tags, 84, 125
Keyboard, placeholders for entering text
    with, 161–162
keyboard text style, 125

keywords, supplying to search
engines, 269
Kinder, Gentler HTML Validator, 315–316
KISS (Keep It Simple, Stupid)
approach, 187

● *L* ●

<LABEL>...</LABEL> (Form field label)
tags, 83, 126–127
labels in HTML documents, 47
LANG="name" attribute, 87
Latin-1 character set (ISO 8859/1), 62
layout, 187
of documents, 40
planning, 359–360
of Web pages, 189–191
layout elements category of tags, 81, 85
left angle bracket (<), 63
levels of HTML, 69
<LI> (List item) tag, 82, 127–128, 231–233
Library of Congress, list of pointers, 18-19
line breaks, forcing, 101–102
line.gif (rainbow line), 205–207
linear structure for Web pages, 223
linear text, overcoming the limitations of,
48–51
linear thinking, avoiding, 358
<LINK> tag, 80, 128–129, 230–231
link anchors. *See* anchors
linked locations, 46
linked TOC, providing, 227–228
links, 47–48
checking, 288, 316–318, 367
examples of, 29
flavors of, 198
testing the operation and content of, 292
types of, 28
visual clues for, 28
links category of tags, 80–81
<LISTING>...</LISTING> tags, 129
lists
bulleted, 196–198
compared to tables, 179
creating in a fixed width font, 129

nesting within lists, 231–233
providing pickable, 141–142
replacing with colored dots, 208
setting off elements in, 127–128
of short elements, building, 109
styles for building, 85
unordered, 196–197
lists category of tags, 82, 85
listserv, 12
local files, opening, 18
local link checkers, 317
local links, checking, 367
location reference, 46
logical and (and) metacharacter, 75
logical or (or) metacharacter, 75
logos, 209–211
long documents
adding structure, 276
splitting, 363
Lorie, Ray, 66
Lotus Word Pro 97 for Windows, 348–349
low scroll rule, 357
LView for Windows, 35, 213
LView Pro, 212
Lvrfy link-checking program, 288
Lycos Search Engine, URL for, 270
Lynx, 14

● *M* ●

MacHTTP, 339
Macintosh
HTML authoring tools, 331–337
HTTP server software for, 339–340
hypertext applications, 30
mailto: in URLs, 16
mailto: link, 219
maintenance, importance of, 358
majordomo, 12
malls, online, 271
management tools for Web sites, 318–320
<MAP>...</MAP> (Client side image map)
tags, 82, 129–130

map files
  absolute URLs in, 260
  building and linking to NCSA map files, 261–262
  for CERN httpd servers, 260–261
  creating and storing, 262
  creating for clickable maps, 257–258
map regions, selecting boundaries for, 259
mapedit program, 257
MapMaker program, 259
markup, 39, 69
markup language, 24, 28, 61
markup tags, 61, 78–79
markup text, 24
Melotti, Bill, 340
<MENU>...</MENU> tags, 82, 130–131
menu.gif (button), 205–207
menu lists, enclosing, 130–131
menu (menu.gif) icon, 209
messages, establishing key, 42–43
<META> tags, 80, 131–132, 268–269
  placement of, 268
  preventing robots from analyzing, 271–272
metacharacters, 75–76
meta-information
  embedding, 131
  identifying, 268
METHOD attribute in forms, 244
Microsoft Internet Explorer. *See* Internet Explorer (IE)
Microsoft Office 97, inserting documents from, 345
Microsoft Waveform (WAV) format, 32
Microsoft Web site, 16, 346
Microsoft Windows, Help utility, 30, 31
Microsoft Word for Windows, 348–349
  technical support options, 30
MIME format, 31–32
Minar, Nelson, 327, 328
Minnesota, University of, 11, 12
MIT Artificial Intelligence Laboratory, online searchable index, 275
MOMspider link checker, 317, 367

monospaced (teletype) font, enclosing, 160
Mosaic, 15
Mosher, Ed, 66
Motif, 323
motion-video formats, 32–33
MOV format, 33
movers and shakers, making friends with, 305–306
MPEG format, 33
MPG format, 33
Muenkel, Heiko, 327, 328
multicolumn tables, 185
multimedia files, size of, 36–37
multiple, 50
Multipurpose Internet Mail Extensions format. *See* MIME
multirow tables, 185

• *N* •

NAME="text" attribute, 226
  with the <LINK> tag, 230
  in an anchor tag, 226
NAME attribute with the <INPUT> tag, 245–246
NAME values in <META> tags, 268
named anchors
  browser behavior with, 226
  naming, 229
names
  of home page files, 216
  of named anchors, 229
  of tags, 63
National Center for Supercomputing Applications (NCSA), 15
navigation
  aiding, 362
  double-checking, 294
navigation bars, 276, 357
navigational aids
  including, 357
  rules regarding, 278–279
Navigator Gold, HTML editing in, 337
NaviPress HTML editor, 324, 332

NCSA, 15
NCSA HTTPD, 330
NCSA httpd servers, building and linking
    map files to, 261–262
nested lists, 231, 233
nesting
  during table building, 185
  tags, 78–79
NetCarta site management tool, 319
netiquette, 12
NetObjects Fusion, 334
Netscape Communications, 176
Netscape Communicator Internet Suite,
    346–347
Netscape Composer, 346–347
Netscape Navigator, 15, 176
Netscape Navigator Gold, 337
NetWings HTTP server for the
    Macintosh, 340
Network News Transfer Protocol
    (NNTP), 17
networks, protocols for, 21–23
Newberg, Lee, 324
news:// in URLs, 17
next.gif (button), 205–207
next (next.gif) icon, 209
<NEXTID> tag, 80
NNTP. *See* Network News Transfer
    Protocol
NOFOLLOW value in the <META> tag, 272
NOINDEX value in the <META> tag, 272
non-http objects, embedding, 132
non-text objects, linking to, 47
NotePad text editor, 54
NOWRAP attribute in table cells, 184
numeric entities, 163–164, 166

• *O* •

<OBJECT>...</OBJECT> (Non-http object)
    tags, 81, 132–134
object name in URLs, 18
objects
  embedding non-http, 132
  linking to non-text, 47

<OL>...</OL> (Ordered list) tags, 82, 135
on-screen check box in forms, 245
online focus group, 305
online malls, 271
online payments, capability to accept, 340
online searchable index at the MIT Artifi-
    cial Intelligence Laboratory, 275
Open file, 18
<OPTION> (Form list choice), 83, 135–136
or (logical or) metacharacter, 75
ordered lists, 135
O'Reilly WebSite site management
    tool, 319
organic acceptance, 357
organizational style for Web pages,
    222–224
outline, creating, 42
outside the boundaries, testing, 285

• *P* •

<P> tag, 81, 136–137
page design, top-down, 354
page footers. *See* footers
page-level information, defining, 117
PageMill, 332, 334, 335
pages. *See also* Web pages
  chaining sequentially, 48
  layout of, 40
  stringing together, 48
Paint Shop Pro, 212
paragraph boundaries, defining for HTML
    text, 136–137
paragraph headings of Web pages,
    192–193
paragraphs
  creating hypertext links within, 228
  defining, 136–137
  writing better, 196
<PARAM> (Applet and object parameters)
    tag, 81, 137
parameters, defining your own for tag
    display, 145
parentheses ( ) metacharacters, 75
parser, 63

PDF format, 32
peer and management review, 368
performance and functionality testing, 292
personal Web page URL, syntax of, 297
personal Web pages, bodies of, 193, 194–195
Personal Web Server, 345
Phoenix X-Windows-based HTML Editor, 324
Photo Styler, 212
physical links. *See* full links
physical tags, compared to descriptive tags, 361
"pick lists", generating, 243
pickable lists, providing, 141–142
pipe, connecting to the Internet, 25
pixel coordinates, displaying, 257
placeholders, indicating for keyboard input, 162
<PLAINTEXT>...</PLAINTEXT> tags, 137–138
plain-text HTML editors for UNIX, 323
platforms, delivering content to a variety of, 68
plug-in applications, 33–35
point region in clickable maps, 259
pointers, list of, 19
polygon region in clickable maps, 259
port address in URLs, 17
Portable Document Format. *See* PDF
POST value in the METHOD attribute, 244
PostScript, viewing, 35
pound sign (#) in entities, 164
<PRE>...</PRE> (Preformatted style) tags, 81, 138–139
preformatted text, 138, 179
prioritized problems, batch-processing, 303
procedural markup language, 61, 62
program code, enclosing, 104–105
programs, 65
project folders in FrontPage 97, 344
protocol/data source in URLs, 16
protocols, 21
PS (PostScript) format, 32
published copy of your Web site, 304
Punin, John R., 324

• Q •

Quadralay Web site, URL for, 329
QuickTime for Windows, 35
QuickTime format, 33
quoted material, setting off, 99

• R •

RA (RealAudio) format, 32
radio buttons in forms, 245, 250
rainbow lines, adding, 205–208
ranges and values, testing predicted, 285
RealAudio (RA) format, 32
rectangle region in clickable maps, 259
red dot (dotred.gif), 205–206
red dot graphics, 208
registering Web sites, 271
relative addressing, basis for, 97–98
relative links, 198–199
relative URLs
  example of, 204
  versus absolute URLs, 295–296
remote Web pages, jumping to, 229–231
rendering, versus emphasis, 361
request message type, 23
Requests for comment. *See* RFCs
RESET attribute in forms, 243
reset button, creating in forms, 245
response message type, 23
return page of index hits, 274
revision dates, placing in footers, 218
revisions, cycling, 303
RFCs, 22-23
right angle bracket (>), 63
road map for all HTML documents, 365–366
robots, 132, 270
Robots Exclusion Protocol, 272
robots.txt file, 272
root level of a hierarchy, 222
ROWSPAN attribute in table cells, 184
Rule number 1, 284
ruler lines, colored, 207

• S •

<S>...</S> (Strikethrough text) tags, 84, 139
<SAMP>...</SAMP> (Sample text) tags, 84, 140
sample text, reproducing, 140
SBI (Sound Blaster Instrument), 32
Schales, Jochen, 332
screen appearance, testing, 292
screens, common controls for all, 43
<SCRIPT>...</SCRIPT> (Inline script) tags, 81, 140–141
scripts
  inserting, 140–141
  placing comment tags around, 141
search engine robots, gathering information from <META> tags, 268
search engines, 19, 43, 270
  supplying keywords to, 269
  URLs for, 207
search pages on the Web, 19
searchable indexes, 124–125, 276
Security Kit for WebSTAR, 340
<SELECT>...</SELECT> (Select input object) tags, 83, 141–142
  defining values for, 135–136
  selecting values in forms, 243, 248–250
semicolon (;)
  closing character entities, 75
  in entities, 164
semi-WYSIWYG programs, 324
servers, 20. See also Web server
  forms-handling capability of, 240–241
  image map formats and, 258
  maximizing the performance of, 20
SGML, 25, 66
  origins of, 66
  relationship to HTML, 67–68
SGML documents
  increasing portability of, 164
  parts of, 67
shapes in clickable maps, 259
SHE (Simple HTML Editor), 332
Shockwave, 37
Shotton, Chuck, 339–340
side effects, unexpected, 303
SimpleText text editor, 54
single screen home page, 189–191

site management tools. See Web site, management tools
SiteMill site management tool, 319, 334
<SMALL>...</SMALL> (Small text) tags, 84, 143
SND format, 32
SoftQuad's download site, URL for, 325
Sound Blaster Instrument (SBI) format, 32
sound formats, 32
"space.gif" file, getting a "tab" key effect, 235
spaces
  placement around tags, 208–209
  in tags, 77
<SPAN>...</SPAN> (Style area) tags, 81, 143–144
spell checkers
  HTML-aware, 316
  running Web pages through, 286
spell-checking Web pages, 366
spiders, 132, 270
spot in URLs, 18
square brackets [] metacharacters, 75
SRC attribute, 74
stand-alone authoring tools for the Macintosh, 332
stand-alone UNIX HTML editors, 322
Standard Generalized Markup Language. See SGML
standardization levels of HTML, 69
standards, adding enhancements to, 1 75
standards for browsers, evolution of, 174
still-video formats, 32
storage off your home directory, 297
storyboard for Web pages, 225–226
strikethrough text, rendering, 139
<STRONG>...</STRONG> (Strong emphasis) tags, 84, 144
structure, providing for HTML documents, 84
STYLE="text" attribute, 87
<STYLE...</STYLE> (Style sheet) tags, 81, 144–145
style sheets
  backwards compatibility with, 110
  defining, 144–145
_{...} (Subscript) tags, 84, 145–146
SUBMIT attribute in forms, 243

submit button, creating in forms, 246
subscript, rendering text in, 145–146
^{...} (Superscript) tags, 84, 146
SuperCard, 30
superscript, rendering text in, 146
superstructure of documents, 43
symbolic link, creating, 298
syntax, 62
  elements of HTML, 63–64
syntax conventions, 74–76
system configurations for testing, 291

● *T* ●

"tab" key effect in HTML, 235
<TABLE>...</TABLE) tags, 83, 146–148,
    181, 182
table data tags, 182
table header tags, 182
table of contents. *See* TOC (table of
    contents)
table row tags, 182
table rows, defining, 158–159
tables, 179
  alternatives to, 179
  attributes used with table tags, 183–184
  building, 184–185
  caption information for, 102
  coding elements on separate lines, 185
  creating, 146–148
  defining data cells within, 149–151
  examples of stunning, 186
  grouping different types of content with,
    148–149
  mixing with graphics, 185
  multirow and multicolumn, 185
  nesting tags during creation of, 185
  padding cells in, 183
  parts of, 181
  planning the layout of, 184
  providing an alternative for the visually
    impaired, 180
  reproducing formatted, 138
  setting the width of, 183
  sticking to the basic table elements, 180
  uses of, 180
tables category of tags, 83, 85
tags, 39, 63
  attributes of, 63–64, 74

categories of, 80–86
double-checking, 294
embedded blanks in, 77
enclosing in angle brackets (<>), 46
example code on the CD, 89
generic form of, 63–64
in HTML files, 24
inserting one set within another, 78–79
keeping track of, 354
names of, 63
nesting, 78–79
pairs of, 74
placement of spaces around, 208–209
spaces in, 77
syntax for, 73–79
<TBODY>...</TBODY> (Table body) tags,
    83, 148–149
TCP/IP, 22–23
<TD>...</TD> (Table cell) tags, 83, 149–151,
    181, 182
teletype font, enclosing, 160
telnet:// in URLs, 17
/Template directory on the CD, 57
template files, included on the CD, 57–58
template for Web pages, 188–189
test plan
  methods and evaluation, 291–292
  performance and functionality
    testing, 292
  purpose and scope of, 289
  schedule and resources, 290
testing
  areas for, 285
  generic alpha test plan, 289–292
  priorities assigned to problems, 292
  system configuration for, 291
text
  associating a single term or line with a
    block of indented, 108
  boldfacing, 96–97
  centering across the page, 103
  creating short lines of, 102
  defining fonts for, 113–114
  defining paragraph boundaries for,
    136–137
  fixed-width font, 137–138, 162
  in HTML, 24
  in HTML tags, 64

(continued)

text *(continued)*
 italicizing, 119–120
 linking to, in another page, 226–227
 linking to, within a page, 227–229
 making one size larger, 98–99
 mastering the mechanics of, 366
 reducing by one size, 143
 sample, 140
 subscript, 145–146
 superscript, 146
 tagging, 46
 underlining, 160–161
text area, providing free-form feedback in
  a form, 251–252, 253
text-based links, adding below image
  maps, 263–264
text controls category of tags, 83–84
text documents, converting into HTML,
  349–350
text editor, creating HTML pages with,
  53–54
text entry, producing a one-line area for in
  forms, 246
text input area, defining, 151–153
text-only information, presenting, 139
text tags in the body, 71
<TEXTAREA>...</TEXTAREA> (Text input
  area) tags, 83, 151–153
 in forms, 243, 246, 251–253
<TEXTFLOW>...</TEXTFLOW> (Applet
  alternative) tags, 153
<TFOOT>...</TFOOT> (Table footer) tags,
  83, 154–155
<TH>...</TH> (Column head) tags, 83,
  156–158, 181, 182
<THEAD>...</THEAD> (Table body) tags,
  83, 155–156
thumbnails, 36, 362
THX demonstration, 44
time, placing in footers, 218–219
timed out, getting, 18
TITLE="text" attribute, 87
<TITLE>...</TITLE> (Document title) tags,
  70, 80, 158
titles
 constructing for Web pages, 191–192
 of HTML documents, 46–47, 158
tmpl-minor-mode.el macro package,
  327, 328

TOC (table of contents), 43
 linking to sections, 195
 links, 227–228
top-down page design, 354
<TR>...</TR> (Table row) tags, 83,
  158–159, 181, 182
traffic, projecting and monitoring, 372–373
Transmission Control Protocol/Internet
  Protocol. *See* TCP/IP
Transparency program for the
  Macintosh, 213
transparent background, creating images
  with, 213
tree structure. *See* hierarchical structure
troff UNIX markup language, 62
<TT>...</TT> (Teletype text) tags, 84, 160
TYPE attribute with the <INPUT> tag,
  245–246
typographic emphasis, 112

• *U* •

<U>...</U> (Underline text) tags, 84,
  160–161
<UL>...</UL> (Unordered list style) tags,
  82, 161
underlining text, 160–161
unexpected side effects, 303
Unicode character set, 62–63
Uniform Resource Locators. *See* URLs
UNIX
 HTML authoring tools for, 321–330
 HTML editors, stand-alone, 322
 HTML syntax checker, stand-alone, 288
 hypertext applications, 31
UNIX-based WWW (HTTP) servers,
  information on, 330
unordered list, 196–197
"URL encoding", 125
URL line
 in footers, 217
 linking a home page to itself, 216
URLs, 16–17
 clickable maps and, 264–265
 composition of, 16–18
 entering, 18
 linking to, 29–30

punctuation for local file access, 18
referencing, 30
syntax of, 18–19
Usenet, 12
users, 284. *See also* audience
feedback from, 304–306, 363–364
projecting the number of
simultaneous, 375
soliciting input from, 114–116
UTC (Universal Time) format, 218–219

• *V* •

validation of Web pages, 294
Validation/Checkers page on Yahoo!, 318
VALIGN (vertical alignment) attribute with
tables, 184
values
in attributes, 86
defining for a <SELECT> field, 135–136
vanity pages, 41
<VAR>...</VAR> (Variable text style) tags,
84, 161–162
variable names, highlighting in HTML text,
161–162
variable text style, 162
VB script, inserting, 140–141
"Venetian blind" look, 214
version numbers, placing in footers, 218
vertical bar (|) metacharacter, 75
vi text editor, 54
video files, size of, 36–37
Video for Windows format, 32
video formats, 32–33
View Source, selecting, 20
visually impaired, providing alternatives
to table data, 180
vocabulary of graphical symbols, 360
VRML (Virtual Reality Modeling
Language), 37

• *W* •

W3. *See* Web
W3C site, 18
WAIS, 13
WAIS:// in URLs, 17
WAV (Microsoft Waveform) format, 32

WAXweb, 51
Wayfinding Toolkit, 277–278
Web, 10
accessing, 25
big deal because, 13
copyright law and, 218
disclaimers on, 217
growth of, 19
history of, 9–10
"home truths" about, 277
how it works, 20–21
linking to other pages, 29
list of common file types on, 32
navigation of the Internet prior to, 11–14
search pages on, 19
structure of, 21
survey of, 20
uniform resources on, 16–19
Web browsers. *See* browsers
Web client. *See* browsers
Web page URL, syntax of, 297
Web pages. *See also* HTML documents;
pages; Web sites
adding forms support, 241–243
adding graphics, 204
adding icons, 209
analyzing sophisticated, 233–238
basic template for, 188–189
bodies of, 193–195
building, 54–57, 356
building clickable maps, 257–259
checkups for, 312–318
constructing titles of, 191–192
content of, 37–38
controlling long, 195
designing, 42–44
drawing the structure of, 224–225
elements of, 45–51
evolutionary changes in, 357
examining code from other, 204
graphics in, 35–36
headings of, 192–193
intent of, 42
jumping to remote, 229–231
layout of, 189–191
moving to the storage area on your
ISP, 298
non-text files in, 31–37

(continued)

Web pages *(continued)*
  open-ended, 51
  organizational style, 222–224
  organizational techniques for building,
    48–51
  rules for creating bodies, 195
  rules for designing small graphics,
    214–215
  sections of, 188–189
  sketching the layout of, 190
  specifying the background color of, 100
  spell-checking, 366
  testing, 174, 283–292
  titles of, 46–47
  uploading to your ISP, 299–300
  validation of, 294
Web Publishing Wizard, 345
Web Robots Pages, URL for, 271
Web root, 297
Web server, 330. *See also* servers
  building or buying, 372
  co-locating your own, 297
  control over, 374
  pipe, matching with potential users, 375
  securing hard drive space on, 296–298
  selecting, 376
  software, testing, 291
  storage on a dedicated, 297
  transferring HTML documents to, 58
Web services, build or buy, 371–376
Web site. *See also* Web pages
  changes, managing and scheduling,
    373–374
  design desiderata for building, 359–364
  excluding robots from, 271–272
  going live, 293–300
  hosting on your own PC, 345
  hypertext links to, 229–230
  maintaining two separate copies of, 304
  management tools, 318–320
  registering, 271
  testing checklist, 293–295
Web structure, 223–224
WebCrawler Searching, URL for, 270
Webcrawlers, 270
Weblint Perl script, 287
WebMaker FrameMaker converter,
  328–329, 350

Webmasters, 21
  maintenance tools for, 309–320
WebSTAR Macintosh Web server, 258,
  339–340
Webtor HTML editor, 332–333
WebWalker link checker, 317
WebWorks Publisher, 329
white space, 190–191, 360
Wide-Area Information Service. *See* WAIS
WIDTH attribute inside the <TABLE>
  tag, 183
Wilbur HTML code name, 69
Windows HTML authoring tools, URLs
  on, 342
Windows. *See* Microsoft Windows
Windows-based HTML authoring systems,
  341–347
Wingif, 212
word-processing add-in functions, 337–339
word processors
  as HTML editors, 348–349
  saving HTML files, 54
working copy of your Web site, performing
  changes on, 304
World Wide Web. *See* Web
write permissions on a server, 262
WS_FTP Pro FTP utility, 299
WYSIWYG authoring systems, 322
WYSIWYG Web authoring systems for
  Windows, 342–347

X

XBM (X-Windows Bitmap) format, 32
<XMP>...</XMP> (Variable text style) tags,
  84, 162
X-Windows Bitmap format, 32

Y

Yahoo!, 19
  tables in, 186
  URL for, 270
  Validation/Checkers page, 318
Yale C/AM Web Style Guide, URL for, 215

Wiley Publishing, Inc.
End-User License Agreement

5. **Limited Warranty.** (a) WPI warrants that the Software and Software Media are free from defects in materials and workmanship under normal use for a period of sixty (60) days from the date of purchase of this Book. If WPI receives notification within the warranty period of defects in materials or workmanship, WPI will replace the defective Software Media. (b) WPI AND THE AUTHOR OF THE BOOK DISCLAIM ALL OTHER WARRANTIES, EXPRESS OR IMPLIED, INCLUDING WITHOUT LIMITATION IMPLIED WARRANTIES OF MERCHANTABILITY AND FITNESS FOR A PARTICULAR PURPOSE, WITH RESPECT TO THE SOFTWARE, THE PROGRAMS, THE SOURCE CODE CONTAINED THEREIN, AND/OR THE TECHNIQUES DESCRIBED IN THIS BOOK. WPI DOES NOT WARRANT THAT THE FUNCTIONS CONTAINED IN THE SOFTWARE WILL MEET YOUR REQUIREMENTS OR THAT THE OPERATION OF THE SOFTWARE WILL BE ERROR FREE. (c) This limited warranty gives you specific legal rights, and you may have other rights that vary from jurisdiction to jurisdiction.

6. **Remedies.** (a) WPI's entire liability and your exclusive remedy for defects in materials and workmanship shall be limited to replacement of the Software Media, which may be returned to WPI with a copy of your receipt at the following address: Software Media Fulfillment Department, Attn.: *HTML For Dummies, 3rd Edition*, Wiley Publishing, Inc., 10475 Crosspoint Blvd., Indianapolis, IN 46256, or call 1-800-762-2974. Please allow four to six weeks for delivery. This Limited Warranty is void if failure of the Software Media has resulted from accident, abuse, or misapplication. Any replacement Software Media will be warranted for the remainder of the original warranty period or thirty (30) days, whichever is longer. (b) In no event shall WPI or the author be liable for any damages whatsoever (including without limitation damages for loss of business profits, business interruption, loss of business information, or any other pecuniary loss) arising from the use of or inability to use the Book or the Software, even if WPI has been advised of the possibility of such damages. (c) Because some jurisdictions do not allow the exclusion or limitation of liability for consequential or incidental damages, the above limitation or exclusion may not apply to you.

7. **U.S. Government Restricted Rights.** Use, duplication, or disclosure of the Software for or on behalf of the United States of America, its agencies and/or instrumentalities "U.S. Government" is subject to restrictions as stated in paragraph (c)(1)(ii) of the Rights in Technical Data and Computer Software clause of DFARS 252.227-7013, or subparagraphs (c) (1) and (2) of the Commercial Computer Software - Restricted Rights clause at FAR 52.227-19, and in similar clauses in the NASA FAR supplement, as applicable.

8. **General.** This Agreement constitutes the entire understanding of the parties and revokes and supersedes all prior agreements, oral or written, between them and may not be modified or amended except in a writing signed by both parties hereto that specifically refers to this Agreement. This Agreement shall take precedence over any other documents that may be in conflict herewith. If any one or more provisions contained in this Agreement are held by any court or tribunal to be invalid, illegal, or otherwise unenforceable, each and every other provision shall remain in full force and effect.

CD-ROM Installation Instructions

For Mac OS users

1. **Insert the CD into your CD-ROM drive.**

2. **When the HTML For Dummies icon appears on your desktop, double-click it.**

   A window opens revealing the contents of the CD.

3. **Please read the ReadMe file and End User License file. (Just double-click their icons.)**

To view the examples and templates on the CD, including the *HTML For Dummies* Web page, open your Web browser, and with its Open or Open File command, open this file on the CD: HTML4DUM.HTM. This file is in the H4D3E folder, which is in the HTML4DUM folder at the root level of the CD (HTML4DUM/ H4D3E/ HTML4DUM.HTM).

To install any of the software programs included on the CD, double-click the SOFTWARE folder at the root level of the CD.

For Windows 3.1x and Windows 95 users

1. **Insert the CD into your CD-ROM drive.**

2. **Windows 95 users: Wait a minute or two while your drive reads the CD. Double-click the My Computer icon on your desktop and then double-click the icon for your CD-ROM drive.**

2. **Windows 3.1x users: From File Manager, double-click the icon for your CD-ROM drive (usually drive d).**

   A window opens revealing the contents of the CD.

3. **Please read the ReadMe file (readme.txt) and End User License file (license.txt). (Just double-click their icons.)**

To view the examples and templates on the CD, including the *HTML For Dummies* Web page, open your Web browser, and with its Open or Open File command, open this file on the CD: HTML4DUM.HTM. This file is in the H4D3E directory, which is in the HTML4DUM directory at the root level of the CD (HTML4DUM/ H4D3E/ HTML4DUM.HTM).

To install any of the software programs included on the CD, double-click the SOFTWARE directory at the root level of the CD.

Notes